Foreword

One community leader once told me that the role of the community press, and the *Nichi Bei* in particular, was to "validate our experience." I initially scoffed at that concept, momentarily tossing it aside as an overreach of self-importance. However, given the closure of Northern California's two historic Japanese American publications in 2009, I've found that notion to not only be true but essentially serve as a mantra for our nonprofit rebirth after the inevitable dissolution of the *Nichi Bei Times*.

This tome in your hands epitomizes the importance of the community press in preserving history.

On behalf of the Nichi Bei Foundation, its nonprofit publication the *Nichi Bei Weekly*, its predecessor the *Nichi Bei Times* (1946–2009), and, before that, the *Nichi Bei Shimbun* (1899–1942)—what the author of this book refers to as our current publication's "grandfather"—I'm proud to introduce Greg Robinson's new volume of groundbreaking work based on his column "The Great Unknown and the Unknown Great" in the *Nichi Bei Times* and *Nichi Bei Weekly*.

"The Great Unknown and the Unknown Great" has been one of our most popular columns, and I'm grateful that fellow *Nichi Bei* columnist Chizu Omori had introduced Greg to me back in 2007, when Greg and I first discussed the idea for his column. His work truly reinforces our newfound educational mission as part of our nonprofit rebirth, and he writes in an accessible manner as well. A quick survey of his work clearly shows that he has written on a diverse array of topics (women, arts, literature and journalism, sports, activism, non–Japanese Americans who helped Japanese Americans, civil rights, etc.).

Over the years, some of his pioneering work has uncovered some hardly known figures in Japanese American history, such as the first professional football player of Japanese descent (Arthur Matsu), those who helped to defend the rights of the Japanese American community (such as African American attorney Hugh Macbeth), and comic artist Robert Kuwahara, who was featured in our "The Many Faces of Manga" exhibit at the Napa Valley Museum, National Japanese American Historical Society, and other locations. His pieces on Louisiana's Japanese American community and the Japanese American community in prewar Chicago were especially eye-opening, as are his pieces on Japanese Americans who played roles in landmark events shaping American history such as the Oyama family—the family behind the historic case that overturned California's Alien Land Act—and pioneer multiracial Japanese Americans. In addition, he has brought attention to the important intersections of Japanese Americans and African Americans, such as Mervyn Dymally, an unsung hero of the Japanese American Redress Movement.

Greg's work not only pulled these historical figures out of the margins or footnotes but also helped us to realize that the deeper richness of the great Japanese American mosaic goes well beyond stories found within the model minority stereotype.

But perhaps I'm most proud of creating a space for his annual LGBT history column, which for several years we have intentionally placed in our most widely (geographically) distributed issue of the year, our Obon and Summer Festivals Guide.

Greg's column adds so much depth to our publication and helps us fulfill our goal of giving a voice to the voiceless. And he also understands the role that the *Nichi Bei* has played in terms of providing him access to the community and creating a welcome place for his research.

THE
GREAT
UNKNOWN

Japanese American
Sketches

GREG ROBINSON

UNIVERSITY PRESS OF COLORADO
Boulder

Published by University Press of Colorado
5589 Arapahoe Avenue, Suite 206C
Boulder, Colorado 80303

 The University Press of Colorado is a proud member of
Association of American University Presses.

The University Press of Colorado is a cooperative publishing enterprise supported, in part, by Adams State University, Colorado State University, Fort Lewis College, Metropolitan State University of Denver, Regis University, University of Colorado, University of Northern Colorado, Utah State University, and Western State Colorado University.

∞ This paper meets the requirements of the ANSI/NISO Z39.48–1992 (Permanence of Paper).

ISBN: 978-1-60732-428-7 (cloth)
ISBN: 978-1-60732-429-4 (ebook)

Library of Congress Cataloging-in-Publication Data
Names: Robinson, Greg, 1966– author.
Title: The great unknown: Japanese American sketches / by Greg Robinson.
Description: Boulder: University Press of Colorado, 2016. | An anthology of articles that originally appeared in the column, "The Great Unknown and the Unknown Great," in the Nichi Bei Times and the Nichi Bei Weekly, and several articles that appeared in other periodicals, as well as some previously unpublished material. | Includes bibliographical references.
Identifiers: LCCN 2015043305 | ISBN 9781607324287 (cloth) | ISBN 9781607324294 (ebook)
Subjects: LCSH: Japanese Americans—United States—Biography. | Japanese Americans—United States—History.
Classification: LCC E184.J3 R6352 2016 | DDC 973/.04956—dc23
LC record available at https://lccn.loc.gov/2015043305

Credits

Nichi Bei Times: Arthur Matsu, Masuji Miyakawa, Hugh MacBeth, Queer Heritage 2007 (Kiyoshi Kuromiya, etc.), Robert Kuwahara, Kathleen Tamagawa, Guyo Tajiri, Eddie Shimano, Isamu Noguchi, Kajiro/Fred Oyama, Ina Sugihara, John Maki, Basketball (Wat Misaka/Dr. Yanagisawa), S. I. Hayakawa (2 parts), Paul Robeson, Baseball (Jose Nakamura, Bill Nishita, Yosh Kawano), Women lawyers (Tel Sono, etc.), Milton Ozaki, Conrad Yama (Hamanaka), Queer History 2008 (Noguchi, etc), Kay Karl Endow, Ralph Carr/Earl Warren, Jun Fujita, Alan Cranston, Prewar Chicago, Chino/Ohi Family, Koji Ariyoshi, Miné Okubo, Hood River Japanese, Queer 2009
Nichi Bei Weekly: Reiko Sato, Jenichiro Oyabe, Ayako Ishigaki, Lincoln Seiichi Kanai, Queer 2010, Norman Thomas, Anne Reeploeg Fisher/Morton Grodzins, Issei women overview, Fuki Endow Kawaguchi, Shio Sakanishi, Sam Hohri, Hisaye Yamamoto, Gordon Hirabayashi, Yoné Stafford, Queer 2011–, Naomi Nakano, Louisiana, Robert Chino, Research methods, Queer 2012—Same-sex JACL, Mervyn Dymally, Gyo Fujikawa, Shinkichi Tajiri, Stanley Hayami, Yasuo Sasaki, Footnotes, Clifford Uyeda/Ben Kuroki, Bowling, Setsuko Nishi, John Franklin Carter, *Regan v. King*, Afterword
Discovernikkei: Buddy Uno/Bill Hosokawa
Nikkei Heritage: Death penalty
Feminist Press at CUNY: Ayako Ishigaki
History News Network: McCloy Memo, Michelle Malkin
Densho Encyclopedia: Eleanor Roosevelt

**THE GREAT
UNKNOWN**

To Casey,

Good reading and best

wishes to a fellow

historian,

To Thanapat Porjit, with deepest affection

Contents

Foreword by Kenji G. Taguma   xi

By Way of Introduction   xv

1 A NEW LOOK AT ISSEI WOMEN   3

   Issei Women: An Overview   3

   Shio Sakanishi: Library of Congress Official and Scholar   6

   Fuki Endow Kawaguchi's Diary   9

   Tel Sono: Issei Woman Lawyer and Missionary   13

   Ayako Ishigaki: Feminist and Peace Activist   17

2 MIXED-RACE JAPANESE AMERICANS   21

   Isamu Noguchi's Struggle against Executive Order 9066   21

   Kathleen Tamagawa: First Nisei Author   24

   The Chino and Ohi Families   28

   Milton Ozaki: Mystery Writer (coauthored with Steven G. Doi) 39

   Yoné Stafford: Pacifist Militant   43

3   LITERATURE AND JOURNALISM   49

Jenichiro Oyabe: Japanese Yankee at Howard University   49

Eddie Shimano: Crusading Journalist and Poet   53

Kay Karl Endow: Novelist, Aviator, and Con Man   56

John M. Maki: Writer and Educator   60

Buddy Uno and Bill Hosokawa: Two Nisei Journalists
    in Occupied China   67

The Hidden Contributions of Guyo Tajiri   77

The Tragic and Engaging Career of Sam Hohri   83

Hisaye Yamamoto and the African American Press   86

4   WARTIME CONFINEMENT AND JAPANESE AMERICANS:
    NISEI STORIES   93

Mitsuye Endo: Plus grand dans son obscurité?   93

Lincoln Seiichi Kanai's Act of Conscience   95

The Exclusion of Naomi Nakano   98

Koji Ariyoshi: A Hawaiian Nisei in Mao's China   109

Sanji Abe and Martial Law in Wartime Hawai'i   113

5   WARTIME CONFINEMENT AND JAPANESE AMERICANS:
    FRIENDS AND FOES   119

The Case against Michelle Malkin   119

The McCloy Memo: New Insight into the Causes of Removal   123

Norman Thomas and the Defense of Japanese Americans   125

Eleanor Roosevelt and Japanese Americans: A First Look   129

Paul Robeson: "Your Fight Is My Fight"   133

Alan Cranston and Japanese Americans   136

Two Wartime Governors and Mass Removal of Japanese Americans   139

Hugh Macbeth: African American Defender of Issei and Nisei   143

John Franklin Carter: The Real-Life Lanny Budd   148

6   POLITICAL ACTIVISM AND CIVIL RIGHTS   153

Masuji Miyakawa: First Issei Attorney   153

The Family behind *Oyama v. California* 157

Regan v. King: When Birthright Citizenship Was Last Tested 160

Yasuo Sasaki: Poet, Physician, and Abortion Rights Pioneer 166

Ina Sugihara: Interracial Activist 173

Mervyn M. Dymally: Unsung Hero of Redress 177

Setsuko M. Nishi: A Life of Service 180

7 SPORTS 193

Arthur Matsu: First Japanese American in the National
    Football League 193

Nisei in Pro Basketball: Wat Misaka and Dr. Yanagi 196

Early Japanese Americans in Organized Baseball 199

The JACL and the Integration of the American
    Bowling Congress 202

8 ARTS 207

Jun Fujita: Poet and Photographer 207

Robert Kuwahara: Cartoonist and Animator 210

The "Double Life" of Conrad Yama 213

Reiko Sato: Actress and Dancer 217

The Unknown Life and Art of Miné Okubo 220

Gyo Fujikawa: Artist and Author 229

Shinkichi Tajiri: Sculptor 232

9 THE QUEER HERITAGE OF JAPANESE AMERICANS 241

Kiyoshi Kuromiya: A Queer Activist for Civil Rights (2007) 241

Sexuality from Issei to Nisei (2008) 244

The Rise of Homophobia in Japanese American
    Communities (2009) 248

The Rise of Homophobia: Part 2 (2010) 251

Hawai'i 1986: The Shift to Equal Rights (2011) 257

The JACL's Historic Vote for Equal Marriage Rights (2012) 261

10 A New Look at the Unknown Great   267

The Astonishing History of Japanese Americans in Louisiana   267

Japanese Americans in Prewar Chicago: An Overview   275

Japanese Americans and the Death Penalty   279

The Other Side of the Hood River Story   284

S. I. Hayakawa: Jazz Specialist and Civil Rights Supporter   288

Anne Reeploeg Fisher and Morton Grodzins: The Censorship
  of Confinement   296

Gordon Hirabayashi's Surprising Postwar Career   300

Afterword   309
Selected Bibliography   313
Index   321

Seeing Greg's *Nichi Bei* columns published in book form is akin to seeing a baby grow up and set out on its own in the world. I'm truly humbled that Greg has asked me to write a brief foreword to this marvelous collection of his work, and we are proud to see his important work reach and engage a broader audience.

One heavy responsibility of the Nikkei community press, I feel, is documenting the community's history for generations to come. Years from now, researchers will still refer to print publications for research purposes, just as they do today. And so we are grateful that alongside our day-to-day documentation of our community's history, we have Greg Robinson's columns to provide added depth and research into yesteryear, revealing hidden or unknown truths of how we came to be, where we've gone, and the people who shaped the development and advancement of our communities. Many of them may be unsung heroes, but thanks to Greg Robinson's work, they are no longer *unknown*.

Kenji G. Taguma
President, Nichi Bei Foundation
Editor-in-Chief, Nichi Bei Weekly

By Way of Introduction

It is now more than twenty years since I began working as a professional teacher and writer of history. During most of that time, a central focus of my attention has been the historical experience of Japanese Americans (and more recently, Japanese Canadians). Why is this so? Mainly because I am fascinated by the vital and often-ignored role that the so-called Nikkei have played—despite their small numbers—in shaping North American culture, law, and politics. I have done a great deal of research on the subject and have written a set of scholarly books of which I am proud as well as editing reprints of classic texts, directing anthologies, and contributing articles to journals.

While I have found my writing to be useful and important—along with teaching classes and giving lectures and attending conferences and doing other sorts of academic things—it is not quite enough for me. The problem is, first of all, that these kinds of books and papers take quite a long time to write and publish, and for good reason: they need to be checked and rechecked for accuracy. Because of this time lag, scholarly authors tend to lose the experience of regular contact with an audience. A more serious

DOI: 10.5876/9781607324294.c000

problem is that academic monographs about Japanese Americans, even good ones, only reach a relatively small number of people. Often they simply are not designed to attract many readers who might be interested in this history, whether they are themselves ethnic Japanese or not.

As a result, ever since I began working as a historian, I have looked for ways to connect with people outside of the typical academic audience, such as talking to community groups, writing magazine articles, and (particularly) blogging. When the conservative columnist Michelle Malkin published a book in mid-2004 that tried to justify and defend the wartime roundup of Japanese Americans and their confinement in government camps (aka Japanese internment), I joined forces with renowned legal scholar Eric L. Muller to write a series of blog posts that critiqued her arguments and pointed out the many errors in her book. It was a revelation to discover, once we finished, that our blogs had reached a whole new public. Many people who had never seen my books now knew my name because of Malkin. It seemed clear that online posts represented a worthwhile means of discussing history, and I accepted an invitation to contribute to *Cliopatria*, a historical blog. Over the following months, I posted on a wide variety of topics linked to history before family responsibilities forced me to withdraw.

In the process, I realized that beyond reaching a larger audience, I really wanted to find a new and different way to write history. One thing that has struck me over the years is that being a good historian—anywhere—has a lot to do with storytelling: it is no accident that many languages use the same word for both *story* and *history*. In the course of my ongoing scholarly research, I regularly came across compelling stories about individual people and their uncommon lives. (The English sections of the old Japanese American press contain a treasure trove of information, especially for the period before World War II.) I wanted to tell these stories, and it was frustrating to have to lay them aside because they did not fit comfortably into the structure of an academic book or historical blog.

It was thus fortunate that in early 2007, Kenji Taguma, the intrepid editor of the *Nichi Bei Times* in San Francisco, contacted me about writing a regular column. It was a flattering offer for a historian, especially as the name *Nichi Bei* carried the weight of tradition. The first newspaper of that name, the *Nichi Bei Shimbun*, founded by Issei businessman Kyutaro Abiko in 1899, was the oldest and, by consensus, the best of the vernacular journals serving the prewar West Coast Japanese community. Shut down during the mass wartime removal, Shichinosuke Asano revived it in 1946 under the name *Nichi Bei Times*, publishing separate weekly editions in English and Japanese into the new millennium. Kenji had been named editor of the newspaper's English section some years previously while only in his mid-twenties (this still made him a graybeard in comparison to Larry Tajiri, the most renowned *Nichi Bei* editor, who was still in his teens when recruited for the editorship in 1934). Kenji was very conscious that the journal should address new issues and audiences and thought I might provide something different. As a non–Japanese American, I was especially touched by his invitation to become a visible member of the community.

We agreed to try an experiment: I would write a set of columns about exceptional people and things in Japanese American history, stretching from the late nineteenth century to the present day. Each column would be about 1,000 words in length—short enough to read easily in a single sitting (the columns grew gradually to 1,500 words or more). I would also assist in finding images to include with the columns. Although Kenji approved a list of proposed topics at the outset, he set no limits and, in fact, encouraged me to write however I saw fit. He also agreed to let me call my column *The Great Unknown and the Unknown Great*. The first installment appeared in print in April 2007 and was soon after posted on the *Nichi Bei Times* website.

My work soon achieved a certain success, at least judging by the letters from readers and the various reprints elsewhere. The columns became a regular feature of the newspaper—they eventually appeared approximately every month, though with no set interval. A hiatus of several months occurred in late 2009, when the *Nichi Bei Times* closed its doors, a sad victim of declining community size. Its website, which had been the main place where people outside the community could see my columns, became inactive. Kenji boldly resolved to carry on, and he founded an all-English successor publication, *Nichi Bei Weekly*. I moved to the new publication and resumed my column there.

What you hold in your hands now, dear reader, is the first-ever anthology volume of the columns that I wrote for the *Nichi Bei Times* and *Nichi Bei Weekly* between 2007 and 2012, plus a selection of others that appeared in outside periodicals or which are published here for the first time. More than any other book that I have written, *The Great Unknown* is a collection of stories designed to make Japanese American history come alive; my late friend Setsuko M. Nishi referred to these pieces as my "bonbons." As the title suggests, the stories bring to life unsung but fascinating people in Nikkei history, shedding light on a galaxy of real-life characters: Milton Ozaki, pulp fiction writer from Wisconsin; Tel Sono, a Meiji-era Japanese woman lawyer who became a teacher in Brooklyn; Art Matsu, a college football star in the 1920s and the first Japanese American in the National Football League; Hugh Macbeth, the maverick African American attorney who was a major wartime defender of Nikkei; among many others. Additional topical essays bring to light unusual information about Nikkei experience. For example, one piece recounts the prewar history of ethnic Japanese in Chicago. Another traces a trio of ethnic Japanese murderers who helped shape public discussion of the death penalty.

The other side of the stories in this book concerns "the unknown great": unusual glimpses that show us new sides of people and things that we thought we already knew. Who would have guessed that conservative US Senator S. I. Hayakawa was once a jazz aficionado who wrote for an African American newspaper? Or that his future Senate colleague Alan M. Cranston joined forces with Eleanor Roosevelt in spring 1942 to dissuade President Franklin Roosevelt from signing Executive Order 9066? Or that Robert Chino, a biracial Nisei from Chicago, thought up the name of the civil rights group the Congress of Racial Equality and joined CORE's first sit-in?

Besides being entertaining (as if that was not reason enough!), *The Great Unknown* has a serious purpose: through the tales it recounts, the work as a whole reframes the familiar narrative of Japanese Americans. Popular ethnic histories, such as Bill Hosokawa's *Nisei: The Quiet Americans* or Paul Spickard's *Japanese Americans: The Formation and Transformations of an Ethnic Group*, center on the impressive success story of Japanese communities. In contrast, I focus my attention on the unusual and often rebellious sorts of characters who deviated from community norms (the "misfits," in artist Miné Okubo's piquant self-descriptive term). In the process, my work challenges one-dimensional model-minority stereotypes of ethnic Japanese as conformist or colorless and reveals the complex and wide-ranging nature of their experience. I also go against the West Coast–centric focus of standard works by devoting attention to Nikkei throughout the country—notably the cosmopolitan communities of New York and Chicago. Finally, most works on Japanese Americans concentrate on the saga of immigrants or the confinement of West Coast Japanese Americans during World War II. If these areas naturally receive due attention in my narrative, my work breaks new ground in its extended investigation of Japanese Americans in the postwar years—an all-but-ignored period in conventional histories.

By highlighting a series of original themes, my work suggests new directions for further study. For instance, a central element in these stories is the experience of Nikkei women and their role in shaping community life. From the first arrival of women from Japan, a durable (if often contested) strand of feminism has been present in ethnic Japanese communities, which have given rise to surprising numbers of women artists, writers, and professionals. Another theme treated at length in this book is the continuing encounter of Japanese Americans with African Americans. The presence of black Americans and their struggle for equality has remained a vital reference point in the consciousness of so many Nikkei, who have defined themselves alongside blacks, and even sometimes against them. Perhaps the most original aspect of my work, and certainly the most audacious, is the set of articles that explores the evolution of dominant attitudes toward sexuality—including homosexuality—within Nikkei communities. I am conscious that I have done little more than scratch the surface of a still largely unrecorded (and partially taboo) history, one that calls out for intensive research.

Before I start, let me offer a few caveats about this book. First, it is a selection of sketches written for easy reading. While I attach an overall bibliography, I do not include footnotes or specific citations for the numerous newspaper articles and other sources consulted. Also, I have taken the liberty of incorporating additions or corrections in the chapters in those cases where I learned more information after the original column appeared in print, and I have also added a few updates that seemed relevant.

I recognize that there are some important omissions in the text. Most notably, the history of the "local Japanese" population in Hawai'i is underrepresented here in proportion to its importance, for reasons having mainly to do with accessibility of sources. I admit to a certain embarrassment over this (relative) absence, as I have sometimes criticized historians who aim to speak about Asian Americans yet leave out Hawai'i, the nation's most established and concentrated ethnic Asian community. At the same time, not without regret, I have omitted some writings I have done specifically on Japanese Canadians (including those from the column I write for the Toronto-based monthly *Nikkei Voice*), as I think they require their own separate study. Furthermore, from the beginning I chose to not write about living people for various reasons, and with very few exceptions, I have followed that rule.

I close by thanking some key supporters. Obviously, my chief gratitude goes to Kenji Taguma, for welcoming my columns in the first place, and to the staff of *Nichi Bei Weekly*, especially Heather Horiuchi and Tomo Hirai, for continued support and editorial assistance. I likewise am obliged to Yoko Nishimura and Vicki Murakami-Tsuda, of Discover Nikkei, and Ben Hamamoto, editor of *Nikkei Heritage*, for commissioning other pieces, as well as Eric L. Muller for making it possible for me to post on his blog *The Faculty Lounge*. Ralph Luker, the presiding spirit of *Cliopatria*, helped me begin blogging on its pages. Steve Doi, who kindly shared his accumulated information on Milton K. Ozaki and served as cowriter with me on the Ozaki piece, graciously consented to its republication here. Maxime Minne prepared the index.

THE GREAT UNKNOWN

1

A New Look at Issei Women

ISSEI WOMEN: AN OVERVIEW

This overview introduces a series of portraits from a whole class of "unknown greats": Issei women. Of all the ethnic Japanese in the United States in the first half of the twentieth century, the lives and experiences of immigrant women have been arguably the least studied by family and community historians, despite notable efforts by such scholars as Akemi Kikumura-Yano and Evelyn Nakano Glenn. The reasons for this, even leaving aside simple sexism or denigration of women, are not hard to find. Most Issei women generally spoke and wrote English badly, if at all, and thus left few readily accessible primary sources behind. In keeping with popular ideas of the female role in both the American and Japanese societies of the day, they were largely relegated to the care of families and as unpaid labor on farms or in shops. Although I will focus on some outstanding individuals, comparatively few were able to establish themselves in careers. Yet it would be a great mistake to dismiss these women or to minimize their contributions. For Issei women, as a whole, were extraordinary.

DOI: 10.5876/9781607324294.c001

First, they were a uniquely educated set of women. As a result of the establishment of universal education in late Meiji- and Taisho-era Japan, they were almost entirely literate—far more so than the average white American of that period. Further, a large fraction of these women continued their education in Japan beyond primary school into high school and normal school, where they studied to become schoolteachers, the only independent career open to Japanese women at that time. (Moreover, because the national universities were closed to women, they studied, in many cases, at Christian schools or with help from Christian missionaries, which facilitated their subsequent familiarity with and embrace of Christianity once in the United States.)

It was precisely these patterns that led them to marry overseas Japanese. That is, because of their extended studies, masses of Japanese women remained single into their early to mid-twenties, which was considered too old for a respectable bride in Japan. Thus, their only remaining option, if they wished to marry, was to look abroad and unite with Japanese immigrant men. Their prospective husbands, themselves generally much older, could not afford to be so choosy about the age of the women who would agree to leave Japan and join them in North America. They gladly tapped into this available pool of potential partners, even though it meant arranging marriages with women they had never seen—women whose educational background, and sometimes class origins, were generally superior to their own. The mass of Issei women wed by proxy came to North America as "picture brides," to be greeted upon entry by their new husbands. (Many are the stories of shock and disappointment experienced by women who discovered that their spouses were not so young or prosperous as they had made out, and had sent faked, misleading, or outdated photos.)

We can only begin to imagine the difficulties that these women experienced, suddenly stuck in a new country with an unfamiliar language and customs, trying to build new lives among foreign (and sometimes hostile) natives. Locked into wedlock with strangers, their adjustment to married life was difficult—as in other immigrant subcultures, wife beating and abandonment were legion in Japanese communities—and they had little recourse besides giving up everything and making the long trip back to Japan. Such drastic action became exceedingly more complicated once these wives became mothers; the immigrant women were at the height of their age of fertility, and so the average birthrate in Japanese communities was considerably higher than that among native-born whites. As Issei men, in most cases, did not participate in child care, the women had to shoulder alone the double burden of working and raising a family.

Still, whatever the rigors and trials of their existence, these women not only adjusted with fortitude to their new circumstances, but they pursued social and intellectual interests. Unlike their husbands, who generally had much less education, Issei women remained devoted readers and writers in their native tongue. They faithfully wrote diaries, a number of which survive. (For example, Susan L. Smith's *Japanese American Midwives: Culture, Community, and Health Politics, 1880–1950* (2005), features the diaries of Toku Shimomura, a midwife in Seattle, which furnish considerable information on birthing practices.) They also wrote letters, especially to friends and family members in Japan. They composed a large proportion of the audience for Japanese-language newspapers and magazines, and they long remained impassioned contributors to the haiku and tanka poetry contests run by these newspapers, one of which is poignantly dramatized in Hisaye Yamamoto's famous story "Seventeen Syllables." In response to such demand, the West Coast Japanese press not only expanded its coverage of sections deemed "women's interests," but newspapers engaged feminists such as Mei Tanaka (Ayako Ishigaki) of *Rafu Shimpo* and Misatoshi Saijo (Miyatsa Asano Saijo) of *Sangyo Nippo* as regular columnists. Indeed, after the death in 1936 of founding editor Kyutaro Abiko, San Francisco's *Nichi Bei Shimbun*, the leading organ of the West Coast Nikkei press, was edited by his widow, Yonako Abiko (who was the sister of the notable feminist educator Umeko Tsuda, founder of Japan's Tsuda College), until its forced dissolution in spring 1942. Issei "aunts" also published in the English-language press.

The extraordinary creativity of the women of the Issei generation was most powerfully demonstrated, ironically, by their wartime confinement. Released from farm labor and shop duties and relieved of the need to cook by communal mess halls, these women were able to take advantage of a measure of leisure to cultivate activities they previously engaged in only in stolen moments. They both practiced and taught ikebana, Japanese dance, theater, and folk arts, all of which had been less present in communities during the prewar era.

Finally, the Issei women, to the extent that they could communicate with their Nisei children, were responsible for passing on their interest in education and its value. The stellar educational record of the Nisei generation, especially women, very soon became evident; despite areas of discrimination and exclusion, such as quotas for ethnic Japanese in West Coast medical schools, Nisei attended institutions of higher education in disproportionate numbers well before Pearl Harbor. Researchers in American education have long agreed that the most important variable in determining the educational success of children is the educational level and interest of their parents. Because fathers were more often absent or emotionally distant in Japanese communities, mothers bore responsibility for their children's achievement and encouraged them to succeed.

SHIO SAKANISHI: LIBRARY OF CONGRESS OFFICIAL AND SCHOLAR

In his April 1939 *New York Times* column, Edward Larocque Tinker offered a laudatory account of a new book, *The Spirit of the Brush: Being the Outlook of Chinese Painters of Nature, from Eastern Chin to Five Dynasties, A.D. 371–960*, a collection of commentaries on art by Chinese classical painters. Tinker noted that the editor of the collection, Dr. Shio Sakanishi, was to be congratulated. He had not only edited and translated the pieces but had added a set of richly anecdotal biographical essays on each artist that explained their work and ideas on art and nature, thereby transforming the Chinese artists from foreign and exotic figures to accessible ones. Two weeks later, Tinker made a shamefaced apology after discovering that Sakanishi was a lady—and a scholar—and not a gentleman as reported. Tinker was not alone in his astonishment at Sakanishi's gender, for she ultimately spent a lifetime challenging conventional ideas of women's role and abilities.

Shio (Shiho) Sakanishi was born to a Christian farming family in Hokkaido, Japan, in 1896. She achieved distinction in her early twenties, when she became the first Japanese woman ever hired to teach at a boy's preparatory school. She came to the United States in 1922 and enrolled at Wheaton College, where she graduated in 1925 with a degree in aesthetics and literature. During her time at Wheaton, she attracted publicity because of a speech at Mount Holyoke College on the need to encourage women writers, and she announced that she had undertaken a Japanese translation of a biography of that school's founder, pioneering educator Mary Lyon. After leaving Wheaton, Sakanishi enrolled at the University of Michigan, where she received her doctorate in 1929.

In 1930, after a short stint as a professor of English at Hollins College in Virginia, Sakanishi was hired by the Library of Congress as a librarian in its Asian Reading Room, then called the Orientalia Division (as a noncitizen, her hiring by the federal government required a special act of Congress). Her first task was to sort through some 15,000 Japanese books collecting dust on back shelves. Her skilled and thorough organization of the collection led to her being named director of the division in 1935. In this job, Sakanishi mixed and grew friendly with government officials as well as writers and intellectuals such as Archibald MacLeish (who became her boss as librarian of Congress in 1939) and Ezra Pound. In addition to aiding researchers, she offered public programs on events such as Buddha's Birthday and gave outside lectures on Asian literature, especially women writers. For example, in 1935 she served as a lecturer at Yale University's Institute of Human Relations. While researching the origins of printing and papermaking, her passion turned to science. In 1941 she supervised a series of experiments designed to duplicate the process of the "million paper charms," a set of Buddhist prayer charms printed by order of the empress of Japan in AD 770 and thought to be the oldest extant examples of woodblock printing. The team discovered that the printing involved baking clay tablets carved with a stylus, then pouring metal over the tablet to create a crude form of type.

Meanwhile, Sakanishi continued translating and began selecting outstanding pieces of Japanese literature for rendering into English. Her first effort, a Japanese comedy called "The Ribs and the Cover," appeared in the *Golden Book Magazine* in 1932. (Soon after, she undertook a multiyear project with collaborators to produce an authoritative list of translations of Japanese drama into English, French, and German, which was released in 1935.) Meanwhile, she received a contract for a set of translations of modern Japanese poets. The first of her translations to appear was that of Meiji-era poet Ishikawa Takuboku's *A Handful of Sand*, in 1934. The next year, she completed a translation of Yasano Akiko's *Tangled Hair* and Sachio Ito's *Songs of a Cowherd* followed in 1936. A small volume of comic playlets, *Kyôgen*, appeared in 1938. Sakanishi served as a regular book reviewer of Chinese and Japanese literature for the *Washington Post* and in 1939 she was invited by the *New York Times* to report on contemporary literature in Japan in a set of articles, "The Japanese Literary Scene." Both her incisive criticism of literary movements and her polished English prose drew respectful attention.

In addition to her translations of Japanese works, Sakanishi turned to a compilation of Chinese art criticism—in the process, demonstrating an impressive command of classical Chinese. Her first effort in this field, which appeared in 1935, was an English edition of Kuo Hsi's *An Essay on Landscape Painting*, a short book in which the eleventh-century Chinese landscape painter conveyed his aesthetic doctrines. *The Spirit of the Brush*, Sakanishi's best-known work, followed four years later.

Although Sakanishi expressed approval of American democratic society, her exalted government position did not isolate her from suspicion due to her Japanese ancestry and Japanese embassy connections. As 1940 dawned, war broke out in Europe and relations between the United States and Japan grew increasingly strained. Sakanishi found ways to assist her adopted country and ease tensions. First, she engaged in historical research that underlined the ties between the United States and Japan. In 1940 she published an edition of the private journal of John Glendy Sproston, who accompanied Commodore Matthew Perry on his historic mission to "open" Japan. The following year, Sakanishi edited an edition of the unpublished letters of Townshend Harris, the first US consul in Japan.

She also engaged in more confidential intelligence work. In 1941 William J. "Wild Bill" Donovan, who had been selected as Coordinator of Information, started putting together a team (his agency would soon morph into the Office of Strategic Services, wartime ancestor of the Central Intelligence Agency). In desperate need of agents to collect information and offer advice on Japanese threats to French Indochina, Donovan recruited as his Southeast Asia regional expert Kenneth Landon, who had recently returned to the United States after he and his wife, Margaret, had served for several years as missionaries in Thailand. (Margaret would draw on her experience in Asia for her 1944 bestseller *Anna and the King of Siam*.) Sakanishi immediately offered Landon, a fellow Wheaton College alum, an office at the Library of Congress and assisted him in his intelligence work. Indeed, in his 1967 book *The Broken Seal*, historian and intelligence officer Ladislas Faragó asserted rather doubtfully that Sakanishi had been a double agent aiding the US Office of Naval Intelligence (Farago claimed that she fingered a Japanese courier carrying the keys to diplomatic codes, thereby enabling naval intelligence officials to copy the documents and break the code).

Whatever the extent of Sakanishi's efforts to assist the federal government, she was targeted once war broke out between the United States and Japan in December 1941. Arrested by the Federal Bureau of Investigation, she was detained indefinitely without charge. Archibald MacLeish protested unavailingly on her behalf while First Lady Eleanor Roosevelt wrote Attorney General Francis Biddle to ask if anything could be done to help her and whether naval intelligence files revealed any suspect conduct. Her political opinions and the reasons for her custody are unknown, though it is likely that her name figured on a list of Japanese immigrants (plus a few Nisei) whom Tokyo demanded be repatriated. What is certain is that, realizing that the war would be protracted, she accepted repatriation, and in August 1942, sailed on an exchange ship to Japan, where she had not lived for two decades. Sakanishi maintained a low profile during the war, though according to one source, she was conscripted into service for Japan's war effort as a translator and propagandist.

Following Japan's defeat, Sakanishi emerged as a liberal and pro-American voice. The occupation government selected her as an advisor, and she was appointed to the Foreign Affairs Committee of the House of Councilors of the Japanese Diet as a specialist on women's issues and international relations. Drawing on her familiarity with American society (a rare commodity in occupation-era Japan), she published a trilogy of studies on American women and popular history: *America no josei* (1946), *Jugonin no Americajin* (1946), and *America shi* (1947). In the years that followed, she produced some two dozen books on social reform issues such as child-rearing, young people, and women's rights, plus translations of numerous American books (as well as the daily *Blondie* comic strip). Sakanishi became best known as a broadcaster and television interviewer. She would question foreign visitors in English, then interpret both questions and answers for her viewers.

In 1963 Sakanishi made a triumphal return visit to the United States. She died in Japan in 1976. Her unique career and success provoked admiration and challenged easy assumptions about gender roles among Japanese.

Fuki Endow Kawaguchi's Diary[1]

As I mentioned in the overview of Issei women, one field of creative work common among immigrants was keeping a diary. We are fortunate to have various surviving journals. Beyond their value as literature, they help fill a

FIGURE I.I. Fuki Endow Kawaguchi, California farm wife and diarist, with her husband.

significant gap in our historical understanding of the removal of West Coast Japanese Americans during World War II: how ordinary people perceived events as they occurred.

In the decades since the war, former camp inmates have produced an enormous corpus of literature dealing with their wartime experiences, including oral histories, memoirs, essays, plays, poetry, and fiction. These have provided valuable insight as to how the government's policy played out in the lives of its victims and included a store of information useful in reconstructing the overall camp experience. Still, memoirs are, by nature, products of hindsight and recollection, formed of material drawn from the untidy storehouse of human memory. They inevitably give an incomplete and less than trustworthy accounting of past sensations, especially the traumatic emotions and painful human relations that characterized the camp experience. In contrast, the contemporary written record of wartime Japanese Americans is both relatively sparse and uneven. Surviving letters, essays, and journals stress the experience of the Nisei, who comprised the majority of camp inmates. Members of the Issei generation, less long-lived and fluent in English than their children, have produced much less accessible material despite various oral history collections and a few published memoirs.

Nowhere is the documentary record, for both groups, barer than that for the period before mass confinement took place. Although government documents and newspaper accounts provide a certain amount of data regarding developments within Japanese communities during this turbulent time, it is very difficult to determine what was happening "on the ground," in ordinary people's lives.

The Japanese attack on Pearl Harbor on December 7, 1941, and the outbreak of war transformed the lives of West Coast Japanese Americans—especially the Issei, who bore the brunt of official repression. Barred on racial grounds from becoming American citizens despite their long residence in the United States, they suddenly were designated *enemy aliens* once war began. Their bank accounts were frozen; many of their newspapers and business establishments were closed; they were subjected to a strict curfew; and their homes were opened to random searches. A total of 1,370 West Coast Issei were rounded up and interned by the FBI in the period after Pearl Harbor, an action that created individual hardship as well as deprived the community of much of its leadership and cohesion in the weeks that followed.

Some time ago I came across a wonderful bit of historical material: the diary of Fuki Endow Kawaguchi (in a translation by her daughter, Sanae

Kawaguchi Moorehead). With the family's permission, I proceeded to edit a section of it. The text offers a rare contemporary portrait of a family of Japanese American farmers in Southern California during the period following Pearl Harbor.

Fuki Endow was born February 6, 1905, in Miho, a peninsula jutting into Suruga Bay on the island of Honshu, about one hundred miles south of Tokyo. Her parents were small shopkeepers. Sickly as a child, she was indulged and received an unusually extensive education for a woman of her time and background. In 1923 she met Sakujiro Kawaguchi, a native of Miho who had immigrated some years before to the United States and had returned to Japan to find a bride. Fuki thought going to America was a very exciting idea and agreed to marry him despite their brief acquaintance. Soon after, she gave birth to a daughter, Kazuko, who died within a month. Daughter Toshiye came a year later, followed by Haruko, Sanae, and Michiko. Fuki found relations with her husband difficult and the strains of constant pregnancy and childbirth were hard on her health. In 1933 she returned to Japan, taking her four daughters with her, a common practice among immigrants who felt a Japanese education would be better for their children. However, life in Japan proved even more difficult. The children were almost constantly ill, and one-year-old Michiko died. In 1935 Fuki agreed to return to her husband. Two years later, they acquired a farm in Dominguez Hills, now part of Los Angeles, where they grew flowers. Life on the farm was hard on Fuki, who was often ill.

She maintained a daily journal, with some interruptions, for forty years, although only the volumes from the 1940s survive. What struck me most powerfully in the existing diary was the section dealing with the period between the onset of the war in the Pacific and the mass removal of West Coast Japanese Americans. The journal's entries trace the author's growing awareness that she and her family might be taken away from their land and her uncertainty over what action to take, as the shadow of expulsion loomed ever nearer. Kawaguchi's text offers a vivid picture of the confusion and anxiety felt by Issei in Southern California as they faced business closings, alien registration forms, and evacuation from defense areas; but it shows the resilience and vitality of their community life. It also refutes popular images of the Issei as passive in the face of mass expulsion. In particular, the text reveals that many families did seriously consider and plan for "voluntary evacuation" from the West Coast, regardless of the considerable difficulties entailed in such an operation, during the short window of time in early 1942 that it was possible. The Kawaguchi family did just that: organizing a caravan and migrating to Utah, where Mr. Kawaguchi had old friends from his days working on the railroad.

I find a thrilling tension in the author's description of the unfolding events, lending her narrative the character of a detective story. Yet the journal's force does not result simply from its immediacy. While the entries stand as they were written at the time, without subsequent correction, the diary is by no means an unconscious or unskilled text. Fuki came from an educated background and was an avid reader and letter writer as well as an accomplished poet of haiku. (On at least one occasion, local Japanese American newspapers offered to publish her work, but her husband forced her to decline such offers because he thought them unseemly for a woman.) Her journal weaves together daily weather reports and a precise accounting of each day's planting with details of the larger world, firmly grounding the historical events leading up to the expulsion of Japanese Americans in the day-to-day experience of ordinary people. Her prose, couched in the Japanese idiom of her youth—one already growing old-fashioned by 1941—features colorful and evocative language. Thus, in addition to its value as a historical resource, Fuki Endow Kawaguchi's diary represents a precious example of *women's literature*, giving voice to the unique perspective of Issei women.

TEL SONO: ISSEI WOMAN LAWYER AND MISSIONARY

One area of professional life in the United States in which women have become most visible is law. Within recent generations, women attorneys have passed from being a rarity, greeted with condescension and often unemployable, to forming the majority of new law school graduates. Nisei women formed part of this wave of courageous pioneers.

Interestingly, the first Nisei woman in the law was not an American but rather Maria Arai of Mexico. She was born circa 1915, the daughter of Kinta Arai, a Japanese foreign ministry diplomat who ended his career as an embassy counselor in Madrid. During those years, Maria received a degree in literature from University of Madrid. In 1933, after her father accepted a new chair in Oriental studies at the National Autonomous University of Mexico,

FIGURE 1.2. Tel Sono, the first Japanese American woman lawyer.

she enrolled at the university and earned a degree in international law. In 1935 the Mexican government hired her as a counselor in the Department of Agriculture and the director of the marine industry bureau. In 1936 she was named chief prosecutor in the Mexican government's crime bureau. She subsequently went by the name Hisa Arai, spending a long career as an advisor on Mexico's international trade for the Instituto Mexicano de Ejecutivos en Comercio Exterior; her fluent Japanese helped her with negotiations on trade missions to Japan. She died in 2007.

Chiyoko Sakamoto (Takahashi) (1912–1994), a Los Angeles native, was the first Japanese American woman to practice law (although Elizabeth Ohi of Chicago, discussed in chapter 2, was admitted to the bar a few months before her). Sakamoto graduated from American University and passed the California bar exam in October 1938. Unable to find a job with a law firm, she worked as a legal assistant to a Japanese American community leader who provided translation services. After being incarcerated during the war at the Santa Anita and Granada camps, she returned to Los Angeles and was hired by African American attorney Hugh E. Macbeth as his associate. She later opened her own law office in Little Tokyo and was one of the founders of the Japanese American Bar Association and the California Women's Bar Association.

Other women followed Sakamoto. Rei Kihara Osaki obtained her law degree and was admitted to the bar in Idaho in 1943, in the teeth of wartime anti-Japanese prejudice. She worked for the Office of Price Administration before retiring to raise a family. Patsy Takemoto Mink, who received her JD from the University of Chicago in 1951, became the first Japanese American woman lawyer in Hawai'i—although she had to go to court to win the right to practice there. In 1964 she became the first woman of color elected to Congress. Nikkei women of subsequent generations also made important contributions. Peggy Nagae served as lead counsel in Minoru Yasui's coram nobis case in the early 1980s to overturn the wartime Supreme Court ruling against him. In the mid-1990s, Susan Oki Mollway, director of the American Civil Liberties Union of Hawai'i, became the first Japanese American woman on the federal bench.

But the first women lawyer of Japanese ancestry in America, Cassie Tel (aka Teru) Sono, lived long before the 1930s. By her own account, Tel Sono was born in Tokyo (then called Edo), Japan, in 1846 and grew up in Ebalaki. Her father, Tesai Sono, was a doctor and philosopher. When she was nineteen, her parents arranged for her marriage to an imperial court officer, with whom she had a daughter. Her husband proved to be an alcoholic, and in 1871

Sono took her daughter and moved back into her family compound. In order to support herself and her daughter, she undertook the study of law with her father. Japan at the dawn of the Meiji restoration had no law schools, and (as in America) most lawyers learned their trade by reading law.

In 1873 Sono moved to Tokyo, and after spending three months clerking as a "Secretary of Judgment," she began her practice. As the first and only woman lawyer in Japan, she later recalled, she made such a startling spectacle in the court of assizes that two poets wrote about her in a volume about novelties in Tokyo, thus bringing her nationwide fame. She also attracted attention for her charitable work and received a letter of commendation from the emperor. Sono practiced law in Japan for twelve years, frequently defending women. She became increasingly frustrated with sex discrimination and the lack of educational opportunity for women. She determined to travel to the United States and study so that she could educate Japanese women.

Sono arrived in San Francisco in 1886. Three months later, the Bank of Japan, in which she had put her savings, failed. Impoverished and speaking no English, she was forced to hire herself out as a domestic to earn a living. She rented a room with an African American family and went to the city's Japanese (Christian) mission to look for work. After her bad experience working for an abusive farm family, the pastor of the Japanese mission found her a free room in the cellar of the Chinese (Christian) mission. She remained there for several months, working during the day and studying English with a white woman at night. After enrolling in public school and being expelled as too old, Sono entered a private women's classical school, supporting herself by domestic work.

Sono's experience with a Japanese missionary led to her conversion to Christianity and her entry into the Japanese Methodist Church in October 1887. She then joined the Woman's Christian Temperance Union (WCTU). According to one source, she studied for a time at a deaconesses' training school in Chicago. In 1889 Sono began raising money to create a Japanese benevolent society in San Francisco and opened a school and daycare center to pursue missionary work among Issei "fallen women." She soon moved to Brooklyn, New York (then an independent city), and began teaching Japanese language at Mrs. Osborn's Missionary Training Institute. At that time she began the Tel Sono Association, with the goal of establishing a Christian missionary training school for high-caste women in Japan. In order to support herself, she produced a 66-page autobiography, *Tel Sono: The Japanese Reformer*, which appeared in 1890 and is almost certainly the first published work by an Asian woman in the United States. It serves as the major biographical source on her life.

Sono attracted widespread attention after she spoke at an international convention of the WCTU in Boston in 1891. Soon after, she embarked on a fundraising tour under WCTU auspices. In her speeches, she wore Japanese dress and spoke of her experiences. Newspapers reported on her speeches in cities such as New York; Washington, DC; and Los Angeles and praised the opportunity she presented for Christianizing the natives of Japan, especially her access to elite women. In January 1893, she set sail for England, where she addressed the famed Mildmay Conference of evangelical missionaries. She then went on to Japan. In September 1893, her girl's boarding school, the Eshowin Geogaku, opened in Tokyo, with two "lady teachers" and a male minister. However, the Women's Board of Foreign Missions complained the following year that Sono was living comfortably on the money she had raised, without pursuing further efforts at fund-raising. Sono's later life lies unrecorded, and she remains largely forgotten—modern Japanese histories of women lawyers list the first women as beginning in 1940.

AYAKO ISHIGAKI: FEMINIST AND PEACE ACTIVIST

In the decade surrounding World War II, the Japanese-born feminist and activist Ayako Ishigaki lived in the United States, where she distinguished herself as a radical intellectual and an outspoken opponent of Japan's military occupation of Manchuria and China. She joined dockside protests aimed at preventing Japanese ships from landing and transporting cargoes and barnstormed the country on lecture tours to raise public awareness and earn money for Chinese war relief. She was equally forceful as an author, both in English and Japanese. She attracted attention within the community—not always favorable—for the columns she contributed to the Los Angeles newspaper *Rafu Shimpo* and became known for her semi-fictionalized 1940 memoir, *Restless Wave: My Life in Two Worlds*.

Ayako Ishigaki was born Ayako Tanaka on September 21, 1903, in Tokyo, Japan. Her mother died when she was young. Although her father, a university professor, did allow her to attend school, he made sure she absorbed

FIGURE 1.3. Ayako Ishigaki, *far left*, circa 1964, at a party in Japan.

conventional wisdom about women's social role. The key event in Ayako's life came when she was around sixteen. Her adored older sister gave into family pressure for an arranged marriage and wed a man in the diplomatic corps. Ayako declared that she would not accept any such union. Instead, she enrolled at Jiyu Gakuen, a new progressive girl's school founded by educational reformer Motoko Hani (artist and musician Yoko Ono would later study there). She also insisted on choosing her own spouse and became enamored of a local doctor's son despite his family's opposition. Meanwhile, she took paid jobs outside the home and was attracted by Japan's radical Farmer-Labor Party. In 1926, after spending a night in jail because of her activities, she agreed to move to the United States with her sister. Her brother-in-law secured a diplomatic passport for her, thereby enabling her to enter the country despite Japanese exclusion. Although Ayako's fiancé thereafter secured his family's consent to their marriage, she refused to return to Japan.

Soon after arriving in America, Ayako abandoned her sister's family and moved to New York, where she met and rapidly married a radical Issei artist, Eitaro Ishigaki. Ayako learned to do household chores and took various shop and factory jobs to support the couple while Eitaro painted. In the summers they worked as concessionaires at Coney Island. The Great Depression hit the Ishigakis hard, and Ayako later claimed that at one point they survived entirely on extra food that their waiter friend Jack Shirai brought home from work (Shirai subsequently volunteered for service on the Republican side in the Spanish Civil War and died in Spain).

Following Japan's 1931 invasion of Manchuria, Ayako began reporting for the radical publications the *New Masses* and *China Today*. In 1937 the American League for Peace and Democracy recruited her to organize against Japanese aggression. She moved to Los Angeles, where she began a column for the *Rafu Shimpo*'s Japanese section. In her column, Jinsei Shokan (Women's Thoughts), written under the pen name May Tanaka, Ayako spoke as a housewife to other housewives. She used informal language and homey metaphors to advocate birth control and women's equality and to oppose militarism. Her column soon became popular—the common discrimination faced by Issei women erased the class barriers that might otherwise have separated them. Despite the column's popularity, the Japanese community's overwhelming support for Tokyo's invasion of China in July 1937 led her to give up in despair, and she returned to New York. In the following years, she undertook fundraising tours in support of China alongside dancer Si-Lan Chen and writer Helena Kuo and began the work that emerged as *Restless Wave*.

Restless Wave, published in 1940 under the pen name Haru Matsui, ranks among the earliest books by an Asian American woman. Mixing autobiography, fiction, and reportage, it recounts the author's coming of age as a feminist and activist in Japan and the United States. The work remains notable for the ways the author associates Japanese military aggression abroad with "feudal" restrictions on women and the poor at home. The work also painted a sympathetic and poignant picture of Little Tokyo in the 1930s. While Ayako criticized the Issei for supporting Japanese militarism, she made clear that their pro-Japanese attitude stemmed from their race-based isolation—and their children's—within American society.

In 1942, following the outbreak of war between the United States and Japan, painter Yasuo Kuniyoshi recruited Ayako to make anti-Axis broadcasts. She thereafter joined the Office of War Information (OWI) as a translator and writer. She worked for the OWI and the War Department for the following five years. During this time, she evidently started a novel about Japanese

Americans, but the project was never realized. In the years following the war, Ayako revived her Jinsei Shokan column for New York's *Hokubei Shimpo*. She and Eitaro faced increasing harassment by the US government due to their political views, including their friendship with radical writer Agnes Smedley. They had already planned to leave the United States when Eitaro was summarily expelled in 1951. Ayako joined him in Japan.

Once in Japan, Ayako became renowned as an informed interpreter of American life as well as for her writings in the women's magazine *Fujin Koron*. In a controversial 1955 article, *"Shufu to iu dai-in shokugyō-ron"* ("Housewife: The Second Profession"), she complained that Japanese women's minds had "turned to mush" from staying at home, and she urged women to take up outside work, whether paid or unpaid.

In later decades, Ayako became a familiar Japanese television personality and women's advisor and authored over twenty Japanese-language books, including diaries, memoirs, essays, and biographies. Following Eitaro's death in 1958, she also dedicated her efforts to building a museum of his artwork, which opened in Wakayama in the 1980s. Ayako revisited the United States on a few occasions and contributed to the Japanese American literary anthology *Ayumi*. She died in a nursing home in 1996. In 2004 the Feminist Press of the City University of New York published a new edition of *Restless Wave*, by then long out of print. Two years later, it won a special citation as a "lost Asian American treasure" from the Association for Asian American Studies. (Full disclosure: I collaborated on the afterword to the new edition.)

NOTE

1. This piece is adapted from Greg Robinson, introduction to "On the Brink of Evacuation: The Diary of an Issei Woman, by Fuki Endow Kawaguchi," with Sanae Kawaguchi Moorehead, in *Prospects: An Annual of American Cultural Studies* 28 (October 2004): 359–82, which includes the text of the diary entries.

2

Mixed-Race Japanese Americans

Today's "great unknown" concerns an unknown aspect of Isamu Noguchi's life. An internationally renowned sculptor, landscape architect, and theatrical and industrial designer, Noguchi (1904–1988) was perhaps the most famous and visible Japanese American during his long lifetime, but he remained largely estranged from the ethnic community, in part because of his mixed ancestry. Yet he threw himself into advocating for his fellow Nisei after Pearl Harbor, an effort that was a notable failure. His generous, if perhaps starry-eyed, wartime activism has been all but erased from his biography.

Born of a liaison between the Japanese poet Yone Noguchi and Léonie Gilmour, the white woman he hired as his assistant, Isamu Noguchi was abandoned by his father when he was only two. He grew up between Japan and America, never feeling truly accepted; he later referred to himself as a "waif." After studying in Paris, where he worked with the sculptor Constantin Brancusi, Noguchi settled in New York. He established himself as a modernist sculptor while making his living doing portrait busts of rich Manhattanites.

DOI: 10.5876/9781607324294.c002

During the 1930s, Noguchi worked on various projects, flirted with leftist politics, and settled for a time in Mexico City (where he allegedly had an affair with Frida Kahlo). He gained additional fame when his stainless steel frieze was picked for installation at Rockefeller Center.

Noguchi remained largely aloof from Japanese communities during the prewar decades. A thoroughgoing democrat, he bore little love for the Japanese society that had rejected him and his mother. He became acquainted with a few Issei in New York, such as bacteriologist Hideyo Noguchi (whom he claimed as a distant kinsman), modern dancer Michio Ito, and the radical painter Eitaro Ishigaki and his wife, feminist/writer Ayako Ishigaki. Noguchi also became friends with the brilliant Nisei journalist Larry Tajiri, who moved to New York in 1940 to work for a Japanese news service.

The Japanese attack on Pearl Harbor forced Noguchi to take stock of his identity and convictions. Now that America was at war with Japan, Noguchi considered it his responsibility to help spread democratic ideas in Japanese communities. At the same time, he felt solidarity with members of the younger generation who were experiencing discrimination and alienation—as Noguchi later put it, "I became a Nisei." With help from Tajiri (who lost his job with the outbreak of war and had time to organize), Noguchi formed an antifascist group, the Nisei Writers and Artists Mobilization for Democracy. Tajiri wrote a manifesto and attracted a set of West Coast intellectuals, including journalists Eddie Shimano and Kazu Ikeda, to sign on. In early 1942, Noguchi traveled to the West Coast to help build the organization. Working in partnership with Shuji Fujii, the Kibei editor of the prewar left-wing magazine *Doho*, Noguchi commissioned a series of reports on the state of the Nisei in California agriculture and employment and housing conditions, which were put together under the direction of Los Angeles minister Fred Fertig and submitted to local authorities.

As February 1942 dawned and the menace of expulsion grew more apparent, Noguchi sought allies to defend Nisei civil rights. First, Noguchi wrote directly to President Franklin D. Roosevelt, asking him not to violate the civil rights of American citizens through arbitrary action. With assistance from author Clare Boothe Luce, whose bust he had once sculpted (and allegedly retouched after she had plastic surgery), Noguchi also requested help from Archibald MacLeish, director of the Office of Facts and Figures (later the Office of War Information [OWI]) and a Roosevelt speechwriter. Meanwhile, he met with progressive writer Carey McWilliams, who suggested that his group assemble an all-star panel of non-Japanese to testify before the Tolan Committee, the congressional committee set up to explore the question of mass relocation. Noguchi contacted Paul Robeson, the famous African American singer/actor/activist, who agreed to testify. University of California, Berkeley physicist J. Robert Oppenheimer, who would soon be called upon to lead the atomic bomb project in Los Alamos, offered his assistance as well.

On February 19, 1942, Roosevelt signed Executive Order 9066. Noguchi was in Los Angeles that day, helping to organize a mass meeting of Nisei. One Nisei later claimed that MacLeish tipped off Noguchi in advance about the order. While this is unlikely, he was surely aware that such action was probable. Once the order was announced, Noguchi's proposed panel was moot. He returned to New York and developed a new strategy. On a trip to Washington, DC, he would lobby for permission to establish a pro-allied vernacular newspaper and make a film of the "evacuation," both in order to teach democracy to Japanese Americans and secure their early release.

Once in Washington, Noguchi met first with OWI staffers, including Alan Cranston, the future US senator, who gave him an official letter asking government officials to assist him with travel arrangements and making his film. Noguchi also made an appointment with John Collier, director of the Office of Indian Affairs (OIA). It was a fateful encounter. Collier was a visionary thinker who had organized an "Indian New Deal." Abandoning past government paternalism, he promoted Native American self-government and respect for Indian art and culture. When Noguchi met him, Collier had just been assigned the task of building a "relocation center" at Poston, on the Colorado River Indian Reservation. Collier intended to organize a model resettlement community—he told his War Relocation Authority (WRA) colleagues that he was not interested in running a concentration camp—complete with agricultural cooperatives, schools, and housing. He was in the midst of hiring numerous social scientists to plan and organize camp governing structures. Collier fired up Noguchi with enthusiasm for Poston: he could teach art, design the community, and inculcate democratic spirit among the Nisei, to whom he could be a model. Although, as an East Coast resident, Noguchi was not subject to Executive Order 9066, he volunteered to be placed in camp. He considered it a worthy sacrifice for Japanese Americans, whom he now felt were his people.

Noguchi arrived at Poston in mid-1942 with all sorts of beautiful plans for parks and agricultural cooperatives, prepared to make a life in the community. Alas, it was not to be. Noguchi soon found that he could not work effectively in the heat and primitive conditions at Poston. Worse, he was viewed with suspicion and hostility as an outsider by many of those whom he had romantically imagined as "his people." Not only was Noguchi thirty-seven years old—old for a Nisei—and an easterner, an artist, a political activist, and biracial to boot, he was regarded as part of the camp administration. (John Collier soon mirrored Noguchi's disillusionment, ironically, once Dillon Myer broke the WRA's original deal with the OIA and ordered that Poston be managed like the other camps.) Within weeks of his arrival, Noguchi asked his friends to get him out of camp. He left camp sometime in fall 1942, having stayed just six months, and swiftly returned to the East Coast, where he remained for the rest of the war. Noguchi found small ways to assist Japanese Americans—making speeches, writing an article on the camps for the *New Republic* (he completed another, commissioned by *Reader's Digest*, but it was never published), and joining an antifascist group, the Japanese American Committee for Democracy. However, his leadership role in community affairs had dissolved, and he never again felt so close to the Nisei.

KATHLEEN TAMAGAWA: FIRST NISEI AUTHOR

Today, when all sorts of astronomical estimates are thrown around on intermarriage rates among Japanese Americans—70 percent, 80 percent, or more—it is curious to reflect that not so long ago, white-Asian intermarriage was illegal in many places, stigmatized in more, and almost everywhere rare enough that those of mixed parentage became objects of curiosity and scrutiny. Precisely wanting to describe her difficult experience as the product of such an interracial marriage, Kathleen Tamagawa Eldridge wrote *Holy Prayers in a Horse's Ear: A Japanese American Memoir*, the first published Nisei autobiography. It poignantly described her sense of being nowhere at home and her yearning to be ordinary.

Kathleen Tamagawa was born in 1893. As she recounted in her memoir, during the 1880s, her father, Sanzo Tamagawa, a Westernized Japanese, settled in Chicago and met her Anglo-Irish immigrant mother. The two fell in love and ultimately married, although her family's opposition delayed their

FIGURE 2.1. Kathleen Tamagawa, first published Nisei autobiographer, and son.

union for several years. (Tamagawa's mother was actually shipped abroad to help her forget her Japanese beau.) After their wedding, the Tamagawas opened a store in Cape May, New Jersey, where Kathleen was born. They soon returned to Chicago, where her father gave lessons in artistic needle-work and subsequently became a silk buyer. Kathleen spent her childhood years in Chicago, living at her maternal grandmother's house. (She achieved local celebrity when she provided the first recorded contribution to support Japan in the Russo-Japanese war, asking that the money go to soldiers "still able to fight.") Kathleen's family dressed her in kimonos and gave her Japanese hairdos. Thus, to her annoyance, friends and neighbors regarded her as an exotic—a living "China doll."

Kathleen was delighted when her father decided to move the family to Japan in 1906. Since she had always been identified as Japanese, she assumed she could now be with others of her kind. Once in Japan, however, she felt even more foreign. Unable to speak the language or communicate with the Japanese, whose customs and ways of life were a mystery to her, she felt her-self without any "race, nationality, or home." For a time, the Tamagawas tried living in a Japanese-style house, but they eventually made a comfortable place for themselves in Yokohama's multiracial foreign section. Kathleen, however, considered the international group a twilight zone of outcasts. In particular, she refused to "add an additional hyphen" to her identity by marrying any of her various international suitors. Instead, she deliberately chose to marry an American diplomat, Frank Eldridge, because she perceived him (mistakenly, she later admitted) to be "ordinary." "To be simple—insignificant—and to melt inconspicuously into some environment—seemed to me worth the ambition of a lifetime," she wrote. "Try as I would I could never find the charm of being raceless, countryless, and now to all intents and purposes relativeless as well."

In 1912 Kathleen returned to the United States with her husband. The Eldridges spent the succeeding years in Washington, DC, and Tennessee, where they had four children. Frank worked for the US Commerce Department and wrote books on trade with Asia. Kathleen, distancing her-self from her Japanese heritage, blended into white middle-class American life and motherhood. Meanwhile, amid the devastation of the 1923 Tokyo earthquake, Kathleen's mother was cut off from her husband. Although she had previously refused to admit the estrangement in her marriage, she finally took the opportunity to leave her husband and moved in with the Eldridges to help care for her grandchildren.

In 1928 the Eldridges moved to the New York City area. Following the onset of the Great Depression, Kathleen took a part-time job as a librarian at Columbia University to help family finances, and enrolled in a creative writing class. There she began work on her memoir. She took as the title a literal translation of a Japanese proverb for fruitless attempts at communication. Beginning in October 1930, she published her story in three installments in *Asia*, a popular magazine. Numerous readers wrote in to praise the author. The positive reception encouraged Kathleen to sign a book contract. She later added a section covering her 1927 trip to Asia, plus letters from her mother describing the Tokyo earthquake.

Holy Prayers in a Horse's Ear, the first mainstream book by an American-born Japanese, appeared in February 1932. Kathleen recounted her life in Japan and America as an "accident of nature." She preferred to treat her racial and cultural difference as an incidental or trivial phenomenon, rejecting all reference to it as an absurdity. She expressed particular irritation with "anthropologists" and "modernists" who tried to determine her character based on her racial background and made fun of the "dramatists" who asked her about the "racial pulls" she felt from her Japanese or European sides. She expressed strong opposition to interracial marriage as a source of grief and confusion (ironically, she did not perceive her own marriage to a Caucasian as an interracial union): "I do not approve of Eurasian marriages. I do not approve of inter-national marriages . . . because there are so few among the many in Europe, in Asia or America who have the wit and ability or the moral and spiritual stamina and determination, or the keen, blind, deaf and dumb intellect that will allow them to drive their psychological horse in triumph to its goal." The book featured a surprise ending, in which the author "disappeared." Speaking in her husband's voice, Kathleen noted that the Japanese government had informed her that, because she was not registered at the time of her birth, for official purposes, she did not exist. She presented that statement as the apex of the absurdity surrounding her mixed heritage.

The book attracted significant popular attention and went through several printings. The publishers invited Kathleen to write a second book, and she began work on a novel about Japan. However, family responsibilities and her own lack of commitment to her writing eventually led her to lay down her pen, and she never wrote again for publication. In 1934 she moved to Washington, DC, where she spent the rest of her life caring for her husband and family. She died in 1979. Rutgers University Press published a new edition of *Holy Prayers in a Horse's Ear* in 2008, with a collective introduction and notes by Floyd Cheung, Elena Tajima Creef, Shirley Geok-Lin Lim, and Greg Robinson.

THE CHINO AND OHI FAMILIES

One of the rare Japanese American family sagas from prewar Chicago was that of the connected Chino and Ohi clans. Frank and Mercelia Chino gave birth to a trio of mixed-race Nisei sons. Mercelia's sister Louise married another Japanese immigrant, Sidney Tokichi Ohi, and had four *hapa* children of their own, three daughters and a son.

The story of the Chino family in the United States begins with the 1883 birth of Haruka (aka Gen) Chino, who traveled from Kanagawa-ken to Seattle in 1899. The youthful Chino, youngest son of a samurai-class family from Odawara, scandalized his family due to his attraction to Christianity. He took passage to the United States with the announced intention of pursuing his studies. (Like so many other Japanese and other emigrants of the period, he may also have emigrated in order to escape the military draft in his native land.) If, like other converts, Gen expected to find America a promised land of Christianity, he must have been rapidly disillusioned by the racial prejudice he faced. He soon adopted the American name Frank H. Chino and found work as a valet to a member of the McCormick family, Chicago's powerful industrial and newspaper clan. According to family legend, Frank visited Alaska with his young employer and earned his gratitude by stepping in to protect him during a brawl.

What is certain is that Chino settled in St. Louis (evidently for the 1904 World's Fair, which featured a Japanese pavilion), where he met and married a local white woman, Mercelia Hicks, descended from a distinguished New England family. Soon after, he introduced Mercelia's sister Kate to another Japanese immigrant, Sidney Tokichi Ohi, who arrived in 1906. The Ohis moved to Chicago, where Sidney Ohi took a job as a chemist in a steel mill.

By 1910 the Chino family had likewise moved to Chicago, where Frank opened a Japanese dry goods shop and worked as a tea "solicitor" for the Jewel Tea Company. (Family legend states that the grateful McCormicks brought him to Chicago and set him up in business.) Frank's business prospered. He served a multiethnic clientele and built his popularity by giving away fruit baskets. Despite being estranged from his Japanese family, he also

FIGURE 2.2. Robert Chino, in Europe with the US Army.

helped support an older brother through medical school in Japan. The Chinos bought a house in a largely Jewish area on Chicago's South Side. Frank was elected president and treasurer of the Japanese Association of Chicago during the 1920s. Unfortunately, according to one history of Japanese Chicago, he became enmeshed in a financial dispute after he invested $1,000, half of the association's funds, in stock that was later discovered to be worth far less.

Chino's store, like so many other businesses, crashed with the Great Depression. He found work as a salesman for a toy company. Rejecting friends' advice that he declare bankruptcy, he labored endlessly peddling toys in order to repay off his store's debts, ruining his health in the process. He and Mercelia ultimately retired to Arizona, where he died in 1954.

Sidney Tokichi Ohi worked for many years in Chicago as a master drafts-man and designer of streamlined trains for the Pullman Palace Car Company, before dying prematurely in the 1930s following a freak accident. The Ohis had four children, who remained close to their Chino cousins. Their eldest daughter, Kamatsu Elizabeth Ohi, attended the University of Chicago and John Marshall Law School, where she was named class valedictorian. In 1937 Elizabeth became the first Nisei woman admitted to the bar in the United States. Dubbed by the *Chicago Tribune* newspaper a "Nipponese Portia," Elizabeth took a job as a secretary for a local attorney, Max Liss, and later served as legal assistant for another attorney, future Supreme Court justice Arthur Goldberg. According to Goldberg, the FBI arrested Elizabeth on the evening of the Pearl Harbor attack, and only Goldberg's threat to bring an immediate habeas corpus petition on her behalf prompted her release. During the 1940s, the family migrated to the region surrounding Washington, DC. Elizabeth changed her last name to Owens, which made it easier to con-ceal her Japanese ancestry, and later served as a Labor Department attorney. She died in 1976.

The stories of the three Chino sons—James Elbert Chino, Franklin Kiyoshi Chino, and Robert Asahi Chino—are worth exploring at length. The excep-tionally divergent life paths they took, which give their family history almost the flavor of a Russian novel, highlight the complexity of the Japanese American experience. The oldest son, Elbert (known in the family as Yoneo or Yone) was born in St. Louis in 1906. He discovered early that he was mechanically inclined and began working in his mid-teens as an aviation mechanic at a local airport before getting his pilot's license (family lore has it that he worked in legendary aviator Charles Lindbergh's team). In 1932 he publicly announced his dream of making a nonstop transpacific flight to sur-pass Lindbergh's feat, though his flight was never realized. Elbert ultimately joined American Airlines as a mechanic. Whether because of disagreements with his demanding father—whom he later described as giving the brothers a "hard time" during their teenage years—or simply weariness with the problems caused by his Japanese ancestry, at some point in the 1930s Elbert began to hide the Asian portion of his racial identity (which did not appear strongly in his features). By 1942, when he adopted a son, Marvin, he had already changed his last name to Cheyno.

Elbert continued to advance in the aviation industry during the postwar years. In 1955 he was selected as a special assistant to the president of Allegheny Airlines. In 1957 he became vice president of maintenance and engineering for Alaska Airlines. Some years later, he moved to Los Angeles, and Lockheed Corporation hired him as an engineer. His paper on vertiports (urban airplane terminals) from 1967 still survives on the Internet.

Elbert retired in 1971, at age sixty-five. Fascinated with Native American art and culture, he started a successful second career painting and sculpting horses and Native American themes. He founded the American Indian and Cowboy Artists Society and in 1974 helped lead "A Bicentennial Moment," a notable show of art on white-Indian relations at Los Angeles's Downey Museum of Art. In 1977, in partnership with John Walgren of the San Dimas Chamber of Commerce, the Society began an annual San Dimas Festival of Western Arts, which continued for two decades. Clad in Stetsons and boots, groups of artists would drive vintage cars of the Atchison, Topeka and Santa Fe Railway to town and set up exhibitions of work to sell.

By this time, Elbert identified himself as "Easy Cheyno," a Cherokee Indian. He insisted that the Chinos inherited Cherokee blood through their mother, and he worked to retrace the Hicks' Native genealogy. In part as a result of Elbert's denial of his Japanese side, he remained distant from his brothers in later life—Robert refused to speak to him for twenty years—although he remained in contact with his Ohi cousins. Elbert died in California in 1992.

In the years preceding Pearl Harbor, three Nisei lawyers worked in Chicago. (To put this fact in perspective, San Francisco, despite a Japanese population twenty times that of Chicago, was then home to a single Nisei attorney.) Minoru Yasui remains known primarily for his courageous Supreme Court challenge to Executive Order 9066. Elizabeth Ohi was the second. The third was Ohi's first cousin Franklin Chino, whose career stands as an intriguing counterpoint to both his peers and his two brothers.

Franklin (who styled himself Franklin H. or Frank Jr.) was born in Chicago in 1911, the second Chino son. He attended Walter Scott and Hyde Park High Schools and grew interested in legal work. Following a period of self-study, he enrolled at John Marshall Law School (where he was a classmate of Elizabeth Ohi) and was admitted to the bar in December 1937. Soon thereafter, he opened a law office, Chino, Iversen and Shultz, with former classmate Peter Shultz, and worked with the Interstate Commerce Commission. No doubt out of a mix of self-interest—the needs of building a business—and principle, Franklin embarked on a path that appears contradictory, at least in retrospect. On one hand, he connected with Japan. He became active in the Chicago Forum of International Relations at the University of Chicago and the International Club at the Chicago YMCA. He was hired as an attaché with the Japanese consulate in Chicago (likely due to his father's connections) and served as a "Public Relations counselor" during 1938 for a monthly salary of $20. The following year, another young Nisei attorney, Minoru Yasui, five years Frankin's junior, moved to Chicago from Oregon. Yasui's father's connections also secured him a job at the consulate, and he and Franklin became warm friends.

Simultaneously, Franklin sought to promote the status of Nisei as Americans. In 1937 he became president of a club for local Nisei, the Japanese Young People's Association. He organized the construction of a community center, formed a Nisei Boy Scout troop (with Yasui as scoutmaster), and in early 1940, proposed a nationwide contest to select a Nisei of the Year—a forerunner of the later Japanese American Citizens League (JACL) Nisei of the Biennium competition. His goal was to both celebrate the achievements and point up the Americanism of "second generations." Franklin wrote to Eleanor Roosevelt to ask her advice on the plan. He described the psychological malaise of the Nisei, who were American citizens, yet not fully accepted:

> On the one hand it is charged that we do not "assimilate" and on the other, social barriers are erected against us to rebuff our attempts to take a real place in the American scheme of things. The result has been that many of us have a definite inferiority complex and persecution mania, all of which is bad not only for the individual but also for Society as a whole.

With the endorsement of the First Lady, who praised the project as inspirational and a "splendid idea," the Sansho Yamagata Award (named for a local Issei businessman) was created. It sparked nationwide interest and nominations among Japanese Americans. The award was given twice, to JACL president Walter Tsukamoto in 1940 and to Mike Masaoka in 1941, before it stopped with the coming of the war.

In developing the award, Franklin had hoped to persuade white citizens, in a time of "rabid nationalism," that the Nisei could be true Americans. Meanwhile, whether out of pacifist principle or concern for Japanese Americans, he spoke out against US intervention in World War II. In a letter published in the black newspaper *Chicago Defender* under the name "F Chino," he recounted incidents in which free speech had been crushed in Japan, France, and Germany. Franklin concluded that Americans should "mind our own business," for once war came "we can say good-bye to the Bill of Rights and the last remaining vestige of democracy on the globe."

The Japanese attack on Pearl Harbor and the American entry into war, though it did not extinguish American democracy, justified Franklin's fears somewhat. Not only was his cousin Elizabeth arrested by the FBI, but his colleague Minoru Yasui was subjected to legal difficulties. Yasui resigned from the consulate and returned to Oregon to join the Army, but he was refused enlistment despite holding a commission in the Reserve. The arrest and indefinite detention of his father forced Yasui to assume family leadership, and he resolved to resist Executive Order 9066. On March 28, 1942, he walked the streets of Portland and pressed local police to arrest him for violating the special curfew declared for Nisei so that he could mount a court challenge. Yasui's challenge was turned aside because of his work in Chicago. In fall 1942, federal judge James A. Fee ruled that the president's order was unconstitutional when applied to US citizens but held that Yasui's employment by the Japanese consulate amounted to a renunciation of his US citizenship. The Supreme Court subsequently reversed both propositions. Still, Franklin, who had been employed in the same consulate, may have had cause to feel vulnerable. He withdrew from public activities, apart from assisting the Chicago Commission on Civil Defense.

Franklin continued his law practice in Chicago after the war and was active in the local bar association. He did not involve himself deeply in Japanese community activities, although he did join other Nisei lawyers in signing amicus briefs prepared by the JACL in a pair of Supreme Court civil rights cases, *Stainback v. Mo Hock Ke Lok Po* and *Takahashi v. California Fish and Game*

Commission, and he participated in political education programs with the Chicago JACL.

In 1948 he drew derision from the *Chicago Shimpo* newspaper and Nisei intellectuals for his public statements urging Nisei to support the Republican Party, on the grounds that the Roosevelt administration had been responsible for Executive Order 9066 while the Republicans had passed evacuation claims legislation. Despite his previous appreciation for Eleanor Roosevelt, he blamed removal on the president: "An arrogant man, who brooked no will but his own, who professed to be a political seer, omniscient and above criticism, [who signed] an executive order." Franklin insisted that the Nisei should be hardheaded and vote "selfishly" for those who best serve their interests. His position reflected his difficult circumstances: "Having been born and reared in Chicago and having been too busy struggling to make a living in this realistic world, I frankly don't have the time to engage in armchair theories or idealistic discussion." In 1950 he wrote a letter to the *Pacific Citizen* advising Nisei to not form separate political organizations but to participate in elections through existing interracial groups.

Much of Franklin's professional efforts in the postwar years were devoted to serving as village attorney for several incorporated towns in the Chicago suburbs. In particular, he helped establish Hoffman Estates, a new suburban housing development, as a legal entity and sued a local water utility to establish public control. Meanwhile, under the guidance of his wife, Marie, an Italian American, he became a devout Catholic. He spent a good deal of time in church activities, such as directing his parish's Holy Name Society and joining the Knights of Columbus. Franklin died suddenly of a heart attack in December 1962—ironically, just as his big water utility case was coming to trial. Hoffman Estates honored him by naming a playground—Franklin Chino Park—after him.

Although Franklin Chino publicly warned of restrictions on civil liberties in case of war during 1940, the Chino who was most directly touched by official action was his brother Robert, born in Chicago in February 1919. A strapping youth and star athlete at Hyde Park High School, Robert also wrote poetry and stories. He became politically involved as a professional labor organizer and activist in left-wing causes. At the age of fourteen or fifteen, during the depths of the Depression, Robert ran away from home for several months and lived as a hobo, eventually sharing a house with an older woman in New Mexico. He returned to Chicago and took a job as a clerk. According to one account, he founded a Chicago chapter of the American Lincoln Brigade (the name given to the American volunteer battalions in the Spanish Civil War). He married a fellow activist, Marilyn Fillis, the daughter of a distinguished local doctor and medical school professor. (According to family accounts, after Robert began dating Marilyn, her father expressed his opposition to the couple keeping company on racial grounds, whereupon they responded by immediately eloping.)

Like his brother Franklin, Robert opposed US intervention in the war in Europe during 1940–1941, and he became active with the pacifist group War Resisters League (WRL). After Pearl Harbor, Robert was assigned a draft classification of 3-A (deferred due to dependents)—unlike other Nisei, his classification was not set at 4-C (enemy alien). Although barred from conscription, he nonetheless returned his draft card to his draft board and continued assisting the WRL in draft counseling. As a Nisei, Robert faced additional burdens due to his actions because they could be read as support for the Japanese enemy.

On February 17, 1942, a fellow pacifist, David Nyvall, who had sent a letter to federal agents stating that he could not support government-sanctioned murder, was arrested for failure to register and was taken to the US courthouse in Chicago. Robert accompanied Nyvall there as his "friend and advisor" and was, in turn, taken into custody by US Commissioner Edwin K. Walker.

The arrests attracted significant media attention. The *Chicago Tribune* alternately described Robert as a "Japanese who said he was an American citizen" and an "American-born German-Japanese." Although he was ineligible for conscription, he was charged with failing to keep his draft card on his person. Federal agents accused him of setting up a group to oppose the draft. Lawyer Francis Heisler, a World War I veteran who defended conscientious objectors, took Robert's case—his brother Franklin was inexplicably absent throughout these events—and entered a plea of not guilty. Nyvall and Chino both remained in jail for several days (during which time President Franklin D. Roosevelt signed Executive Order 9066). Nyvall's parents, who deplored his actions, openly opposed bail for him, while Chino could not meet the $5,000 bond initially required. Finally, the radical millionaire Georgia Lloyd provided bail funds for their release. She also provided bail for another resister, Hugo Victoreen, who subsequently registered for the draft.

Robert's trial was set for May, after those of other resisters. He attended the other trials, where his presence attracted extra attention because of his ancestry. Nyvall pleaded guilty and was given a suspended sentence, on the condition that he thereafter register for the draft and avoid all further contact with Chino. On May 12, 1942, when resister Lauren Wispe's case went to trial, Judge Michael Igoe did not even wait to hear arguments before denouncing the defendant and the "south side clique" influencing him. Spotting Robert in the courtroom taking notes, the judge expelled him, shouting, "You half-alien, you half-Jap, you have no right here! Go on, I don't want you in my courtroom! Get out of here!" (Igoe also scolded Lloyd and the other women witnessing the trial, claiming that they were "encouraging slackers.") Igoe sentenced Wispe to three years in prison.

On May 26, Francis Heisler appeared before Judge William Holly and informed him that Chino wished to plead nolo contendere, in essence, leaving his sentence to the judge—Chino presumably believed that the judge would be less hostile than a jury. He admitted that he had returned his draft card but now insisted that he had done so in protest against the board's discriminatory treatment of him. His case was continued while the probation board examined his record. On June 25, Robert appeared before Judge Holly, who denounced him as a "showoff," lectured him about his duties as a citizen, and then sentenced him to three years in prison for failing to carry a draft card. Refusing Chino's application for probation, he noted that the defendant could not be considered a true pacifist since he had previously enlisted in the Illinois National Guard (such enlistment presumably referred to the military training obligation imposed on all male students at land-grant institutions such as the University of Illinois).

Robert was sent to prison in Minnesota, where he spent the next eighteen months. He was then offered a chance to leave prison if he would join the Army. He accepted the deal and was immediately enrolled in the celebrated all-Nisei 442nd Regimental Combat Team. (According to one story, Robert's father saw him off as he was being shipped out. The elder Chino, whose attachment to samurai *bushido* values had remained strong, did not embrace his son but instead gruffly told him to fight and die "like a Japanese.") Because of his mixed-race ancestry and midwestern background, Robert cut an unusual figure in the 442nd. He served as supply sergeant with the unit in Italy and France. He was wounded on three occasions and received the Silver Star, the Bronze Star, and the Purple Heart for his bravery. Among his Nisei comrades in the 442nd Robert found a sense of belonging, even more than among the pacifists and idealists in prison. In a letter to Georgia Lloyd explaining his Army service, he paid tribute to the decency and good sense of his comrades, which he compared to the strained personal relations among the resisters:

> Like every place else, sweeping generalizations become meaningless, yet thus far I have found our GIs somehow a little more considerate, a shade more socially responsible, than the pacifists as a group. Again I mean the combat troops; the few who undergo the intense sharp experience of war, the ones who do the killing and are killed . . . I don't know where these men came from, what they were before—but they were probably ordinary men. They are still ordinary and yet they do look out for one another and they try to share. Perhaps that doesn't sound so important yet it is. Remember, these men are not out to save the world or even to rework it . . . But they have learned to live together.

In early 1945, while his regiment was stationed in Nice, Robert met a French woman, Susanne Rieufly. The two remained in touch even after his regiment moved to Italy. He returned to Nice in January 1946 to marry her while serving in Livorno guarding supplies. Fluent in French and German, Chino announced that he had been invited to work for a newspaper in Nice and write a novel. In the end, neither marriage nor employment seems to have occurred. Instead, he decided to remain with the Army and applied for a promotion. Despite letters of endorsement from generals and others, however, he was denied advancement due to his conviction on draft charges, even though his sentence had been commuted when he joined the Army—the very act over which he had originally been imprisoned. He left the Army in 1948 and settled in Nice with his wife, Claude. They soon had twin sons, Denis and Bruce, but the marriage did not work out. He left the family after a few years and remarried. He and his third wife, Gisele, had a son, Philippe, in 1954. Shortly thereafter, his widowed mother, Mercelia, moved in with the family and remained with him until her death.

In the decades that followed, Robert occupied various jobs and moved several times. For a while, he specialized in electronics. He kept up his military connections, and in 1954 he was named adjutant of the French division of the American Legion. His real love nevertheless remained fly-fishing, and he pursued his interest frequently. (One family story reveals that he fished with Ernest Hemingway when the writer was in France; Chino described Hemingway as an extraordinary fisherman but always drunk.) He published articles and letters on the subject in such diverse periodicals as *Fly Fisherman*, *Fly Tyer*, and *Gordon's Quill*. He likewise translated French pediatrician Jean-Paul Pequegnot's book, *French Fishing Flies: Patterns and Recipes for Fly Tying* (1987).

In 1987, while living in the south of France, Robert fell ill. Although he had not been to the United States for many years, the family arranged a military plane to fly him to Walter Reed Army Medical Center, where he died in December 1987. His lonely episode of draft resistance, like his proud military service, remained long forgotten among the Japanese Americans in whom he had expressed such pride, yet his acts of principle make him a fitting subject of respect for admirers of both draft resisters and veterans.

Robert Chino Postscript

Some time after I completed my initial article on Robert Chino, I was looking at *Lay Bare the Heart: An Autobiography of the Civil Rights Movement* (1985), the memoir of James Farmer. Farmer was the founding director of the Congress of Racial Equality, the nonviolent protest group that became one of the major forces in the black civil rights movement of the 1960s. In his memoir, Farmer notes that, in April 1942, he came up with the idea for a Gandhian civil rights protest movement, and a group of a half-dozen activists met to form its steering committee. Farmer states that one of the group was "Bob Chino," whom he characterizes as a "University of Chicago student who was half-Chinese and half-Caucasian" and that Chino's fellow resister Hugo Victoreen was another. He adds that Chino came up with the idea of calling the group CORE, as representing the center of things and the place of action. Chino was then one of twenty-eight activists who participated in the very first civil rights sit-in, in May 1942, at Jack Spratt's Coffee House in Chicago, a restaurant that did not serve blacks. Chino went to jail only a few weeks after for draft resistance (eventually so did all the male members of the first CORE "cell," except Farmer), so he did not have time to participate further.

It is probable that Farmer simply did not recollect that Chino was Japanese American, forty years after the events described in his memoir, and misremembered him as Chinese because of his name. It is unlikely that Chino would ever have passed for Chinese, given both the publicity about his Japanese background during his trial and his own strong feelings against passing (he stopped speaking to his older brother once Elbert began to pass as Native American). It is also not clear why Farmer recalled him as a University of Chicago student, as no evidence of his enrolment has come to light. Despite these errors, Farmer's identification of Robert Chino as "present at the creation" and birth of CORE deepens our understanding of Chino's history as a man of principle. More importantly, it reshapes our historical understanding of CORE and the civil rights movement. The mass of history books and encyclopedia entries that have been produced on the subject tends to paint the original CORE as made up entirely of middle-class black and white (mainly Protestant) religious activists. The revelation that a secular Japanese American like Chino played such an important founding role allows historians a larger understanding of civil rights struggles and the place of Nisei in them, even as it challenges larger (and unjust) stereotypes about Asian Americans as fundamentally hostile to blacks.

Milton Ozaki: Mystery Writer (coauthored with Steven G. Doi)

The time was the early 1950s. The place was Chicago. For all the street gangs and tough guys around, it was in some ways an innocent age. You couldn't turn on a television and see hours of raw violence. *Playboy* magazine was just appearing (with Vince Tajiri, Japanese American editor of photography) and hadn't yet started printing three-page color centerfolds. Yet millions of male readers would reach into their pockets for the quarter that would buy 180 pages of crime, sex, and murder. Hundreds of pulp mystery writers made a living cranking out material for an audience hungry for titillation, violence, and sleaze. Their hardboiled detective novels featured nearly identical plots and language, with page after page of scantily clad women in smoke-filled bars, con men, and crooked cops who used them both.

Amid this crowd was one improbable biracial Nisei: Milton K. Ozaki. Writing from his apartment at Elm and State Streets, Ozaki turned out twenty-five detective novels from 1946 to 1960—the first mass-market genre fiction by a Japanese American since actor Sessue Hayakawa's 1925 potboiler *The Bandit Prince*—in which he intoned with zeal the rhythmic jargon of

FIGURE 2.3. Milton Ozaki.

1950s cop-talk. It is too easy to say that Ozaki's mixed ancestry led him to specialize in tales involving mystery and outlaws, but it may have contributed to his apparent rootlessness and his lifelong compulsion for self-creation (down to devising a personal letterhead with an invented motto).

Milton K. Ozaki was born on June 14, 1913, in Racine, Wisconsin, northwest of Chicago. His father, Frank Jingoro Ozaki, emigrated from Japan in 1899, worked as a houseboy for a wealthy Racine family, then later opened a restaurant in nearby Kenosha. Frank married a local white woman, Augusta Rathbum. (It is not known whether Frank and Augusta had a happy marriage. Augusta would draw widespread attention in 1942, when she publicly announced that she was suing for divorce because after Pearl Harbor she could no longer stand to be married to a Japanese.)

Milton, the couple's only child, lost a leg in early childhood. Nevertheless, he became an active Boy Scout, and in 1927 he was crowned the town's marbles champion. Meanwhile, he developed a love of reading and writing. He was named editor of the Kenosha Senior High School newspaper and worked briefly for the *Racine Times*. In 1933 Ozaki entered Ripon College, a small liberal arts college, where he majored in English. Although he attended only two years, he joined the college debate team and worked for the school newspaper. He later reminisced in a letter to a friend about the "tranquil days at Ripon."

Meanwhile, Ozaki became passionate about bridge and studied many books on the game. He later said that he and his Alpha Lambda Delta fraternity brothers got "free dinners around the town by playing bridge." In 1935 Ozaki left school and moved to Chicago, where he worked as a hairdresser at Burnham's School of Beauty Culture. He subsequently opened Monsieur Meltoine Beauty Salon. Ozaki claimed, however, that he earned his living largely by playing bridge for money. He became a National Master by 1941 but then gave up playing once World War II came. Exempted from military service due to his handicap, Ozaki remained in Chicago. While visiting New York during this period, Ozaki ran across a book by James M. Cain, author of *Double Indemnity* and *The Postman Always Rings Twice*. "Overwhelmed," as Ozaki put it, by Cain's thrillers, he rushed out, bought everything he could find by Cain, and spent the week reading. He resolved to write such stories himself.

In 1946 Ziff-Davis published Ozaki's first mystery, *The Cuckoo Clock*. The dust jacket described the author as a "newspaper man, artist, writer and . . . well-known Chicago tax accountant." The plot revolved around three characters: the narrator, Bendy Brinks, a graduate student at North University; Professor Caldwell; and Detective Phelan of the Chicago Police Department. Ozaki used his own apartment and shop as settings for the story. Ozaki soon published two more novels, *A Fiend in Need* (1947) and *The Dummy Murder Case* (1951), using the same characters. These novels seem rather naïve today, with their simplistic portrayal of good against evil. The cops—even college-educated detectives—are too stupid to tell victims from perpetrators, and they need assistance from Professor Caldwell. Stepping from a crowd of suspects, the guilty party confesses on the last pages.

Meanwhile, beginning with *The Black Dark Murderers* (1949), Ozaki wrote a series of books featuring private eye Carl Good, who solves murders from his downtown office even as he mixes in Chicago's sleazy underworld. Ozaki published these books under the pen name Robert O. Saber—a pun on his name, as *zaki* in Japanese can be translated as "knife" or "saber." (Ozaki denied that he used a non-Japanese pseudonym to increase sales, asserting that all prolific writers used aliases to mask their rapid production.)

Altogether Ozaki published twenty-five novels, plus short stories, in serials such as *Detective Story*. He was president of the Chicago Chapter of the Mystery Writers of America. His works were translated into German, Swedish, and Finnish. Ozaki stated that it took about three weeks to write a book. The hurried pace showed: editing was practically nonexistent and sometimes it seemed as if Ozaki simply wrote enough to meet the editor's page-length requirement before giving the mystery away on the last two pages. Sex plays a central role in Ozaki's works. Women fall into two categories: the innocent student and the working girl (always with a vengeful spurned lover), both of whom are favored suspects. In *The Cuckoo Clock,* the murder victim is a part-time artist whose library walls are covered with nude sketches of female models. Bendy Brinks is assigned to interview each model as to why they would pose nude. The reader is given a detailed narration of how Brinks imagines each interviewee naked. Two books in a series featuring Detective Rusty Forbes show how Ozaki riffed on classic pulp language: "Her white satin dressing gown draped a creamy body with more curves than the engraving on a thousand dollar bill" (*Sucker Bait*, 1955); "The car was hot and so was the blonde who drove it" (*Dressed to Kill*, 1954).

Conversely, race is largely invisible in Ozaki's works. There are few minority characters, although they are portrayed realistically—Ozaki avoids the derogatory stereotypes and racist terms endemic to the genre. For example, in *The Scented Flesh*, (1951), Carl Good visits the China Inn, a lunchroom operated by "a young American-born Chinese": "A seedy-looking character in a dirty army overcoat came and stamped his feet noisily. The Chinese looked up and shouted: "Why don't you take your goddam dirty feet over to Thompson's Charlie? What do you want? A quart of coffee?" Still, in *The Case of the Deadly Kiss* (1957), Ozaki did what no mystery writer had ever done: he used an Asian American character in a non-stereotyped role. Ozaki's protagonist is Detective Lieutenant Ken Koda, a Nisei detective. Koda is just another cop in suburban Stillwell, Illinois—no accents, proverbs, or anything but his name to suggest his ancestry. Although Osaki later claimed he could not remember the character, Koda resembled the author in his grizzled appearance and love of cigars. (Koda may also have been inspired by Detective Anthony Muranaka, the only Nisei on the Chicago police force.) Koda and his partner, Sergeant John D'Alessandro, continue through several later novels.

By 1960 the hardboiled detective industry had declined, a casualty of television and the increased availability of soft-core pornography. Ozaki realized he could not make his fortune by writing, so he put away his typewriter and moved back to Kenosha before eventually relocating to Colorado. He renewed his interest in bridge and wrote widely on the subject, including a humorous guide, *Bridge for Absolute Beginners* (1963): "It's my opinion that any stupe can learn to play contract bridge. As a matter of fact, many do. Ask any player." He also became a stamp broker, published the guidebook *Making Money from Stamps* (1964), and founded the magazine *Philatelic Investor*. He subsequently moved to Nevada, where he opened various businesses. One had its shady side: the Society for Academic Recognition sold honorary degrees from fictitious universities to gullible individuals until local authorities closed it in 1974.

When Milton Ozaki died in 1989 in Sparks, Nevada, his work had been forgotten. However, amid renewed popular interest in the hardboiled detective genre, Ozaki has made a minor comeback. His name appears in reference works and *Dressed to Kill* was reissued in 2008. It is time to recognize this pioneer Nisei writer within Asian American literature.

YONÉ STAFFORD: PACIFIST MILITANT

One of the more pleasant aspects of writing The Great Unknown are readers' responses to my columns from readers, including friends and family members of the people whom I write about. They not only offer praise but provide additional information and inspire further work. In 2011 I wrote a column about the late Hisaye Yamamoto, in the course of which I mentioned Yoné U. Stafford, Yamamoto's warm friend and political collaborator, who seems to have served as her model. I was then asked by different readers about Stafford and her career. I lacked a complete picture of this versatile Nisei activist, whose writing covered a multitude of fields. But it seemed useful to make a first attempt to piece together some of her contributions, with the added hope that readers would be able to assist me in fleshing out more of the picture.

Yone Ko (or Yone-Ko) Ushikubo was born on July 24, 1902. She was a rare native-born Nisei New Yorker. Her father, Daijiro, a Japanese of samurai ancestry, came to the United States in 1890 and settled on Manhattan's Upper West Side. In 1894 he was employed by the New York branch of Yamanaka and Company as an importer of Japanese art and ceramics, a field in which he flourished; according to one source, by the 1920s, Ushikubo became one of the richest Japanese in the United States. He also published books about Japan, including *Life of Kôyetsu* (1927). Like many Issei businessmen outside the West Coast, Ushikubo took a white American wife, Louisa Ushikubo, the daughter of German immigrants. Yoné was their only child.

The family traveled back and forth to Japan several times in Yoné's early years. In 1918 her parents sent her to Japan, where she attended the Sacred Heart Academy for two years before returning to the United States. Sometime in the 1930s, Yoné married another New Yorker, Bradley Stafford, and moved with him to Springfield, Massachusetts (a passenger list from her return visit to Japan in early 1937 recorded her name as Yone Ushikubo Stafford). Bradley would later run a paper factory.

Yoné was long attracted to social reform. (She later recalled that while staying in Kyoto in 1924 she was inspired by a book of speeches from religious reformer Robert Ingersoll, which she read because few English-language works were available.) Some time afterwards, she joined the Socialist Party. It is possible that, like other Nisei such as Kiyoshi Hamanaka and Sam Hohri, she was drawn to the Socialists by their belief in pacifism, since the party followed an antiwar platform in the period before Pearl Harbor. She also became involved in the Women's International League for Peace and Freedom (WILPF). She and her husband were active in the local branch of the America First Committee, the isolationist group that opposed all intervention in Europe's wars. Yoné idolized Charles A. Lindbergh, who led isolationist efforts.

The anti-Japanese climate after Pearl Harbor caused Yoné to reach out in support of other Japanese Americans. Although as an easterner, Yoné was exempted from Executive Order 9066, she reacted strongly and immediately to what she termed the "atrocity." First, she sought to influence public opinion against the action by writing protest letters to newspapers. The *Springfield Republican* refused to publish any of her letters, though one of her letters ran in the *Springfield Union*. Meanwhile, she wrote several letters to the Wisconsin-based weekly the *Progressive* (under the name Mrs. Bradley Stafford), in hopes of persuading its editors and readers to pay more attention to the treatment of Japanese Americans. Several pro–Japanese American letters from writers in neighboring towns soon began to appear in the *Progressive's* letters section as well, a fact that suggests Yoné had a hand in organizing the authors. Yoné's challenge to official policy caused a local weekly to undertake a smear campaign against her, and locals regularly reported on her to the authorities (a local government worker told her that she was known around the post office as the "FBI's sweetheart" because of all the letters it received about her). It also caused considerable strain in her marriage, especially when the president of her husband's company threatened to discharge him if Yoné continued writing letters. She refused and even offered to leave her husband rather than give up her struggle. Instead, the Staffords compromised, and Yoné continued her letters to newspapers but signed them under the pseudonym America (the Japanese character, or kanji, for the name was identical to that for "Yoné").

Less controversially, Yoné worked with the WILPF and the Fellowship of Reconciliation (FOR) during 1942 to collect a 250-pound shipment of clothing and blankets, which were sent to the Heart Mountain camp. She meanwhile worked with the American Friends Service Committee (sending "all the money I could," as she put it, plus writing friends and speaking in public) to allow Nisei students to leave the camp to attend college. She also wrote to the inmate newspaper *Heart Mountain Sentinel* to encourage individuals to resettle and agreed to help sponsor newcomers. When two young Nisei women were authorized to leave camp and settle in Springfield, Yoné labored to assist them. She was outraged when the discriminatory treatment the two resettlers experienced from townspeople led them to leave. Yoné complained of widespread prejudice in Springfield, in spite of its development of the famous "Springfield Plan" for race relations. Similarly, Yoné struck up a friendship with writer Hisaye Yamamoto after she and her brother moved to Springfield. While family needs forced Yamamoto to return to camp, the friendship between the two women remained strong.

In 1945, after the government finally allowed confined Japanese Americans to return to the West Coast, the War Relocation Authority (WRA) announced that the camps would be closed at the end of the year and began reducing services in the camps. Yoné was furious over the WRA's policy of forcing destitute Japanese Americans to vacate the camps and resettle in hostile surroundings. Since the United States was busy educating Germans and Japanese in the ways of democracy, she snapped, perhaps they could "spare a few gauleiters for our Department of the Interior and the War Relocation Authority?"

During the postwar years, in the shadow of the atomic bombing of Japan, Yoné returned to her primary interest in pacifism, which she had not altogether abandoned during the war. (In April 1944, she wrote a letter to the editors of *Christian Century* in support of the Peace Now Movement, which called for immediate cessation of hostilities.) Yamamoto, who had taken a position as a columnist with the African American newspaper *Los Angeles Tribune*, recruited Yoné to write guest columns. In a 1947 column (written under the pseudonym H. Nagasaki), she deplored the movement for peacetime military conscription. In 1948 Yamamoto left the *Tribune*, and Yoné was engaged to replace her. Yoné's column, titled I Go Crying Peace, Peace, ran off and on for the next few years. She continued to publish letters in *Christian Century* and other journals. She was tart-tongued in her criticism of the Cold War. In 1949 she wrote a letter to the *Berkshire Eagle* criticizing NATO. In 1953 she wrote to *Time* magazine that US senator Margaret Chase Smith's proposal to use the atomic bomb in the Korean War "made me ashamed for my sex."

She also associated herself with diverse domestic reform movements. She became involved with Dorothy Day's Catholic Worker (CW) movement (she told Day she had a soft spot for Catholics because of her Japanese convent school experience) and inspired Hisaye Yamamoto to join as well. When Yamamoto moved to the CW's collective farm in Staten Island, New York, she wrote to her friend, "You are really the reason I am here, Yone." In the 1960s, she sat on the national committee of the War Resisters League.

Yoné's primary tool of political activism took the form of letters to the editor. Playing on Thomas Jefferson's famous quote about democracy, she quipped "eternal letter-writing is the price of decency." Her ideas remained tied to her prewar isolationism and her feelings about Japan as well as her continued outrage over the treatment of Japanese Americans. In 1970 she accused American leaders of having introduced Jim Crow practices to Japan, which was left "embittered and pauperized" by the occupation. Similar feelings surfaced when, in 1973, she wrote a letter to the conservative *Chicago*

Tribune to complain (with some exaggeration and inaccuracy) that she was sick of hearing about President Richard Nixon and Watergate. "We have been conditioned to so much worse under former presidents, beginning with F.D.R., who gave away 50 destroyers without a 'By Your Leave,' imprisoned and impoverished citizens because of their race, and dropped atomic bombs on people already beaten." The next year, she deplored an environmentalist proposal to boycott Japan because its fisherman killed whales: "We should mind our own business and stop telling other nations what to do." In the early 1970s, Yoné joined the national committee to secure a pardon for Iva Toguri d'Aquino, convicted of treason as "Tokyo Rose," and supported the successful movement to win her a presidential pardon. In one of her last interventions, she joined the National Council for Redress Reparations.

Yoné and her husband retired to Cape Cod in the 1960s. She died in West Chatham, Massachusetts, in 1981, nine years before her husband.

3

Literature and Journalism

Jenichiro Oyabe (1867–1941) was among the first people of Japanese ancestry to write about his life in the United States. His memoir, *A Japanese Robinson Crusoe*, first published in 1898, offers a picturesque account of the author's experiences. It also is a fascinating example of the dark side of Americanization—how immigrants seeking liberty and enlightenment can absorb conventional social views and imitate elite snobbery against those considered inferior.

Oyabe opens the narrative of *A Japanese Robinson Crusoe* by describing his boyhood in Meiji-era Japan. His mother dies early in his life. Abandoned by his father, who joins the new imperial civil service, Oyabe is raised by various relatives. After attending different schools, he rejoins his father, who has become a judge on the northern island of Hokkaido, then largely frontier territory inhabited by Ainu (Japanese aborigines). Oyabe soon breaks with his father and decides to devote himself to missionary work among the Ainu. He travels to an Ainu region, is adopted by a chief's family, and takes on Ainu

DOI: 10.5876/9781607324294.c003

FIGURE 3.1. Jenichiro Oyabe.

dress and speech. After several months, he resolves to seek education to uplift the Ainu (whom he calls a good-natured but "stupid" people).

Inspired by American missionaries, Oyabe expresses interest in Christianity and decides to travel to America for enlightenment. After several detours, he arrives in New York in 1888. He explains that he initially believed that all Americans were as enlightened and Christian as the missionaries and ship captains he met in Asia, who paid his fare to America. He is thus dismayed by the various forms of immorality and criminality he observes in New York—his pocket is picked; he sees young boys smoking and having to work to earn a living shining shoes; he sees scantily clad women at a theater; and he visits an opium den in Chinatown, where white women mingle with their Chinese boyfriends.

Oyabe's negative impression of America climaxes a few weeks after his arrival, when he goes to get his hair cut and is insulted: "'Aee, John, git out from here. Oi don't cut a China man's hair!' I was scorned by the old barber. I told him that I was not such a man, but a Japanese. 'Ou, ye Javanese, a country of lots coffee! All right, sit dan, my good fellar.'" Oyabe is charged a quarter, pays a dollar, and gets his change. However, he quickly discovers that the fifty-cent piece the barber gave him is counterfeit. When he returns to the barbershop to challenge the barber, the man denies any wrongdoing and says that his business is as honest as the Bible.

The lesson Oyabe takes from this, however, is not that racism exists in America but that racists are not truly American: the barber is a new immigrant and low class and thus not representative. Conversely, Oyabe immediately jumps back with an endorsement of American democracy and the melting pot—something that attracts even such curious people as African Americans and Jews:

> Once I heard a speech from a curly-headed black man at the anniversary
> of Washington's death-day. "Gent'men! We are born 'merican citizen, de
> chi'dren ov George Washin'ton' The name *American citizen* was a matter of
> pride even to that black man. I knew a young Jew in New York, whose father
> had lived in that city about fifteen or sixteen years, who was forbidden to
> eat pork or anything that was cooked with lard, and who had no knowledge
> of English. Still, he did a large business in the city, and called himself an
> American citizen." (121)

It is during his time in New York that General Samuel Chapman Armstrong, president of Hampton Institute, recruits Oyabe to study there. He enrolls as Armstrong's special student and protégé. After two years at Hampton, he transfers to Howard University and becomes president Jeremiah Rankin's protégé and companion. Oyabe carefully conceals in his memoirs that both these institutions are historically black colleges.

After receiving a degree in divinity from Howard in 1893, the author enrolls at Yale University. (In a fascinating passage, Oyabe describes his joy in playing basketball, then newly invented, during his student years; he is pleased to hear a fellow student say "that Jap plays like a tiger.") Shortly before graduating, Oyabe reads an article in a California newspaper about the "threat" posed by the large Japanese plantation worker population in Hawai'i (then an independent republic), who were bringing "their idols and heathen customs to this country." Unfamiliar with endemic anti-Asian prejudice on the West Coast, he doesn't realize that the journalist is in fact targeting all Japanese Americans. Instead, Oyabe resolves to defend Christianity in the islands, and he travels cross-country to take up the assignment (while in Utah, he visits Native villages and is congratulated by a pro-Japanese American Indian on Japan's victory in the Sino-Japanese War). However, once his boat arrives in Hawai'i he is chagrined to discover that Christianity is widespread on the islands. Oyabe takes up a pulpit in Maui and spends two years preaching to Japanese laborers. He ultimately finds life in the islands too easy and comfortable, and his missionary instinct bids him leave for further training. The book ends with Oyabe at Yale, taking sociology courses on American Indians and expressing uncertainty about his future path. Although he expresses zeal about doing missionary work with native peoples in Japan, he shares white paternalist views of their capacity:

> In my future, besides my pastoral work among my own race, I desire to establish a manual training institution for aborigines in the Orient, like the Hampton and Carlisle institutions in America . . . Let it produce many trained native workers, who know something about manual labor to support themselves, and scatter them everywhere among their own people.

Shortly after publishing *A Japanese Robinson Crusoe*, Oyabe returned to Japan and built a model Ainu school, which he operated for ten years. He later became well known in Japan as a nationalist scholar and historian. In 1924 he published a book arguing that the Mongol chieftain and conqueror Genghis Khan was actually Japanese—Minamoto Yoshitsune, younger brother of the first Minamoto shogun. His nationalistic tone was also evident in his 1929 book *Nihon oyobi Nihon kokumin no kigen* (*Origin of Japan and Japanese*), in which he explored the influence of the ancient Hebrews on the development of Japanese civilization. He never returned to the United States, though one son emigrated to Seattle. Jenichiro Oyabe died in 1941. When Howard University president Mordecai Johnson invited Oyabe to the school for its commencement in 1933, he declined but expressed his pleasure. Ironically, his son, Masayoshi "Joe" Oyabe, came to the United States in 1920, married, and produced three children; he remained in America until his death in 1989. In 2009, the University of Hawai'i Press published a new edition of *A Japanese Robinson Crusoe*, edited by Greg Robinson and Yujin Yaguchi.

EDDIE SHIMANO: CRUSADING JOURNALIST AND POET

The young Nisei who came of age in 1930s America included a selection of nonconformists—individuals who lived outside Japanese neighborhoods, expressed interest in larger social and political questions, and challenged established community leadership. At the same time, many young Nisei turned to art and literature as a means of expressing themselves and their difficulties in finding a place within the larger society. One of the most brilliant, and certainly the most flamboyant, of these twin groups was Eddie Shimano, a self-described rebel and advocate of intellectual freedom.

Eddie Tokato Shimano was born in Seattle on May 28, 1911, one of four children of Hosei Shimano, a baker. He grew up in the city. After obtaining his diploma at Franklin High School, he started college at Ellensburg Normal School (now Central Washington University). However, he soon tired of it and dropped out when the Great Depression was at its height. After a short trip to Japan with his family, Eddie started on a cross-country tour of the United States that took him through forty states. According to one story, he traveled to New York to find work as a journalist, but the editor with whom he met refused to engage him, assuming that no Japanese American could possibly write good English. At this time he also spent a stretch living in California with the writer William Saroyan. Ultimately, he returned to school and in 1934–1935 enrolled at Cornell College, in the tiny Iowa town of Mount

Vernon. (He was marked by his time in the Midwest. When, in the weeks after Pearl Harbor, a group of bigoted whites told him to "go back where he came from," Eddie responded with mock horror, "Oh, no, not Iowa again!")

Eddie was a striking figure on Cornell's campus. Many of his classmates had never seen an Asian before. He joined the English Club and soon impressed his classmates so greatly with his tales of talented Nisei writers that they agreed to produce a review of Japanese American literature. Eddie contacted Mary (Molly) Oyama, who directed the Los Angeles literary club Writers of Southern California. She agreed to merge the club's literary quarterly, *Leaves*, with Eddie's new magazine and to recruit contributors. Henry Tatsumi, a lecturer at the University of Washington, not only found Seattle-based contributors but chose a title for the magazine: *Gyo-Sho*.

Gyo-Sho, twenty-four pages long, appeared in May 1936, in a handsome, hand-bound edition. As Eddie explained in his foreword, "GYO-SHO, literally Dawn-Bell, means 'the peal of the gong at the break of day.' In Japan the temple bell is struck at the first glimmerings of the break of dawn to announce to the inhabitants that a new day awaits. And so we think of this magazine as the bell which we strike to announce to the world a new day, symbolizing the awakening of the Nisei." It was not the first Japanese American literary magazine—that honor belonged to the Salt Lake City–based quarterly *Reimei*. However, *Gyo-Sho* remains notable for its diversity of literary styles and genres.

"Coming of Age," Mary Oyama's story portraying the experience of a Nisei voting for the first time, is a particular highlight. Another is a long poem by a Nisei alumnus of Marquette University with a delightfully exotic name: the late Ambrose Amadeus Uchiyamada. Eddie himself contributed a (not very interesting) set of verses.

After leaving Cornell, Eddie moved to San Francisco, where the Nisei newspaper the *New World Sun* hired him as a journalist/editor. Soon after, the Japanese Army invaded China. Eddie bravely took a public stand against the Japanese occupation and the atrocities in Nanking. Calling for a boycott of Japanese goods, Eddie joined Chinese colleagues in demonstrations on the San Francisco docks. For his activism, community leaders ostracized him. Worn out from the ordeal, Eddie spent parts of 1939–1940 in a tuberculosis sanitarium. During this time, he wrote a short novel, "Bread," for which he was unable to find a publisher. To support himself, he took a job contributing to the series of monographs on the history of California theater that Lawrence Estavan produced for the New Deal–era Works Progress Administration.

After the United States declared war on Japan, Eddie helped his friends, journalist Larry Tajiri and sculptor Isamu Noguchi, to form an antifascist political group, the Nisei Writers and Artists Mobilization for Democracy. Their goal was, simultaneously, to stimulate democratic sentiment among Nisei and avert mass removal. Despite his efforts, Eddie was rounded up with other Nisei and sent to the Santa Anita Assembly Center. There, he won the coveted position of editor of the center newspaper, the *Santa Anita Pacemaker*. (He chose the title, he explained, in hopes that the newspaper would "set the pace" for Nisei and encourage them to overcome their difficulties.) After several weeks, he was sent on to the Jerome camp in Arkansas, where he was named editor of its newspaper, the *Denson Communique*.

Not long after he arrived, the Common Council for American Unity—a New York-based group organized to defend immigrants and minorities—recruited Eddie for the job of assistant editor of its journal, *Common Ground*. Once settled in New York, Eddie organized a public forum on Japanese Americans, which attracted some 200 people, and worked with *Common Ground*'s editor, M. Margaret Anderson, on a special journal issue titled, "Get the Evacuees Out!" Eddie contributed the essay "Blueprint for a Slum." It described the harsh psychological toll of mass incarceration on the Nisei in the camps and advocated full integration of resettlers into the larger society. Although Eddie prided himself on his friendships with people of different backgrounds, he also became active among local Nisei—notably with the New York–based political group Japanese American Committee for Democracy. When the progressive community newspaper the *Nisei Weekender* was organized at the end of the war, Eddie was named editor. Unfortunately, the newspaper soon folded.

I would like to report that Eddie Shimano went on to realize the promise of his talent. However, writer's block and physical and emotional difficulties increasingly restricted him, especially the breakup of his marriage to his first wife, Kitty. According to one legend, Eddie grew so tired of his wife's many cats that he told her that either he or the pets had to go—whereupon she kept her cats and threw him out. (The couple's divorce was secured in Alabama, whose divorce laws were less restrictive than New York's.) He later lived in upstate New York, where he married his second wife, Virginia, and worked as a freelance editor and ghostwriter. He died in 1986, a late casualty of the war.

KAY KARL ENDOW: NOVELIST, AVIATOR, AND CON MAN

One of the notable qualities of the Nisei as they came of age in the prewar United States was their passion for literature. Sunday editions of the *Nichi Bei Shimbun* and other newspapers featured stories by community writers while circles of authors formed groups and published magazines containing short works. Critics debated which young author would write the Great American Nisei Novel. Yet mainstream presses expressed little interest in their work. Although Toshio Mori's volume of short stories was accepted for publication shortly before Pearl Harbor—and then languished several years, amid the hostile wartime climate, before being released—no prewar writer who graced the Nisei press would produce a novel that was considered publishable. Still, one Nisei, a somewhat obscure and mysterious figure even in life, managed to publish not just one but two books of fiction during this period.

He was born Shigeru Nakagawa in 1906, not long after his parents, Nosoke Nakagawa and Mito Sato, immigrated from Japan to the Sacramento, California, region. Within a few years, three brothers and a sister joined the family. Nakagawa grew up in Yolo County, where his father farmed, and he apparently attended Sacramento High School. At some point he took the name Karl, though his friends knew him as "Johnson" because his baseball pitching speed suggested that of Walter Johnson. According to a later interview with the *San Francisco Chronicle*, in 1925 he visited Japan as part of Sacramento's Nippon Stars baseball team.

In 1928 the young man who now called himself Karl S. Nakagawa self-published a mystery novel, *The Rendezvous of Mysteries*, with Dorrance & Company of Philadelphia. This was the first book of fiction ever published by a Nisei, at least in English (French-born Nisei writer Kikou Yamata published the novel *Masako* in 1925). Dorrance was a subsidy publisher, so Nakagawa presumably contributed funds of his own toward publication. The author later claimed variously that he had sold 35,000 to 50,000 copies of his book, but this is certainly exaggerated because first, the book received no reviews or publicity in the mainstream press, and second, in purely literary terms, it was—to be frank—terrible.

The plot, worthy of a *Scooby-Doo* episode, revolves around a house in Sacramento, the Rendezvous, which is reputed to be haunted. The hero has inherited it and wishes to move in, but strange noises and apparitions terrify him and his friends. (At the risk of spoiling the story for potential readers, I will reveal that the apparition turns out to be a disguised criminal and his ventriloquist henchman, who hope to buy the house cheaply.) One feature of interest is that, while there are no Japanese American characters, there is a significant African American character, the janitor and former prizefighter Jeff Jenkins. Although Jenkins speaks somewhat distorted English and furnishes comic relief, he is not altogether a stereotyped African American; at the story's climax he even saves the girl. The novel was not generally discussed in the Japanese American press, though its appearance did give rise to considerable debate among Sacramento Nisei about which house was the basis for the mystery.

In the aftermath of Charles Lindbergh's transatlantic solo flight, Nakagawa became entranced by aviation, and in 1929 he moved to Lincoln, Nebraska, to take flying lessons. By April 1930, he was working as an aviator in California. Meanwhile, he claimed to have received a contract from Dorrance for a second mystery novel, "The Phantom Fox." With this success in hand, he penned an article, "How Stories Are Written," for the 1931 New Year's Day edition of the *Nichi Bei*. While he claimed that he was merely a "novice" and that writing was a "hobby," he produced a list of hints to budding authors. The last may have pointed at some of his own difficulties: "Don't be too optimistic . . . Always bear in mind that your story must be many times better than you think it is, in order to have it accepted." A few weeks later, his gloomy mood was confirmed, he later noted, when Dorrance informed him that his manuscript had burned up in a fire. Although Nakagawa stated that he had a rough draft, the destroyed text represented his only complete manuscript. He was evidently too discouraged to rewrite the book, for it was never published. Instead, he began work on a new novel about aviation, *Grim Wings of Destiny*.

It took four years for Nakagawa to receive public attention, with an announcement in February 1935 that the author, who now called himself Kay Karl Endow, had been offered a contract by a Los Angeles press—Wetzel Publishers—for both the aviation novel and a second work, "Love is Love." The aviation novel, renamed *Transpacific Wings*, appeared later that year. Like

FIGURE 3.2. Kay Karl Endow.

its predecessor, it possessed dubious literary merits. Indeed, the plot, which revolved around two friends organizing a nonstop transpacific flight, contains multiple devices of melodrama—a chase scene, mistaken identity, an attack of amnesia, and the miraculous recovery from disease. One interesting fact is that the original manuscript featured a love poem, which Endow later cut. A Nisei composer, John Kuwamoto, subsequently set those lyrics to music.

Again, like *The Rendezvous of Mysteries*, *Transpacific Wings* was very white. While one character states offhandedly that she has a Nisei friend, Endow depicts no Asian characters, even in the portions that take place in Japan. Perhaps he was saving all his thoughts on racial issues for his next book, *Love is Love*, whose imminent appearance was advertised at the end of *Transpacific Wings*. According to the blurb, the new novel charted the interracial love affair of Lydia Meadows and Lonnie Matsuda, "their trials and tribulations, parental obstacles encountered, jealousy aroused, and conflicting outside influences." The advertisement promised that "the surprising and unexpected climax will please you, regardless of race or creed." For unknown reasons, this romance never actually appeared in print. It would have been an interesting addition to the literature on miscegenation.

Whether to gain attention for his novel or from ambition, in late 1935, Endow announced his plans to make an unprecedented solo flight from Seattle to Tokyo, as an expression of Japanese American friendship and international peace. Sales of *Transpacific Wings*, he pledged, would help raise money for the trip. Endow succeeded in selling a reported 11,000 copies and acquiring a set of backers, who allegedly raised $20,000 to purchase a special Bellanca airplane. He made friends with baseball star Lefty O'Doul and boxing champion Max Baer, who publicly expressed confidence in him.

In February 1936, Kay Karl Endow Day was held at the Sacramento airport. Endow took several dozen passengers, mostly Japanese, for airplane rides in his Fokker Trimotor. The event proved so popular that a second commemorative day was held the following weekend. This time Endow climaxed the day with a parachute jump. Supporters such as Howard Imazeki of the *New World Sun* affirmed that Endow would manage a transpacific flight. Yet, observers such as *Nichi Bei* columnist Larry Tajiri remained skeptical that Endow could complete the feat. Endow promised that he was serious and would make the attempt or "my future as a writer or as an aviator will be completely washed up." In July Endow announced that the aircraft manufacturer had advised him to postpone his flight for a year due to poor weather conditions in the North Pacific. Although he promised to refund donations if he did not make the flight then, no more was heard of Endow's flight. In July 1937, he was arrested in Los Angeles on a forgery charge. While he was ultimately acquitted, his already damaged reputation was further tarnished.

Surviving relatives state that he moved to New York and worked in a business office, then made at least one trip back West, possibly when his family was confined in the War Relocation Authority camps. There is no sign of him in the 1940 census. According to the family, he died in obscurity in New York circa 1948.

If Karl Shigeru Nakagawa, alias Kay Karl Endow, was unable to realize his project of heroism, his family did. Two of his brothers, Itsuo and Kazuo Nakagawa, served in the 442nd Regimental Combat Team during World War II. Moreover, his nephew, the late Gordon R. Nakagawa, later became a war hero as a pilot in Vietnam.

John M. Maki: Writer and Educator

The career of pioneering writer, scholar, and educator John McGilvrey Maki offers an unusual twist on the classic narrative of Asian Americans. Maki, the first Nisei to earn a doctorate from Harvard University, taught at the University of Washington (UW) for many years before being named a professor of political science and vice dean of Arts and Sciences at the University of Massachusetts Amherst during the mid-1960s. Despite his years living and working in Japanese American communities and his service as a "bridge" to Japan, Maki considered himself grounded in neither an ethnic identity nor a Japanese one but always insisted that he was classically American.

Maki's claim of an exclusive American allegiance is worth study, since in the opening phases of his long career, he was faced with the condition of the "marginal man," in sociologist Robert Park's famous formulation. Park noted the marginal man (he did not elaborate on marginal women) is a cultural hybrid caught in the interstices between two societies, connected to both but accepted by neither. Park noted, "The marginal man is a personality type that arrives at a time and a place where, out of the conflict of races and cultures, new societies, new peoples and cultures are coming into existence. The fate which condemns him to live, at the same time, in two worlds is the same which compels him to assume, in relation to the worlds in which he lives, the role of cosmopolitan and stranger." If many Nisei in those years occupied a marginal position in both Japanese and American society, Maki's case was extreme, since as an adoptee in a white family he also maintained an uncertain position within Japanese American communities. His embrace of an exclusively American identity can thus be termed strategic as well as emotional, while his development and eventual career path were marked by a succession of paradoxes and no small amount of irony.

John Maki was born Hiroo Sugiyama in Tacoma, Washington, during the first decade of the twentieth century. His birth parents were Japanese immigrants who already had other small children and lacked the money and stability to care for him. Thus, while still an infant, he was taken in by Mr. and Mrs. Alexander McGilvrey, a middle-aged white couple of Scottish ancestry whose children were already grown. His birth parents ultimately broke off contact with him, and in 1918 his foster father legally adopted him as John McGilvrey. John (universally known as "Jack") later stated that the McGilvreys did not provide him any education in his Japanese heritage—he never ate Japanese food and seldom met any Japanese Americans during his boyhood. Instead, he lived a typically American life. Outside of one or two incidents where he was targeted by exclusion, he faced no racial prejudice.

Mrs. McGilvrey died when Jack was still quite young, and he and "Dad McGilvrey" moved to Seattle, where they supported themselves by running rooming houses and through menial labor (such as working for a time as packers in a china shop). By working part time and living at home, the young McGilvrey was able to enroll at UW at the end of the 1920s. Jack, who had helped edit his high school newspaper, originally chose to major in journalism, but the dean of the journalism school soon informed him bluntly that such a major would be useless because no newspaper would hire a Japanese American. He therefore switched his major to English literature. He was honored as an outstanding English Department graduate in 1932.

Although the Depression was then at its depths, Jack parlayed his academic celebrity into a job working for the *Japanese American Courier*, the Seattle Nisei weekly run by the blind former boxer James Sakamoto and his wife. Jack was charged with drafting editorials and writing essays and filler material. His *Courier* job brought him into regular contact with Nisei for the first time. According to Robert Hosokawa, who knew him during those years,

FIGURE 3.3. John M. Maki.

Jack McGilvrey stood out from other Nisei not only because of his name but because of his accent and body language. Meanwhile, Jack contributed to several end-of-the-year literary sections of Nisei newspapers and placed poems in *Gyo-Sho*, the Nisei literary anthology produced by Eddie Shimano in 1936.

At the same time, Jack began graduate school in English at UW. However, the following year, the secretary of the English Department (no doubt at the behest of higher-ups arranging a deal) told him that as a Nisei he would never be able to get a job in English and proposed that he accept instead a fellowship in Oriental studies. Although he had taken an elementary Japanese language course as an undergraduate, he had no experience with Asian civilizations—clearly, his ancestry was his only qualification. He nonetheless agreed to her recommendation and began to absorb Japanese culture. (Shortly afterward, he accompanied Bill Hosokawa, a young journalist he had met at the *Courier*, to a Japanese student conference in Oregon. During the trip, Hosokawa introduced Jack to Mary Yasumura, the daughter of a Seattle Japanese American family, who would marry him soon after.) On the advice of his new father-in-law, Jack again changed his name. In order to be more credible as a scholar of Japanese, he adopted the name John M. Maki, Maki being a Japanese version of his previous name.

In 1937, thanks to the fellowship (sponsored by the Japanese government, whose leaders were eager to gain favorable publicity and Nisei support for their China policy), Maki and his wife began a two-year residence in Tokyo. Ironically, while Mrs. Maki, who had attended Japanese school growing up in Seattle, was familiar with Japanese language and customs, and made friends easily, Jack, the nominal specialist, felt alienated from his surroundings and was slow to learn Japanese (which he would always speak with a poor accent) or choose a research project. He did take massive notes on Japanese literature and culture, some of which he used to draft an article for the scholarly journal *Monumenta Nipponica* on Lady Murasaki Shikibu's classic novel *The Tale of Genji*, then largely unknown in the West. In 1939, upon his return home, Maki was offered a position as a lecturer in Oriental studies at UW. Given his own cursory study of Japanese culture, he later said, as a teacher he felt like the fabled one-eyed man in the kingdom of the blind.

In the aftermath of Pearl Harbor, Maki was caught up in the widespread wave of anti–Japanese American panic. His wife's father was arrested and interned in Montana, and Maki himself needed a special permit to attend his own adoptive father's funeral. In May 1942, he was confined with his wife, her family, and other West Coast Japanese Americans in Washington's Puyallup Assembly Center. He later stated that he never thought to challenge evacuation or incarceration, this being long before the civil rights movement. Rather, he said, he and his wife accepted that they were inescapably identified with the Japanese enemy and so placidly prepared for removal. After a few weeks in the center, however, Maki was recruited by a UW friend who worked at the Federal Communications Commission (FCC) to serve as a specialist on

Japan. He and his wife were thereby permitted to leave Puyallup and proceed to Washington, DC.

This series of events is redolent with irony. Maki, unlike the mass of Nisei, got himself and his wife out of camp based on his familiarity with Japan, although it was precisely such perceived closeness that fed the suspicions that resulted in the mass confinement of Japanese Americans as well as the indefinite internment of Mrs. Maki's father. Conversely, Maki's adoption by a white family, which prevented his immersion in Japanese culture as a youth and limited his actual familiarity with Japan, almost certainly served to reassure anxious government officials of his pro-American attitude. Interestingly enough, although one official at the Office of Naval Intelligence did ask Maki to teach him Japanese, none of his colleagues asked him to offer briefings on his life in Japan. Instead, Maki worked for a year analyzing translated Japanese propaganda for the FCC's Foreign Broadcast Intelligence Service. (Given his limited Japanese, he was not asked to do the actual translating himself.) In June 1943, the Japan desk of the Office of War Information (OWI), headed by his former UW colleague George Taylor, hired him to put together directives and scripts for shortwave news broadcasts to Japan.

While at the OWI, Maki spent his off hours writing a mass-market work on Japan in preparation for the postwar American occupation. (According to his sister-in-law, Michi Yasumura, who moved in with the family after being released from the Minidoka camp, Maki formulated the book's material on his daily bus ride to and from work, wrote the text rapidly once at home, and was so focused that he could chat about other things as he typed the manuscript.) Alfred A. Knopf published the book in May 1945 as *Japanese Militarism: Its Cause and Cure*. Other than small-press literature, it was the first English-language book ever published by a West Coast Nisei. The work gave a historical analysis of Japanese development. Maki argued that militarism, far from being an ideology imposed from above by a small coterie of leaders, was so deeply embedded in Japanese culture that the work of democratization would require revolutionary change in Japan's social structures. In one notable passage, Maki stated that the emperor was a bulwark of militarism, and the ideal solution would be for an internal movement in Japanese society to arise for his removal. Yet Maki argued that having the occupying powers execute the emperor would be a tragic error, and he prophetically recommended transforming the emperor into a vessel for democracy. The book was widely reviewed, including the *New York Times*, and Maki received favorable attention (such as interviews in the *New York Post* and on radio talk shows). Within a short time, the book sold out its initial run of 5,000 copies.

The book is interesting to read even today. Beyond the content, what is particularly striking is the form and tone of the book. Maki claimed no connection with Japan and did not even mention his prewar residence there. Instead—audaciously, in light of the stigmatization of Japanese Americans—he presented himself on the cover as an American of Japanese descent "completely enlightened about the Japanese nation, and ardent in his desire for complete victory." Yet, even in the climate of wartime censorship and hunger for victory, it is striking that Maki made no comment about the treatment of Japanese Americans—and certainly not their mass confinement—except for a vague suggestion that Japan's protests over the 1924 US immigration law excluding Japanese immigrants on racial grounds were irrational, and, in light of Japan's own racialist ideology, unjustifiable. Rather, he identified entirely with the United States.

In early 1946, Maki was sent to Japan for work in the American occupation. He later said that it took him so long to get from the United States to Japan, because of shipping shortages and other complications, that he was not able to be present for work on the drafting of the constitution itself. Instead, he devoted much of his time to reporting on the structure of Japan's central government and its surviving agencies and their response to the emergency situation. (Because of Maki's lack of Japanese fluency, Nisei translators accompanied him during his studies and interviews of Japanese bureaucrats.) After six months in Japan, Maki decided to study for a doctorate. He moved to Boston and entered the Political Science Department at Harvard. Midway through his studies, he received word that Harvard's faculty would accept *Japanese Militarism* as equivalent to a thesis, once he added footnotes to the text. Thus, in the end, Maki spent less than two years at Harvard before earning his doctorate in 1948.

Following his graduation, Maki launched his academic career. With the support of his former OWI boss, George Taylor, Maki accepted a job as an assistant professor of Asian studies at the University of Washington and became a leading expert on Japanese politics and constitutionalism. Among his noteworthy contributions was the 1962 book *Government and Politics in Japan: The Road to Democracy*. He also remained conspicuously active in faculty governance, and in 1962 he became the first nonwhite professor to chair the faculty senate. He and his wife raised two sons.

In 1966 Maki was persuaded to accept a position directing the new Asian studies program at the University of Massachusetts Amherst. During his time at UMass, he produced a number of articles as well as *We, the Japanese: Voices of Japan* (1972), a book of quotes from young people. He served on the faculty of UMass until his retirement in 1980 and remained exceedingly active professionally through the years that followed. Most notably, he brokered a novel sister university agreement between the University of Massachusetts and the University of Hokkaido, two institutions created by nineteenth-century educator William Smith Clark. For his services uniting Japan and the United States, Maki was decorated by the emperor of Japan in 1985.

In 2002 the nonagenarian Maki published *A Yankee in Hokkaido: The Life of William Smith Clark* as well as a book on the Japanese constitution, *From Imperial Myth to Democracy: Japan's Two Constitutions, 1889–2002*, in partnership with scholar Lawrence W. Beer. Two years later, he privately published a moving memoir, *A Voyage through the Twentieth Century*, compiled from oral interviews. In November 2006, Maki suffered a bad fall at his home and was taken to the hospital. He died of complications from the injury a few weeks later. In a climactic irony to his career as a bridge between Japan and the United States, he died on December 7, 2006, the sixty-fifth anniversary of the Japanese attack on Pearl Harbor.

John M. Maki's development and career trajectory foreshadowed the complex acculturation and ambivalent belonging of current-day Asian-born adoptees. Raised by a white family, without access to his ancestral culture (although largely without prejudice), he remained somewhat apart from the Nikkei community. He did not deny his identity as a Nisei, and he remained proud of his early writings for the *Japanese American Courier* and occasionally reviewed books on Japanese Americans in the years after the war. Yet Maki saw himself fundamentally as an American. As he later put it, "I figured that if it walks like a duck, and talks like a duck, it is a duck." Neither his involuntary shift of college majors nor his acceptance into the Seattle Japanese community, nor even his brief imprisonment on racial grounds, altered his unproblematic and confident sense of himself as American—one so solidly implanted that he felt able to write about Japan without fearing accusations of double allegiance.

Buddy Uno and Bill Hosokawa: Two Nisei Journalists in Occupied China

On August 20, 2011, the Heart Mountain Interpretive Learning Center opened its doors. The center, located on the site of the War Relocation Authority camp at Heart Mountain, sheds new light on the history of the wartime camps. Its creation was an impressive achievement and a major labor of love by the board of directors of the Heart Mountain, Wyoming Foundation. I followed the project throughout its development with great interest, especially because of the presence on the board of Eric Muller, my past collaborator—I jokingly refer to him as my partner in crime—in refuting Michelle Malkin's absurd charges of widespread prewar subversive activity by Nikkei. Eric is a scholar of Japanese Americans whose passion and work I have long admired.

One of Eric's great concerns is that chroniclers of Japanese Americans, in trying to debunk racist wartime images of Nisei as disloyal and pro-Japanese, have gone too far in the other direction. He points out that books, plays, and exhibits have largely erased the Japanese connections of prewar Nisei and have tended to portray them in almost Hollywood-style terms as assimilated small-town Americans, "a group composed entirely of bobby-soxers drinking malteds, jitterbugging, and reading comic books."

Eric's point is well taken. Although such stereotypes are not altogether without foundation, they reduce and distort a complex reality. In fact, the mass of Nisei maintained close connections to various aspects of both Japanese and American culture. They ate Japanese food, performed Japanese plays, learned Japanese arts and crafts, watched Japanese films, and cheered Japanese athletes in international competitions. They attended Japanese language schools—willingly or unwillingly—and while most youngsters spoke Japanese poorly, their lingo was studded with Nihongo. The ethnic press, both English and Japanese language, featured extensive coverage of news from Japan. Numerous Nisei traveled back to their ancestral homeland for visits or education, although they often faced prejudice and isolation as Americans there, and some moved there permanently—according to one estimate at the time, 5,000 Nisei lived in Tokyo alone in 1940. Others settled in Japanese-controlled Korea and Manchuria.

As a result of their grounding in Japanese culture and the influence of their parents, many Nisei, especially older ones, felt a certain sense of identification with Japan during the 1930s. Although such feelings did not by any means translate automatically into support for the Japanese government's foreign policy, a review of the ethnic press does indicate that most Nisei journalists and speakers publicly defended Japanese expansionism and the occupation of China during those years. We can only guess at their motivations: sentimental attachment to family, self-interest, political analysis, racial pride, or, at times, professional duty. Even so, the Nisei did not cease to regard themselves as Americans—any more than did the other Americans of all stripes who favored Japan over China. Instead, as Tokyo and Washington, DC, moved toward confrontation at the end of the decade, the Nisei were caught between the two and felt pressure to choose sides. While the large majority reaffirmed their primary attachment to America, a fraction of the group continued to support their ancestral homeland, especially those who had lived in the Japanese empire and absorbed some of the dominant militarist philosophy.

The dilemma over what position to take was especially keen for the phalanx of educated adult Nisei, blocked by racial discrimination from taking jobs with American companies, who were hired by Japanese consulates and businesses in the United States and abroad. Nisei such as T. Scott Miyakawa, an employee of the Japanese-dominated South Manchurian Railway, or Larry Tajiri, a correspondent for Japan's Asahi news empire, either tried to avoid taking sides openly until imperatively necessary or sought to distance themselves from their Japanese sponsors without giving up their employment.

A revealing, if possibly extreme, case study of this complex reality lies in the contrasting careers of a pair of notable journalists, Buddy Uno and Bill Hosokawa. Both were hired to work in Asia in the late 1930s and both reported from Japanese-occupied China. Both also were recruited in turn as contributors by a pro-Tokyo newspaper, the *Far Eastern Review*. Yet their paths diverged in striking fashion. Uno cast his lot with Japan during World War II, while Hosokawa returned to the United States and proclaimed his support for America, even after being confined at the Heart Mountain camp.

Kazumaro "Buddy" Uno (whose career has been extensively studied by the late Yuji Ichioka) was born in 1913, the eldest of ten children; his siblings included future journalist Robert Uno and activists Edison Uno and Amy Uno Ishii. In the early 1930s, he became a well-regarded feature writer for the West Coast Nisei press as the author of the column A Nisei Melodrama. In

FIGURE 3.4. Bill Hosokawa.

1937, following the outbreak of the Sino-Japanese War, Uno traveled to Japan, where he secured permission to visit China as an accredited war correspondent. After touring the battlefront for several weeks, the young reporter published a series of pro-Japanese dispatches in the Nisei press, which, according to Ichioka, consisted largely of slightly altered Japanese Army press releases. On the strength of these accounts, Uno was invited to make a second tour of the front in 1938. Following his tours, Uno returned to the United States for lecture tours up and down the West Coast to speak of his experiences and defend Tokyo. He spoke in Japanese communities (often with the support of local branches of the Japanese American Citizens League) and participated in public debates with Chinese Americans.

In fall 1939, Uno returned to Asia and published a series of articles in the *Far Eastern Review*, an established English-language monthly magazine based first in Shanghai and later in Manila. Due to the secret subsidies the magazine received from the Japanese government, writer Peter O'Connor later termed it a "semi-official organ" for Tokyo. In his series, "A Nisei Visits China," Uno described his travels around China, lauding in the process the impressive activities of the Japanese occupier. The series is remarkable for Uno's blindness about the impact of the occupation, mixed with a wide-eyed naïveté so absolute that in our current, more ironic age it would be read automatically as satire.

In his first piece, for example, Uno recounts his stay in Hangchow (Hangzhou), and notes excitedly how the exchange rate fostered by occupation makes the prices of Chinese goods extremely cheap. The highlight of the article is his description of his conversation with an American missionary, Miss A.R.V. Wilson. When Miss Wilson states that she wants nothing to do with the Japanese military, Uno insists that, ever since occupying Hangchow, the Japanese soldiers have been devoting themselves to aiding war refugees by distributing food and medical care and opening an employment bureau. When she remarks that she is prevented from traveling to her mission, Uno closes with indignation at the idea that religious leaders are so narrow-minded that they can only see matters from a religious angle.

In a second article, "A Nisei in Hangkow," Uno tells the story of traveling to the city (present-day Wuhan) and lauds the enterprise of the Japanese businesses that have set up there, following the struggle of the brave soldiers to take the city, and proceeded to dominate the local economy: "Expansion of Japanese business into Hangkow was only made possible at the cost of thousands of Japanese lives dedicated to peace and goodwill." (The loss of life by the city's Chinese defenders in the face of the massacres perpetrated by the agents of such "goodwill" apparently did not similarly impress him.)

The two other articles in the series, describing Uno's visits to Formosa (i.e., Taiwan) and Hainan, are similar in tone. Both feature the author's breathless descriptions of Japan's efforts to unite the regions under its rule into a place where "all peoples are prospering under a single government based in freedom and justice" as well as his occasional pained incomprehension when the non-Japanese he interviews are reticent in their responses to his position. An interesting aspect of the final entry is how Uno touches on the startling news of the German-Soviet pact and the outbreak of war in Europe at the end of summer 1939. An American consul says hopefully that the German "insult" to Japan in allying with their Russian enemy will bring Tokyo to forge better relations with the United States. Uno, for his part, states candidly that while he is uninformed on the actual cause of events, he sympathizes with Germany. If the United States stays neutral, he continues, as no doubt it must for domestic reasons, Germany and the Soviet Union could together "have the advantage over" Great Britain and France, whom Uno considers the true enemy.

In January 1940, Uno joined the Japanese Army Press Bureau in Shanghai as a civilian journalist and was detached as a liaison for Japan's military with foreign correspondents. In early 1941, he was drafted into the Japanese Army. Although he was discharged after a single day to return to his Press Bureau activities, his enlistment caused him to be stripped of his American citizenship. The loss was evidently a decisive step for Uno, already bitter over the discrimination he had found in the United States, in cementing his growing allegiance to Japan. During World War II, the Press Bureau named Uno editor-in-chief of a seized local Anglophone newspaper, the *Shanghai Evening Post & Mercury*, which he made into a collaborationist organ. He also edited a pro-Japanese photo magazine titled *Freedom*. He subsequently served in Tokyo, where he organized pro-Japanese radio broadcasts with coerced labor by POWs, and later did similar work in Manila. Captured by Filipino forces at the end of the war, he was ultimately deported to Japan, where he spent his final years. He died in 1954.

Kumpei William Hosokawa was born in Seattle on January 30, 1915. Although he did not begin speaking English until kindergarten, he developed an early interest in reading and sports. He excelled in basketball and later helped found a local Nisei basketball league. Like many young Nisei, he spent several summers in Alaska working in salmon canneries. In 1933 Hosokawa entered the University of Washington to study journalism, although he was warned that no mainstream newspaper would ever hire a Japanese American (Hosokawa's younger brother Robert, universally known as "Rube," would follow him into journalism). Soon after, Hosokawa took a part-time job working for the Seattle Nisei newspaper *Japanese American Courier*. When Buddy Uno visited Seattle in 1936, he met Hosokawa, who befriended him, took him home for the night, and lent him pajamas.

In 1937, after earning his BA degree, Hosokawa was hired by the Japanese consulate in Seattle. Shortly thereafter, he moved to Singapore to found an English-language newspaper, the *Singapore Herald*. A column written shortly before his departure reveals his state of mind. A convinced pacifist, Hosokawa called on his readers not to be "suckers" taken in by war propaganda coming from many sides: "The Japanese people are suffering, and the government is doing its best to keep up the war spirit with its National Spiritual Mobilization campaign. The Chinese people are suffering from marauding armies, exploiters, warlords, taxes and invaders. The Germans and Italians are suffering from rigidly controlled economies and regimentation. And the people of the so-called democratic nations, the United States, the British Commonwealth, and France, are suffering from acute and chronic cases of jitters brought on by the soaring imaginations of those who pull the strings to make you and me and two billion other guys dance." Hosokawa affirmed that ordinary citizens should resist being manipulated into a war spirit and recognize that those on the other side "are not bloodthirsty plunderers at all, but just like the rest of us who've been foxed."

In 1940 Hosokawa sent his family back to the United States and migrated to Japanese-occupied Shanghai, where he wrote for the English-language *Shanghai Times*, which operated under Tokyo's censorship. In early 1941, Hosokawa began writing for the *Far Eastern Review*, the same journal that had earlier featured Uno's dispatches. These monthly pieces, likewise written under censorship by the occupying power, united his existing pacifism with the "realistic" vision that many international correspondents then held of China as a backward region requiring uplift by Japan, despite the evidence of brutality by the occupiers.

For instance, in May 1941, in "The Future of a 'Democracy,'" Hosokawa complained that Americans had been misled by pro-Chinese propaganda to view China as a democracy. In fact, China had no history as a democracy and was not likely to develop one. Japan, in contrast, was the closest thing to an American-style democracy in Asia. Although Japan had been forced to suspend many constitutional rights—like any other country at war and was now "in many respects totalitarian," Hosokawa admitted—it had a solid previous record as a democracy on which it could build (implicitly under the incentive of a favorable policy). In his June 1941 article, titled "Pacific Factors for Washington to Weigh," Hosokawa explicitly called on the United States to work for friendship with Japan. He claimed that the China question was not an insoluble barrier; there was room for negotiation between American demands that Japan respect China's territorial integrity and Japanese demands that America withdraw aid to the Chinese government: "Somewhere between the two points of view lies the compromise that must be reached if a solution by force of arms is to be avoided." He concluded that if the United States and Great Britain could meet legitimate Japanese concerns, Japan could be induced to detach itself from the Axis and become an ally, or even a friendly neutral. This would enable the British and Americans to reduce their forces in the Pacific and concentrate their forces on the conflict with Germany, the real enemy.

In July 1941, Hosokawa published "China and Her Foreign Masters." In it, he drew a parallel between the Chungking government, which received aid from the United States, and the collaborationist Nanking government of Wang Ching-Wei, which benefited from Japanese "guidance and assistance." In both cases, he added, technical advisers from "mentor governments" were performing the work of "guiding and counseling a less advanced administrative regime." While Hosokawa did not state openly that Wang's government was a puppet regime, he admitted the realities of the occupation: "Little can be said in praise of Japan's military occupation of China except that the intentions expressed at various times have been good." However, he claimed that with the stabilization of Wang's regime, Japan's positive plans to reconstruct China from the bottom up (which he claimed were more realistic than the vain efforts of the Americans to treat China as a modern nation) were becoming more visible.

In August 1941, Hosokawa followed with an article titled "Tokyo in the Shadow of War," which was perhaps his most overtly propagandistic in tone. In it he praised the ability of the Japanese to withstand war-inspired hardship: even under the increased stress of conflict they presented themselves as more orderly and united than they had been a year previously. He repeated his thesis that war turned all states totalitarian: "The Germans have proved to the world's satisfaction that the totalitarian state, bereft of all democratic impediments, is the most efficiently streamlined body politic for the pursuit of a war. So, like many another nation at war or still on the brink of a precarious peace, Japan is at work building up what is called the most efficient national defense state." In that sense, he insisted, Japan was no different from Britain or the United States, which had built up their own military forces.

As part of its "national defense" state, he noted, Tokyo created neighborhood councils to offer the people productive work: "Since speculation, either verbally or in the press, regarding government policy has been forbidden in Japan, [semiofficial] Neighborhood Groups serve as a convenient outlet for the natural anxiety and nervous energy of the people. The very fact that every individual can help with the national defense through these groups has given the patriotic and energetic Japanese much comfort." Hosokawa concluded that while the Japanese people did not seek war with the Western powers, they would have no hesitation in taking it up if it were to come and that they would be able to triumph through their will: "While officialdom may know Japan's limitations, the people have the utmost faith in their ability to withstand further hardships and carry on for the Emperor. Material difficulties are of secondary importance to their way of thinking. This is not to imply any fanatical desire for conquest and glory; I merely wish to point out that to the Japanese mind the material factors retreat before the will and spirit to succeed."

A month later, Hosokawa contributed another article, "The Fates at Work in Washington and Tokyo," in which he expressed his hope that negotiations between Japan and the United States would lead to a fundamental settlement and a durable peace. He reminded his readers of "the awful cost of a shooting war" and expressed cautious optimism as to the possibilities of settlement and the potential benefits: "A settlement which will lead to the end of the Sino-Japanese War, and the solution and clarification of such long-pending issues as Manchukuo, the New Order, and Japan's southward expansion policy cannot but open the way to an era of peace and mutual prosperity and progress so long overdue in the Far East." However, despite his use of the word *Manchukuo* (the name of the puppet state created by Tokyo and unrecognized by Western democracies, rather than *Manchuria*, as in his earlier writings), here he drew less of an equivalence between the respective justice of Japan's position and that of the United States than in his July piece: "It has long been obvious, despite Chungking's [i.e., the Nationalist Chinese government's] ill-disguised concern, that the United States is not going to abandon or compromise the principles of international morality she has risked thus far to uphold. Wishful thinkers in Tokyo may not realize this but the government would not be worthy of its name if it were similarly deluded."

In October Hosokawa wrote what would be his final article, "'Good Old Days' for the Foreigner in China—are Gone," which presented the Chinese as barbaric and prone to looting. As he stated, with some exaggeration, "In both 1932 and 1937 when Sino-Japanese hostilities broke out, foreign troops [in Shanghai] were stripped for action, not against the danger of a Japanese invasion, but to defend the city against victory-drunk Chinese troops . . . Opinion as to the respective merits of the Chinese and Japanese cases was widely split even then [among "Old China Hands"], and those who supported Japan . . . were not few." Hosokawa described Japan as a nation unfairly condemned by Western countries, not out of true morality but because she threatened their own imperialistic interests. He praised Japanese transformation of the Far East into a sphere of influence: "Under the ideas embodied for the still-undefined 'Co-Prosperity Sphere' it is to be presumed that here will be a happy hunting ground of commercial enterprise with resultant uplifting of the masses."

In October 1941, Hosokawa returned to Seattle, where the *Japanese American Courier* rehired him. After the onset of war, he assisted with the dissemination of *Courier* editor James Sakamoto's abortive plans for the formation of Nisei agricultural colonies. After being sent to Puyallup (i.e., Camp Harmony), Hosokawa was separated from the inmates headed for Minidoka—he later explained that authorities feared him as a potential troublemaker—and sent to confinement at Heart Mountain. He was named editor of the camp newspaper *Heart Mountain Sentinel*, where he defended enlistment of Nisei in the military. After the war, Hosokawa became an esteemed journalist and editor for the *Denver Post*. Within the Japanese community, he established a reputation as an American patriot and stalwart of the Japanese American Citizens League. In his long-running *Pacific Citizen* column Out of the Frying Pan and in books such as *Nisei: The Quiet Americans* (1969) and *JACL: In Quest of Justice* (1982), Hosokawa praised the Americanism of the Nisei and the glories of US democracy. He continued to write until nearly the end of his long life and published his last book, *Colorado's Japanese Americans: From 1886 to the Present* (2005), at the age of ninety. He died in 2007.

In conclusion, Bill Hosokawa, who ended up a staunch supporter of the United States against Japan, worked in the Japanese empire, where he wrote for the same collaborationist journal as Buddy Uno, who remained pro-Japanese. To be sure, the tone of Hosokawa's writings clearly differs from Uno's. Uno was an unabashed defender of Japan and its military and gullible as to the nature of the occupation. Hosokawa's stated goal was maintaining international peace and uplifting the Asian masses. Like many liberals of all shades, he welcomed the end of white domination and racial chauvinism in the Far East. His writings called on both Washington and Tokyo to follow realistic policies and compromise in the name of peace. Despite the cloud of official and unofficial censorship around him, he bravely (if fleetingly) expressed his distaste for Japan's military occupation of China. While he expressed skepticism about the anti-Japanese position of imperialist Western powers, he also stated that the position of the United States was based in international morality. In notable contrast to Buddy Uno, he approved the struggle to resist Nazi Germany.

All the same, Hosokawa's writings, doubtless subjected to surveillance by Tokyo, edged at times toward what would have been considered enemy propaganda under true wartime conditions. Long after most Nisei on the West Coast had ceased to justify Japan's imperial expansion in Asia against Washington's demands for withdrawal, he continued to extol Japanese efforts, even in the face of Japan's brutality in China and occupation of French Indochina. Conversely, he deplored pro-Chinese propaganda and repeatedly described the Chinese as backward and incapable of self-rule. He even drew a clear equivalence between the aid and technical advice furnished by Japan and the United States to their respective Chinese clients (a textbook example, to paraphrase Winston Churchill, of remaining neutral as between the fire brigade and the fire). His words also reflected a subtle pro-Japanese bias. Not only did he praise Japan's efforts in occupied Manchuria, but in some cases he referred to the area as Manchukuo. He also made favorable references to Japan's plan for a "Greater East Asia Co-Prosperity Sphere" as a sincere effort at regional leadership rather than a mask for exploitation.

Worse, Hosokawa soft-pedaled the totalitarian nature of Japanese society, portraying it as a response to war no different from that of other countries. He made only the most glancing reference to press censorship, which he mixed with glowing accounts of neighborhood councils giving anxious people patriotic work (he passed over entirely the activities of the network of informants developed by the councils). His disquisition on the advantages of the invincible Japanese spirit over material difficulties resembled a good deal of Tokyo's official propaganda.

What do we make of this apparent contradiction? It should be stressed that Hosokawa was neither a shill for Japanese militarists nor a hypocrite—he was a man of genuine principle who later displayed moral courage in expressing opinions at times that were not popular among the Nisei. (In the interests of full disclosure, I should note that I met Hosokawa on two occasions and he helped publicize in his newspaper column some of my findings about the causes of wartime Japanese removal.) Rather, it seems clear that, like many young Nisei—Hosokawa was just twenty-two when he moved to Asia—he felt a certain connection with Japan. Hosokawa's own experience of discrimination on the West Coast due to his Japanese ancestry, though less decisive than Buddy Uno's, would surely have promoted his expressed sympathy with Japan as a "have-not country," denied its fair share of resources by jealous "have countries," as well as his skepticism about the motives of the anti-Japanese press. These factors, as well as his sincere pacifism and fear of another world war, made Hosokawa slow to appreciate fully the nature of Japan's domination of Asia. In contrast, once Japan attacked Pearl Harbor, he became a convinced opponent of Japanese militarism.

THE HIDDEN CONTRIBUTIONS OF GUYO TAJIRI

One "great unknown" that we all come up against is the nature of other people's marriages. Nobody outside, not even friends or children, can really be certain what occurs between husbands and wives behind closed doors. This seems to be equally true, though in a different sense, when the spouses are professional collaborators: How do we know who is responsible for what? There are cases, still fairly rare, where both spouses receive equal authorship credit, such as historians Charles and Mary Beard, screenwriters Albert and Frances Hackett, or sociologists Robert and Helen Lynd. More often, however, the husband appears as the sole visible partner and reaps the recognition for the couple's joint work, while the wife is content (or constrained) to stay in the background. A particularly compelling case of a self-effacing wife is that of Guyo Tajiri, who joined her husband, Larry Tajiri, in building the *Pacific Citizen* into a newspaper of nationwide interest and importance during the 1940s but whose contributions as a writer and editor have been obscured.

She was born Tsuguyo Marion Okagaki in 1915—the second child of nine and the oldest daughter—and grew up in an integrated neighborhood in San José, California. Her father, Kichitaro Okagaki (1884–1947), who had come to the United States in 1904, covered local news for the San Francisco–based Japanese-language newspaper *Shin Sekai* (*New World Sun*). Guyo worked as an unpaid assistant for the newspaper during her teen years, writing and fact-checking—doing "a bit of everything," she later said—its

English-language section. Attracted by journalism, she decided to make a career of it. Upon completing high school, she was accepted into the University of Missouri's prestigious School of Journalism in fall 1932. While she loved the university, she was forced to leave after only a single semester— no doubt the Great Depression pushed tuition and board beyond the family's means. She returned home and briefly attended San José State University before enrolling the following fall at the University of California, Berkeley, where she remained for two years before graduating in 1936.

During her college years, Guyo continued to work summers at the *New World Sun*. (She worked briefly and explosively as an assistant to the editor of the English section, James Omura.) At this time she met a young journalist from Los Angeles, Larry Tajiri. Although barely older than Guyo, he had started working full time as a columnist and assistant editor at *Kashu Mainichi* at age seventeen and had become a seasoned professional. Despite (or because of) his lack of formal education, he was extremely well-read and passionate about literature and theater. (An account Guyo wrote for the *New World Sun* of the Sayonara Ball at the close of the 1934 Japanese American Citizens League [JACL] convention portrays Larry hurriedly scribbling words for a song that would be sung.) Soon after, Larry was recruited to be a columnist and coeditor of the English-language section of the *Nichi Bei Shimbun* in San Francisco, whose staff Guyo also joined. In 1937 the two were married.

In 1940 Larry and Guyo moved to New York, where Larry became the local correspondent for Japan's Asahi newspaper chain. Guyo enjoyed walking the streets of Manhattan and visiting the World's Fair and she made several lasting friendships—notably with artists Isamu Noguchi and Chuzo Tamotsu. She and Larry continued to write for the *Nichi Bei*. In one article, Guyo lyrically described her shock over the city's poverty:

> Down toward the waterfront the buildings grow even drabber, their outlines monstrous and black against the sky, with the deserted elevated tracks above them. Bent old men come timidly out of the buildings like rats in a deserted house.

The Japanese attack on Pearl Harbor in December 1941 brought a rapid end to Larry's job. Over the following weeks, Guyo and Larry gradually worked their way west (they stopped en route in New Orleans, where the racial segregation horrified them). Following their return, Larry formed organizations

FIGURE 3.5. Guyo Tajiri and her husband, Larry.

and campaigned without success to avert mass removal. As the exclusion date neared, Larry was offered a job with the Office of War Information (OWI). He was at the point of accepting when the JACL invited both spouses to transform the *Pacific Citizen*, the organization's tiny monthly newsletter, into a full-fledged weekly to replace the shuttered West Coast press. Working on forty-eight hours' notice, they packed their belongings, and on March 29, 1942—the last day before such "voluntary evacuation" was banned—they left the West Coast. Once they arrived in Salt Lake City, where the JACL had moved its operations, they rented a home from an elderly German widow, opened an office in three rooms adjoining JACL headquarters in the downtown Beeson Building, and hired a printer. The revamped weekly version of the *Pacific Citizen* reappeared on June 4, 1942.

From the *PC*'s first issue, Guyo and Larry put together the entire newspaper by themselves. It lost money at first, and the hard-pressed JACL had no extra money for reporters or features. Thus, in addition to printing government bulletins, the Tajiris read through mountains of outside reports, newspaper pieces, camp papers, and other sources for Nisei-related material to reprint, and they maintained a steady stream of correspondence to solicit information or columns. They also wrote an enormous amount of original material. Larry drafted editorials and wrote a regular column, Nisei U.S.A. Guyo had her own recurring column, under the pen name Ann Nisei, and did regular book reviews and features. She also was largely responsible for proofreading each issue for the printer—who had trouble spelling all the Japanese names. Eventually, finances improved enough for them to hire a single part-time secretary and they persuaded writers such as Joe Grant Masaoka, Bill Hosokawa, and Dyke Miyagawa to contribute columns. Still, for their extraordinary burden of work, the Tajiris were paid only $100 per month—Larry $75 and Guyo $25—plus rent on their home. (Legend has it that Larry supplemented family budgets through winnings at weekly poker sessions.)

The Tajiris succeeded in making the *PC* both entertaining and intelligent, and it provided a broad liberal forum for opinion. Under their direction, the paper was singled out for praise by OWI Director Elmer Davis as "the finest weekly newspaper in the United States," and in 1946 it was nominated for a Pulitzer Prize (apparently the first minority newspaper to be so honored) by Friends of the American Way, a West Coast group. During the postwar years, even as other Japanese American newspapers appeared, it maintained its strong focus on civil rights. In summer 1949, Guyo traveled to San Francisco as a special correspondent, reporting on Iva Toguri d'Aquino's "Tokyo Rose" trial.

Guyo's writing was admirably sharp. As Ann Nisei she presented information for women in camp—discussing such topics as makeup, romantic problems, and family life—and underlined the importance of Nisei women's development. Before the war, she commented bitingly in 1943, the perception of the Nisei woman was "vague, dull, stolid—a modernized version of her mother, and exuding withal the faint odor of cherry blossoms." Now, however, Nisei women were relocating and were "anxious and eager to meet the world, expectant that they could conquer it." She was not starry-eyed, however. In a 1946 review she commented, "For the Nisei, the evacuation was a horrible experience in humiliation. The remembering of the incredible humiliation and agony of that experience must be, to the Nisei who went through it, an experience that burns upon the heart." Her most reprinted contribution was the lyric she penned in 1948 for the JACL hymn (though in later years, an easy way to make her cringe was to repeat it to her):

There was a dream my father dreamed for me
A land in which all men are free:
Then the desert camp with watchtowers high,
Where life stood still 'mid sand and brooding sky.
Out of the war in which my brothers died,
Their muted voices with mine cried;
This is our dream, that all men shall be free,
This is our creed, we'll live in loyalty.
God help us rid this land of bigotry,
That we may walk in peace and dignity.

In 1952 Larry and Guyo left the *Pacific Citizen*, victims of burnout and an internal power struggle. They worked a short time for a newspaper in Colorado Springs before the *Denver Post* hired Larry, and the couple moved to Denver. Guyo kept house and painted and Larry was named the *Post*'s entertainment columnist and drama critic, a job he held until his untimely death in 1965. At the time Larry died, Guyo recalled, she had not worked in a long time and had no "marketable skills." By then in her fifties, she bravely went back to school and earned a degree in education. Settling in the

Berkeley Hills, she took a job as a public school teacher in Oakland, where she remained for twelve years before retirement. Always modest and reticent about her own role with the *Pacific Citizen*, she remained in her later years a generous resource for historians and a joy to her many friends.

Postscript

Guyo Tajiri was both my friend and a great supporter of my work. In late summer 2007, after I learned that she was terminally ill, I quickly drafted the above article. I made an exception to my usual rule against writing about living persons, as I thought the time had come to set the record straight about Guyo's role in publishing the *Pacific Citizen* and her importance in Japanese American life. Guyo was in the hospital, but her family kindly agreed to share the column with her. They reported to me that she said it was a nice article but (with typical modesty) had insisted that I had greatly exaggerated her contributions.

Guyo died in September 2007, shortly after my article appeared. I wrote a brief tribute to her for the *Nichi Bei Times*. I began by declaring bluntly, "Putting it in the nicest possible way, Guyo Tajiri was a fraud: she posed as an ordinary person and covered her tracks, minimizing and disclaiming credit for her contributions." I concluded that even if she preferred to remain in her husband's shadow, during his life and in her long widowhood, she was his full partner in informing and uniting the Japanese community in a time of trial and helping it recover and grow afterward. Her service could therefore equally merit the famous inscription on the tomb of the architect Christopher Wren in St. Paul's Cathedral in London, which he built: *Si monumentum requiris, circumspice* (If you would seek his monument, look around you).

Guyo's death powerfully influenced the direction of my professional life. In 2006, with the encouragement of the Tajiri family, I began work on a book composed of the writings of Guyo's husband, Larry Tajiri. When I asked Guyo for permission to reprint those of Larry's wide-ranging articles for which the JACL did not hold copyright, she immediately granted me the rights without charge. After her death, and in the wake of my article "outing" her as an important figure in the *Pacific Citizen*, it became painfully obvious that the book should include a section of her writings as well, which Guyo's family generously granted me permission to reproduce. The book was eventually published as *Pacific Citizens: Larry and Guyo Tajiri and Japanese American Journalism in the World War II Era* (2012). I incorporated much of the information in this chapter in the book's introduction. In the afterword, I recounted the story of my initial meeting and friendship with Guyo and noted the irony that, as sorry as I was that she did not live to see the book and its celebration of Larry's work, her own self-effacing character would likely have led her to oppose my including her or paying her deserved homage.

THE TRAGIC AND ENGAGING CAREER OF SAM HOHRI

Like many other people, I was saddened by the news of William Minoru Hohri's passing in fall 2010. I greatly respected Hohri's contributions to the Japanese American redress movement through his work in founding and operating the National Council for Japanese American Redress as well as his various other activities on behalf of social justice in the United States. I was interested to read the various memorial tributes.

One element that seemed absent from his obituaries was a discussion of the Hohri family. In particular, none of the pieces mentioned the tragic and engaging figure of William's eldest brother, Sam Hohri. Sam lived barely thirty years and much of his life lies unrecorded. Nevertheless, he left a deep impression—not only on his young brother but on countless others both inside and outside Japanese communities. Sam's friend Hisaye Yamamoto, herself no slouch as a writer, later referred to Sam as "our Orwell," for his mix of tough-minded independence and literary skill.

Samuel Shiro Hohri was born in Japan on July 4, 1916. His father, Daisuke Hohri, was a Christian convert who became a Methodist preacher. In 1921 the Hohris moved to the United States with five-year-old Sam and his two younger siblings. Three more siblings would be born in the United States. Although the Hohris lived for a time in Sierra Madre, the family ultimately settled in West Los Angeles. A newspaper described Daisuke, a veteran of the Japanese Army, as in broken health when he arrived in the United States. Once in America he turned to sketching and painting on velvet and silk. According to his children, he was not a worldly man—his salary as the itinerant minister to his tiny flock did not begin to cover the expenses of a family of eight. Thus, the family lived in poverty, especially after the onset of the Great Depression. Sam nonetheless managed to finish high school and enrolled as a journalism student at Pasadena Junior College, where he wrote for the school newspaper, *Chronicle and Campus*. However, he finished only one year of school before he was struck down with tuberculosis, a deadly scourge in those pre-antibiotic days. The next years he spent time in sanitoriums. As a result, Takuo, the next oldest brother, took a job mowing lawns to support the family after he finished high school.

Being "an involuntary hermit," as Sam termed it, in the Olive View Sanitorium, he struggled to pass the time. He received letters and listened to the radio. He devoted a fair share of his attention to political interests, becoming a devoted pacifist and antifascist. At some point during this period he joined the Socialist Party. He also kept busy reading and writing. He served as a columnist for the sanitorium's publication, also called the *Olive View*, and as the editor for the short-lived quarterly publication *Tab*.

On March 13, 1940, while still confined in the sanitorium, Sam took a bold step by undertaking a regular column in the English section of the bilingual Los Angeles newspaper *Sangyo Nippo* (*Industrial Japan*). He joked that the column, which he dubbed Rambler's Nemesis, would differ from others in not centering on what the writer ate for breakfast. It would soon become notable for its powerful support of racial democracy and intergroup alliances with "Nisei" from other racial groups. As Sam stated in July 1940, "We should recognize the fact that we are only a segment of the minorities that abound in this nation. When we face this situation and unite our activities with that of the other minorities, we will extend the realization of that more perfect democratic state so vigorously attributed to Jefferson and Lincoln et al." He criticized the Japanese American Citizens League (JACL) and other groups for supporting a proposed all-Nisei housing development in Jefferson Park that excluded other racial groups. Meanwhile, he took a maverick position on national issues. Like other Socialists in the prewar period, Hohri denounced Republicans for reactionary politics and the Roosevelt administration for excessive militarism. In mid-1941, he complained that the JACL had no business claiming to speak for the Nisei in support of White House policy in the Pacific, when many Nisei were skeptical or hostile regarding such a position.

The coming of war deeply scarred the Hohri family. On the day after Pearl Harbor, Daisuke, who had figured on government lists as a Japanese Army veteran and a minister (thus, a community leader) was arrested and sent for internment in Montana. Sam managed to find work as a publicity agent with his old adversaries, the JACL. In early 1942, he wrote a letter to Eleanor Roosevelt on behalf of the JACL, complaining that the San Francisco Red Cross was excluding Nisei on racial grounds from donating blood. He ultimately succeeded in reversing the policy.

In the wake of Executive Order 9066, the Hohri family was removed from their home and sent together to Manzanar. Sam immediately joined three other Nisei in publishing a mimeographed sheet, which they dubbed the *Manzanar Free Press*. Soon after, he was named the paper's features editor. Meanwhile, he began a correspondence with Socialist Party leader Norman Thomas about the plight of Japanese Americans. In his letters, Sam described the grim conditions in camp, though he added that Manzanar was relatively restrained: "In other camps they have the whole shebang that you associate with Germany: division of the camp in sections, each fenced and intra camp visiting verboten; sentry towers with searchlights and machine gun crews."

Too ill to work for much of the first summer, Sam returned to the *Manzanar Free Press* in fall 1942. He aroused the ire of the camp administration by his investigation of the unprovoked shooting of a Nisei youth, Hikoji Takeuchi, by an armed sentry. In the wake of the December 1942 "Manzanar Riot," Hohri wrote an insightful account of the event for Thomas. He deplored the tactics of pro-Axis thugs who had profited from the atmosphere of tension in the camp but did not spare camp officials and soldiers for their poor handling of the situation: "When the MPs fired several of the casualties were among the ranks of the onlookers who were neither demonstratively supporting nor opposing the storming of the Bastille."

Sam remained in Manzanar throughout the balance of the war, then prepared to move back to the West Coast. He considered return a moral duty for Nisei. When New York–based activist Ina Sugihara published an article in the Catholic magazine *Commonweal* in September 1945 entitled "I Don't Want to Go Back," claiming that mass return to the West Coast by Japanese Americans would lead to intergroup tension and rioting, Sam took up the challenge. In a letter to the editor, he responded that the way for Nisei to fight discrimination was by returning to their homes, despite threats from white racists: "The night riding terrorists of the West Coast would like to spread the miasma of the South to the West. In choosing to stay away and avoid this unpleasantness, there is the danger of reverting to isolation . . . if the terrorists succeed in intimidating the Nisei . . . their success will validly encourage and incite them to depress others—the Negroes, the Mexicans, other Orientals, Jews."

He restated his case soon after in the *Pacific Citizen*. In a review of African American writer Richard Wright's memoir, *Black Boy*, Sam called for interracial action against discrimination: "If we join our waiting friends (many of whom we must acknowledge are new and formerly rejected or uncultivated) to engage in creating a clean healthy social climate in California, we can go on to claim the swampland [the South]."

Despite his powerful will, Sam's health, never strong, soon began to give out. He suffered a recurrence of tuberculosis and was forced to return to a California sanitorium. He wrote little afterward, though he did contribute a pair of pieces to the African American newspaper *Los Angeles Tribune* at the invitation of his friend Hisaye Yamamoto (who had taken a job as columnist with the newspaper in order to act as a bridge between blacks and Nisei).

Sam Hohri died of tuberculosis on March 19, 1947. His integrity and support for black-Nisei unity helped inspire not only his friends but his brother William, who became active in the civil rights movement of the 1960s and marched in Mississippi with James Meredith in 1966. When William moved to Los Angeles in the mid-1990s and began writing a newspaper column for *Rafu Shimpo*, he named it Rambler's Nemesis in tribute to his admired brother.

Hisaye Yamamoto and the African American Press

Hisaye Yamamoto DeSoto, who died on January 30, 2011, at the age of eighty-nine, remains known primarily as a literary artist, a crafter of powerful short fiction—including her signature stories "Seventeen Syllables" and "Yoneko's Earthquake"—as well as assorted newspaper columns. Yet the story of her development as a writer is less known and bears exploring, especially since it ties in with the many other lives that she led. For she was the last, and quite possibly the greatest, representative of a whole generation of Nisei literary and political thinkers who were featured in the Japanese vernacular press in the prewar years, and the only one who achieved mainstream renown with her writing after the war.

Hisaye was born on August 23, 1921, in Redondo Beach, California. Like the family she depicted in "Seventeen Syllables," her father, Kanzo Yamamoto, was a farmer. Her mother, Sae, better educated than her husband, was attracted to literature and inspired her daughter to take an interest in learning. At just fourteen years old, Hisaye began writing a regular column for the local newspaper *Kashu Mainichi* under the pen name Napoleon. Her column went through a variety of handles, from Napoleon's Last Stand to Don't Think it Ain't Been Charming, before finally settling on Small Talk. Much of it was, indeed, of little lasting interest: chatty anecdotes of her dialogue with brothers Johnny and Yuke (i.e., Frank Yukata Yamamoto), plus a running mock feud with fellow columnist Kenny Murase (in later life, the distinguished educator Kenji Murase, but then—to hear Napoleon tell it—a pimple-faced stuffed shirt).

Like the other Nisei press writers—Sam Hohri, Mary Oyama Mittwer, Eddie Shimano, Chiye Mori, George Furiya, Yasuo Sasaki, Joe Oyama, Ayako Noguchi, and the rest—Hisaye was caught up in endless discussions of who would write the Great American Nisei Novel, but she did not publish much in the way of fiction during the late 1930s. Yet she read widely and seized on the chance to educate herself. After finishing high school, she enrolled at Compton Junior College, where she specialized in foreign languages—German, French, and Latin. In the process, she was exposed to modern literature, especially from Europe, with new political ideas. For example, she was greatly impressed by Erich Maria Remarque's antiwar novel *All Quiet on the Western Front*, which she read in an uncut German version. She was enchanted by the existential novels—little known in America—of the French writer André Malraux, such as *Man's Fate* (*La condition humaine*).

By mid-1940, Yamamoto had begun to expand her column to include a discussion of literature. Her columns contained reviews of works by Thomas Wolfe, then recently deceased, and the African American novelist Richard Wright. She also inserted commentary on political issues. A self-described cynic, she adhered to no definite platform but indirectly made her views known by citing letters from friends. One piece from December 1940 deplored the national climate of militarism and the danger that Nisei would be forced to abandon their dream of democratic treatment and conform in the name of patriotism: "Maybe it is a fortunate thing that the nisei are yet to come to a political awakening, that the nisei are yet to experience 'social consciousness' and that the few nisei who are liberals are too disorganized to effect any influence on the rank-and-file nisei."

The coming of war turned Yamamoto's life around. Even before the West Coast press was shuttered, she abandoned her column and turned toward her family. In 1942 the entire Yamamoto clan was sent to Poston. Hisaye soon found work as a reporter for the *Poston Chronicle* and restarted her Small Talk column. Although the *Chronicle* was less strictly controlled than other camp newspapers, she was careful about her presentation of subject matter: "We knew what we could and could not print," she later commented. Still, Yamamoto managed to write some powerful stories. In an October 1943 article on the deportation of the "segregants" to confinement at Tule Lake, she vividly underlined the cruel impact of the move by her description of the tears of inmates separated from friends and loved ones: "A young girl sobbed so hard that the comic books in her arms—saved to shorten the journey's length—fell to the ground. And her friends, crying, bent to pick them up." She also wrote a serial novel set in camp, a potboiler called "Death Rides the Rails to Poston" (probably the first hard-boiled detective tale with Japanese American protagonists, and surely the first to mention André Malraux).

In 1944 Yamamoto relocated to Springfield, Massachusetts, with two younger brothers and found work as a domestic. Despite the city's famed "Springfield plan" for improving race relations, she found the town unfriendly and conditions harsh. During her time there, she befriended Yoné Stafford, a biracial Nisei Socialist and pacifist who was active in organizing aid for inmates. Soon after, Yamamoto's eldest brother, Johnny, who had joined the 442nd Regimental Combat Team, was killed in combat. She decided to return to camp and help care for her family. She adopted a young Sansei boy, whom she raised as her own.

In 1945 Yamamoto returned to Los Angeles, first living at the Evergreen Hostel and then settling in Boyle Heights. She learned that the African American newspaper the *Los Angeles Tribune* was in search of a Nisei columnist for its staff. The *Tribune* had distinguished itself during 1942 as the sole Los Angeles newspaper to formally oppose Executive Order 9066, and columnist Erna P. Harris had subsequently contributed numerous pieces supporting the rights of Japanese Americans. Meanwhile, thousands of black workers had moved to Los Angeles during the war and found housing in the evacuated Little Tokyo district, which was redubbed "Bronzeville." As Japanese Americans moved back to their old homes, they entered into close contact with their new black neighbors. Now the *Tribune* sought a columnist to serve as a bridge between the two communities.

Hisaye later related that when she applied for the job, she doubted strongly that she would be chosen. First, she had very little experience with African Americans, apart from a few students in school and a set of black War Relocation Authority employees at Poston. (Perhaps because the Office of Indian Affairs, under the direction of the progressive activist John Collier, first established Poston, it featured a more intellectual and racially diverse staff than other camps. Black employees in Poston included Ora A. Dennis, a teacher and sanitation engineer; nurses Lydia Vance and Beatrice McMillan; and schoolteacher Manila Smith.) Also, as she went for her job interview at the *Tribune*'s office, she saw that Bean Takeda, an experienced Nisei journalist and editor, was also in contention. Yet Yamamoto was hired. Since the *Tribune* had a female editor, Almena Davis, and featured columnists Erna Harris and Minnie Lomax, she may have faced less of a handicap as a woman there than elsewhere.

Hisaye started work for the *Tribune* in June 1945 at the munificent salary of $35 per week. Other Nisei later joined her on the *Tribune*'s staff, including sports editor Chester Yamauchi (nicknamed "Cheddar") and his then-wife, writer Wakako Yamauchi (whom Hisaye referred to as "Wacky"). Both became her close friends. Hisaye meanwhile solicited other writers to contribute to the *Tribune*, including her brothers Yuke and Jemo (James Tsutomu Yamamoto), Jeanne Naito, Edith Fukuye, Yoné Stafford (who ultimately replaced her as columnist), and Sam Hohri, who published a pair of pieces before his early death of tuberculosis. On her recommendation, the paper also featured a piece about life on a goldfish farm—the first publication of budding Nisei writer and columnist Chizuko (Chizu) Omori, the future cocreator of the documentary film *Rabbit in the Moon*. Hisaye had grown close to Chizu at Poston and had housed her briefly in Los Angeles, after the independent-minded teenager left her family behind in camp to return alone to the West Coast. The two would remain lifelong friends.

Yamamoto found working at the *Tribune* a transformative experience. Although she had been hired to produce a column about Japanese American issues, on the model of Larry Tajiri's *Pacific Citizen* pieces, she quickly branched out to cover other topics, including existential philosophy and Arab-Jewish relations in Palestine. She also not-so-delicately approached the touchy issue of Nisei prejudice against blacks. In the process, as she later recounted in her 1985 memoir *A Fire in Fontana*, she began to feel like an African American herself. The climax of her identification came out of a hate crime. She was visited at the newspaper's offices by an African American couple who had bought a house in a suburban white district and who feared violence. She was deeply stunned shortly after when the house burned to the ground, killing three family members inside, in a clear care of terrorism.

In part as a response, she became active with the civil rights and pacifist group Fellowship of Reconciliation (FOR) (and reported on FOR activist Bayard Rustin's lecture to the Japanese American Citizens League). With assistance from the Yamauchis, in 1947 she helped organize a Los Angeles chapter of the Congress of Racial Equality (CORE). In July of that year, CORE began a series of Saturday sit-ins in the restaurant of the downtown Bullock's department store, which refused to serve its black patrons. A mixture of white, black, and Nisei patrons took up seats and refused to leave until they were served. Yamamoto publicized the group's activities in her column (to the consternation of *Tribune* editor Davis, who disagreed with CORE's direct action tactics). After several weeks, Bullock's capitulated and ended its segregation policy. In early 1948, Yamamoto organized a new set of pickets at the Bimini Baths, a popular swimming resort that restricted both black and Asian patrons. The campaign lasted several weeks and ended inconclusively.

In mid-1948, Yamamoto published her first short story, "The High-Heeled Shoes," in the prestigious New York intellectual journal *Partisan Review*. Encouraged by this success, in 1950 she left her job at the *Tribune* to devote herself to writing full time, with help from a John Hay Whitney Foundation Opportunity Fellowship. She remained interested in pacifism and social justice. Impressed by the ideas expressed by social activist Dorothy Day in her journal, *Catholic Worker*, in 1953 Yamamoto moved to New York and took a job as a laborer on a farm run by the organization. There she met Anthony DeSoto. In 1955 she married DeSoto and returned to Los Angeles. While she found time to produce an occasional column—mostly Christmas pieces for *Rafu Shimpo*—she devoted herself to caring for her husband and raising five children. Although her small corpus of stories from the postwar period continued to be anthologized, it was not until 1985 that her writings were first collected into a book, *Seventeen Syllables*. Published in a condensed edition in Tokyo in 1985, a new edition appeared two years later by

Coffee Table Press, with an introduction by scholar King-Kok Cheung. The work won the American Book Award and relaunched Yamamoto's fame. Although family concerns, accompanied by poor health, limited her work, she remained a vibrant writer and speaker (she can be seen in interviews in *Rabbit in the Moon*).

Postscript

I first met Hisaye Yamamoto in Los Angeles in January 1999, when a mutual friend brought us together. We decided to attend the opening of the new wing of the Japanese American National Museum and arranged to meet first for lunch at an old udon restaurant that Hisaye knew in Little Tokyo. I felt both excitement and considerable apprehension as I drove to our date with my sister-in-law, Tracy. Although I had read and admired Hisaye's writing, I was a young *hakujin* from the East Coast working on a dissertation about Franklin Roosevelt and Japanese Americans. I had not published anything at that point and had no professional reputation. I feared that she might consider me an interloper among Japanese Americans.

Hisaye immediately impressed me. It was not the brute force of her personality, for she came off as a bit shy and unassuming—I inwardly recalled a classic description of writers as phlegmatic people who put their main passion into their writing. Rather, I was enchanted by her eager friendliness and her gift for immediately finding in-jokes we could laugh at together, like an old friend. Her genuine interest in my research also touched me; she said she was pleased to be dealing with a historian of Asian Americans for once rather than another literature scholar. As sincerely grateful as she was for her readers and their embrace of her, she told me that literature students all tended to ask her the same general questions, especially since the corpus of her work was so small.

After lunch, we visited the museum. I pointed out a descriptive plaque that quoted her writing, which seemed to gratify her. After a little while, though, she said that the exhibition was making her sad. Clearly, the memory of the camp years was still vivid—and searing. We decided to leave, and Hisaye gave me a hug and told me to stay in touch. After returning to New York, we began corresponding. Over the next several years, she sent several letters, plus Christmas cards and other greetings. When my book *By Order of the*

President: FDR and the Internment of Japanese Americans was in press, she kindly sent the publisher a blurb for it. I felt so proud that this great writer was someone I actually *knew* and who had publicly praised my work.

After a while, Hisaye's letters ceased, and I knew that her health was declining. I visited her twice more at her home, carrying archival materials to show her. She had told me that her memory was diminished, so even though she greeted me cheerfully and seemed to know me, I took care always to reintroduce myself. Although Hisaye's powers of recall were indeed reduced, at times something I read to her or a question I asked would strike a long-dormant memory, and she would regale me with a story. She also allowed me to look through some of her scrapbooks as we chatted and to make copies of material. I wanted to find time to visit her one final time, but the distance to Los Angeles, mixed with my shyness about bothering her, meant that it did not happen. I remain thankful that I got to know her and touch the person inside the magic name.

4

Wartime Confinement and Japanese Americans

Nisei Stories

DOI: 10.5876/9781607324294.c004

MITSUYE ENDO: PLUS GRANDE DANS SON OBSCURITÉ?

Mitsuye Endo (Tsutsumi), who died in fall 2006, represents an unusual case of heroism—a hero both self-effacing and effaced by others. In the case of *Ex parte Endo* the US Supreme Court finally ruled that the government could not confine citizens whom it conceded to be loyal (although the Court dodged addressing the essential question of the government's power to issue military orders against citizens). This case was fundamental to the trajectory of Japanese Americans, as it led to the opening of the camps and the return of inmates to the West Coast.

On the one hand, Endo was largely disconnected from the actions connected with her name. Indeed, the fact that her case was brought at all, let alone before the Supreme Court, was in some sense a matter of chance. Her original intent was not to challenge confinement as such but to regain the civil service job in California from which she had been arbitrarily dismissed. Recruited as a test case by lawyer Jim Purcell, Endo either never met her lawyer or did so on only one occasion (according to differing testimony). Purcell decided that the most promising way to proceed was to contest Endo's confinement in the War Relocation Authority (WRA) camps—Endo was willing to serve as a plaintiff. Once her case was decided, she shied away from public scrutiny and did not participate in the annual protests and commemorations that the Japanese American redress movement began in the 1970s (although she did produce a short oral history for John Tateishi's 1983 anthology *And Justice For All: An Oral History of the Japanese American Detention Camps*). Furthermore, because she won her case, she was not connected with the coram nobis petitions through which her fellow wartime plaintiffs— Gordon Hirabayashi, Minoru Yasui, and Fred Korematsu—challenged their convictions and were vindicated. Partly because she remained so private, and also, no doubt, partly because she was a woman and not a convenient symbol of manly self-assertion, she remained largely excluded from the pantheon of internment resister glory—the honor roll of those who "stood up."

Yet, for all that her presence in the case was largely accidental, and her involvement in its preparation incidental, Endo showed at least as much courage and dedication to principle as any of the more prominent male Nisei plaintiffs. First, she came into contact with the lawyers because she was prepared to challenge her arbitrary dismissal from a California civil service job. The possession of such a job was an unusual achievement for a Nisei woman in the prewar days, when discrimination was the rule. Thus, in addition to her desire to hang on to such a prized position for herself, she was surely actuated by the need to defend her rights on behalf of the larger group. After she brought her petition, Endo was moved from the Tule Lake camp to the camp at Topaz to remove her from the jurisdiction of the California court—a bit of government skulduggery with later echoes to *Rumsfeld v. Padilla*. The WRA's chief attorney traveled to see her and tried to persuade her not to continue, offering her an immediate "leave permit" if she would abandon the case, but Endo stuck to her principles. She remained in confinement for over eighteen months so the case could be brought and argued before the high court. Even after her victory, she did not return to the West Coast and the job she left; instead, she settled permanently in Chicago (and lived and worked alongside African American colleagues as an assistant to the city's Commision on Human Relations).

Not long ago, I was discussing the wartime Supreme Court Japanese American cases with a distinguished Nisei historian, who posed a somewhat tendentious question that nevertheless zeroed in on the legacy of those cases: Why is it that men like Gordon Hirabayashi and Minoru Yasui, who challenged Executive Order 9066 and arbitrary government power entirely on principle, have their contributions ignored while Fred Korematsu, who challenged Executive Order 9066 in order to stay with his non-Japanese girlfriend, became renowned and was awarded the Presidential Medal of Freedom? I answered as best I could that these things were partly a matter of luck—Korematsu's case turned out to be the decisive one in its long-term impact—but were also a product of a person's willingness to stand up when the decisive time came. Korematsu, once he decided to appear publicly and talk about his case after many years of silence, was mobilized over the years to speak about his experiences and raise his voice against the mistreatment of Japanese Americans. An ordinary man—not an intellectual—he served as an eloquent symbol. It is interesting that the historian did not mention Mitsuye Endo in his litany. She was, after all, a classic case of an ordinary person who stuck up for principle. Might this be another case of the unfortunate obscuring of Endo and her case? Or was Endo herself (to paraphrase the title of the aria from Charles Gounod's *La Reine de Saba*) "more great in her obscurity"?

LINCOLN SEIICHI KANAI'S ACT OF CONSCIENCE

In the annals of Japanese American history, a great deal of attention has been justly devoted to the four wartime "internment cases," in which individual Nisei—Gordon Hirabayashi, Minoru Yasui, Fred Korematsu, and Mitsuye Endo—challenged mass removal before the US Supreme Court. In contrast, several other Nisei brought cases in the lower courts. However, because these cases were not brought up to the "major leagues" of the high court they have been all but erased from history.

The first of these cases was that of Mary Asaba Ventura of Seattle, a Nisei married to a Filipino American. In March 1942, with the help of her husband, she brought a habeas corpus petition challenging the official curfew and restrictions imposed on American citizens of Japanese ancestry under Executive Order 9066. Her petition was denied by a local judge, Lloyd D. Black (who would later preside over Gordon Hirabayashi's trial and pronounce sentence on him). While, officially, Judge Black rejected the petition on the grounds that the restrictions on Ventura did not amount to imprisonment, he also proclaimed that the order and the underlying laws were constitutional and rather gratuitously suggested that if she really was as loyal as she claimed, she ought to gladly cooperate with the government. After being confined (solo) in Minidoka, she moved to Illinois, where she died in 2000.

Shortly afterward, in Los Angeles, African American attorney Hugh Macbeth joined American Civil Liberties Union (ACLU) attorneys A. L. Wirin and Edgar Camp in bringing a habeas corpus petition on behalf of Ernest Kinzo Wakayama, a Hawai'i-born Kibei union official and World War I veteran, and his wife, Toki. Wirin and MacBeth argued that the Army had not demonstrated any military necessity for mass evacuation and likewise charged that race-based confinement constituted unconstitutional discrimination. In October 1942, a three-judge panel heard the petitions and finally granted a writ of habeas corpus on February 4, 1943. However, by then, the Wakayamas, worn down by beatings and ostracism at Manzanar, had withdrawn their suit and requested repatriation to Japan. Ernest Wakayama was over one hundred years old when he died in Japan in 1999. His son, Edgar (named for Edgar Camp), returned to the United States and is a career Army officer.

Perhaps the most unusual challenge to Executive Order 9066 came from Lincoln Seiichi Kanai, a YMCA secretary in San Francisco. Instead of waiting for the government to expel him from the West Coast, Kanai challenged the president's order "with his feet" by leaving the area without official permission and had to be extradited to California to stand trial.

Kanai was born in Kauai, Hawai'i, in December 1908. According to one source, he was a foundling of uncertain Asian ancestry, while another claimed his mother was Chinese and his father was mixed-race Japanese. He later explained that he had been named not for the Great Emancipator but for an African American school principal. He was one of four children. His older brother, Matsukichi Kanai, later became a doctor and practiced during World War II as a medical officer in the Office of Indian Affairs. Lincoln grew up in Hawai'i and later stated that the racial tolerance he found in the territory shaped his conviction that all Americans, regardless of color or background, deserved equal citizenship rights. He majored in science and social work at the University of Hawai'i, where he graduated in 1930. In 1937 he moved to San Francisco and was named secretary of the Buchanan (aka Japanese) YMCA.

In the weeks following Pearl Harbor, Kanai joined various efforts to organize assistance for needy Japanese Americans and avert mass removal. Once removal became a *fait accompli*, he wrote General John L. DeWitt, the West Coast defense commander, to object to the indiscriminate identification of loyal citizens with aliens. Kanai asked that the evacuation order be changed to provide for loyalty hearings for aliens and citizens, especially those with family members serving in the armed services, and for the appointment of a property custodian to hold the belongings of Japanese Americans.

He meanwhile turned his attention to the mission of encouraging resettlement. Kanai decided to tour the country and feel out the attitude of public officials, social workers, college presidents, and law enforcement authorities on arranging the absorption of Japanese Americans, especially college students. He decided that he would first go to Chicago and then, if he could find money for his expenses, to New York City and Washington, DC, to meet with War Relocation Authority officials. In addition to his wish to help other Nisei, he was driven by the determination to speak out against official policy, whatever the consequences. As he wrote his friend Galen Fisher, "It would be easy for me to just go to camp but I can't have my conscience bother me the time I am in there for accepting that the decision has been the wisest thing." The renowned Bay area community figure and YMCA leader Fred Hoshiyama later wrote, "I am probably the last remaining person alive who worked with, was influenced by, and talked to Lincoln Kanai. I still remember his last advice and words in April 1942: 'Fred, your job is to stay with the evacuees and support them. My job is to visit as many college presidents as possible to try to open admissions. I have a higher authority than the US government AND I MUST FOLLOW IT.'" Hoshiyama's eyewitness account underlines the moral dimensions of Kanai's protest.

Kanai left San Francisco on June 1, traveling in an old car. During his trip he conferred with the faculties of twenty-one midwestern colleges and with representatives of other groups. In July 1942, while attending a YMCA convention in Geneva, Wisconsin, FBI agents arrested him. Kanai stated publicly that he was motivated by loyalty: "I am in full sympathy with the United States. I am a citizen of the United States and many of my friends were killed in the attack on Pearl Harbor. How could I feel anything but loyalty to the United States?" Unable to afford bail following his arrest, he was held in the Milwaukee County Jail. With aid from ACLU lawyer Perry

Stearns, Kanai's attorney, Arthur W. Richter, submitted a habeas corpus petition on his behalf. Arguing that the necessities of war should apply to "enemies, not races," and noting that German Americans were permitted to roam the country without restriction, Richter noted that Kanai was already outside the military area and requested that he be allowed to remain in the "free zone." Nevertheless, on July 29, federal judge F. Ryan Duffy quashed the petition. Although he agreed that Kanai was a loyal citizen, Duffy insisted that if he were permitted to remain, other Japanese Americans would be encouraged to disobey military orders; he commanded that Kanai be extradited to California to stand trial for disobeying laws forbidding him to leave the military area without a permit.

A pair of federal marshals escorted Kanai by train to San Francisco, where he pleaded guilty to the charge of violating military orders by traveling without a permit and defended his action in court by stating, "I shall oppose any such action willfully whenever it is detrimental to our country's welfare and injurious to the basic democratic ideals . . . This is my native land and in violating that restriction I had to choose either to support the Constitution and my convictions or to temporarily suspend them." On August 27, 1942, he was sentenced to six months in prison. He decided not to appeal and instead was incarcerated at Fort Lewis, where he served four months before being released for good behavior in January 1943. Once released from prison, he was immediately handed over to the Army's prisoners of war escort team for confinement in the camp at Heart Mountain.

Kanai's later life remains fairly obscure. After being confined at Heart Mountain, he relocated to Milwaukee as a boys' advisor and teacher for the Norris Foundation, a local school for underprivileged youth. Sometime in the 1950s he moved to Battle Creek, Michigan. He died there in February 1982, shortly before his fellow Nisei defendants undertook their coram nobis campaign. Perhaps if Kanai had survived, his conviction would have been overturned, like those of Fred Korematsu and Gordon Hirabayashi. Instead, his example of calm courage against injustice remains for us to rediscover.

The Exclusion of Naomi Nakano[1]

Philadelphia, the City of Brotherly Love, was far removed from the endemic anti–Japanese American prejudice that marked the Pacific coast during most of the twentieth century. During World War II, Philadelphia's tiny Japanese American population remained free from mass removal, although certain travel and economic restrictions were imposed on enemy aliens. The city eventually received a stream of resettlers who local Quakers and other sympathizers welcomed, opening hostels and offering other assistance. The handful of Nisei students enrolled at the city's proud Ivy League institution, the University of Pennsylvania, remained fully integrated in their classes and campus activities.

Nonetheless, Penn was touched during the war by the same conflicts between military security, race, and citizenship that fueled the larger confinement. Even as the White House instituted mass removal of West Coast Issei and Nisei, Penn's leaders adopted an unjust and undemocratic blanket exclusion policy on new admissions. Paradoxically, this very action, approved by Penn's administration in order to avoid trouble, embroiled the university in nationwide controversy during spring 1944. Under the provisions of its policy, the university denied admission to its graduate school to an existing student—Naomi Nakano—whose personal and academic credentials were so uncannily perfect that the university's refusal to admit her appeared to Americans throughout the country to be motivated entirely by racism.

Penn's singling out of its Japanese American students began well before Pearl Harbor. According to documents in the school's archives, in early June 1941, Administrative Vice President Paul Musser received a confidential memo from the Fourth Naval District's Intelligence Office requesting the university's help in keeping tabs on its Japanese students. Musser immediately furnished the addresses and enrollment status of all Japanese nationals. On June 9, 1941, naval intelligence then requested information from Musser on the six Nisei students enrolled at Penn. Although the legality of such surveillance of American citizens was questionable, Musser again complied. During fall 1941, with the university's knowledge and, presumably, consent, naval intelligence officers checked up in some fashion on at least four of these students.

By December 1941, only a handful of Nisei studied at Penn (plus a single student from Japan—Noboru Kamirya—listed as "withdrawn as of December 6, 1941"). On December 9, the day after Congress declared war, the school provided the same information on its Nisei students at the request of the Federal Bureau of Investigation (FBI). Significantly, in his letter to the FBI, university vice president William H. DuBarry referred to all these Nisei as "Japanese."

FIGURE 4.1. Naomi Nakano with Thomas Sovereign Gates.

At some time in the following weeks, Penn's administration decided on the unwritten, unannounced policy of refusing admission to all Japanese American students for the duration of the war (a rule apparently adopted as well by other elite universities, such as Harvard and Yale). As a result, over the following two years, Penn's admissions office responded negatively to all Nisei applications for admission and requests for enrollment information. The administration announced that Nisei students already enrolled would be permitted to finish their degrees but that they could not continue their education in another part of the university—these would constitute new admissions. Thus, in 1942–1943, the Executive Committee of the Board of Trustees refused to grant Robert Yoichi Sato, a graduating senior, permission to enroll in the graduate school and graduate student Koshi Miyasaki was not allowed to pursue further studies after receiving his MBA.

It is not clear precisely when and how the decision to exclude was made: no mention of the subject appears in the minutes of trustee meetings. University administrators later variously claimed that they had received orders from the War Department and informal instructions from the Navy to exclude Japanese Americans. In truth, the military issued several confusing and contradictory directives.

The first came in May 1942, when the new National Japanese American Student Relocation Council (NJASRC), founded to help Nisei students transfer to colleges outside the West Coast, inquired whether Penn would accept any students from the camps. Since Philadelphia was in a special defense area, the administration asked the Army's opinion. On May 11, 1942, General Hugh Drum of the East Coast Defense Command recommended that new Japanese Americans should not be "encouraged" to enter the defense zone. The university then declined to accept any such students. By August 1942, however, that directive had lapsed, and Nisei from the camps enrolled at other colleges in the area—for example, future writer and educator Kenji Murase entered Temple University, where he soon received honors. Once the Army withdrew its opposition, the Navy interposed an unspecified objection to students from the camps. The university made no further inquiries regarding the Navy's objection and continued to refuse admission to all Nisei students. In October 1943, the Army's provost marshal general issued a directive requiring universities that engaged in important defense work to obtain his approval before admitting Japanese American students. The NJASRC, which still hoped to enroll Nisei students at Penn, informed the university that it was exempt from the requirement and that it did not appear on any Army or Navy excluded list. DuBarry nevertheless informed naval intelligence that Penn had ceased all such admissions after

Pearl Harbor, in accordance with orders from the War Department, and would continue to do so.

Clearly, the Army and Navy orders represent, at best, only one element in the university's policy and may have served as a pretext for exclusion rather than the actual reason. For one thing, the military's jurisdiction covered only Nisei from the camps, not Japanese Americans who applied to Penn from outside the excluded areas. Certainly, there was no military reason for the university to deny Koshi Miyasaki and Robert Sato, Hawai'i-born students already enrolled at Penn, permission to continue their studies. Moreover, in 1943 the university gained military approval to retain Warwick Sakami, a Nisei PhD student working on a secret government research project at the school's Laboratory of Physiological Chemistry.

The ban was also not universally enforced, as Mitsu Yamamoto was permitted to enroll in the graduate school after receiving her BA. Yamamoto was a biracial Nisei whose Japanese father, Sannosuke Yamamoto, was employed by Penn's Linguistics Department during the war to teach Japanese to Army translators and develop a Japanese dictionary for the Army. Yamamoto (who would go on to contribute to the *New Yorker* in the postwar years and later became a noted children's book author) subsequently insisted that she was never informed of any exclusion policy: "I signed up for graduate work with complete freedom and took classes in the English department." Perhaps because of her mixed ancestry and what she called her "white-bread appearance," Yamamoto was not troubled by the administration despite her unmistakably Japanese name.

All these contrary facts suggest that the university based its blanket exclusion policy on factors other than national security: misinformation and confusion over government policy, eagerness to support the military, ignorance of Japanese Americans, bureaucratic rigidity and reluctance to take initiative, and the general desire to avoid trouble. In addition, the policy reflected an indifference to the equal rights of American citizens that was informed by prejudice and racial animosity, as indicated by the numerous references to the Nisei as "Japanese" and "foreign students" in administration correspondence during 1942–1943.

In spring 1944, Penn's exclusion policy rebounded strongly against it after Naomi Nakano, a senior majoring in philosophy in the College for Women, applied for admission to graduate school. Nakano, born in 1921, was a

Philadelphia-area native who grew up in the only Japanese American family in the Philadelphia suburb of Ridley Park. Her father, Yosuke "Nick" Nakano, was a distinguished Penn alumnus who had immigrated from Japan to the United States at nineteen and worked his way through college. After receiving a master's degree from Penn's architecture school in 1916, he joined the firm of Wark & Company. During the 1920s and 1930s, he helped construct a significant chunk of Philadelphia's skyline, including the Sun Oil Building, Presbyterian Hospital, the Bell Telephone buildings, and, according to one source, the Christian Association building on Penn's campus—later the home of Penn's Asian American Student Center. Nakano was so greatly respected by industry giant Edward Budd that, during World War II, Budd insisted that he be granted a security clearance for defense work—even though he was an enemy alien—and Nakano supervised the Budd Company's construction of Philadelphia's Quartermaster Depot.

Naomi, the eldest of two daughters, entered Penn in 1940 (she was granted a scholarship for academic excellence, but her affluent father insisted on donating the price of her tuition). A brilliant student, she was admitted to Phi Beta Kappa in her junior year. In addition, she was involved in a wide variety of student activities. For example, she worked as a Red Cross volunteer, tried out for the women's hockey team, and served as associate editor of the *Bennett News*, the College for Women's weekly. She was especially active in the Student Christian Movement, under whose auspices she toured campuses along the East Coast, propagandizing for admission of Nisei students to universities. In her senior year, Nakano became vice chair of the group's Middle Atlantic regional council. In tribute to both her accomplishments and her warm personality, she was elected president of her junior class and as a senior, became president of the Women's Student Government Association.

Nakano later spoke fondly of her student days at Penn: "There were some good restaurants around campus. My favorite was called the Lido. I made friends through the Christian Association, which was a center for socially minded students, and through other student activities." She said she never felt any hostility as a Japanese American during the war from other students or faculty. "There was no prejudice, although there was one woman librarian at Penn who panicked after Pearl Harbor and wanted to deny me access to the library—until cooler heads prevailed," she recalled. "Actually, I felt more the discrimination against women students. For instance, in those days the men had the student union at Houston Hall to themselves! Women were restricted to the basement, which was where the campus bookstore was."

In early 1944, Nakano filed an application to Penn's graduate school. The Philosophy Department voted to recommend her for a scholarship, which was then approved by the Graduate Council. Soon after, however, the dean of the graduate school, Edwin P. Williams, summoned Nakano and explained to her that university rules required that her application be denied. Nakano at first took the news calmly, believing that the university was under explicit military orders: "I thought that it was a bureaucratic administrative decision."

However, Carolyn Merion, women's chair of the Student Cabinet of the Christian Association and editor-in-chief of the *Bennett News*, was outraged by the rejection. Merion, Nakano's good friend, had helped manage her campaign for junior class president. She also was an outspoken opponent of anti-Semitism and racial prejudice and had helped persuade Nakano to join her own sorority—Alpha Omicron Pi—the previous year in order to racially integrate it. Nakano agreed to Merion's request to be the "guinea pig" in a challenge to the exclusion policy, although she had decided by that time to accept a graduate fellowship in sociology at Bryn Mawr College.

Merion proceeded to organize a group of students from the *Bennett News* and the Christian Association to discuss the exclusion policy with Dean Williams. Williams told them that because of the official Navy exclusion order, the university had no choice. Accompanied by George H. Menke, the regional secretary of the Student Christian Movement, Merion then met with Provost George W. McClelland to ask why Nakano had been excluded and the reasons behind the university's actions. McClelland insisted that the board of trustees had decided on the policy after informal conversations with the Navy and referred all further inquiries to Penn's president, Thomas Sovereign Gates.

On April 27, 1944, Merion published the editorial "An Issue to Face" in the *Bennett News*. She expressed her "respect and admiration" for the university's wartime accomplishments but explained, "Because of what is said to be an unwritten,unofficial request of the Navy," Penn excluded all people of Japanese ancestry. While the editorial did not mention Nakano by name, it deplored the fact that such an "arbitrary ruling" had prevented an honor student with a high record of leadership and service from applying for graduate school: "What good does it afford to talk of postwar ideals, for the future, if our very educational policies now are discriminatory? Why not practice democracy now?" There was no immediate response to the editorial. "*Bennett News* was pretty unimportant," Merion later recalled, "so the University authorities felt, no doubt, that the affair was a pin-prick."

In the wake of the administration's silence, on May 16, Merion and Walter Speake, the men's student cabinet chair of the Christian Association, wrote Gates a joint letter protesting the exclusion policy. Noting that, despite what they had been told about naval orders, there was no legal basis for any such action, they asked whether the board of trustees would accept responsibility for excluding Japanese Americans from admission. They conceded that the university, as a private corporation, could legally discriminate but that in such a case the trustees should openly admit that they were barring students on a racial basis. When Gates failed to acknowledge or reply to the students' letter, Merion published its text in the May 25 issue of the *Bennett News*. The editorial pleaded with the administration to issue a statement justifying its policy and clear up the "fog of confusion" created by its contradictory statements. It warned darkly that "silence gives assent to responsibility by the University." When Merion failed to receive any response, she put a front-page editorial, "Paging Dr. Gates," in the June 1 issue. The piece recounted in detail Merion's attempts to discover who was responsible for the exclusion policy and how Gates and the administration had ignored her efforts. The editorial was to have closed with an appeal to students and faculty members to see President Gates and request an official statement. However, Arnold Henry, dean of student affairs, insisted that the passage be removed—the administration's sole response to Merion's campaign.

Meanwhile, Menke's attempts to obtain a satisfactory answer as to the reasons for the exclusion policy were equally unsuccessful. During early May, he made several appointments to meet with Gates, but each time the president's office canceled. Finally, on May 16, Menke wrote Gates a formal letter, asking for a specific statement explaining which government agency was responsible for ordering exclusion. Menke added that Nakano's case would be the subject of a discussion at the next regional student conference. On May 20, Gates sent Menke a brief and evasive response, in which he stated that Nakano had accepted a scholarship at Bryn Mawr and disingenuously presented the issue of exclusion as arising from her request to attend certain classes at Penn under an agreement between the two institutions. He explained that certain unspecified "government relationships" limited the university's freedom of action. Menke immediately wrote asking clarification regarding such "government relationships." When he received no response, he wrote once more on May 25, asking the university to justify its action and that he would "seek the information through other channels" if he did not receive a reply.

In the face of continued administration stonewalling, Merion and Menke ultimately took their story to the press. On June 2, the *Philadelphia Record* featured a long piece on Penn's exclusion of Nakano, accompanied by a large photograph of her in a Red Cross uniform. The *Record* recounted Merion's and Menke's fruitless efforts to obtain information from the administration (the article reprinted their correspondence with university officials in full) and highlighted a statement from the head of the Navy security program, Bureau of Personnel Chief Admiral Randall Jacobs: "I never heard of such a[n exclusionary] rule—it sounds cockeyed to me." Nakano (whom the article described as an "attractive, dark-eyed, slender brunette") expressed great disappointment at not being able to continue at Penn, where she had spent four happy years: "The principle of discrimination hurt me very much. I have lived all my life on the East Coast and haven't been too much aware of it. This is the first time—the only time, in fact—that it ever touched me." The Associated Press immediately picked up the story, and within twenty-four hours an abbreviated version of the article had appeared in newspapers throughout the nation, as well as in *Yank* magazine and the military press overseas.

The news aroused a wave of public indignation, especially as it followed on the heels of a well-publicized incident in which a Nisei war veteran was driven off a New Jersey farm by bigoted neighbors. Editorials condemning the university's action appeared in the *Record* and in such diverse newspapers as the *Des Moines Tribune* and the Dayton (Ohio) *Daily News*. Gates received protest letters from Penn graduates and alumni chapters in such diverse cities as New York, Chicago, Los Angeles, Philadelphia, and Cleveland, opposing the policy as biased and undemocratic. An alumnus in Chicago wrote that the exclusion policy represented the "ugly, caste-creating, stranger-hating sort of *Rassenpolitik* which is as close akin to Hitler's worst vagaries as it is foreign to democracy." When a group of Penn alumni in Los Angeles met to draft a protest, George Winfield Scott, an eminent graduate, became so agitated by discussion of the university's policy that he collapsed and died.

Until the story of her exclusion was broadcast nationwide, Nakano had been, by her own admission, rather removed from the controversy. She had not participated in the protests and the *Bennett News* had been careful to not reveal her name. "I was pleased that the challenge was carried forth by the Student Christian Movement, and brought to national attention. I knew why they were protesting, and I was happy to provide the test case—that's how I viewed it," she later recalled. Now she was a public figure, dazzled and a bit disturbed by her sudden fame: "I used to do a lot of commuting late at night. I remember being dismayed at seeing my picture in newspapers strewn around trolley cars and in trash cans." She was nonetheless grateful for the letters of sympathy and support she received from high school friends, American soldiers overseas, and Japanese Americans: "I was very touched by the letters from people in the camps. I actually received several proposals of marriage from men in the camps who offered to protect me!"

In the glare of bad publicity, the administration backpedaled. On June 2, Gates stated publically that the university had only just learned of a change in military regulations under which a student and a university could apply for clearance. Such an application had been made on behalf of Naomi Nakano. The *Philadelphia Record* reported on June 4 that a spokesman for the Army's Office of the Provost Marshal had denied there had been any recent change in policy, and that no application had been filed on behalf of Nakano, or for Koshi Miyasaki or Robert Sato, whom the university had previously barred from continuing their education. Gates immediately issued an additional statement, asserting, "Under recent Governmental regulation, applications for permission to continue their studies have already been filed jointly by the students and the University in the Philadelphia office of the Provost Marshal, in the Bankers Securities Building—not in Washington, as was the mistaken impression in some quarters." He offered to admit Nakano forthwith and reiterated the university's "impartial" attitude toward its students of Japanese ancestry.

In fact, according to official files, the university had been informed of the provost marshal's policy long before. However, it did not file an application on behalf of any student until mid-May 1944, well after Carolyn Merion's first editorial on the exclusion policy, when Vice President DuBarry met with naval intelligence officers to discuss the Nakano case. On May 19, DuBarry asked Nakano, as well as Hajime Honda and Mitsu Yamamoto—the two other students of Japanese ancestry then enrolled at the university—to make appointments to visit his office in order to provide "additional information" of an unspecified nature. Thus, on May 29, Nakano finally filled out a worksheet for a Personnel Security Questionnaire, and she returned to sign the completed form on June 1. (Even then, the university listed her on the form as a student in the College for Women, not as a prospective student in the graduate school.) On June 8, the Army's Security and Intelligence Division informed President Gates that it had no objection to Nakano's attendance at Penn. By that time, it was too late—Penn had already been exposed to nationwide criticism for racial bias. It was also too late for Nakano, who had already committed to attend Bryn Mawr.

In an ironic coda to the controversy, on June 9, Penn held its Hey Day exercises. A contingent of reporters and photographers from the *New York Times* and other national newspapers, lured by the Nakano controversy, were in attendance. During the festivities, Thomas Gates was honored for his years of service as university president. Naomi Nakano, acting as president of the Women's Student Government Association, appeared onstage to present Gates with an engraved tray and was fiercely applauded by spectators.

Following its embarrassment in the Nakano case, the university officially opened its doors to Japanese Americans. In October 1944, after being cleared by the provost marshal, Chieko Shigekawa, Lily Sakaguchi, and Chihiro Kikuchi became the first Nisei students since 1940 to enroll at Penn. Shortly afterward, the War Department rescinded its order requiring military approval for admission of Japanese Americans. Students of Japanese ancestry became commonplace at Penn in the years after 1945. Still, the wartime discrimination left its traces. In 1949 a Nisei scholarship student publicly accused Penn of ignoring her application for admission, reviving memories of the Nakano controversy. This time, the administration moved quickly to demonstrate that it did not discriminate and pointed with pride to its Japanese American students, including Nakano's younger sister, Teru. University president Harold Stassen called on his chief political lieutenant, future Supreme Court Chief Justice Warren E. Burger, to launch an investigation. When Burger determined that the reason no action had been taken on the protesting student's application was that she had failed to take her College Board exams, the matter was resolved amicably.

Naomi Nakano attended Bryn Mawr in 1944–1945. During this time she took an evening course at Penn and frequently visited the campus. After receiving a master's degree in philosophy from Bryn Mawr, she briefly studied at Columbia University. In 1947 Nakano returned to Penn as an instructor in sociology. (Aside from the celebrated diplomat and economist Eleanor Lansing Dulles, who taught at the Wharton School of Business in the 1930s, Nakano was, apparently, the first female faculty member at Wharton, where the Sociology Department was then located.) She later said that she never felt any hesitation about returning or bitterness over the wartime events: "I had family ties to Penn. It was my university." During the postwar period, she became active with the Philadelphia chapter of the Japanese American Citizens League and served as a chapter president. A few years later, she married Joseph Tanaka, a St. Louis native and a professor of architecture at Washington University, and moved with him to St. Louis. Her sister, her daughter, and her sister's son all attended Penn, marking three generations of the Nakano family at the university. Nakano died in St. Louis in 2006.

KOJI ARIYOSHI: A HAWAIIAN NISEI IN MAO'S CHINA

An underappreciated element of Japanese American life is the enormous gulf that separates communities in Hawai'i from those on the mainland. The gap was even stronger in the first half of the twentieth century, before the coming of statehood to the Islands in 1959 and the advent of regular jet service linking the islands with the continent, which made mass tourism possible. During the prewar years, a small circle of white businessmen—the so-called Big Five—dominated the Territory of Hawaii's plantation-based economy. While the populations of Japanese in the islands and on the mainland were about equal, the two were markedly different. First, Nisei "buddhaheads" in the islands were some years older on average compared to their mainland "kotonk" counterparts. Also, while the mainlanders came of age as members of a tiny and despised minority group, the "local Japanese" made up the territory's largest ethnic group—almost 40 percent of the total population—and were the mainstay of the local workforce (their indispensability as laborers was a major factor deterring mass confinement during World War II). Racial lines in Hawai'i were more fluid than in California and intermarriage among nonwhites fairly common. Nisei became teachers, police officers, and postal clerks and several candidates even won election to the territorial legislature. Communities of artists, writers, and political activists flourished despite lack of public support, while newspapers run by Japanese American journalists occupied a prominent position in the life of the territory.

Still, if race-based exclusion played a less direct role in Hawai'i, Japanese American achievement was limited by the problems of access to quality education (generally restricted to whites plus the small percentage of Nisei who spoke standard English rather than pidgin) and the availability of decent jobs. As a result, dozens of ambitious Nisei left the islands every year, hoping to attend college or make good, and settled permanently on the mainland. With the aid of their greater age and experience, Hawai'i-born Nisei such as attorney Saburo Kido, YMCA officer Lincoln Kanai, union official Ernest Kinzo Wakayama, and businessmen Joseph Kurihara and Kiyoshi Okamoto became well known among West Coast Nisei. Each also played a visible role following the mass removal of Japanese Americans from the West Coast: Kido, as president of the Japanese American Citizens League (JACL), promoted accommodation; Kanai and Wakayama brought legal challenges to Executive Order 9066; and Kurihara and Okamoto led protest movements at Manzanar and Heart Mountain, respectively. (As an aside, it might be noted that many current-day Nikkei scholars of the mainland Japanese American experience are Hawai'i-born, including Ronald Takaki, Gary Okihiro, Tom Fujita Rony, Franklin Odo, Steven Sumida, and Gail Nomura.)

Conversely, one Hawaiian Nisei who moved to the mainland—a leader in the wartime camps and in military service—returned to Hawai'i after the war and became a legendary activist. His name was Koji Ariyoshi. He was born in 1914 on a coffee farm in Kona, on the Big Island. During the 1930s, he worked on coffee plantations and in a pineapple cannery and general store. In 1935 Ariyoshi moved to Honolulu and found work as a stevedore. Shocked by the conditions he saw, he wrote a series of exposés about life on the plantations and docks that was published in the *Honolulu Star-Bulletin*. Hoping to further his education, he enrolled soon after at the University of Hawai'i. In 1940, with encouragement from a sympathetic YMCA worker, he applied for and won a YMCA fellowship to study at the University of Georgia in Athens, Georgia.

Once enrolled, he made a close study of racial discrimination against blacks and toured the homes of white sharecroppers (writer Erskine Caldwell's parents served as his guides). The poverty and oppression made him resolve to fight on behalf of minorities and the poor. In summer 1941, Ariyoshi left Georgia and settled in San Francisco (in response to the entreaties of a white friend who had joined the Marines and wanted company, he attempted to enlist in the Marines but was refused entry on racial grounds, as he had predicted he would be). In San Francisco he worked as a stevedore, engaged in political organizing with Kibei Communist and labor leader Karl Yoneda, and was active in the International Longshoreman's and Warehouseman's Union (ILWU), under the direction of President Harry Bridges. He continued working on the docks and was subjected to some workplace harassment after Pearl Harbor.

In spring 1942, following Executive Order 9066, Ariyoshi moved to Los Angeles with Karl Yoneda to help organize mass migration, and in April he joined a volunteer battalion that mobilized to build the camp at Manzanar. He would remain at Manzanar for several months, punctuated by a furlough harvesting sugar beets in Idaho. He joined the staff of the *Manzanar Free Press* and later served as a camp policeman. While in camp, he helped form the Manzanar Citizens Federation, an antifascist organization that battled pro-Japanese inmates and championed Nisei civil rights. He and Yoneda meanwhile circulated a petition calling for the invasion of Europe and the establishment of a "second front" to aid the Soviet Union.

In November 1942 Ariyoshi traveled to Salt Lake City for an emergency meeting of the JACL, where he reported on his experience on agricultural projects. Meanwhile, the Military Intelligence Service recruited him as a Japanese translator. (He left for the Army just days before the "Manzanar Riot," when he would undoubtedly have been a target for beatings by disaffected inmates.) After training at Camp Savage, he joined a unit sponsored by the Office of War Information (OWI) to work in psychological warfare overseas. He then traveled to different posts in India and to the Burma-India border, where he wrote propaganda pamphlets and interrogated Japanese prisoners. In June 1944, he volunteered to join the OWI mission in China and spent the next months in Kunming and Chungking. In October 1944, he was assigned to carry on his work in the distant outpost of Yenan, an area controlled by Chinese Communists, as part of the US Army Observer Group (popularly known as the Dixie Mission). The Mission explored whether to connect formally with the Chinese Communists, who were living in caves and engaging in guerilla warfare against their Japanese occupiers. Ariyoshi was struck by the better status of peasants and small farmers under the Communists compared to the Nationalist government of Chiang Kai-Shek and was impressed by the Chinese Communist leaders he worked with, Mao Zedong and Zhou Enlai. He reported favorably on the Communist regime to his Army and diplomatic superiors.

Ariyoshi remained in Yenan until spring 1946. After returning from overseas, he settled in New York, where he worked as an activist with the progressive Japanese American Committee for Democracy. Meanwhile, on the invitation of editor Larry Tajiri, he began writing a regular column for the JACL newspaper, the *Pacific Citizen*. He returned to Hawai'i in 1948. With backing from the ILWU, he founded a radical weekly newspaper, the *Honolulu Record*. As editor, Koji crusaded for union organization (in collaboration with the Democratic Party), better conditions for workers, and racial equality. In keeping with his interest in interracial coalitions, he hired Frank Marshall Davis as a columnist. (Davis, a black poet and journalist, would later serve as a mentor of sorts to a young Hawaiian African American, Barack Obama.) Koji's newspaper earned widespread influence, if small profits. However, in 1951, as McCarthyism spread to Hawai'i, Ariyoshi and six others—the so-called Honolulu Seven—were arrested under the Smith Act and charged with being Communist Party members. During this time, he published his memoirs in serial form in the *Record*. In June 1953, a jury found Ariyoshi guilty. He appealed the ruling and his conviction was eventually overturned. He kept the *Record* going until 1958 when, unable to make a living, he ultimately folded it.

In 1960 Ariyoshi opened a flower shop/liquor store in Waikiki, which he ran for ten years. As McCarthy-era tensions faded, he became increasingly glorified as a victim of the blacklist. In 1969 he was appointed to the board of directors of the Hawaii Foundation for History and the Humanities. Shortly afterward, he founded the US-China Peoples Friendship Association. In mid-1971, he became one of the first US citizens invited to visit the People's Republic of China after it reopened to Americans. Aided by credentials from the *Honolulu Star-Bulletin*, Ariyoshi reached China in January 1972 and secured a four-hour interview with Chinese Premier Zhou Enlai. According to Ariyoshi's son, the premier remembered Koji from Yenan and assured him that the Chinese government would grant entry visas to any American whom he would vouch for. After his return from Asia, Koji opened a travel agency, which devoted most of its business to arranging passages to the country. That same year he was invited to teach the first ethnic studies class at the University of Hawai'i. Ariyoshi died of cancer in 1976. *From Kona to Yenan: The Political Memoir of Koji Aruiyoshi*, published by the University of Hawai'i Press, appeared in book form in 2002.

SANJI ABE AND MARTIAL LAW IN WARTIME HAWAI'I

This chapter covers the tragic story of Senator Sanji Abe as a way to understand the plight of Japanese Americans in Hawai'i during World War II. People who study Executive Order 9066 and the wartime Japanese American camp experience often present as a contrast the treatment of Japanese Americans in the Territory of Hawaii. In Hawai'i, which had an even larger ethnic Japanese population than the West Coast, no mass removal took place, and only some 3,000 individuals of Japanese ancestry were ever confined in camps, either on the islands or on the mainland. General Delos Emmons, the territory's wartime military governor, well understood that, apart from removal's moral or constitutional dimensions, any such policy would be doomed to failure on practical grounds. Putting together, in time of wartime scarcity, the resources in food and materials needed to either maintain 150,000 people in close confinement (from which they could be liberated by any Japanese invader) or transport them to the mainland would be costly, if not impossible. Furthermore, the territory's leaders simply could not afford to incarcerate the bulk of its labor force if they needed to keep up war production and the politically powerful five families who made up Hawai'i's ruling class were opposed to losing their plantation workers. Emmons preferred to trust Japanese Americans, and they amply repaid that trust by contributing massively to the war effort in terms of their labor in defense industries and by enlisting as soldiers.

As countless numbers of latter-day scholars and activists have pointed out, the fact that Japanese Americans were left at liberty in Hawai'i—a territory attacked at Pearl Harbor and that remained the most exposed to invasion during the war—lays bare the hollowness of the case for military necessity made by the Army and those West Coast whites who agitated for the wholesale removal of ethnic Japanese. Put another way, if they could be left alone in Hawai'i, where Japanese Americans constituted some 40 percent of the population, why could not 1 percent of the West Coast population be similarly trusted? This argument, to be sure, carries a great deal of truth, but it tends to ignore two essential (and related) points.

First, averting mass confinement in Hawai'i was a near thing, despite the unrealistic nature of any such project. Plans for the mass roundup and confinement of "local Japanese" were drawn up in spring 1942 by the Joint Chiefs of Staff, approved by Secretary of the Navy Frank Knox, and endorsed by President Franklin D. Roosevelt. General Emmons (with help from Assistant Secretary of War John McCloy) succeeded in scuttling the plan by a stalling policy, though he did ultimately send 1,000 "potentially dangerous" Japanese Americans and family members—the sacrificial victims of the policy—to camps on the mainland as a gesture of compliance. Emmons deserves enormous credit for his cool-headed balancing of the needs for labor and materials against fears for security.

A second and related point is that Japanese Americans, like others in Hawai'i, remained only partly free under wartime military rule. Indeed, beginning in the first moments of the war, their presence gave the Army the pretext to grab absolute power in Hawai'i and cling to it. On December 7, 1941, as the bombs fell on Pearl Harbor, the commander of operations in Hawai'i, General Walter Short, visited Territorial Governor Joseph Poindexter and warned of the urgent menace of sabotage by local Japanese. He insisted that, unless the governor granted full powers to the Army, he would not be responsible for guaranteeing the territory's safety and then threatened to take power unilaterally. Short then pressured Poindexter to sign a special martial law proclamation that the governor had never seen. Once Poindexter had been bulldozed into signing the proclamation, Short declared himself the military governor, abolished Hawai'i's government, dismissed the legislature, and suspended the US Constitution.

When General Emmons arrived ten days later to replace Short, he took on the title and powers of a military governor. Military officials, led by Provost Marshal General Thomas Green, imposed a set of general orders to govern the territory. Army rule was marked by harsh and often arbitrary regulations. Newspapers remained heavily censored and criticism of military officials forbidden. The regime imposed stringent labor rules and bans on strikes. Despite promising to restore civilian government, military governors held power for three years, long after any threat of Japanese invasion had passed.

While Japanese Americans were not singled out for different treatment in most cases, some special restrictions were placed on them. Japanese American farmers in the West Loch area near Pearl Harbor were banished from their homes, though they were permitted back during daytime hours to farm on their property. Japanese churches and language schools were shuttered. Community leaders such as school principal Shigeo Yoshida, knowing that Japanese Americans were vulnerable, led "speak English" campaigns and war bond drives.

It is incontestable that in certain cases the commanders of the military regime used their great power in unjust and arbitrary fashion against Japanese Americans. A case in point is the story of Sanji Abe. Born in Kailua Kona to immigrants from Fukuoka Province on May 10, 1895, he was granted US citizenship after the United States annexed Hawai'i in 1898. He later moved to Hilo, on the Big Island. After serving in World War I, Abe joined the conservative veterans' group the American Legion to assist in the Legion's Americanization program. Meanwhile, he was named president of the Nisei Club, a well-known civic group in Hilo. Hired as a patrolman by the Hilo Police Department, he was later promoted to the position of clerk of the police court and was subsequently named a deputy sheriff. He also bought a home and various other properties. Meanwhile, he married and had six children.

In 1940, running on the Republican ticket, Abe sought election to the territorial Senate. After being repeatedly attacked by a race-baiting white Democratic opponent for his (pro forma) dual citizenship, Abe agreed to formally renounce his Japanese nationality as a gesture to appease nativists—his expatriation notice arrived a few days before the election. In November 1940, he defeated his opponent, thereby becoming Hawai'i's first-ever Nisei senator. After the Pearl Harbor attack the following year, Abe (who was well beyond military age) volunteered as a civil defense worker.

Abe seems to have been closely watched by military authorities once war began. According to Hawai'i historian Bob Dye, on July 21, 1942, Abe's son, Stanley, accompanied military intelligence agent Samuel H. Snow on an inspection of the Honolulu theater Yamatoza, of which Abe was part owner. While looking among various stage properties, Snow announced that he had found a Japanese flag—Abe, who had become familiar with the theater's backstage by playing there, was certain that the flag had been planted. On

August 2, he was arrested and charged with possession of a Japanese flag, for which the penalty was a fine of up to $10,000 and/or a one-year prison term. Abe protested that he had never bought or flown any Japanese flag—and had indeed ordered his theater checked carefully for just such contraband. He also pointed out that the military orders making possession of Japanese flags a crime were not issued until August 8, six days after his arrest. Army officials were thus forced to release him on August 19.

Even after he publicly burned the offending flag, Abe remained under suspicion. In September 1942, military officials ordered him to be rearrested—this time without charge—and brought before a board made up of both officers and civilians. The kangaroo court considered evidence against Abe based on rumor, vague accusations by informants, and a broad dose of racial prejudice. The chief charges against him were that in the prewar era he had studied in a Japanese-language school, traveled to Japan, shown Japanese-language motion pictures in his theater, and served on a reception committee for officers of a visiting Japanese naval vessel in 1939. Abe responded by producing white witnesses who testified as to his loyalty to the United States. Despite the lack of any evidence regarding Abe's purported disloyalty, let alone formal charges against him, the board recommended that he be interned for the duration of the war. As a result, Abe was placed in "custodial detention," where he remained for nineteen months—first at the Sand Island camp and later at the Honolulu Federal Detention Center.

Bob Dye's hypothesis is that Abe's detention was part of a larger campaign by military officials to pressure all Japanese American legislators into resigning their seats or withdrawing from the legislature. After elections were held in November 1942, not a single Japanese American assemblyman was returned. Despite the pressure, Abe, who was not up for reelection, refused to resign his seat. But in February 1943, he was barred from taking his seat in the new legislature when it convened, and he reluctantly resigned in order to spare his district from further reprisals. In March 1944, Abe was granted parole. As a condition of his release, he was required to sign a form waiving any challenge to his detention. During the postwar years, Abe concentrated on his business affairs and did not speak publicly about his ordeal. When interviewed about his detention in 1968, he insisted that the reasons for his detention were still a mystery to him. When his interviewer asked whether it was the work of his political opponents, he responded, "I assume so."

Wartime Army rule in Hawaii Territory represents a unique case in modern US history: Army commanders exercising unchecked power overthrew an elected government. Throughout the war, the Army in Hawai'i used Japanese Americans as scapegoats, and they became proxies in the larger struggle for the constitutional rights of all groups. Sanji Abe, despite being a war veteran and a duly elected territorial legislator, was subjected to arbitrary arrest and imprisonment without charge. His case reminds us that even if Japanese Americans in Hawai'i were not confined en masse, they remained subject to official denial of their fundamental rights on racial grounds.

NOTE

1. This article is adapted from Greg Robinson, "Admission Denied," *Pennsylvania Gazette* 98 (January–February 2000), 38–41.

5

Wartime Confinement and Japanese Americans

Friends and Foes

THE CASE AGAINST MICHELLE MALKIN

Several years ago, I wrote a book on the decisions behind the mass removal and confinement of the Japanese Americans, commonly (if inaccurately) known as the Japanese American internment, and in particular on the role of President Franklin Roosevelt. I based it on several years of research in a number of archives around the country. The book was published under the title *By Order of the President: FDR and the Internment of Japanese Americans* (Harvard University Press, 2001). In the time since, I have preferred to let the work speak for itself [and have not responded to critics, even when I felt they distorted what I said]. However, I have felt obliged by the publication of Michelle Malkin's *In Defense of Internment: The Case for Racial Profiling in World War II and the War on Terror*, to break my silence.

First, Malkin is a bestselling author whose book is being put out by an established publisher (Regnery), and her status as a celebrity will make many undiscriminating or unknowing people buy the book and take her arguments at face value. Also, Malkin, unlike all other writers I have seen, deliberately

DOI: 10.5876/9781607324294.c005

impugns the motives of those who disagree with her. She proclaims herself a disinterested seeker of truth with an open mind. However, she is gratuitously nasty toward all others:

> Unlike many others who have published on this subject, I have no vested interests: I am not an evacuee, internee, or family member thereof. I am not an attorney who has represented evacuees or internees demanding redress for their long-held grievances. I am not a professor whose tenure relies on regurgitating academic orthodoxy about this episode in American history.

This is an outrageous slur, not only on Japanese Americans but on scholars. I myself am in none of the categories she mentions, apart from being a professor, and I was not even that when I researched and wrote my book. (As far as my tenure is concerned, moreover, I can say with confidence that the University of Quebec does not take a position on the internment.) I am mindful, however, of Sidney Hook's admonition: "Before impugning an opponent's motives, even when they legitimately may be impugned, answer his arguments." Since there is a great deal to criticize in Malkin's arguments from a logical and historical point of view, I will focus on that.

An analysis of Malkin's book should start with the material the author includes on MAGIC (the decrypted intercepts of the Japanese code), which by her own statement constitutes the heart of her argument. There is a certain repetition in my response here, since the author further states that her material is mostly if not entirely lifted from the work of the late David Lowman, to whom the book is dedicated. Lowman first tried in the 1980s to make a case that the MAGIC cables justified Executive Order 9066. His work has been repeated and decisively refuted, most recently by James C. McNaughton, Command Historian of the United States Army, Pacific.

Since there is nothing new in the author's case for MAGIC, my rebuttal will be brief. Let me divide it into three parts: first, that the MAGIC cables do not present the image of a Japanese American spy network; second, that the people who pushed the case for evacuation would not have had access to the MAGIC excerpts in any case; third, that those who did have access to MAGIC did not base their decision on it.

First, an examination of the MAGIC cables provided by the author does not provide any solid case for implicating the Japanese Americans in espionage activities. Only a tiny handful of the thousands of decrypted messages detail efforts by Japan to build networks among Japanese Americans, and those list hopes or intentions more than actions or results. For example, the author relies most strongly on a memo from the Los Angeles consulate to Tokyo from May 1941. The author claims "the message stated that the network had Nisei spies in the U.S. Army" (p. 44). In fact, the message states: "We shall maintain connection with our second generations who are at present in the U.S. Army . . ." This speaks of agents to be recruited. There is no evidence that any individuals had been recruited as agents, still less that they were actively giving information. Further replies from Los Angeles and Seattle state that they had established connections with Japanese and with "second generations." Again, there is no description of agents nor information from them.

The rest of the cables she cites recount information given to Japan in the fall of 1941, long after any discussion of recruiting Japanese Americans had ceased, with no clue as to the source of the information given. The sum total of the information is that Tokyo unquestionably tried to build a spy network in the United States during 1941. The bulk of their efforts were devoted to recruiting non-Japanese. One of the MAGIC cables instructed Japanese agents to emphasize recruitment of groups other than Issei and Nisei, particularly "Negro, labor union members, and anti-Semites."

The vague mentions of Japanese Americans may have simply amounted to agents in the consulates puffing their activities for their bosses at home, or they may have tried to recruit Nisei. There is no evidence that they had any success. The American occupation authorities in Japan after the war who studied captured Japanese documents found no evidence of any giant spy rings among American citizens of Japanese ancestry.

Next, those who made the case for internment did not rely on MAGIC. The author herself notes that access to the MAGIC encrypts was limited to a dozen people outside the decrypters. This leaves her in the position of asserting that the essential reflection and decision was made by those figures alone—that is, President Roosevelt, Secretary of War Stinson, and Assistant Secretary of War McCloy—and the reasons or motivations of any other actors were irrelevant. It defies credulity that in a military system the commander on the spot would not be relied on. In any case, the record amply demonstrates that West Coast Defense Commander General John DeWitt (and his assistant Karl Bendetsen) were largely responsible for making the case for "evacuation" (i.e., removal), and that their judgment of the situation and their recommendation for mass evacuation overcame the initial opposition of McCloy and Stimson. DeWitt's motivations for urging evacuation—notably, his comment to McCloy that "a Jap is a Jap" and his reliance on arguments about the "racial strains" of the Japanese in his Final Report justifying his actions—indicate that his conduct was informed by racism.

Finally, the MAGIC excerpts did not influence the figures who did have access to them to fear a Japanese American threat. Malkin does not, as she must, show any *direct evidence of influence* here—it cannot simply be assumed, with the burden of proof on the other side. (The 9/11 commission's work demonstrates the fallacy of saying that since documentary evidence existed and government officials had access to it, they must have seen it and reacted accordingly—the president and his advisors had access to evidence that Al-Qaida planned to attack but did not act on it.) There is, instead, considerable evidence that leads to a contrary inference. Throughout all the confidential memoranda and conversations taking place within the War Department at the time of the decision on evacuation, transcripts that show people speaking extremely freely, the MAGIC excerpts are not mentioned a single time. Logic further refutes Malkin's claims. If the prewar MAGIC excerpts had been all-important in establishing a threat from Japanese Americans, Roosevelt and his advisors would have ordered mass removal of Japanese Americans directly after Pearl Harbor, not two months later.

In sum, Malkin's book is not a work of history but a polemical argument with evidence tortured or ignored to fit a predetermined and ideologically driven thesis. Malkin must thereby ignore significant evidence that cannot be reconciled with her argument. For example, she does not explain why the Canadian government, whose leaders did not have the benefit of the MAGIC cables, nonetheless went through the process of relocating and incarcerating their ethnic Japanese residents. Furthermore, she does not explain why immediate loyalty hearings were not granted to the Japanese Americans, whether citizens or aliens, the way that they were to *all* other enemy aliens, or how it was that if Japanese American loyalty could not be determined, they eventually were granted hearings. Most of all, the author does not deal at all with the long, extensive, and very well-documented history of anti-Japanese American racism on the West Coast. This absence is so glaring as to constitute bad faith.

The McCloy Memo: New Insight into the Causes of Removal

The removal and confinement of some 120,000 American citizens and permanent residents of Japanese ancestry from the Pacific coast during 1942—popularly, if imprecisely, known as the Japanese American internment—remains a powerful event in the nation's consciousness. In the decades since the war, historians have exhaustively documented the primary role of anti-Japanese prejudice and war hysteria by West Coast Army officers and civilians in bringing about the issue of Executive Order 9066, which authorized removal.

Yet, in recent times, a series of "internment revisionists," led by journalist Michelle Malkin, and building on the work of David Lowman, have loudly argued that mass removal was a justified and positive example of ethnic profiling. The keystone of their argument is that a few White House and War Department authorities—notably Assistant Secretary of War John McCloy—made the decision to confine West Coast Japanese Americans based on their reading of the MAGIC Intercepts, top-secret Japanese diplomatic messages decoded by American cryptographers. The MAGIC cables, these revisionists claim, provided clear evidence of mass espionage by aliens and American citizens during the prewar period. Although the revisionists' evidence is predominantly old and discredited, in the current mood of insecurity and wartime nationalism they have attracted significant attention.

Some years ago, I was at the Library of Congress researching my book *By Order of the President: FDR and the Internment of Japanese Americans*. I discovered a set of documents in the papers of Robert Patterson, then under secretary of war. Among them was a file copy of a memorandum, dated July 23, 1942, that John McCloy sent Patterson in response to inquiries about the expense of feeding Japanese American "internees." McCloy noted that since 70 percent of those in the camps were citizens, and most were women and children, the government should provide them with sufficient food. This was neither novel nor relevant to my project, so I filed the document without thinking. Recently, I was surprised to discover that the memo also included what was marked as a handwritten postscript, where McCloy admitted that military security was not a primary factor in triggering the removal of West Coast Japanese Americans:

"These people are not 'internees': They are under no suspicion for the most part and were moved largely because we felt we could not control our own white citizens in California."

Since the revisionists credit McCloy as the chief decision-maker on removal, his admission fatally discredits their argument about national security. (They cannot escape this reality by claiming that McCloy was protecting the secrecy of MAGIC. Patterson probably was aware of MAGIC; and, in any case, the spectacle of McCloy lying to his superior officer, who supported removal on national security grounds, to preserve secrecy over its causes enters the realm of the ludicrous.)

For more thoughtful students of history, this postscript raises questions of interpretation. McCloy's explanation about protective custody does not square with the evidence—it does not seem that Army officers discussed removing Japanese Americans to protect them, and it is certain that if protection had been the goal, Japanese Americans would have faced very different conditions following removal. Conversely, how do we account for the evidence that War Department leaders genuinely feared pro-Japanese subversion during early 1942? Or the fact that McCloy continued, then and in later years, to defend the government's actions as based on military security—even manipulating evidence before the Supreme Court to bolster the government's case against a legal challenge?

There are no simple answers to these questions. Yet the note—especially the intimacy of a handwritten afterword—testifies powerfully to McCloy's bitterness against the Californians who had forced Washington to take extreme action. Perhaps it is not too much to say that McCloy's memo reveals remorse—a realization that he had been misled about the Japanese threat. So why did he not publicly reveal the truth about removal? As a patriot and military loyalist, McCloy believed in defending the White House and the War Department at all costs. To confess that the Army had acted in response to popular prejudice would discredit the war effort and stain the reputations of America's leaders.

Yet McCloy's postscript may help explain why that normally supercautious man twice went out on a limb during mid-1942 to support Japanese Americans. McCloy and the commanding general of the Hawaiian Department, Delos Emmons, together thwarted Franklin D. Roosevelt's orders for the mass confinement of Japanese Hawaiians. Meanwhile, McCloy overrode Army opposition to Nisei soldiers and brokered the creation of the famous 442nd Regimental Combat Team. The possibility that these actions represented a concealed form of contrition lends them a special poignancy.

NORMAN THOMAS AND THE DEFENSE OF JAPANESE AMERICANS[1]

Norman Mattoon Thomas (1884–1968), leader and perennial presidential candidate of the Socialist Party, distinguished himself by his tireless defense of the human rights of Japanese Americans during World War II. He was the only national political figure to take a public position against Executive Order 9066, which he decried as "totalitarian justice." In newspaper articles and public speeches, including some delivered on the West Coast, he decried the government's action and warned that it was a precedent for other arbitrary action against American citizens. Thomas was also active in organizational efforts against mass removal and confinement. So active, in fact, that all I can do here is begin to explore his involvement.

By the time of Pearl Harbor, the Socialist Party—and Norman Thomas in particular—faced a crisis. The party had been reduced from a once-impressive political force to a small and largely powerless group and Thomas's pacifism and long opposition to American military intervention against Nazi Germany publicly discredited him. Although he announced his support for the war after its declaration, he feared for the survival of civil rights at home and campaigned against wartime censorship and for the rights of minorities. While the treatment of Japanese Americans deeply and sincerely troubled Thomas, it also demonstrated for him the potential for government abuse of power under the cover of war.

Thomas knew few West Coast Nisei before the war, although during 1941 he corresponded with Sam Hohri, columnist for *Rafu Shimpo* and a Japanese American Citizens League (JACL) activist, who reported on the conditions facing Japanese Americans. In mid-January 1942, Ann Ray, a Socialist activist in Santa Barbara who served as the secretary of California's Race Relations Commission, began sending Thomas reports from the commission's chair, African American attorney Hugh Macbeth, on the growing public calls for removal of all people of Japanese ancestry from the West Coast and the greed and racism that underlay them. Thomas was further energized when

FIGURE 5.1. Norman Thomas.

his colleague Harry Fleischmann took him to task for ignoring the question of Japanese Americans in a radio broadcast Thomas made at the end of January 1942 supporting antilynching legislation: "how about Americans of Japanese descent, who are today being discriminated against even more violently and cruelly than Americans of Negro origin . . . Children of Japanese descent are now being put out of public schools in New York. God knows what is happening in California—where at least one man has been murdered for being of Japanese origin."

Thomas was concerned but failed to respond publicly until Executive Order 9066 was publicly announced. He then quickly denounced the order before audiences in Detroit and Chicago and drafted a series of articles for the Socialist Party newspaper *The Call.* He also instructed his assistant, Mary Hillyer, to immediately send letters to all the people on his mailing list, asking them to write the government and "bring pressure for sanity and fair play" on the government. Thomas considered the order not just an injustice to Japanese Americans but a shocking example of the violation of individual rights in the name of patriotism. As he put it, even if there was a risk of subversion, "So drastic a provision is a good deal like burning down Chicago to get rid of gangsters." He was even more uneasy about the lack of visible public outrage and protest.

Thomas tried to persuade the American Civil Liberties Union (ACLU), of which he was a founding executive board member, to fight mass removal, but in June 1942, the ACLU National Board of Directors voted by a decisive margin to not oppose the constitutionality of Franklin D. Roosevelt's order, although local ACLU lawyers were still permitted to bring test cases to oppose the arbitrary application of the order to Japanese Americans. Thomas later protested to ACLU lawyer Ernest Besig that such a position was illogical "for that order was clearly intended to make possible just what has been done, which in every respect has had presidential backing." He seriously considered resigning from the ACLU as a public protest, which "amounts objectively to betrayal of a cause," but decided against it. When Thomas learned that the ACLU had sent a message congratulating General John DeWitt, who led the Western Defense Command, on the efficiency and humanity of the removal operation, he hit the roof and fired off a letter dripping with sarcasm to ACLU Executive Director Roger Baldwin, asking whether he had also praised Nazi commandants for their humane operations: "Better keep your letter of thanks to a form letter. In the years to come there may be many humane American army officers engaged in establishing ghettoes."

Blocked by the ACLU, Thomas mobilized the Post War World Council, a Socialist Party–affiliated planning agency. In May 1942, Thomas drafted a petition for the council that called for rescission of Executive Order 9066, on the grounds that it "approximates the totalitarian theory of justice practiced by the Nazis in their treatment of the Jews." Within a few weeks, over 200 people agreed to sign, including such notable figures as John Dewey, Reinhold

Niebuhr, Ruth Benedict, and W.E.B. Du Bois. Encouraged, Thomas scheduled a forum on "the Japanese Question" in New York the following month. At the meeting, guest speaker Mike Masaoka, of the Japanese American Citizens League (JACL), stated that the treatment of Japanese Americans was "a test of democracy" and warned, "If they can do that to one group they can do it to other groups." With Masaoka's support, Thomas introduced a resolution calling for the immediate establishment of hearing boards to determine the loyalty of the "evacuees" and warning against the "military internment of unaccused persons in concentration camps." However, representatives of the Japanese American Committee for Democracy (JACD), an antifascist group close to the Communist Party that favored full war mobilization, introduced a counter-resolution approving mass removal. Although the JACD resolution was defeated handily by those assembled, Thomas was unable to persuade the other groups at the meeting to support his demand for the "reconsideration" of Executive Order 9066. In the end, the meeting settled on a weak compromise resolution that avoided criticizing the government and called for resettlement of Japanese Americans away from the West Coast.

Meanwhile, Thomas turned to the press. In addition to his articles in *The Call*, in July 1942, he published the pamphlet *Democracy and Japanese Americans*, in which he repeated his description of Executive Order 9066 as "totalitarian justice" and described the difficult conditions facing inmates in the assembly venters. He devoted the last several pages to a program promoting immediate resettlement, including provisions to reimburse the dispossessed Japanese Americans through government grants of land. The pamphlet enjoyed wide circulation (in part, interestingly enough, through the financial support and distribution efforts of the JACL). Its influence was limited by attacks from Army officials, who unsuccessfully sought to discredit the information it contained, and by scurrilous commentary in the West Coast media. One of the most damaging attacks on Thomas was a letter to the *San Francisco Chronicle* sent from the camp at Manzanar by Nisei Communist Karl Yoneda.

Throughout the years that followed, Thomas continued to receive reports from inmates and their supporters. In return, he pressed the government to respect the civil rights of the inmates and speed resettlement. He also attempted to put together an estimate of the financial losses incurred by Issei and Nisei and supported compensation for those who had lost property. He even defied hostile West Coast opinion. In September 1944, he made a speech at San Francisco's Commonwealth Club in which he denounced the "racism" of Californians who wished to prevent inmates from returning to their homes "legally if possible, illegally if necessary."

Norman Thomas's actions, and the opposition he faced, demonstrate the nature and extent of dissent over the wartime treatment of Japanese Americans. Thomas never wavered from his position that Executive Order 9066, more than an injustice to Japanese Americans, was a disturbing sign of totalitarian rule, and he deplored the lack of public opposition. As he stated during the war, "In an experience of nearly three decades I have never found it harder to arouse the American public on any important issue than this." Although his dissent was little noticed by most Americans and won him few supporters—even among Japanese Americans—it stands for us as positive evidence of a road not taken.

ELEANOR ROOSEVELT AND JAPANESE AMERICANS: A FIRST LOOK

The attitudes and activities of Eleanor Roosevelt—wife of President Franklin D. Roosevelt and a celebrated activist First Lady—in regard to Japanese Americans during World War II remain quite shadowy, not least because she was largely silent on the issue in the years after FDR's death and completely avoided the topic in her memoirs. What is clear is that Executive Order 9066 left her in a quandary, which she was unable to resolve. On the one hand, she strongly opposed the policy. Beginning in the first days after Pearl Harbor, she publicly defended Japanese Americans and sought ways to help them. On the other hand, as the president's wife, she could not publicly oppose the administration's policy, and there were limits to what she could do even in private.

Until the dawn of World War II, Eleanor had virtually no contact with Japanese Americans. A notable supporter of equal rights for black Americans, she seldom addressed the problem of anti-Asian discrimination during her first eight years in the White House. However, in October 1941, Togo Tanaka, editor of *Rafu Shimpo*, and Gongoro Nakamura, of the Central Japanese Association, came to Washington, DC, to inquire after the fate of Japanese Americans in case of war. Eleanor agreed to meet them and promised her assistance. At a press conference following the meeting, she praised the patriotism of the Nisei, who had joined the Army in large numbers, and added,

"The Issei may be aliens technically, but in reality they are Americans and America has a place for all loyal persons regardless of race or citizenship."[2]

After Pearl Harbor was attacked, Eleanor immediately flew to the West Coast to assess the situation and coordinate civil defense efforts. When she discovered that Treasury Department orders freezing "enemy alien" bank accounts were causing unnecessary hardship to Issei farmers, she quickly contacted department officials and had the orders relaxed sufficiently to permit Issei to withdraw $100 per month for living expenses. While on the West Coast, Eleanor also publicly defended Japanese Americans and warned against war hysteria. Photos of her posing with Nisei representatives appeared on the front page of West Coast newspapers. In a national radio broadcast on January 11, 1942, she spoke out on behalf of the Issei, who, she reminded her listeners, were longtime residents who were prevented from becoming citizens.

Executive Order 9066 took Eleanor by surprise. When she protested to her husband, he told her peremptorily that he did not wish to discuss the subject with her.[3] She tried to get around this block by meeting with FDR's friend Archibald MacLeish, director of the Office of Facts and Figures, and his aides (including Alan Cranston, the future US senator) to put together arguments against mass removal, but without success.

In the months that followed, Eleanor remained publicly silent but troubled. She privately lamented that innocent people were being made to pay for the crimes of the guilty and kept herself informed of Japanese Americans and their problems to help where she could. She authorized the transfer of money from the special projects fund she maintained with the American Friends Service Committee to pay for emergency programs. She supported the efforts of the National Japanese American Student Relocation Council to find colleges willing to accept Nisei students so that they could continue their education. She intervened to aid Japanese Americans threatened with dismissal from government jobs. She asked the War Department for permission to visit an assembly center, a request that was declined. And she corresponded with individual Nisei.

At the same time, she made no overt criticism. When black civil rights activist Pauli Murray wrote FDR in July 1942, proposing that the government relocate southern blacks to save them from lynching, just as it had removed West Coast Japanese Americans to protect them from racist attacks, she unleashed her deep frustration and defensiveness about internment. In a rare display of anger (mixed with some very odd ethnic categorization), Eleanor wrote Murray, "How many of our colored people in the South would like to be evacuated and treated as though they were not as rightfully here as other people? I am deeply concerned that we have had to do that to the Japanese who are American citizens, but we are at war with Japan and they have only been citizens for a very short time. We would feel a resentment if we had to do this for citizens who have been here as long as most of the white people."

In March 1943, Eleanor received a letter from Harriet Gipson, asking about rumors of Issei and Nisei fifth columnists. After checking with Rep. John Tolan, she discovered, to her surprise, that there had been no incidents of sabotage and no Japanese Americans convicted of disloyal acts. This discovery seems to have pushed her into action. In the wake of charges by the Chandler and Dies Committees that the War Relocation Authority (WRA) was "coddling" Japanese Americans, FDR agreed to let her visit one of the camps (though he nonetheless refused her plea to bring a Japanese American family to live in the White House as a symbolic gesture). On April 24, 1943, Eleanor visited the Gila River camp. By her presence and her interest, she made clear to the internees her sympathy for their plight. In a speech, she told the internees that their residence in Japanese neighborhoods, "in communities within a community," had delayed their assimilation into "the American society" and recommended that they scatter and assimilate once released. While she genuinely meant well, one inmate who was present when Eleanor spoke believed she was blaming the victims for their own incarceration.

After she returned from Gila River, Eleanor campaigned to assist confined Japanese Americans. In her syndicated daily newspaper column, she lauded the efforts of the inmates to grow their own food, ameliorate the harsh desert climate and the ugliness of the hastily constructed camps, and police and educate themselves. In an interview published in the *Los Angeles Times* three days after her visit, she was more frank. She described the inmates as living in conditions that were not indecent, but "certainly not luxurious," and added, "I wouldn't like to live that way." She strongly recommended that the camps be closed as soon as possible: "[T]he sooner we get the young [native-born] Japanese out of the camps the better. Otherwise if we don't look out we will create another Indian problem." It was her most open public expression of opposition during the war.

Following her return to Washington, Eleanor persuaded her husband to meet with Dillon Myer—the first and only time the president did so—to build support for the beleaguered WRA leader and to push for Myer's proposal that the Army permit the release of the inmates. She also wrote an article for *Collier's* magazine, in which she publicized the plight of the inmates and the policy's historical background. Calling attention to the sacrifices the Japanese Americans had made, including their often-forced disposition of property, she urged her readers to live up to "traditional American ideals of fairness" in dealing with them once they left the camps. She met with Japanese American Citizens League representatives at the White House; invited Hawaiian YMCA worker Hung Wai Ching to Washington to brief the president on the condition of Nisei soldiers; and invited wounded soldier Jack Mizuha to tea. She received Michio Kunitani at the White House to discuss the problems of resettlers. In June 1944, when debate arose within the administration over lifting exclusion, Eleanor helped bring pressure to bear on FDR for opening the camps in the form of a proposal by NAACP Executive Secretary Walter White for mass demonstrations by blacks on behalf of Japanese Americans, a proposal that the president turned aside.

Following the death of her husband in April 1945, Eleanor left the White House. Late that year, President Harry Truman appointed her to the United Nations General Assembly and in 1946 she was chosen president of the UN commission charged with drafting a Universal Declaration of Human Rights. She considered the ratification of the declaration on December 10, 1948, her greatest achievement. She remained a delegate until 1952. While she served at the United Nations and afterward, she maintained her newspaper column and public speaking tour schedule and wrote books and magazine articles.

As FDR's widow, Eleanor took on the role of public custodian of her husband's memory during the postwar years. She avoided commenting on her wartime involvement with Japanese Americans, even in her memoirs. In her solitary public discussion of the question, in her introduction to Allen H. Eaton's book *Beauty Behind Barbed Wire: The Arts of the Japanese in Our War Relocation Camps* (1952), Eleanor's comments struck an oddly false and defensive note.

Although Eleanor Roosevelt carefully concealed many of her activities to avoid giving the impression of interference, the surviving evidence indicates her sincere public support of Japanese Americans and her considerable efforts on their behalf.

Paul Robeson: "Your Fight Is My Fight"

Paul Robeson, longtime hero and friend of Japanese Americans (both individuals and the community generally), was (after Joe Louis) the most popular and visible African American of the 1930s and 1940s. He was a celebrated stage actor and movie star, an internationally famous folk singer, a champion athlete, a lawyer and orator, a civil rights activist, and a linguist conversant in some two dozen languages. Robeson is remembered today chiefly as an uncritical supporter of the Soviet Union and the US Communist Party. Because of his left-wing sympathies and advocacy of civil rights, he suffered severe repression during the 1950s. Although he had been the highest-paid black entertainer in the nation during the prewar years, he was blacklisted and effectively unemployed for ten years, harassed by the FBI, and stripped of his passport.

While Robeson's advocacy of friendship with the Soviet Union aroused the greatest public attention, his primary interest on the international scene during the 1930s and 1940s was Africa, whose nations were then struggling for liberation from European colonialism. Robeson considered himself an African, and he championed the rediscovery of traditional culture as a tool to give Africans the self-esteem necessary to achieve independence. He argued that the interest of Africans (and thus African Americans) lay in coordination with other groups, particularly those with powerful cultural traditions from which Africans could draw strength. For example, he was a fervent admirer of Jewish culture and worked to build coalitions between blacks and Jews in the United States. He also admired China, studied Chinese language, and sang Chinese folk music in his concert programs. During the years 1939 to 1941 (when he followed the Communist Party's overall antimilitarist line), he supported the Chinese struggle against the Japanese occupation. Robeson appeared at rallies for China relief and recorded an album of Chinese songs in both English and Chinese.

Despite his concern for Asian liberation, Robeson was largely silent during the 1930s about racial discrimination against people of Asian ancestry, especially on the West Coast. Nevertheless, many Japanese Americans admired his talent and insistence on racial equality. In 1941 *Nichi Bei* columnist George Jobo rhapsodized about Robeson's singing: "Inadequate vocabulary of your writer fails to describe the rich simplicity of Mr. Robeson's voice as well as his

FIGURE 5.2. Paul Robeson at a Nisei veterans dinner, Memorial Day 1946.

ability to hold the audience spellbound to his very last notes." Meanwhile, the *Nichi Bei* reported exultantly on Robeson's victorious suit against the proprietor of a Bay Area café that had excluded him on racial grounds. In 1942 a club at the Santa Anita Assembly Center played and discussed Robeson records.

Once war began, Robeson interested himself in the condition of Japanese Americans, with whom he felt an immediate kinship. In February 1942, he was approached by sculptor Isamu Noguchi, who had founded a progressive group called Nisei Writers and Artists Mobilization for Democracy. Noguchi asked Robeson to join a blue-ribbon panel of prominent non-Asians who would testify before Congress to the loyalty of Japanese Americans in order to avert mass removal. Robeson readily volunteered. The panel idea was dropped once President Franklin D. Roosevelt signed Executive Order 9066, but Robeson's offer of action impressed many Nisei. He remained attentive to Nisei concerns in the years that followed. In a 1943 speech, he praised "the workers from Mexico and from the east—Japan and the Philippines— whose labor has helped make the west and the southwest a fruitful land." In 1946 he publicly opposed the Canadian government's movement to deport thousands of Japanese Canadians. To demonstrate his solidarity, Robeson accepted an honorary life membership from the Japanese Canadian Committee for Democracy.

Meanwhile, he sang and spoke before Japanese American audiences on several occasions. In April 1946, he gave a concert in Salt Lake City—at that time home to the Japanese American Citizens League (JACL)—for an audience composed significantly of Japanese Americans. While he did not refer directly to the Nisei in his remarks, he spoke out in favor of "equal economic rights" for all races. His talk was widely reported in the Nisei press, and community reaction was so favorable that Japanese American groups in Chicago invited Robeson to be a guest speaker at a Memorial Day banquet honoring Nisei veterans. At the banquet, Robeson denounced racial discrimination in America as a fascist doctrine and reminded veterans that the victorious struggle against fascism had to be continued at home. "Your fight is my fight," he stated.

The following year, Robeson returned to Salt Lake City to give another concert. Afterward, he granted an interview to *Pacific Citizen* editor Larry Tajiri, himself an outspoken partisan of collaboration between Nisei and blacks. Tajiri reported that Robeson was "sharply aware of the evacuation and of wartime prejudice against the Nisei. He said he would like to include a Japanese song in his program, a song of the common people to help fight discrimination against Americans of Japanese origin. It is all part of one problem, he noted, this matter of discrimination and it may be the foremost question facing us today in the atomic age."

Robeson seems not to have found a Japanese American song to his liking, for he did not add one to his repertoire. However, he came into contact with the problems of the Nisei again in 1948, when he became a supporter of Henry Wallace's Progressive Party. At the party's convention in Philadelphia, Robeson joined forces with Dyke Miyagawa and Chiye Mori, delegates from the Nisei for Wallace (aka Nisei Progressives), to push for civil rights planks in the party's platform. The Progressive Party went on the record in favor of evacuation claims for former camp residents, repeal of discriminatory laws against Japanese aliens, and equal immigration and naturalization rights. During the campaign, Robeson organized a fundraising concert tour in Hawai'i. The largely Asian American workforce gave him what he later called the warmest reception of his life. Characteristically mixing music and politics, he added, "I managed to learn some of the songs of the people from the Philippines, of the Japanese Americans."

Paul Robeson showed warm solidarity with Japanese Americans, though their struggles were never a central area of interest for him. In return, many Nisei claimed him as a friend. The Nisei press devoted numerous articles to him and offered other support. In 1949, when right-wing vigilantes disrupted a Robeson concert in Peekskill, New York, numerous Japanese Americans traveled to attend the replacement concert. The next year, when Rutgers College alumni tried to strike Robeson's name from the college roll, Gordon Hirabayashi wrote a column in the Nisei journal *Northwest Times* praising Robeson's Americanism and support for democracy and fair play.

ALAN CRANSTON AND JAPANESE AMERICANS

Los Altos, California, can be said to lie squarely within the geographical orbit of San José, as it is located barely ten miles outside the city limits. Yet, during the first half of the twentieth century, the Issei and Nisei denizens of San José's Japantown, apart from those who worked as gardeners on the estates of Los Altos, had limited contact with its predominantly white population. Still, one famous local son, future businessman and US senator Alan M. Cranston, formed treasured bonds with Japanese Americans during his early years. These friendships inspired him to offer personal and official support to Japanese Americans during the years of World War II, joining in a desperate struggle within government circles to avert mass removal.

Alan MacGregor Cranston was born in Palo Alto in 1914 and grew up in Los Altos. A prize athlete at Mountain View High School, he starred in track at Stanford University. After graduating in 1936, Cranston worked as a journalist for the International News Service. He gained national attention after he published an unexpurgated English translation of Adolf Hitler's *Mein Kampf* as a warning against Nazism, and Hitler's publisher sued him.

In 1940 Reed Lewis, director of the Common Council for American Unity, a New York–based nonprofit group that defended immigrants and promoted American pluralism, hired Cranston as an assistant. Cranston assembled data on the legal and social status of immigrants. In particular, he collected research on Asian Americans as part of the group's lobbying campaign to repeal the Chinese Exclusion Act. Meanwhile, the Council began a new quarterly magazine, *Common Ground*, under the direction of Louis Adamic (whose popular book *From Many Lands* featured life stories of Americans from different ethnic and racial groups, including that of a young Nisei,

Charles Kikuchi). Cranston published several articles in its pages during 1941, including analyses of public sentiment regarding immigrants and a discussion of the impact of new alien registration laws.

In December 1941, the United States entered World War II. Cranston expected to be drafted soon. He resigned from the Council and handed over his job to his wife, Geneva Cranston, whose efforts to champion repeal of Chinese exclusion were ultimately crowned with success in late 1943. (In similar fashion, Adamic left the editorship of *Common Ground*; new editor M. Margaret Anderson published numerous pieces by and about Japanese Americans in the years that followed and sponsored the postwar career of writer and artist Miné Okubo.)

Instead of joining the Army, Cranston was recruited for government service by poet and statesman Archibald MacLeish, who had been impressed by his work with the Council. In addition to serving as Librarian of Congress and sometime advisor and speechwriter to President Franklin D. Roosevelt, MacLeish became, in late 1941, the director of a new agency, the Office of Facts and Figures (OFF). OFF had originally been designed (largely on the initiative of Eleanor Roosevelt) as a clearinghouse for information about government agencies and activities. But with the outbreak of war its mission rapidly expanded to disseminating wartime news and propaganda, monitoring media, and controlling information. It was ultimately folded into a larger group, the Office of War Information.

In mid-January 1942, Cranston was named assistant director of OFF, tasked with managing immigrant and foreign-language groups. In the months that followed, he and his team, which included writer Bradford Smith and cartoonist Lee Falk, designed and executed policies to permit the foreign-language press to continue publishing under government supervision, worked to reconcile competing factions of Italian and Yugoslav antifascists, and disseminated information behind enemy lines and to Axis soldiers.

From the beginning, Cranston and MacLeish recognized the dangers of growing anti–Japanese American sentiment on the Pacific coast. They considered anti-Nikkei campaigns to be both unjust and a threat to national unity and accordingly rushed to defuse the situation. Cranston visited Los Angeles during the third week of January 1942 to meet with city officials and newspaper editors and ask them to tone down sensational stories of arrests and saboteurs. In cooperation with liberal groups such as the Hollywood Writers

Mobilization, Cranston worked to encourage positive coverage of Japanese American loyalty.

Nevertheless, it soon became clear that OFF efforts were insufficient to calm West Coast fears. Thus, in mid-February, MacLeish wrote Eleanor Roosevelt, who had already made public statements on behalf of Japanese Americans, asking her to use her influence to help sway government policy and public opinion. Although she did mention the subject in a radio address, she was unable to provide further help. Not only was she frequently on the road, but she focused on responding to attacks from critics over her direction of the wartime Office of Civil Defense, from which she was forced to resign on February 20. Once freed from her official post, the First Lady agreed to meet with MacLeish and his assistants to discuss helping Japanese Americans. Because he was the only native Californian in the bunch, Cranston was the star witness. He gave Mrs. Roosevelt several arguments against relocation, hoping that she could use his words as ammunition in dealing with the president. Alas, the decision had already been made. According one account, Mrs. Roosevelt protested to her husband that Nisei were good Americans, but he told her the matter was not open for discussion.

Cranston was powerless to prevent the signing of Executive Order 9066. However, with MacLeish's support, he did what he could to aid confined Japanese Americans and give them opportunities to demonstrate loyalty. He provided endorsements for Isamu Noguchi and Larry Tajiri, who sought to document relocation by making a film; he confidentially advised Japanese Americans in New York who had been banned from local victory parades on how to make their presence felt; in late 1942, he toured three of the camps and brought supplies. Meanwhile, he corresponded with his Nisei friends and offered encouragement.

In 1944 Alan Cranston left the government to join the Army. In later years, he became a prominent advocate of world government, an author, and a successful businessman. In 1968, running on an anti–Vietnam War ticket, he became a US senator from California. Cranston became most notable (in contrast to the position of his California Senate colleague S. I. Hayakawa) for his outspoken support for Japanese American redress. He remained in the Senate until 1992, when he was forced to retire due to age, prostate cancer, and fallout from the Charles Keating savings and loan scandal. He died in December 2000.

Two Wartime Governors and Mass Removal of Japanese Americans

One increasingly visible aspect of Nikkei experience during World War II has been the stories of non-Japanese who defended the loyalty and civil rights of Issei and Nisei. Some years ago, local community members in San Francisco founded the Kansha Project to recognize and honor these "righteous gentiles" of Japanese America. Several of these figures were profiled in Shizue Seigel's fine 2006 book, *In Good Conscience: Supporting Japanese Americans During the Internment*. Other notable works on the subject include Joanne Oppenheim's masterful *Dear Miss Breed: True Stories of the Japanese American Incarceration During World War II and a Librarian Who Made a Difference* (2006), which examines the poignant letters of young Nisei to a supportive San Diego librarian, Clara Breed. Franklin Odo's book, *No Sword to Bury: Japanese Americans in Hawai'i during World War II* (2004), and Tom Coffman's documentary *The First Battle: The Battle for Equality in War-Time Hawaii* (2006) recount (in different ways) how FBI agent Robert Shivers and YMCA worker Hung Wai Ching helped Nisei in Hawai'i organize and avert mass incarceration. John Howard's *Concentration Camps on the Home Front: Japanese Americans in the House of Jim Crow* (2008) provides a complex picture of Nisei benefactor Earl Finch. By showing the interplay between Japanese Americans and their supporters, these works help enrich our understanding of events as well as remind readers of the range of responses to official policy.

Following on this question, I wish to look closely at two wartime officials who offered support to Japanese Americans. One is Colorado Governor Ralph Carr. A self-made journalist and attorney, Carr reluctantly ran for and won the governorship in 1938. He helped bring the state's finances into order and was touted within some Republican Party circles as presidential timber in 1940. In the days after Executive Order 9066, Carr became the only chief executive in the mountain states to not oppose resettlement by Japanese Americans fleeing the West Coast. In the face of large-scale demands to refuse Nikkei entry to the state, he retained his devotion to the Bill of Rights, insisting that American citizens had a legal right to settle in any part of the country. Carr was defeated for office in the November 1942 election and never returned to public service. (He was running once more for governor when he died in 1950.) Because of his stand, extolled most notably in Adam Schrager's laudatory biography *The Principled Politician: The Story of Ralph Carr* (2008), Carr has now become something of a folk hero. (Schrager's title implicitly, but firmly, contrasts Carr—not just a, but *the* principled politician—with today's poll-driven and untrustworthy political class.) In a keynote speech at a Japanese American National Museum conference in July 2008, George Takei praised Carr fulsomely as a great man and a model leader.

Carr's decency stands in contrast to the generally racist and craven attitude of his neighbors. Yet it would be a mistake to praise him too highly, based on the record. First, Carr was not altogether welcoming. The governor's principal intervention came on February 28, 1942, when he informed Congressman John Tolan, head of a House committee on labor migration, that *if* the Army considered it essential, Colorado would do its patriotic duty and grant temporary quarters for German, Italian, and Japanese enemy aliens—provided that the federal government also assured that it would provide security for Coloradans. He added that his proclamation was simply a national defense measure, *not* a general invitation. For this grudging and hedged consent, Carr was commended publicly by General John DeWitt and received approving national press coverage. Such a stand, let us note, was neither completely unique nor unsurpassed. North Dakota Governor John Moses assured Tolan that his state would "cooperate to the extent of our ability with the Federal government in every manner possible" and suggested that Japanese American farmworkers could help at harvest season.

Carr's remarks caused a storm of protest in Colorado, and he struggled to defend his policy. He released a letter to US district attorney Thomas Morrissey, demanding that the federal government care for all "undesirable" enemy aliens who entered Colorado. Carr conceded that American citizens had the right to travel freely, but he asked Morrissey to ensure that all those of various nationalities who entered Colorado be "induced to stay in places where their activities may be supervised and guarded" to protect against potential subversion. Carr meanwhile released a telegram responding to DeWitt, assuring him that (for public consumption at least) "the majority of telephone calls, telegrams, and letters I have received commended me on my stand. I believe the great majority of the people of Colorado want to cooperate with the Army and the Federal government in solving any problem at hand." Various newspapers—notably the *Rocky Mountain News*—expressed support for Carr's policy. Within a month, DeWitt relieved Carr of his concerns by freezing "voluntary relocation," which rapidly quieted public debate on the issue.

In the end, Carr's supportive stance had little real impact. Only 1,500 refugees voluntarily moved to Colorado (more went to Utah despite the hostility of Governor Herbert Maw, and their caravans were personally welcomed at the gates of Salt Lake City by Mayor Ab Jenkins). Carr did not object publicly when the War Relocation Authority confined thousands more Issei and Nisei in a camp at Granada, Colorado. Indeed, in September 1942, Carr announced that the state would take no part in protecting Japanese Americans recruited for harvest labor by local communities, stating that the communities would have to assume the task themselves. This regulation severely limited the number of inmates who could accept work furloughs and leave camp, compared to other states such as Idaho and Wyoming, which eased access to such "furloughs" by inmates.

Also, if Carr was outraged by Executive Order 9066, as his admirers insist, he was remarkably restrained in his public silence on it, at least compared to Socialist leader Norman Thomas, who denounced removal as "totalitarian justice," or Republican senator Robert Taft, who questioned the constitutionality of laws to enforce military exclusion orders (though he did not oppose them). Throughout his governorship, Carr had repeatedly warned of federal government violations of the constitution. However, faithful to his conservative Republican principles, he was extreme in his rhetorical defense—not of democracy and civil rights for minorities but of states' rights and private capital against economic reform. In September 1940, Carr called President Franklin D. Roosevelt's "destroyers for bases" deal with Great Britain positive proof that the theories of the New Deal led to totalitarianism. In 1941 he opposed the opening of federal hydroelectric projects on the Arkansas River, modeled on the Tennessee Valley Authority, on the theory that they would interfere with private enterprise and threaten regional development (meaning Colorado's sole control over water resources). In January 1943, in his final statement as governor, Carr warned that federal social planning was part of a scheme to impose dictatorship. The Atlantic Charter, he complained, had not included guarantees of "freedom of enterprise," which undergirded all other freedoms and was thus a blueprint for oppression.

Worse, Carr's admirers seem to accept at face value Carr's bitter (and self-serving) assertions that support for Japanese Americans cost him his political career. Democratic politicians and unscrupulous press barons, they insist, used Carr's principled stand on Nikkei to whip up sentiment against him during fall 1942, leading to his defeat in a race he was expected to win. In reality, Carr damaged himself by choosing not to run for reelection as governor and not taking advantage of his incumbency. Lieutenant Governor John C. Vivian, Carr's handpicked candidate and close advisor, was elected easily. Instead, Carr sought to challenge incumbent Edwin Johnson in the Senate. Johnson was vulnerable due to his prewar isolationism (which Carr had shared) but remained popular. If Carr's party considered that his stand on Japanese Americans in February 1942 made him a liability in the fall elections, it did not stop them from nominating him unanimously as their candidate in September. The state's dominant newspaper, the then reactionary and virulently anti–Japanese American *Denver Post*, supported him editorially, as did the *Rocky Mountain News* and other newspapers. Carr received extra publicity from an admiring spread in *Life* magazine a week before the election. Surviving press accounts of the race in the national press do not mention Japanese Americans as an issue. Rather, Johnson campaigned on full support of the war effort. Carr focused on opposing federal bureaucracy, including wage and price controls that curbed inflation. Nor did defeat permanently damage Carr's prospects. While the loss was a temporary blow to his career, Carr remained well regarded in Republican circles. Had Thomas Dewey won the White House, Carr could have expected a prominent post. He was leading in the polls for reelection as governor when he died.

As a counterpoint to Carr, I wish to discuss a second wartime Republican governor who demonstrated support for the Bill of Rights amid widespread calls for exclusion of Japanese Americans. Although his actions have remained curiously unnoticed, they had a decisive impact on the lives and fortunes of tens of thousands of people. During the last weeks of 1944, well-founded rumors spread over the West Coast that the Army planned to permit "loyal" Japanese Americans to return before war's end. Nativist and agricultural interest groups that had earlier fomented mass removal now campaigned to avert return, many using not-so-veiled threats of violence. They were seconded by a variety of political leaders. Republican vice presidential candidate John Bricker proposed local referendums on whether to permit return and Los Angeles mayor Fletcher Bowron lobbied for extending exclusion to avert race rioting. On November 18, 1944, the governor of the largest western state affirmed publicly that if the Army no longer considered exclusion of Japanese Americans a military necessity, he would ensure returnees "full recognition of their constitutional and statutory rights." When exclusion was lifted a month later, he promised Japanese Americans full protection and called for full and cheerful public compliance with their orderly return. He met personally with state law enforcement officials to handle potential disorders and denounced attacks by vigilantes as "atrocities."

Who was the principled politician whose courageous stand, amid widespread opposition, preserved Japanese Americans from danger? It was California Governor Earl Warren—a man usually considered a villain during the Nikkei saga due to his support for mass removal in 1942. Warren was no sterling champion of equality: even in 1945 he signed legislation to deny fishing licenses to Issei and fund escheat suits to strip Nisei GIs and others of their land. Nevertheless, due to his forthright and timely intervention, mass violence was averted and resettlement succeeded in California. By contrast, north of the Canadian border, in British Columbia, political leaders, citing public opposition, succeeded in forestalling return by ethnic Japanese until 1949.

HUGH MACBETH: AFRICAN AMERICAN DEFENDER OF JAPANESE AMERICANS

Hugh Macbeth, Sr., a black attorney from Los Angeles, is largely forgotten today, but he deserves commemoration as an outstanding defender of Japanese Americans during World War II. Born in Charleston, South Carolina, in 1884, Hugh Ellwood Macbeth attended Fisk University and Harvard Law School, graduating in 1908. After living for several years in Baltimore, where he was the founding editor of the *Baltimore Times* newspaper, in 1913 he headed to California.

In the decades that followed, Macbeth became an important player on the Los Angeles legal and political scene. He concentrated on aiding African American litigants and criminal defendants and represented such notable clients as jazz great Jelly Roll Morton. Macbeth pressed numerous cases challenging segregation laws and restrictive housing covenants. In 1940 he persuaded the American Legion to cease excluding black boxers from fight cards at Hollywood Legion Stadium. Yet his firm had many white clients, and he remained active in the larger society. In 1934 he was named general counsel for the Utopian Society, a largely white economic reform group that claimed 600,000 members. Although Macbeth's reach beyond the black community drew criticism, his broad connections led to his being named resident

FIGURE 5.3. Hugh Macbeth.

consul for the Republic of Liberia in 1936. Two years later, when Governor Frank Merriam created the California Race Relations Commission (CRRC), Macbeth, who had drafted the law establishing the commission, was named executive secretary and was the sole black commissioner.

Macbeth maintained close contacts with Japanese Americans. He settled near Los Angeles's Jefferson Park, then largely Japanese. Macbeth's son, Hugh Jr., who later became his law partner, recalled that as a child he attended Japanese school with his Nisei pals after school—otherwise, he would have had nobody in the neighborhood to play with. There Hugh, Jr. studied Japanese language and judo (and also absorbed community prejudices against Chinese and Filipinos). Meanwhile, the Macbeth family informally took in an orphaned Nisei, Kenji Horita.

In early January 1942, shortly after Pearl Harbor, Macbeth traveled to Guadalupe and Santa Barbara, California, to investigate the cases of Issei rounded up by the government during December and interned in Missoula, Montana. Following interviews with the internees' families, he discovered that those taken were prosperous farmers and that there was no evidence of sabotage. He swiftly concluded that white agricultural interests anxious to grab the Issei farmers' land engineered the removal. Outraged, Macbeth turned to organizing support for Japanese Americans among liberal and church groups. Thanks to Macbeth, the CRRC and the Santa Barbara Minister's Alliance would become the only two Southern California organizations to officially oppose "evacuation."

Macbeth simultaneously organized efforts nationwide. He corresponded with Socialist leader Norman Thomas, who used the information Macbeth provided in radio speeches and newspaper articles to denounce Executive Order 9066. Macbeth later cosigned Thomas's pamphlet, *Democracy and Japanese Americans*. The pamphlet decried the government's policy as "totalitarian justice" and called for an end to forced removal and for reparations.

The announcement of Executive Order 9066 on February 19, 1942, was a blow to Macbeth. On February 22, he sent President Franklin D. Roosevelt a telegram, asking him—now that his order had allayed fears of sabotage—to permit "liberty-loving Japanese" to resume their agricultural activities "under military surveillance and with government assistance." Meanwhile, he spoke privately of his grief at families being "torn up by the roots" and sent off from their homes "they know not where." In March 1942, he wrote General John DeWitt to propose that loyal farmers be permitted to form cooperatives and establish colonies in Utah. (The plan was designed by Hi Korematsu, whose brother Fred would soon challenge Executive Order 9066 in court.) Macbeth lectured the general, writing that removal reflected "general and deep seated

American racial prejudice against orientals and particularly against Japanese." Not unexpectedly, DeWitt failed to reply.

In May 1942, Macbeth visited the Santa Anita Assembly Center with his wife and brother to see friends and collect information on conditions. Shortly afterward, he traveled to Washington, DC, to brief Justice Department officials on Japanese Americans. (Using a White House cook, Macbeth attempted, without success, to secure a meeting with President Roosevelt in order to lobby for an executive order making racial discrimination a military offense.)

Upon returning to California, Macbeth joined ACLU attorney A. L. Wirin in defending Ernest and Toki Wakayama. Ernest Kinzo Wakayama, born in Hawaiʻi in 1897, was a union official, a World War I veteran, and an officer of the American Legion; Toki was a Nisei from California. The Wakayamas filed habeas corpus petitions asserting that there was no military necessity for evacuation and that DeWitt's exclusion order was arbitrary and a violation of their rights. In October 1942, a three-judge panel heard the petitions. In his supporting brief and oral argument, Macbeth charged that race-based confinement constituted unconstitutional discrimination. On February 4, 1943, the judges granted a writ of habeas corpus. However, by that time, the Wakayamas, worn down by large-scale beatings and ostracism at the Manzanar camp, had withdrawn their suit and requested repatriation to Japan.

Despite this defeat, Macbeth continued to aid Japanese Americans. He repeatedly wrote War Relocation Authority Director Dillon Myer with advice. At a public forum in Los Angeles in April 1943, he bravely spoke out in favor of letting Japanese Americans return to the West Coast. In 1943 he cowrote the Japanese American Citizens League (JACL) amicus brief in *Regan v. King* and he later signed briefs in the historic cases of *Hirabayashi v. United States* and *Korematsu v. United States*. Shortly afterward, he traveled to the Amache camp to counsel families of Nisei draft resisters. When Chiyoko Sakamoto, the first Nisei woman to be admitted to the bar, returned from camp in mid-1945 and was unable to find work, Macbeth hired her as his associate.

In 1945 Macbeth and his son joined JACL counsel A. L. Wirin in the case of Fred and Kojiro Oyama, who challenged California's Alien Land Law. In February 1945, they argued *People v. Oyama* in the San Diego County Superior Court. Wirin and Macbeth argued that alien land laws were out of date and penalized the defendants solely because of race. The judge ruled against the Oyamas, at which point Macbeth withdrew from the case. However, the decision was appealed and ultimately reached the Supreme Court. In January 1948, the high court granted victory to the Oyamas. *Oyama v. California* not only ended all enforcement of the Alien Land Law but furnished an important precedent for later rulings striking down racial segregation.

Hugh Macbeth, Sr., died in 1956. Although his career is obscure, his passion for justice remains inspiring.

Postscript

This article appeared in June 2007. It was one of the first that I published in *Nichi Bei Times*, and it really set the tone for the kind of column I intended to produce: more complex views of Japanese American history and rediscovery of unjustly forgotten figures of all backgrounds. It is also the article that has had the greatest impact. It has been linked and reprinted in blogs and cited in encyclopedia entries. I have been invited to speak about Macbeth's career at universities and law schools. I later expanded the *Nichi Bei Times* column into a full-length article, which appears in my 2012 book *After Camp: Portraits in Midcentury Japanese American Life and Politics*. I am gratified that Macbeth's actions have become more widely known among Japanese Americans. He was commemorated at the 2013 Manzanar Pilgrimage and leaders of San Francisco's Japanese community invited his son to be an honored guest at their 2009 Day of Remembrance ceremony for Executive Order 9066, as a gesture of appreciation to the family.

Another nice by-product of this work has been my good fortune to get to know Hugh Macbeth, Jr., who was his father's law associate and partner before setting up his own law office, eventually serving as a Superior Court judge. Hugh Jr. also followed in his father's footsteps in defending the rights of Japanese Americans. Not only did he join the legal team in *People v. Oyama*, he signed an amicus brief in support of the JACL in *Takahashi v. Fish & Game Commission*, in which the Supreme Court formally struck down all state laws that discriminated against "aliens ineligible to citizenship." He has been generous in sharing information and encouraging my research.

JOHN FRANKLIN CARTER: THE REAL-LIFE LANNY BUDD

In a series of popular novels published during the 1940s and 1950s, such as *Presidential Agent* (1944), author Upton Sinclair told the story of Lanny Budd. Lanny was an undercover agent for democracy against fascism, who used his guise as a playboy and an art dealer to infiltrate Nazi circles and perform special missions for the US government. In order to guard his secret, Lanny reported directly to President Franklin D. Roosevelt, who appeared as a character in the novels (Budd also received spirit messages from the ghost of banker and impresario Otto H. Kahn).

Sinclair's works were celebrated in their time as rousing thrillers but not taken as anything but fantasy. And indeed, Sinclair himself may have been unaware of anything more. Yet President Roosevelt made use of a number of confidential agents. Confined to a wheelchair by polio and limited by the demands of his office, he could not easily circulate to investigate conditions outside, although his wife, Eleanor, served as a roving investigator. Thus, he called on old friends such as Vincent Astor and Cornelius Vanderbilt II to collect intelligence on domestic and international affairs and provide reports. However, by far the most important confidential agent was John Franklin Carter, Jr., a novelist, political theorist, newspaper columnist, and government worker. Most notably, Carter and the intelligence team he formed were called on to study Japanese American communities before Pearl Harbor and offer secret guidance to the White House.

Carter was born in Fall River, Massachusetts, in 1897, one of seven children of the Rev. John Franklin Carter. He attended Yale University and was a classmate and pal of Thornton Wilder and Stephen Vincent Benet. During the 1920s, Carter was employed in the American Embassy in Rome and was a correspondent for the *London Daily Chronicle* and the *New York Times*. From 1928–1932, Carter served in Washington, DC, as a State Department official. During this time, he adopted a series of aliases—most notably "Jay Franklin," under which he wrote a series of popular newspaper and magazine articles on political topics to supplement his income. His books *What This Country Needs* (1931) and *What We Are About to Receive* (1932) explored methods of relieving the Great Depression through nonsocialist economic cooperation. (He also wrote a series of mystery novels under the pen name Diplomat.)

After Carter's identity was discovered and he was forced to resign from the government in 1932, he started a nationally syndicated daily newspaper column, We the People, under his Jay Franklin byline. In the late 1930s, Carter also made regular appearances on NBC as a radio commentator. Meanwhile, under the pseudonym The Unofficial Observer, Carter wrote a series of portraits for *Liberty* magazine of staffers from the new Roosevelt administration, which were collected into a pioneering study, *The New Dealers* (1934). An enthusiastic New Dealer himself, Carter was hired by the Department of Agriculture to write speeches and articles championing the conservation efforts of the Tennessee Valley Authority.

Throughout the 1930s, Carter acted sporadically as unofficial idea man and speechwriter for President Roosevelt. In early 1940, he called for the president to be nominated for an unprecedented third term in office and used his column to back Roosevelt's reelection as indispensable to national security. After FDR won the election in November, Carter was emboldened to ask for a reward. Beyond owing Carter favors, Roosevelt was also displeased by the quality of official intelligence reports. Thus, in January 1941, he hired Carter to create and coordinate a secret White House information-gathering operation, making him a real-life precursor of Lanny Budd.

Using State Department and White House funds, Carter set up a secret spy team in the White House basement (even as he continued his newspaper column). His agents were dispatched to investigate such diverse topics as new weapon and ship designs, Nazi influence in South Africa, and political conditions in Martinique. Carter saw the president several times a week and kept him personally informed of his agents' findings. He also attempted to serve as liaison between the White House and Ernst "Putzi" Hanfstaengl, a high-ranking Nazi defector. Furthermore, at the president's orders, Carter oversaw the top secret M Project, a massive series of confidential anthropological reports on migration, which Roosevelt planned to use as a basis for arranging postwar resettlement of Jewish and other refugees in South America.

Perhaps Carter's most significant contribution was his investigation of Japanese Americans. In fall 1941, Roosevelt asked Carter to mobilize his team to report on the loyalty of West Coast Japanese communities. Although various government agencies, including the Federal Bureau of Investigation and the Office of Naval Intelligence (ONI), had been keeping tabs on Issei and Nisei for several years, Roosevelt wanted a clear understanding of their sentiments. Carter sent his top agent, Curtis Munson, to the West Coast and Hawai'i, while agent Warren Irwin checked up on ethnic Japanese in the Southwest and on the Mexican border. In October 1941, Munson visited Southern California, where he met with Col. Kenneth Ringle of the ONI—the most knowledgeable intelligence officer on Japanese communities—plus local FBI agents. He also interviewed various Japanese Americans.

Munson quickly sent a series of bulletins to Carter with the message that West Coast Japanese Americans were overwhelmingly loyal and would support the United States in case of war with Japan. He added that the Nisei in particular were pathetically eager to show their patriotism. In November he sent a full report that amplified the message that there was no threat; he insisted that the greatest danger to security in case of war did not lie in the threat of sabotage or subversive acts by Japanese Americans but in racist mob violence against them. Munson and Irwin, who shared his views, each urged the White House to take action to preserve the loyalty of the Nisei through supportive public statements by political leaders. Munson added prophetically that the best way to ensure such loyalty was to promise Issei and Nisei that they would not be rounded up and put into concentration camps in the event of war. Carter not only passed along Munson's findings to the president, but with FDR's approval he began designing plans to protect loyal Japanese Americans from violence in case of war.

Although the Japanese attack on Pearl Harbor threw new suspicion on Japanese Americans, Carter remained convinced of their Americanism, and he opposed the growing pressure for mass removal of West Coast Japanese Americans. With help from Munson and Ringle, he lobbied Roosevelt to recognize loyal Nisei by placing them in control of community affairs. While FDR initially gave Carter permission to proceed, the opposition of General DeWitt and the War Department stymied him. He was so frustrated that on February 9, 1942, he wrote in his We the People column that, even though the loyalty of Japanese Americans had been reliably estimated at 98 percent before the war, the official harassment they had suffered and the failure of the government to understand them, either as individuals or as a group, led to that figure falling to 90 percent, and the support of the entire community was menaced.

Carter continued to head his service throughout the war years. After Roosevelt's death in 1945, Carter maintained the operation of his intelligence unit for a few months under his successor, President Harry Truman. After leaving the government at the end of 1945, Carter published a fascinating novel, *The Catoctin Conversation* (1947), under the name Jay Franklin, in which Franklin Roosevelt is a central character. Carter's FDR, whose words and ideas drew from Carter's extensive real-life familiarity with the president, agrees that mass removal of Japanese Americans was wrong but that he had no choice but to order it: "The Army asked for special status on the Pacific Coast. After Pearl Harbor, they were entitled to get what they said they needed. Once they had this status, they decided that the Japanese-Americans must move east of the Rockies. I had no choice but to back them or discredit them." On the other hand, when challenged, Roosevelt says, "When the war is over, they'll go back . . . It's a small matter compared to the war itself." Carter's dramatization of Roosevelt's pragmatic and uncaring attitude rings true.

In 1948 Carter signed on as an advisor and speechwriter for Truman in his reelection campaign. Sadly, Carter was fired after the election for writing popular articles on his work that disturbed the president. Carter then switched sides and joined the Republicans, working first for Thomas Dewey—Truman's erstwhile opponent—and later for Nelson Rockefeller. In his later years he emerged as an archconservative. Although Carter was largely forgotten by the time of his death in 1967, he deserves to be rediscovered. He made important contributions to the Allied victory during his wartime stint as a confidential agent, while his writings continue to bear study as an incisive example of American political theory and analysis.

NOTES

1. This article is adapted from Greg Robinson, "Norman Thomas and the Struggle Against Japanese Internment," *Prospects: An Annual of American Cultural Studies* 29 (2004), 419–34.

2. Togo Tanaka, "Mrs. Roosevelt Talks to Local Representatives," *Rafu Shimpo*, November 1, 1941, 3–4.

3. Doris Kearns Goodwin, *No Ordinary Time* (New York: Simon & Schuster, 1994), 323.

6

Political Activism and Civil Rights

In fall 1906, the San Francisco School Board, in a move inspired by anti-Japanese prejudice, excluded all Nikkei children from public schools and ordered them to attend separate "oriental" schools. The children's parents were outraged by the segregation, and with the support of the Japanese consulate, they decided to fight it in court. However, instead of depending on white lawyers, as usual, community leaders decided to approach Masuji Miyakawa, a Japanese immigrant who had already gained a reputation as an attorney. Through the case, Miyakawa gained fame as a defender of civil rights for Japanese Americans, to which he added laurels as journalist, lecturer, and penetrating student of American life.

Born to an elite family in Fukushima, Japan, in 1870, Masuji Miyakawa migrated to the United States in 1896. After settling in San Francisco, where he worked for a short time as a teacher and court interpreter, Miyakawa decided to become a lawyer. With financial aid from local Japanese, he moved east, and over the following years took courses at St. Joseph's College,

DOI: 10.5876/9781607324294.c006

FIGURE 6.1. Masuji Miyakawa.

George Washington University (then known as Columbian University), and eventually Indiana University Law School, where he received his law degree in 1905. After graduation, he was accepted to the Indiana state bar—becoming the first and only Japanese-born attorney permitted to practice in the United States in the first half of the twentieth century—and then returned to San Francisco, where he opened shop.

In addition to pursuing his work as an attorney, Miyakawa hoped to use Western models of constitutional law to promote liberal democracy in Japan. He began writing an English-language book (commissioned, it was rumored, by friends in the Japanese government) that discussed the effects of modernization on Japanese society. *Life of Japan*, published in 1907, earned Miyakawa glowing reviews from American commentators. Its success prompted him to expand on his ideas in a book published the following year, *Powers of the American People, Congress, President, and Courts: (According to the Evolution of Constitutional Construction)*, which analyzed American government and explained American constitutional law to foreigners. The work resembles Alexis de Tocqueville's classic *Democracy in America* in its emphasis on equality in American society and the role of private associations in training Americans for citizenship. Miyakawa's expressed support for democracy was qualified by certain elitist and racist assumptions about the inferiority of blacks and Chinese. Nevertheless, he claimed that by imposing equal treatment under the law, democratic society could breach barriers between diverse cultures.

Miyakawa's cosmopolitan attitude and emphasis on the rule of law in building democracy were underlined by his involvement in a case against the San Francisco School Board. Miyakawa agreed to take the case after representatives of the Nikkei schoolchildren approached him to bring suit against the segregation policy. As he later described it, his reasons were legalistic rather than egalitarian: exclusion of Japanese was clearly illegal, since under California law only Chinese and "Mongolians" could be segregated. (Not only were the Japanese not Mongolians, he added, but they had saved Europe from the Mongol hordes in the thirteenth century by resisting the invasion force of Kublai Khan.) At the same time, Miyakawa shocked his clients by telling them to not rely on the Japanese government to intercede for them but to fight discrimination as Americans, under principles of American law: "An individual Japanese . . . cannot be called great and respectable simply because his nation is great and respectable . . . [he must here prove] that he can speak the English language better than others, that he is more law-abiding than the others, more enlightened in idea and his conception of things American than the others, and that he is educationally, intellectually, morally, and industriously much stronger than the others." Miyakawa's sense of Japanese Americans as models of modernity—more educated and enlightened than

Westerners—was an unusual attitude to take at a time when most white Americans considered Asians to be unalterably backward and foreign.

In November 1906, Miyakawa began arguing the case in circuit court. However, the matter was almost immediately suspended by intervention from the federal government. President Theodore Roosevelt, who worried that the segregation policy might offend Japan and lead to war between the two nations, asked the school board to withdraw its policy. In exchange, he promised to restrict Japanese laborers. When Roosevelt invited San Francisco mayor Eugene Schmitz and city officials to the White House to confer, Miyakawa raced to Washington, DC, to present the case for Japanese Americans and to lobby against total exclusion. In the end, the school board agreed to withdraw the policy. Roosevelt negotiated a deal with the Japanese government—the so-called Gentlemen's Agreement—whereby Tokyo agreed to not grant exit visas to laborers but ensured that immigrants could still bring over wives and children.

Even though the school board case was never argued in court, Miyakawa's defense of Nikkei civil rights made him famous nationally. He received several honorary degrees and was commended by the American Bar Association, which chose him as editor of its comparative law section. He was appointed to the chair of comparative constitutional law at Indiana University and taught there and at Illinois College. Meanwhile, with sponsorship by prominent whites, Miyakawa successfully petitioned for naturalization. (In the process, he became one of the rare Japanese who won American citizenship in the years before 1922, when the US Supreme Court ruled that all Japanese immigrants were racially ineligible for naturalization.) Throughout this period, Miyakawa made Washington, DC, his base and served as an unofficial lobbyist for Japan. He also made several tours as a lecturer and goodwill ambassador for Japan, promoting peace and popular understanding. (Sometimes his appearances were accompanied by a film he had made showing scenes of Japanese life—one of the first Japanese motion pictures.) In 1913 Miyakawa moved to New York City, where he founded a short-lived magazine, the *Japan Review*.

Following the outbreak of World War I in 1914, Miyakawa traveled to Vladivostok on a mission for the Japanese consul. He became ill during his adventure and spent several months resting in Hawai'i and the American South, in hope of regaining his health. He nonetheless remained frail and died suddenly while in Los Angeles on March 1, 1916. Japanese community leaders and influential whites from across the West Coast attended his funeral.

The Family behind *Oyama v. California*

One element that makes American democracy so distinctive is the power our system grants judges. The courts, from the local level up to the US Supreme Court, enjoy great authority to interpret the constitution and to overturn laws they deem unconstitutional. There is a catch, though: judges are dependent upon citizen action. Since the courts can only act when they have an actual case before them, it requires a person to bring suit or appeal for justice to take its course. It is inspiring to note that many of the cases which led to historic reforms were brought by ordinary people, without fortune or great reputation, who stood up for what they believed. Prominent among this small honor roll of everyday heroes are Kajiro and Fred Oyama, who successfully challenged California's Alien Land Law in the Supreme Court.

Kajiro Oyama was born in Wakayama Prefecture in 1899. With encouragement from a teacher in Japan, who suggested he attend the California Institute of Technology, he moved to the United States in 1914. However, he was unable to complete his education and became a farmer to make a living. In 1923 he brought over from Japan a bride—Kohide Kushino—a Wakayama girl whom he had known since elementary school. They settled in Chula Vista, near San Diego, where they had five children over the following years. Their first son, Fred Yoshihiro Oyama, was born in 1926 (1928, according to some sources).

Kajiro worked hard to support his family by growing celery, tomatoes, and other crops. He prospered sufficiently that he and his wife were able to travel to Japan with the younger children in 1935. After returning, the family settled outside San Clemente, near San Juan Capistrano. Meanwhile, Kajiro sought to buy farmland in Chula Vista. Under California's Alien Land Law, enacted in 1913 and upheld by the Supreme Court ten years later, he was forbidden to own agricultural property because he was "ineligible for citizenship" as a Japanese immigrant. However, while the law was seldom enforced against violators—barely a dozen suits were filed in its first thirty years—Kajiro was an extremely methodical man and preferred to use legally sanctioned means. Therefore, when he purchased a plot in 1934, paying $4,000 for it, he gave title

FIGURE 6.2. Fred Oyama.

to his young son Fred, since, as an American citizen, the boy could own property. He then had himself appointed Fred's official guardian in order to hold the land for him. In 1937 Kajiro bought Fred a second parcel of land, worth $1,500, on the farm of Kohide's brother and his family.

In spring 1942, following Executive Order 9066, the Oyamas were forced to leave their land. Unlike the overwhelming majority of Japanese Americans, they were able to avoid camp. Thanks to a seed salesman Kajiro had dealt with, who offered to lease them a farm near Cedar City, Utah, they left the West Coast during the brief period of "voluntary evacuation." After briefly farming that property, they settled in a house near Provo, Utah.

Meanwhile, members of the California Legislature, hoping to prevent excluded Japanese Americans from returning to the state, voted in a series of restrictive laws. One measure funded escheat suits under the Alien Land Law to take away property illegally acquired by Japanese aliens; within a few years, some fifty-nine cases were brought. Many Japanese Americans, faced with such challenges, lost their land or paid extra money to the state to quiet title. In 1944 Attorney General Robert Kenny commenced an escheat proceeding against Kajiro, claiming that he had fraudulently transferred land to Fred in order to evade the law and that the "vacant" property belonged to the state. While Kajiro had little money, he determined to bring a legal case. Upon their return to California, the Oyamas and their neighbors formed the Society for the Promotion of Japanese-American Civil Rights to raise money.

The Japanese American Citizens League (JACL) took up the Oyamas' case; they agreed to fund it because Nisei leaders admired Kajiro's determination. Furthermore, since Kajiro had been officially appointed his son's legal guardian, he had a particularly strong defense. JACL counsel A. L. Wirin (supported by Hugh Macbeth, an African American lawyer from Los Angeles) was engaged to handle the case, which went to trial in San Diego Superior Court in early 1945, along with a sister case. Wirin and Macbeth argued, among other points, that alien land laws were racist in inspiration and unconstitutionally deprived Japanese Americans of equal protection on a racial basis. The trial judge refused to examine the law's constitutionality and ruled against the Oyamas. With the aid of James Purcell (Mitsuye Endo's former attorney), who replaced Macbeth, Wirin then appealed to the California Supreme Court, which nonetheless upheld the Alien Land Law, in the process overturning many earlier court decisions authorizing Issei to serve as legal guardians for minors.

The JACL elected to appeal to the US Supreme Court, which agreed to hear the case in fall 1947. Wirin decided the best strategy was to focus on Fred Oyama and to argue that the law placed an unfair burden on citizens of Japanese ancestry, based on their race, to prove that they had not received property from Issei parents in order to evade the law. Wirin concluded that there was a strong presumption against any "race" legislation and that courts should rigorously scrutinize such laws rather than assume they were constitutional. The JACL scored a further coup when a distinguished lawyer, Dean Acheson (who soon after was appointed US Secretary of State), agreed to present the JACL's appeal before the Court.

In January 1948, the Supreme Court ruled 6–3 in *Oyama v. California* that the Oyamas could keep their land. Chief Justice Fred Vinson proclaimed that only the most exceptional circumstances could constitutionally justify any laws that made "racial classifications" among citizens. This new doctrine (which originated, ironically, in the Court's notorious 1944 *Korematsu* decision upholding Japanese American evacuation) would soon be developed in cases involving African Americans and would serve as precedent for the Court's historic *Brown v. Board of Education* school desegregation decision seven years later. The *Oyama* decision also saved many Japanese Americans. Although the Court did not decide whether alien land laws could be enforced against aliens, California immediately halted all escheat actions afterward.

Kajiro Oyama continued to work his land. He lived to a great age, dying in 1998. Fred Oyama became a schoolteacher. However, he never abandoned his love for farming, and he still grows crops on his property in Escondido. He is modest about his role in his family's case but speaks with pride of his father's achievements.

REGAN V. KING: WHEN BIRTHRIGHT CITIZENSHIP WAS LAST TESTED

One interesting way of examining current-day controversies over race, immigration, and birthright citizenship is through the historical prism of the 1942–1943 legal case *Regan v. King*. In this case, arising in the wake of Executive Order 9066, West Coast nativists from the American Legion and the Native Sons of the Golden West brought suit in federal court to disenfranchise Nisei. Their openly expressed purpose was to erase the citizenship of all Asian Americans by overturning the 1898 US Supreme Court case *United States v. Wong Kim Ark*, which had enshrined the principle of automatic birthright citizenship for all persons born in the United States. The lawsuit thereby brought to an ultimate climax the long-standing campaign by nativists, informed by racism, against all Asian immigrants and their US-born children. In response to the suit, lawyers from the American Civil Liberties Union, the Japanese American Citizens League (JACL), and the NAACP, joining forces for the first time, rallied to defend fundamental citizenship rights. In the end, the suit was defeated at both the district and appellate court level. It is worth looking closely at the *Regan* case, as it not only established the basic constitutional rights of the Nisei in a climate of popular hostility against them, but it reaffirmed the principle of birthright citizenship for all Americans.

How did *Regan* come about? As is well known, during spring 1942, over 100,000 Japanese Americans living across the Pacific coast were removed from their homes by the US Army, under authority of Executive Order 9066, and placed in a series of holding areas, or assembly centers, then shipped inland for confinement in a network of ten government camps. In the wake of these official actions, the Native Sons of the Golden West, a California nativist fraternity that had led the prewar movement for Japanese exclusion, threw themselves into action. In May 1942, their 65th Grand Parlor (i.e., convention) met at Hoberg's resort. The keynote speech was delivered by Ulysses S. Webb, who had served as California attorney general for thirty-six years. After calling for the full prosecution of the Pacific war, Webb turned to his real motivation for action: "The productivity of the Japanese constitutes a definite threat which must be obviated by a reinterpretation of the constitution or a constitutional amendment." The convention officially resolved to have the incoming grand president, Lloyd Congrove, create a committee of five persons to raise money "first to prosecute, then to carry through to the Supreme Court of the United States, if necessary, a suit challenging the United States citizenship of the Japanese; and second to draft and sponsor an amendment to the Constitution of the United States which shall have for its object the exclusion of all persons of Japanese ancestry from American citizenship."

In addition to the prestige lent the case by the presence of Webb, the Native Sons' campaign received important backing from the incumbent attorney general, future US chief justice Earl Warren. According to an account in the *Oakland Tribune*, Warren pledged his support in his banquet speech at the Grand Parlor: "Warren stated he strongly favored prosecution of the suits now pending in the federal courts to determine if any Japanese can become a citizen and vote. Warren said further action depends upon new interpretation of the law by higher courts which now makes it possible for Japanese to hold property and vote. Following the judicial determination, other methods will be studied to meet the situation, he said." Warren then served as keynote speaker at the Native Daughters of the Golden West's convention, in which the resolutions of support were voted.

To be sure, Warren's endorsement was limited. Unlike Webb, he justified action on the basis of security, not race. Also, he did not approve any constitutional amendment; he called only for "study" of other methods should a test case fail. After the convention, he refused to discuss the matter. A fair conclusion is that Warren, who had announced in April his candidacy for governor (to which he was elected that fall), made a single hedged statement supporting the suit as a necessary profession of faith to retain the political support of the Native Sons, long his chief backers. Still, as the state's chief law enforcement official, Warren lent quasi-official status to the lawsuit by his assent.

On May 7, 1942 (a few days before the start of the convention), John T. Regan, longtime grand secretary of the Native Sons, sued Cameron King, as registrar of voters in San Francisco County, to remove ninety named Nisei from the voting rolls for the August 1942 primaries and to deprive them of voting "privileges," at least for the duration of the war. Although the complaint ostensibly touched only on voting, the publicly avowed purpose of the suit was as an initial step toward overturning the 1898 Supreme Court *Wong Kim Ark* decision and annulling the US citizenship of all descendants of "aliens ineligible to citizenship." Webb agreed to act as attorney on the case (as well as a similar lawsuit in Oakland brought by the American Legion, which was later dropped for other reasons).

The *Regan* case was argued in federal district court in the last week of June 1942. Japanese Americans, locked in assembly centers and barred from the coast, were not able to be present at the hearing, and it does not appear that any Japanese American organizations sent non-Japanese observers. Webb told Judge Adolphus St. Sure that the case "involves the citizenship and right to citizenship of all peoples and all races who do not fall within the characterization or description of white people." He then made an argument that rested unabashedly on principles of white supremacy. Pointing to the origins of the nation, Webb insisted that, except where American Indians were involved, the country was settled by "a cosmopolitan population composed of every European people, all of whom were members of . . . the Caucasian race." Only white people had fought at Lexington, Bunker Hill, and Valley Forge. He then added that the Declaration of Independence was made entirely "by and for white people," as was the constitution. Walter Dold, assistant city attorney of San Francisco, responded rather blandly that the Supreme Court had established in *Wong Kim Ark* that all those born in America, irrespective of ancestry, were US citizens.

On July 2, 1942, less than a week after the close of arguments, Judge St. Sure issued his decision in *Regan v. King*. In it, he flatly rejected the Native Sons' plea: "It is unnecessary to discuss the arguments of counsel. In my opinion, the law is settled by the decisions of the United States Supreme Court just alluded to." Webb quickly announced that he would appeal the decision directly to the Supreme Court, which he believed might reverse its previous decision. Instead, in late September, he filed an appeal to the Ninth Circuit Court of Appeals. His brief, submitted just before Christmas, repeated his historical argument that the nation was founded by and for white people only. Using the removal policy as evidence of dangers, he went on to present the case against Nisei citizenship in starkly racist terms: "Because of racial characteristics of the Japanese, assimilation with Caucasians is as impossible as it is undesirable . . . The off-spring of Japanese wherever born are taught the Japanese faith and pledged to its observance. Dishonesty, deceit and hypocrisy are racial characteristics [of all Japanese]."

The Native Sons appeal in the *Regan* case catalyzed the intervention of a notable pair of new players: the JACL and the NAACP. At that point, the JACL, the largest prewar Nisei organization, was financially strapped and embattled—from the outside by mass removal and from inside the Japanese community by its reluctant decision to offer the federal government its assistance with mass removal. Although the JACL did speak out against attempts to restrict permanent citizenship rights of Japanese Americans, the organization apparently did not consider taking part in the *Regan* case until its Special Emergency National Conference, held in Salt Lake City, November 17–24, 1942. A. L. Wirin of the Southern California ACLU (a notable civil rights lawyer who had left his previous law firm in order to defend Japanese Americans in court cases) gave an update on the various test cases challenging Executive Order 9066. He spoke briefly about *Regan* and suggested that in case of an appeal, the JACL might want to intervene.

Soon after, the JACL approved the preparation of an amicus brief in opposition to the Native Sons, and national president Saburo Kido and Walter Tsukamoto, past president, volunteered to draft it. However, both Kido and Tsukamoto were confined in government camps, far from law libraries and proper office facilities. Thus, doubtless at Wirin's suggestion, they reached out to Hugh Macbeth, a maverick African American attorney from Los Angeles who had served as director of the California Race Relations Commission and had been an outstanding defender of Japanese Americans. Macbeth not only agreed to work with the JACL, but in turn recruited the NAACP's Southern California branch president, Thomas L. Griffith. (Loren Miller, another African American lawyer who frequently worked with the NAACP, signed the amicus of the National Lawyers Guild.)

The JACL's amicus, which listed Kido, Tsukamoto, Macbeth, Griffith, and Wirin as counsel, was filed on February 17, 1943, two days before oral arguments began. Perhaps the most striking and original section of the document was located in its latter half. The brief pointed out that the Native Sons' case was, in fact, directed at many other groups, including American Indians and Americans of Chinese, Korean, Filipino, and East Indian ancestry, whose citizenship the Native Sons had declared to be "repellant." The brief then explored what it termed the "Interests of Negroes and this case." In this section—which may well have been drafted by Macbeth—the brief ridiculed the disingenuous suggestion of the Native Sons that the citizenship of African Americans was not in question. Pointing to larger connections between opponents of equality for Japanese Americans and blacks, the authors reminded the judges that Native Sons leaders had claimed in recent testimony to Congress that granting citizenship to blacks after the Civil War had been a "grave mistake." They added that if the Native Sons lawsuit was successful, the next step of such "Hitlerism" would be the introduction of a constitutional amendment to deprive Negroes of citizenship." The brief then made an extended comparison between statements of official Nazi ideology and the arguments of the Native Sons.

The case of *Regan v. King* was set down for oral argument before the court of appeals sitting en banc (that is, by all seven judges). Ironically, the day chosen for the hearing was February 19, 1943, the very same day the court considered the appeals in the "Japanese internment" cases of *Korematsu*, *Hirabayashi*, and *Yasui*, in which Nisei plaintiffs challenged Executive Order

9066. Webb made a thirty-minute presentation of his appeal. He again stated that "without committing treason," it was his contention that *Wong Kim Ark* had been "erroneously decided." Having presented his case, Webb left the podium. Walter Dodd then rose to take the defense case, with A. L. Wirin waiting to present the JACL position afterward. However, no sooner had Webb completed his argument than the judges, instead of taking a recess, put their heads together in hasty conference. After a few minutes, Judge Curtis proclaimed on behalf of the court, "It is not necessary for the court to hear further argument. The decision of the lower court is sustained." The court then immediately called the cases of *Hirabayashi* and *Korematsu*, which occupied the rest of the day's proceedings.

The Native Sons, continuing their campaign for exclusion, launched an appeal to the Supreme Court. Their petition was publicly supported on the floor of Congress by Tennessee senator Tom Stewart, who had previously introduced legislation to confine Japanese Americans in military prisons for the duration of the war. Calling for the Court to take jurisdiction of the case and overturn the "unsound" *Wong Kim Ark* decision, Stewart insisted that Japanese in the United States "[h]aven't got the American ideal, and never can have," since treachery, deception, and arrogance are "inborn characteristics of the race." Webb's petition for certiorari to the Supreme Court was filed on April 28, 1943. However, on May 17, less than a week after it heard arguments in the *Hirabayashi* and *Yasui* cases, the high court refused the petition. The *Regan* case was dead.

The failure of the lawsuit in *Regan* preserved the rights of all Americans to birthright citizenship from challenge. An important share of credit for the defense of basic rights must go to the JACL and the NAACP lawyers who anchored its legal team. (Indeed, the Nisei editor of the *Poston Chronicle*, a War Relocation Authority camp newspaper, declared that the intervention of the JACL in the *Regan* case, and especially the presence of the black attorneys alongside them, was even more significant than the end result.) By both their presence and their arguments, the African Americans dramatized the central role of racist bigotry in the movement to erase birthright citizenship.

Still, even if the judges were unanimous in their decisions, it was a narrow victory. If either the trial court or the Ninth Circuit Court of Appeals had ruled the other way, it is difficult to know what would have ensued and whether there would have been a popular movement to strip citizenship from Asian Americans. The case has considerable contemporary resonance. As recently as 2010, there was still serious talk, in Arizona and elsewhere, of stripping citizenship from native-born children of undocumented immigrants. The *Regan* case provides an essential historical reminder and constitutional reference point.

YASUO SASAKI: POET, PHYSICIAN, AND ABORTION RIGHTS PIONEER

Dr. Yasuo Sasaki was a pioneering Nisei poet and intellectual as well as a scientist, physician, and fighter for reproductive freedom. Beginning at an early age, he worked to unite the twin strands of his family heritage—medicine and literature—and pursued both throughout his career.

Sasaki was the scion of a long line of doctors. His great-grandfather had been a doctor of Chinese medicine in Japan who worked for a samurai family during the Edo period as well as serving the public. Sasaki's paternal grandfather was a physician who studied German medicine at what was then Tokyo Medical School (part of today's University of Tokyo). Yet Yas's father, Shuichi (George) Sasaki, did not practice medicine; instead, he yearned to be a writer. Born in 1883 near today's Iwaki City in Fukushima Prefecture, Shuichi Sasaki traveled to Tokyo in 1902 to study Japanese and Chinese literature at Waseda University (then called the Tokyo Professional School). Three years later, he came to the United States and settled, successively, in Oregon and Idaho, attending school during the winter and working as a picker in the radish fields during the summer.

After sojourning in Japan for eighteen months following his father's death in 1909, he returned to Idaho with a Japanese bride. The couple would eventually have seven children, including three sons. A few years later, the family moved to Salt Lake City, Utah, where Shuichi found work. When he was not struggling to earn money to support his large family, he was employed as a poet and journalist, working under the name Sasabune Sasaki. He later wrote a series of Japanese-language books—notably *Amerika Seikatsu* (*Life in America*) (1937), a set of short articles and essays, and *Yokuryujo Seikatsuki* (*Life in Camp*) (1950), a memoir of his experience as an enemy alien interned at Missoula, Montana.

Yas, the eldest child, was born in Idaho on October 31, 1911, and grew up in Salt Lake City. A skilled violinist, at one time he had ambitions to launch a concert career. After attending Granite High School, where he won a coveted chemistry prize, he enrolled at the University of Utah in the late 1920s. He continued his science education in preparation for a medical career, was elected to Phi Beta Kappa in December 1932, and graduated in 1933 with high honors. At the same time, he wrote for the student literary magazine *University Pen*, won a prize for his poetry in the Gleam Scribbler contest—a university competition sponsored by a pair of literary fraternities—and was selected to read the class poem at Class Day exercises.

Yas's literary activities extended far beyond his campus exploits. With a group of friends in Salt Lake City he founded *Reimei*, the first Nisei literary magazine, in 1931. His goal was to encourage Japanese Americans to take pride in their Japanese ancestry and draw from their cultural heritage in their self-expression. In the magazine's initial issue, he wrote a slightly grandiloquent preface to his Nisei readers: "This is our apology in presenting you the *Reimei*. We only desire you to accept it as your own—for you to gain closer intimacy with the people who harboring under the same Star, have the same problems, a like destiny, the same ideals: for you to become a participant in our effort to ward off all handicaps and strive for the goal—perfection in life." Over the following two years, four issues of *Reimei* were produced, with contributions by such notable Nisei authors as Taro Katayama, Tosuke Yamasaki, and Chiye Mori as well as Hoshina Airan (the pseudonym of a white friend who joined the group). Issues of *Reimei* also featured translated excerpts from French writer Kikou Yamata's 1925 romance *Masako*—the first published novel by a Nisei. In addition to editing the journal, Yas contributed poems, a review of Willa Cather's *My Antonia*, and a pastiche dialogue based on Lady Murasaki's *The Tale of Genji*.

Even as he directed *Reimei*, Sasaki contributed various pieces to West Coast Nisei newspapers. In 1932 he wrote a short tale, "Young Atheists," for the first Sunday literary page of *Kashu Mainichi*. Editor Larry Tajiri later pronounced it "one of the finest short stories to be published by the Nisei press." In 1933, following his graduation from the University of Utah, Sasaki traveled to Los Angeles, where his family had previously moved from Utah. He stayed with the Socialist activist Joseph Hansen, who discussed political theory with him and persuaded him to read the work of Leon Trotsky (to whom Hansen would later serve as secretary). Sasaki would long remain influenced by Trotsky's ideas. Meanwhile, he joined the staff of the Nisei newspaper *Shin*

FIGURE 6.3. Cover of the review *Reimei*, 1936.

Sekai and fell in with a local circle of literary Nisei who called themselves the Nisei Writers Group. Along with Carl Kondo, he edited their mimeographed magazine, *Leaves*. (At least three issues of *Leaves* were ultimately published, but only one exists in any public archive.) Through the writers group, he met a local Nisei writer and columnist, Mary Oyama (later Mary Oyama Mittwer), who in turn introduced him to her younger sister Lily. Lily was a talented artist who had studied for a year at the Otis College of Art and Design. She and Yas were married in 1937 and remained together for over seventy years. They soon had a daughter, Averil Miye (Mimi) Sasaki.

In fall 1933, Yas accepted a scholarship to the University of Cincinnati, where he was also employed as an assistant instructor in the Biochemistry Department. He received his PhD from Cincinnati in 1936. His doctoral thesis, "The effect of vitamin B1 deficiency on the lipides of the central nervous system," concerned the nervous disease beriberi, which had roots in malnutrition. In the process of his doctoral research, Yas grew interested in pellagra, a nutritional deficiency disease widespread in the American South. Following graduation, he spent six months in Birmingham, Alabama, which he later called "a fascinating experience." Working at the Hillman Hospital—a charity hospital—he witnessed the depressed conditions among poor whites and backs, which deeply moved him. Sasaki was a central researcher in a medical team led by Dr. Thomas Spies, and together with Spies and Esther Gross he authored a pair of published medical journal articles on pellagra in 1938. (That same year, Spies and two other colleagues were awarded *Time* magazine's "Man of the Year" distinction for science after proving that vitamin therapy with niacin would cure pellagra in humans.)

Throughout this time, Yas remained absorbed in literary work. In 1937 he began a regular column for *Nichi Bei* titled Bioscheme, in which he discussed literary and political topics, with the goal of awakening his Nisei readers' social conscience. For example, a January 1938 column reviewed John Steinbeck's now-classic novel *Of Mice and Men*—then newly published—and praised its depiction of life among the poor (this included Mexican laborers, he reminded his Nisei audience). In 1939 he toured the Midwest and South and published a series for *Nichi Bei* and *Rafu Shimpo* titled "A Nisei Discovers America." Soon after, in another article in *Rafu*, titled "The Negroes' Problem," he analyzed the different sides of the struggle for racial equality among black Americans. Praising the "surging movement" among blacks "for the ultimate victory of democratic ways," Sasaki argued that the Nisei might do well to consider adopting similar strategies of militant protest.

In May 1939, he returned to Los Angeles, where he organized another literary group, the League of Nisei Writers and Artists, and helped put together its mimeographed publication, *The Letter*, to which he contributed a book review. When the League was attacked as an antifascist group, he commented, "Politically, all we provide for is a defense of democratic ideals, including civil rights and freedom of thought and press. We stand for the highest ideals of the American way and are striving to be loyal, progressive citizens . . . Primarily, of course, we are a fellowship of those who love to write or draw."

There is some uncertainty about developments over the following years. What is clear is that after leaving Birmingham, Yas worked in the dispensary at Cincinnati's Longview Hospital, an institution for mental disorders. He received his MD in 1941 from the University of Cincinnati College of Medicine, and one source from 1941 listed him as being on the staff of St. Mary's Hospital in Cincinnati. He was geographically separated during this time from Lily, who was living with the Sasaki family in Los Angeles. In 1942, when West Coast Japanese Americans were rounded up following Executive Order 9066, Lily and Mimi accompanied the Sasaki family to the Grenada camp. (Shuichi, who had been interned after Pearl Harbor at Missoula, was released after a few months and ultimately joined the family in Grenada.) Presumably in order to complete his medical studies, Yas remained in Cincinnati, outside the excluded zone. After graduation, he opened a medical practice in the nearby town of Covington, Kentucky.

In the years after World War II, the Sasaki family settled in Covington. Lily painted, made clay figurines, and cared for Mimi and a new baby, Brian, born after Lily's release from camp. She also kept up a lively correspondence with her sister, Mary Oyama Mittwer, who worked as a columnist for *Rafu Shimpo*, and engaged in encouraging Nisei littérateurs.

Yas, for his part, also continued his interest in literature and politics. During the 1960s, he published in the Cincinnati-based poetry journal *Mt. Adams Review* and produced a slim volume of verse, *Ascension: Poems of Vintage, 1967* (1968), a set of brief poems that detailed his reactions to the events of the 1960s. Three of his poems later appeared in the 1980 Japanese American anthology *Ayumi*. A second poetry volume, *Village Scene, Village Herd: Poems of Vintage 1968 and Sequel*, though planned for release in the mid-1970s, did not appear until 1986. Still, Yas's literary and political interests took something of a backseat as he concentrated on his family life and burgeoning medical practice (which moved to the neighboring town of Newport and, in 1970, to Cincinnati). Known locally as Doc, he served a widely assorted clientele. As his nephew Richard Oyama later described it, "Yas tended to Kentucky hillbilly patients and jazz musicians alike."

Ironically, Yas's medical practice eventually forced him into the political arena. In August 1969, Kathleen Iatrides, a divorcée with two children living in Cincinnati, consulted Sasaki at his Newport office because she believed she was pregnant. According to Iatrides, Yas examined her, confirmed the pregnancy, and then performed an abortion on her in his office for the fee of $300. At that time, abortion was illegal in Kentucky unless it could be shown to be necessary to preserve the mother's life (thirty-five other states had similar statutes—in 1970 Hawai'i and New York would became the first two states to legalize abortion virtually on demand). Yas was arrested on a charge of "using an instrument with intent to procure the miscarriage of a pregnant woman." After several court-granted delays, on November 17, 1970, he was tried in the Campbell County Court. During the selection of the jury, Yas's attorney, William H. Allison, Jr., asked potential jurors if they were Catholics and, therefore, had religious scruples against all abortions. Four of the panel stated categorically that they were against abortions in all cases. As one put it, "I don't believe in abortions, period." As a result, they were excused for cause. Jury members were also asked about pre-trial publicity and presumption of guilt. Two candidates commented that if Sasaki hadn't performed the abortion he wouldn't be on trial. They too were excused. The judge then called the attorneys into chambers, and when they returned, he took over the examination of the remaining jurors, whom he found competent to serve.

Once the actual trial began, Yas initially denied having performed an abortion. The patient, who agreed to testify against him in court—rather unkindly, under the circumstances—swore that he had given her an abortion at her request. (According to state law, even if a woman consented to an abortion, she was deemed a competent witness and was not considered an accomplice for the purposes of her testimony.) The same day, Yas was found guilty. His sentence was fixed at a $1,000 fine and one year nine months in the state reformatory. Not only did he face prison, but the felony also meant the automatic loss of his medical license.

Yas immediately posted a $25,000 bond and filed a petition challenging the conviction with the state court of appeals. (Even before his trial, he had appealed to a federal district court to quash his indictment on constitutional grounds, but the court had taken the matter under advisement and failed to take any action.) He argued to the Kentucky appellate court that the judge had erred by prematurely cutting off the voir dire examination. More broadly, he took the position that the laws against abortion violated the fundamental rights of women to decide whether or not to bear a child (and also their religious freedom, since the law had no secular purpose). Since the law did not allow for abortion to preserve the mother's mental or physical health, he also claimed that the law infringed on the physician-patient relationship and the rights of physicians to offer the best medical advice. Furthermore, the statutes were overbroad and vague in defining precisely what was necessary to save a mother's life. On October 6, 1972, the Kentucky Court of Appeals issued its opinion in *Yasuo Sasaki v. Commonwealth of Kentucky*. The justices upheld the statute unanimously, finding it consistent with the state's obligation to preserve human life. (Much of the opinion's language was drawn from a similar federal case that had been decided in Kentucky earlier that same year.) They also found that the objection on the voir dire had not been properly preserved.

Yas then appealed to the US Supreme Court, and in early January 1973, his attorneys filed a jurisdictional statement supporting their petition. However, on January 22, the Court ruled in the celebrated case of *Roe v. Wade* that laws limiting abortion, at least in the first trimester of pregnancy, were unconstitutional. On that basis, the Supreme Court took up Yas's petition for an appeal. On February 26, 1973, the Court issued its decision in the case of *Sasaki v. Kentucky* (410 US 951), summarily vacating Yas's conviction and mandating the Kentucky court to reconsider its original decision in light of the new ruling in *Roe*. As a result, on May 4, 1973, Yas's conviction was unanimously reversed by the Kentucky Court of Appeals. The justices found that since the Kentucky abortion law under which he had been charged was identical, for practical purposes, with the Texas law at issue in *Roe*, it was unconstitutional as well, and thus, his conviction could not stand. One member of the Kentucky court, Justice Earl T. Osborne, wrote a concurring opinion in which he issued an ill-tempered denunciation of the Supreme Court and its ruling: "I believe that [the] court, in this instance and in many others, has and is usurping the rights of the several states in this Union to determine for themselves what constitutes a crime and to enforce their own criminal laws. This interference has now reached the point of the ridiculous. The citizens of the several states are forced, more and more, to look to the seat of our National Government for guidance, regulation and control and when they look, they are perceiving [*sic*] more and more of nothing but confusion and incompetence." Through his victorious legal struggle, which helped bring before the Supreme Court the issue of doctors and abortion, Yas had helped establish not only the rights of women to control their bodies but of their doctors to furnish the highest quality medical advice.

By this time, Yas had retired, and he and Lily returned to the West Coast and settled in Berkeley, California. In 1985 he attended a "Coming of Age in the Thirties" symposium at UCLA, where he chaired a panel of prewar Nisei writers that included Mary Korenaga Sutow, James Omura, Hisaye Yamamoto, Mary Oyama, and Joe Oyama. Over the succeeding years, Yas worked with the young scholar Stan Yogi and others to organize an anthology of prewar Nisei writing. A preparatory model for the project, *Nisei Renaissance: An Anthology of Writing by Nisei Before 1942*, coedited by Yas, was issued in 1993. It contained a sampling of poetry, plus notes for prose inclusions. Unfortunately, the larger study never appeared in print. Yas also served on the advisory board of the Japanese American History Archives. Yasuo Sasaki died on May 2, 2008. Lily followed in March 2010, just days before her one hundredth birthday.

INA SUGIHARA: INTERRACIAL ACTIVIST

One essential element of Japanese American community life has been the continuing contribution of women. However, a lot of their work has been in less glamorous and visible positions—the tedious organizing work, event planning, meetings, and administration men have shunned. Even when they have found a public voice, they have not necessarily attracted attention. A good example is the career of the versatile activist Ina Sugihara.

Ina Sugihara, born in 1919, grew up in a small town in Colorado as one of four children, then later moved to Long Beach, California. She said later that UCLA scouted her for a scholarship but rejected her because she wanted to be a lawyer rather than a nurse, which was considered inappropriate for an Asian girl. After attending junior college, she moved to Oakland and enrolled at the University of California, Berkeley. She supported herself by working in the house of a white family and also attended union-backed labor schools. She likewise became friends with members of the pioneering political group Oakland Nisei Young Democrats and attended meetings of the club. After graduation, she worked as a secretary to Ernest Besig, attorney and director of the Northern California branch of the ACLU.

In spring 1942, with Besig's help, John Thomas, of the American Baptist Home Mission Society, hired her, which allowed her to migrate "voluntarily" to New York and avoid confinement in the War Relocation Authority camps. Sugihara subsequently took a job with the Protestant Welfare Council's Human Relations Division and worked with the Federal Council of Churches. As part of her work, she wrote articles and press releases for the Religious News Service.

After the prejudice she had experienced in California, Sugihara enjoyed the cosmopolitan climate of New York. Soon after settling in the city, she grew acquainted with Socialist Party leader Norman Thomas, the only national political figure to oppose mass removal of Japanese Americans. Her talks with Thomas, building on her own experience, inspired her to throw herself into civil rights organizing. In 1943 Sugihara became a founding member of the New York branch of the nonviolent resistance group Congress of Racial Equality. The African American leader James Farmer (who stayed in the apartment of Sugihara and her boyfriend for several months following Farmer's divorce) later marveled at the fierce intelligence and lively humor with which she confronted bigots. The following year, Sugihara helped organize the New York branch of the Japanese American Citizens League (JACL), the organization's first multiracial chapter, and eventually was elected vice president of the JACL's Eastern District. Sugihara also became a frequent contributor to the JACL newspaper *Pacific Citizen*.

Even before the war, Sugihara had spoken publicly in favor of the assimilation of Nisei, and during the war she toured New York State to advocate aid for resettlement. She believed that normal life was only possible for the Nisei if they remained dispersed and centered on the East Coast. In a 1945 article for the Catholic magazine *Commonweal* (titled, rather melodramatically, "I Don't Want to Go Back"), Sugihara insisted that, while Japanese Americans certainly should have the right to return to their homes after the war, the resettlement of masses of Nisei in California would not only spark racial discrimination but would place them at odds with other minorities: "If Japanese Americans return in large numbers to Los Angeles's international ghetto . . . tighter restrictions in the rest of the community against all minority groups will crowd them into an extremely limited territory, and lack of privacy, together with the search for a scapegoat, will cause bloodshed."

In contrast, Sugihara concentrated on multigroup coalition building. In 1945–1946, she led the New York JACL in lobbying for congressional reauthorization of the wartime antidiscrimination watchdog agency the Fair Employment Practices Committee (FEPC). As part of her campaign, Sugihara joined forces with black leaders and contributed an article, "Our Stake in a Permanent FEPC" to the NAACP magazine, *The Crisis*. The article detailed the history and some of the successes of the FEPC. Referring obliquely to the government's mistreatment of Japanese Americans, she not-too-gently reminded her African American readers that they were not the only group in need of redress: "Perhaps the most notable accomplishments of the FEPC is [*sic*] its successful handling of cases involving Japanese Americans [in the face of] war hysteria, hidden circumstances and personalities, and other factors not found in the usual cases." Sugihara concluded that it was in the direct interest of both groups to fight for a permanent FEPC. Beyond easing discrimination, she argued, the agency's efforts helped heighten the consciousness of minority groups about their fundamental interdependence and fostered multiracial alliances to fight discrimination: "One of [the FEPC's] most important functions has been to prove to people, some of whom were previously concerned over the welfare of one community group or another, that the fate of each minority depends upon the extent of justice given all other groups."

In accord with her philosophy, Sugihara helped bring Nisei and black activists together in visible fashion. In March 1947, she attended a conference called by the NAACP on legal strategies to fight restrictive covenants in the US Supreme Court. Sugihara afterward contacted the JACL's Anti-Discrimination Committee and arranged for the organization to submit a supporting brief. Later that year, she convened a meeting of civil rights and church groups in support of the *Takahashi v. California Fish and Game Commission*, the JACL's Supreme Court challenge to anti-Issei discrimination, and she helped persuade NAACP chief council Thurgood Marshall to submit a brief.

Figure 6.4. Mervyn M. Dymally.

Despite the respect she inspired by her efforts, Sugihara became increasingly marginalized during the postwar years within a Japanese American community that she considered intolerant of blacks. In particular, in the early 1950s, she married an African American, Willis Jones. She later stated that she and her husband were made to feel uncomfortable at community events. She thus gradually withdrew from community activism. In later years, she worked for Texaco, lived in African American areas in Queens, and supported open housing. In 1977 the couple moved to White Plains, New York, where Willis died in 1982. Ina Sugihara Jones retired shortly afterward and lived in White Plains until her death in 2004.

Mervyn M. Dymally: Unsung Hero of Redress

During the early 1970s, the movement for Japanese American redress (as it would later be called) was born on the West Coast. It started as a collection of grassroots activists seeking to raise popular consciousness about the wartime removal of Japanese Americans. One notable leader was Sue Kunitomi Embrey, who directed the annual Manzanar Pilgrimages. Another central figure was Edison Uno, who worked to persuade the Japanese American Citizens League to endorse official reparations for confinement. In many ways, the campaign for redress was a fringe movement—many former inmates opposed it, and even those who agreed with the principle of restitution were skeptical that it could ever be realized.

Yet the fledgling movement did attract powerful support from an important outside constituency: African American politicians. During these early years, the black political class, especially California-based officials with sizable groups of Nisei constituents, signed on as endorsers of reparations. Mayor Tom Bradley of Los Angeles offered low-key support for protests. Congressman Augustus Hawkins, who had denounced the original wartime removal as a California state assemblyman during World War II, lent his full backing to the principle of redress. US representative Yvonne Braithwaite Burke was another early convert.

Perhaps the most vital black supporter of redress was Rep. Mervyn Malcolm Dymally. Dymally, born in Cedros, Trinidad, in 1926, claimed both African and East Indian ancestry. He moved to the United States at the close of World War II to attend college, first as a journalism student at the all-black Lincoln University in Missouri, then at Los Angeles State College (now CSLA). He subsequently received a PhD from United States International University (now known as Alliant International University) in 1979. He worked for several years as a teacher of handicapped children in the Los Angeles Unified School District.

Dymally's political career started in 1962, when he was elected to the California State Assembly. Four years later, he won election to the state Senate—the first-ever African American in that body. In 1974 he made history by becoming lieutenant governor of California, one of the first two African Americans to occupy such a position since Reconstruction. After serving one term, he was elected to Congress in 1980 from California's 31st District, which included the heavily Japanese American city of Gardena.

Once installed in Congress, Dymally soon became a leading advocate of redress. According to Miya Iwata, he was first introduced to the issue at a Town Hall in Gardena organized by city mayor Mas Fukai. Iwata asked him what his position on redress was. When Dymally admitted that he was not familiar with the issue, Fukai informed him that it was the most vital question of interest to the Japanese community. Dymally astutely asked to meet with activists from the National Coalition for Redress/Reparations (NCRR) to inform himself.

After his reelection in November 1982, Dymally threw himself into action. In December 1982, following the hearings of the US Commission on Wartime Relocation and Internment of Civilians (at which Fukai and other Gardena residents had testified) Dymally introduced a pair of redress bills drafted by the NCRR. The first, which had provisions similar to a failed bill previously introduced by Washington State congressman Mike Lowry, provided for individual reparations, while the second was designed to provide community-wide benefits to restore "social, economic, and cultural well-being" to Japanese communities. He simultaneously obtained Congressional Black Caucus (CBC) approval for the bills. He meanwhile offered NCRR members facilities in his congressional office for lobbying and other organizational work, hosted receptions for them, and hired Japanese American staffers. In August 1984, Dymally was the lead congressional witness at a US Senate hearing on redress chaired by Alaska senator Ted Stevens. The following year, Dymally went on a well-publicized tour of Manzanar during the annual pilgrimage. He stated at that time, "To me, Manzanar is symbolic of the whole concentration camp experience of the Japanese American people during World War II . . . This is a place where history was made." In addition to seeking support for redress, he added, "I am also going to Manzanar because I would like to bring this experience and this issue to the greater consciousness of the American people."

In 1987, in tribute to his prestige in Congress, Dymally was elected chair of the CBC. However, his activism on redress was by no means universally popular among African Americans. According to Nisei congressman Robert Matsui, most members of the CBC, despite their endorsement of the Dymally bills, were slow to warm to the issue of redress on the grounds that African Americans should have priority on reparations. Indeed, by the late 1980s, *Jet* magazine reported that Dymally himself faced increasing challenges from black officials, who believed that blacks ought to be compensated first for their ancestors' suffering under slavery: "Dymally's response to critics is that talk without action is all he's heard from Black leaders approaching him about similar legislation for Blacks."

Dymally was also forced to contend with anger in the black community over the discriminatory statements and actions of officials and businesses in Japan. These rebounded against Japanese Americans who—as in World War II—were unfairly connected with Japan. In 1986 Japanese prime minister Yasuhiro Nakasone asserted in a speech that Japanese educational success was due to Japan's status as a monoracial society, while "Blacks, Puerto Ricans and Mexicans" held down US education levels. The comments raised a storm of protest. Nakasone ultimately apologized for his words and met with various African American leaders.

Still, the damage was done. The sentiment of mistrust was gravely aggravated in July 1988 when Michio Watanabe, a former finance and trade minister (and future deputy prime minister), publicly charged that, unlike Japanese, black Americans were nonchalant about declaring bankruptcy. As chair of the CBC, Dymally organized a press conference with his colleagues in which they deplored the Japanese attitude and challenged the Japanese government to act forcefully to curb racial bias against blacks, under threat of boycotts of Japanese goods. Dymally was careful to make clear that he did not include Japanese Americans in his strictures against Japan. Rather, he insisted that CBC members spoke for other members of Congress and people of goodwill across America, including Japanese Americans. Two Nisei members of Congress, Robert Matsui and Norman Mineta, joined the CBC in publicly denouncing Tokyo's actions, even as NCRR members and other Japanese Americans in Los Angeles sponsored a protest at the local Japanese consulate.

In August, Congress approved the Civil Liberties Act of 1988, which provided an official apology and a $20,000 redress payment to each person of Japanese ancestry who had been affected by Executive Order 9066. Four years later, Dymally left Congress. In 2002, following a decade-long absence, he returned to political life by running successfully for the California State Assembly. He served three terms before retiring definitively from public life in 2008.

Mervyn M. Dymally's stalwart support for Japanese American redress makes him, in Miya Iwataki's words, the "unsung hero" of the campaign. He certainly backed redress at a time when it was not "safe" to do so and brought the movement a new level of visibility and legitimacy. Yet his activism is

FIGURE 6.5. Setsuko M. Nishi, *center*, with Greg Robinson and Sheila Hamanaka.

largely unknown among Japanese Americans, and he does not figure in the list of outside champions of the community. Worse, the story of his leadership has scarcely percolated within the larger community or among African Americans. I have thus made an exception to my usual rule of not writing about living persons—as Dymally is very much alive—in hopes of helping rectify this injustice. [Representative Dymally died in October 2012, not long after this column was published.]

SETSUKO M. NISHI: A LIFE OF SERVICE

Today's column focuses on the distinguished sociologist and activist Dr. Setsuko Matsunaga Nishi, a pioneering scholar of race relations who died on November 18, 2012. Unlike virtually all the people I write about in The Great Unknown, I knew Setsuko personally. Because of our friendship and my knowledge of her career, I helped the Nishi family put together an obituary for her. I will draw from that obituary and other materials in telling her story here and then will take the liberty of offering some personal glimpses.

Setsuko Matsunaga was born in Los Angeles on October 17, 1921, the second of four children and the eldest of three sisters. Her father, Tahei Matsunaga, was an unusual Issei—after taking sociology classes at the University of Southern California during the 1920s with the renowned scholar Emory Bogardus, he graduated from Woodbury Business College, then became a local real estate dealer and hotel owner. Because of his ability to work among white elites to resolve discrimination and open up opportunities for other Issei, the elder Matsunaga was dubbed the unofficial "mayor" of "Little Tokyo." Setsuko's mother, Hatsu, was an educated woman. The Matsunagas were a musical family: Ernest, the oldest, was an avid singer, while sister Helen Haruko later became a professional violinist. Setsuko dreamed of becoming a concert pianist.

Meanwhile, she became politically aware; she later recounted how her friend Joe Oyama, a progressive Nisei writer, took her to her first union meeting, which fascinated the naïve teenager. She also distinguished herself for her skills as a public speaker. In June 1939, she received first prize in an oratorical contest sponsored by the YMCA-YWCA at the Union Church. *Kashu Mainichi* reported that she had succeeded in "[i]mpressing both the audience and the judges with her sincere and inspired delivery." Her prize was a free trip to the Golden Gate International Exposition in San Francisco. Future Japanese American Citizens League stalwart Masao Satow, the general secretary of the Little Tokyo YMCA, drove Setsuko and the runners-up to the fair. Setsuko also joined a Nisei girl's club, the Tartanettes (she later recounted how poet Chiye Mori had invited the club to her house to instruct them on the art of makeup).

After graduating from high school, Setsuko enrolled at the University of Southern California (USC)—her father's alma mater—as a music major, with a minor in education. During her junior year, the Japanese attack on Pearl Harbor led to war between the United States and Japan. (Setsuko credited Occidental College president Remsen Bird, a friend and supporter of her sister Helen, for intervening with the authorities to save their father from internment in a Department of Justice camp.) In contrast to many Japanese Americans, Setsuko moved to take direct action in support of Japanese American citizenship rights. Joining her friend Masamori Kojima, plus liberal minister Rev. Fred Fertig and a group of sympathetic brothers at the Maryknoll Mission in Boyle Heights led by Theophane Walsh, she organized a speakers' bureau and developed information meetings in various locales

(Masao Satow not-too-helpfully advised them to counter rumors about fifth column activity in Hawai'i by insisting that mainland Japanese Americans were different from those in Hawai'i).

As the shadow of mass removal drifted over the community, Setsuko wired President Franklin D. Roosevelt to urge him to not take arbitrary action. Her telegram, located decades later in White House files, read, "LOS ANGELES, FEB. 10, 1942. THE PRESIDENT: WE NISEI AMERICANS LOYAL. PROTEST INTERNMENT AS UNDEMOCRATIC CURTAILMENT OF CONSTITUTIONAL RIGHTS AND CIVIL LIBERTIES. SETSUKO MATSUNAGO [sic]."

In the wake of Executive Order 9066, Setsuko and her family were forced into confinement. Just before removal, Emory Bogardus, her father's onetime instructor, informed her that she had been admitted to the Phi Beta Kappa honor society. Since she was scheduled to be confined before the date of the official ceremony, Bogardus arranged a special induction for her in the office of USC president Rufus von KleinSmid. (Setsuko later recalled that she was presented with the PBK key by a sometime boyfriend, a white student who carefully concealed their dating from his conservative American Legionnaire father.) Bogardus continued to correspond with her while she and her family were confined at the Santa Anita Assembly Center. Under his guidance, Setsuko became interested in sociology. (Just before being removed, Setsuko was also stricken with pleurisy, which was aggravated by the dusty camp conditions—the damage to her bronchial tubes led to her being hospitalized in the postwar years.)

In fall 1942, after spending several months at Santa Anita, Setsuko and her sister Helen were among the first students permitted to leave camp under the auspices of the National Japanese American Student Relocation Council—she later stated that release involved clearance by five different agencies. Following a harrowing journey across the country, she arrived in St. Louis and enrolled in the MA program in sociology at Washington University. During her months in St. Louis, Setsuko made two important contacts. First, sociologist Tomatsu Shibutani recruited her to report on local communities as an "Assistant Research Collaborator" for the UC Berkeley–based Japanese Evacuation and Resettlement Study (JERS). In 1944 Setsuko would submit a research report for the project, "The Adjustment of Evacuees in St. Louis." Meanwhile, she was invited to speak about Japanese Americans to the Twentieth Century Club, a group of elite black men in St. Louis. (Setsuko later recalled that she was the first woman ever invited to speak to the group. Since the members met in formal evening clothes, and asked her to do the same, she could not wear any of the clothes she had brought from camp and had to scramble to fix up something that could pass as an evening gown.) At her talk, she met P. L. Prattis, editor of the *Pittsburgh Courier*, who was impressed by her speech.

Following graduation from Washington University, Setsuko moved to Chicago, where her parents had settled, and enrolled as a doctoral student in the famous University of Chicago Sociology Department. She participated in JERS seminars with Director Dorothy Swaine Thomas and such eminent staffers as Tamotsu Shibutani, S. Frank Miyamoto, Charles Kikuchi, Togo Tanaka, and Louise Suski. While at the University of Chicago, she teamed up with social scientists George DeVos and William Caudill to launch the interdisciplinary Japanese American Personality and Acculturation Study to study the life experiences of resettlers.

She also became attached to Ken Nishi, a California-born painter who was then serving as a noncommissioned officer in the US Army. The two were married in 1944. In the years that followed, the couple had their first child, Geoffrey. Despite her burden of child care, Setsuko nonetheless took employment outside the home. P. L. Prattis hired her as an assistant (and ghostwriter) for the *Pittsburgh Courier*, and she worked as a research editor for the *Chicago Defender*.

In 1944 Prattis introduced her to the celebrated African American sociologist Horace R. Cayton, who became a longtime friend and collaborator. Cayton engaged her as a staffer at Parkway Community House, a settlement house he directed in the city's "Black Belt." While at Parkway, Setsuko organized community forums on such topics as Gunnar Myrdal's celebrated study of racism, *An American Dilemma: The Negro Problem and Modern Democracy* (1944). With Cayton's guidance, she helped found the Chicago Resettlers Committee, a social service agency now known as the Japanese American Service Committee, for which her father, Tahei, served as president. With funds from the American Council on Race Relations, Setsuko wrote a short book, *Facts About Japanese-Americans* (1946), which received wide distribution. She simultaneously wrote a review of Miné Okubo's graphic memoir, *Citizen 13660*, for the influential *American Sociological Review*.

Through her efforts, Setsuko became both a bridge between black and ethnic Japanese communities and a visible activist in favor of racial equality.

In the late 1940s, she assumed the position of acting head of the Chicago Council Against Racial and Religious Discrimination, a coalition of African American, Jewish, Catholic, Protestant, Japanese American, and labor organizations that lobbied and ran educational campaigns for civil rights legislation. She went on speaking tours and traveled to the state capital at Springfield to lobby for a statewide fair employment practices bill. Setsuko later claimed that the work was an important learning experience for her in building coalitions, as the leaders of each group were aware that if they banded together, they would gain more attention for their concerns but that competing over who was the most oppressed was self-defeating. As she put it:

> I've had a career advocating that minorities (in Louis Wirth's comprehensive meaning) should coalesce in dealing with their common sources of oppression and be aware of and protect against their vulnerability to the "divide and conquer" institutionalized arrangements and practices of those in power. These who-suffered-the-most arguments are counterproductive of our joining forces in holding on to and really enforcing our hard-won civil rights laws, themselves a result of the historic coalition of African Americans, Jews, and other minorities.

Although Setsuko completed her comprehensive doctoral exams at the University of Chicago by 1951, and was able to draw on the research she had conducted with William Caudill for her dissertation, she was obliged to put off completion of her doctoral project because of paid employment and growing family responsibilities. Her husband, Ken, was stricken with a life-threatening infection, one that arose from an untreated injury he had sustained while in the Army; he spent two years in a veterans hospital being treated for his condition and would be hobbled by a frozen knee for the rest of his life. Setsuko relied heavily on her friends Ernest and Chizu Iiyama, who earned her unending gratitude by moving in with the Nishis and helping to care for their young son. Even after his recovery, Ken struggled to support himself as an artist. In addition to working outside the home, Setsuko and her family assisted Ken in producing greeting cards, which helped support the family. The couple soon had four more children: Lisa, Paula, Stefani, and Mia. As Setsuko later described, "[Ken's] paintings from that time are imbued with deeply contained emotion, like his harlquins [sic] in quiet repose. We worked hard together as well as separately, supporting each other with plenty of space.

Sometimes I wonder who else would have found a way to put up with me."

In 1949 the Nishis visited Cape Breton Island in Nova Scotia. The land so enchanted them that they bought land in the village of Mabou and built a house. Setsuko would spend summers there for the rest of her life. The Nishis meanwhile built a home and art studio in Tappan, New York, near New York City, which would remain their home base during the rest of the year. Once in New York, Setsuko was named to a position in the Research Department of the National Council of Churches. She hired Horace Cayton as a research advisor and invited him to collaborate on a book, *The Changing Scene: Current Trends and Issues* (1955), a two-volume study of churches and social service. When Cayton, who was struggling with alcoholism, checked himself into Rockland Psychiatric Hospital for treatment, the Nishis invited him to stay at their house during his weekend furloughs. They also hosted Nisei journalist Eddie Shimano, who had fallen on hard times.

In 1963 Setsuko was finally able to complete her dissertation and receive her long-delayed doctorate. Her dissertation, "Japanese American Achievement in Chicago: A Cultural Response to Degradation," is a case study of the social movement from which the post-camp Japanese American community in Chicago emerged—in opposition to the forced assimilation policy of the War Relocation Authority and Caucasian "friends of resettlement." It forms a notable contribution to the literature on Japanese Americans in its inquiry into the social and cultural factors that aided the postwar resettlement of the community. However, while Setsuko celebrated the community structures that enabled Japanese Americans to reestablish themselves, she was impatient with cultural determinism as reductivist and bitterly criticized "model minority" notions of Asian American success as simplistic and biased. Instead, she explained variations in minority group achievement through a mix of culture and social structure minority achievement. In 2005 Setsuko would enter into a controversy with a young scholar, Jacalyn Harden, over Harden's assertions that Setsuko and other Nisei social scientists had presented Nisei in their theses as culturally superior to African Americans. Setsuko bitterly opposed any such contention, and she went so far as to write an open letter in the pages of *Amerasia Journal*, in which she denounced Harden for distorting her work and strongly requested that the author and her publisher issue a retraction.

In 1965, with support from sociologist Alfred McClung Lee (himself an acerbic critic of wartime confinement), Setsuko was appointed as a professor of sociology at Brooklyn College. She was subsequently admitted as a faculty member at the Graduate Center of the City University of New York. During her tenure at Brooklyn College, Setsuko taught the first courses on Asian American studies and served as a mentor to a generation of scholars. In her later years, she organized and served as director of the Japanese American Life Course Survey, a large-scale investigation into the long-term effects of wartime incarceration on Japanese Americans.

Setsuko did not engage in much academic publishing during the following years. Instead, as in Chicago, she pursued work as a self-described "scholar/ advocate." In collaboration with African American sociologist Hylan Lewis, she reported on methods and strategies for achieving school integration and she subsequently served as an advisor on Dr. Kenneth B. Clark's HARYOU-ACT minority youth aid project. As a senior fellow at the Metropolitan Applied Research Center, the noted think tank of the civil rights movement led by Clark and Lewis, she served as a senior fellow and senior consulting associate. In the process, she collaborated in many studies, including methods and strategies for achieving school integration, institutionalized discrimination in foster care, and inequities in performance evaluation in corporate employment. One of her major interests was the problem of minority group drug use and abuse. As part of her activism, she served as coauthor of the 1976 work *Drug Use and Abuse among US Minorities: An Annotated Bibliography*.

In the 1970s, Setsuko was appointed to the New York State Advisory Committee to the US Commission on Civil Rights. She served for three decades, including six as its chair. She also served on the National Advisory Council of the Center for Women Policy Studies in Washington, DC, and on the board of directors of United Way of New York City. In 1981 she testified before the US Commission on Wartime Relocation and Internment of Civilians. In 1989 she cofounded the Asian American Federation, served as its first board president until 1995, and remained an active board member through the years. She also was an active advisor for the Japanese American National Museum (JANM). In particular, in 1998 she joined the delegation of Japanese Americans in New York who met with Jewish community leaders to discuss the use of the phrase "concentration camps" at JANM's Ellis Island exhibition.

In 1999 Setsuko retired from Brooklyn College. Two years later, her husband died. Setsuko established a foundation to collect and preserve his work, kept up her busy schedule of meetings with community and philanthropic groups, and presented at several academic conferences. She meanwhile plugged away on her study of Nisei life experiences, though she had difficulty making headway on it. She received some important honors for her work over these years. In 2007 Setsuko received a Lifetime Achievement Award from the Association for Asian American Studies. In June 2009, she was conferred the Order of the Rising Sun, Gold Rays with Neck Ribbon by the Government of Japan. In May 2012, she returned to USC as one of the Nisei former students who received honorary degrees in place of the diplomas they had been unable to complete due to mass removal.

In summer 2012, as in previous years, Setsuko traveled to Nova Scotia for the summer. She planned to return to New York in early November, shortly after her ninety-first birthday. However, after receiving news of the destruction wrought by Post-Tropical Cyclone Sandy, she delayed her return by two weeks. She was packing for her delayed trip when her aorta burst, and she apparently died rapidly and, effectively, painlessly.

Postscript

As previously mentioned, most of the individuals I write about in my profiles are people who I never met or knew only slightly. In contrast, I was privileged to become close to Setsuko Matsunaga Nishi, first professionally and then personally, and would like to give some personal glimpses of this extraordinary woman.

Although Setsuko and I both lived and worked in the New York area during the 1990s, we only slowly became acquainted. When I first started doing research on Japanese American history, some Asian American studies scholars recommended that I contact her, though they nonetheless warned me of her fearsome reputation for both intelligence and toughness. Our paths crossed a few times at Day of Remembrance ceremonies and funerals of prominent Nisei. Despite her short stature and polished appearance and manner—Setsuko was very much a lady in the classic sense—she had a no-nonsense aura that made me a bit shy about approaching her. At a book party I had my first real conversation with her. She expressed interest in my research on the historical relations between Nisei and black Americans, as well as my work on Miné Okubo, and graciously offered her help; I have since discovered that I was just one of a number of younger scholars to whom she provided assistance and backing. At any rate, since by that time I had moved to Montreal I did not meet her, but wrote her for information and contacts.

We gradually began exchanging regular e-mails. Emboldened by her interest and encouragement of my research, I gradually started to share drafts of my articles. Setsuko was the best kind of reader because she was both an enthusiast and a thorough critic (informed by her wide reading as well as her own lived experience). She bravely went through the manuscript of *A Tragedy of Democracy: Japanese Confinement in North America*, the book I was then in the process of drafting, reading chapters as I finished them and furnishing suggestions. I paid her back as best I could by relaying greetings from old friends who I met through her or sending tidbits from my research that touched on her own work; she was delighted to see a glamorous photo of her that I located in the *Chicago Defender* taken in her days working at the Parkway Community House settlement. She especially appreciated seeing advance copies of my *Nichi Bei* columns, which we jokingly called my "bonbons." I was honored when she, in turn, consulted me regarding her own work in progress.

It was gratifying to connect with Setsuko. Given her long career, it felt like having a direct link to the Nisei past. In fact, on my first visit to Japan, I had the pleasure of visiting the Japanese Overseas Migration Museum in Yokohama. Shigeru Kojima, the museum's chief researcher, graciously gave me a guided tour of its interesting collections. One of the exhibits concerned Japanese Americans and World War II, which displayed prominently a copy of Setsuko's *Facts about Japanese-Americans*. When I pointed out the volume to him, Kojima-san asked politely, "Do you know this book?" "Better than that," I replied, "I know the author!" I then explained to my amazed guide that not only was Setsuko still alive—over sixty years later—but was still at work on her latest book project. Not for the world would I have explained that she was only twenty-five when *Facts* was published—it was more fun to let him think that she was a supercentenarian!

A turning point in my relations with Setsuko came one year on New Year's Day, when I was in New York City with my partner. She invited us to come up to her family house in Tappan for an *oshogatsu* fete. I was touched by the invitation but apprehensive. Despite my extended correspondence with Setsuko, I didn't know her well and was still somewhat in awe of her. Also, attending the party meant finding our way to Tappan on public transportation (as a true New Yorker, I do not drive). I nevertheless decided to make the trip, and we found a bus to take us. Once we arrived, Setsuko, bustling with preparations and pausing to play with various grandchildren, greeted us briefly, then directed us to the outbuilding that had been the painting studio of Setsuko's late husband, Ken, where the party was taking place.

As I stepped into the crowded studio, I saw an impressive scene. The walls were covered by Ken's paintings. One side of the room contained a spread of American and Japanese food, including piles of fish freshly smoked by family members. Musical entertainment filled the other side, featuring singer Ernest Michio Matsunaga, Setsuko's brother (who I later learned had written the defiant poem "Buddahead Blues" while confined at the Santa Anita Assembly Center in 1942). I had expected to be surrounded by academics and Asian Americanists, but none were present. Instead, various family members came over to introduce themselves. To my surprise, none of them seemed aware of Setsuko's outside identity (one man asked, "However did you get to know Aunt Suki?"). I was struck by her modesty and the line she maintained between her personal and professional life. I felt like shouting that their doting family member was a scholar with a long set of credentials.

Following that (thoroughly enjoyable) New Year's party, I felt I had crossed a line into being accepted as a friend. Setsuko began mixing stories of her family doings into her work e-mails, and I likewise shared some personal news. Of course, I was not personally close to her in the way that her large circle of family and longtime friends were—I never felt comfortable calling her "Suki," as they did. I also was not directly connected to her professionally in the way of some of her old colleagues and longtime collaborators, such as Cao K.O or Barbara Katz Rothman. However, I was a rare person who had a foot in each camp.

Gradually, a kind of rhythm established itself. I would see Setsuko when I came to New York during the school year as well as at her annual New Year's party. We also shared panels at a few conferences in various cities and would go out to eat together afterward. Whenever I saw her, I would pump her shamelessly for stories of her life and experiences. Sometimes she would talk of her early years in Los Angeles. She would tell of visiting her father's office in Little Tokyo and of passing the time by hanging around downstairs at Carl Kondo's typewriter store. (I discovered from her sister Molly that Setsuko had gone out on a date with Frank Chuman, the future attorney and JACL president, the night before Pearl Harbor.)

Setsuko would also describe her days in Chicago. She met the great novelist Richard Wright, who encouraged her to write about the wartime confinement and offered to introduce her to his publisher. She described dressing up to go to Springfield to lobby the state legislature for bills favoring Japanese Americans and others. She also spoke of the veterans hospital where she regularly visited her husband. I marveled at how, in the midst of the years of "the feminine mystique," when women were bullied to stay home and women of color had an even more difficult time, Setsuko continued to work, even as she raised five children. Setsuko especially loved to recount her activities with children and grandchildren at the summer house on Cape Breton Island. I heard the story of how her husband, Ken, gave a seminar on the island in 1948, and they both were so in love with the area that they bought land and built a house there.

I liked to hear stories of her later life. After the great civil rights activist Dorothy Height died, Setsuko recounted a trip they had taken to Paris in 1978 at the invitation of the US State Department to serve on the US Delegation to the UNESCO Intergovernmental Meeting of Experts to prepare a draft declaration on race and racial prejudice. Setsuko presented some conceptual clarifications of racism at the plenary meeting and was impressed that Height, a longtime worker in the field, had approved of and used them. She was even more impressed that when she fell ill on the final day of the trip, Height insisted on watching over her at the hotel and sacrificed her one free day in Paris to offer support.

In addition to Setsuko's wealth of information, I particularly enjoyed her sense of humor. She made me laugh when she told me that she and her dear friends Midori Shimanouchi Lederer (director of the Nisei social service agency JASSI) and Grace Lyu Volckhausen, of the Korean American League for Civil Action, sometimes imagined themselves as three alligators, "tough-skinned and large-mouthed, watching in wait for the right strike." She also told a story on herself about undergoing an operation to repair damage to her eyes from macular degeneration. After the operation, she said, "I discovered suddenly that I have wrinkles on my face, and my office has dust on the windowsill!"

I last saw Setsuko in spring 2012 at the annual meeting of the Association for Asian American Studies in Washington, DC. I had proposed her for a roundtable panel on internment research, as it was always fun to attend conferences with her, and the panel had been accepted. After the panel, we went out to dinner at a Malaysian restaurant with my partner and two friends. Setsuko, I think, had never had Malaysian food before, but she was thrilled to try it and ate with gusto. Meanwhile, she delighted our friends with her stories—she was in rare form. They were stunned that a ninety-year-old woman could be so lively and fun. The next day, I ran into Setsuko as she was heading back home. Normally she was very independent about carrying her own suitcase, but when I offered, she said she would *permit* me to help her, so I took the bags to the taxi, gave her a hug, and sent her off. I will always remember her warmth and class.

7

Sports

ARTHUR MATSU: FIRST JAPANESE AMERICAN IN
THE NATIONAL FOOTBALL LEAGUE

One familiar name in the National Football League (NFL) in recent years was Scott Fujita, formerly of the New Orleans Saints and later of the Cleveland Browns. Adopted in his youth by a Japanese American family, Fujita proudly proclaimed his Nikkei identity. Many fans doubtless figured that Fujita must be the first Japanese American in the NFL. Members of an older generation generally supposed it was Wally Yonamine, the Hawai'i-born Nisei who joined the San Francisco 49ers in 1947 and played a single season before becoming a professional baseball star in Japan. In fact, the ethnic Japanese presence in the NFL dates back all the way to the early years of the league—1928, to be precise, when Art Matsu briefly took the field.

Arthur Matsuzawa, born in 1904 in Glasgow, Scotland, came to the United States as a toddler. His father, Ichezo, was Japanese, and his mother, Agnes, was Scotch. Matsu spent his early years in Cleveland (during which time he shortened his name) and lettered in four sports at East High School. A 1920

DOI: 10.5876/9781607324294.c007

FIGURE 7.1. Arthur Matsu, *right*, with two teammates.

census form indicates that he lived with his father, a servant in the house of local whites. In 1923 Matsu enrolled at the College of William & Mary in Williamsburg, Virginia. While William & Mary excluded African American students, it was open to him. Matsu's athletic talent and good looks assured him campus celebrity, and he pledged two fraternities. Nevertheless, fears that his popularity would spark interracial fraternization may have prompted Virginia's legislature to pass the Racial Purity Act in 1924, extending the state's miscegenation law and explicitly forbidding intermarriage between Asians and whites. (This same act would be overturned in the landmark 1967 US Supreme Court case *Loving v. Virginia*—a case in which the Japanese American Citizens League played a crucial role.)

In 1924 Matsu took the field as quarterback of the William & Mary team, then known as the Indians. In November, William & Mary shut out the heavily favored King College 27–0, with Matsu drop-kicking the extra points, and almost beat Navy's powerful team. The next year, Matsu helped take the Indians to the state title. In 1926, at the start of his senior year, Matsu was named team captain. In his final game, the team beat Chattanooga for bragging rights as best of the South.

Although he was short even among football players of his day, Matsu was renowned for his keen passing ability and his skill as a kicker. He converted eighteen extra points during a single season and kicked three fifty-three-yard field goals. His talent, plus his unusual racial heritage, earned him national attention. The *Washington Post* enthused that "[t]he Jap is probably the most consistent extra-point man in the state," while *Time* magazine called him a "clever quarterback and captain." In 1935 Matsu was named second-string quarterback on the all-time-best William & Mary team. In addition to football, Matsu excelled at golf (a talent he attributed to his Scottish ancestry) and diving. In the fall of 1927, following graduation, Matsu became William & Mary's golf and swimming coach.

In fall 1928, Matsu joined the NFL's Dayton Triangles. The Triangles were in desperate need of good players: they had managed to win only one game out of twelve in their previous two seasons. Matsu was placed at fullback. He was not the team's only Asian American player—the Triangles also featured Hawai'i-born Chinese American running back Walter Achiu (nicknamed "Sneeze" because of his name). Unfortunately, Matsu did not do well as a professional—he played in only two games. Although he made two receptions, for a total gain of fifteen yards, and returned a pair of kickoffs, he completed only one of eight passing attempts and threw two interceptions. (His teammates did not do much better. Dayton lost all of its seven games that season and was shut out in all but one. The team later moved to New York and became the Brooklyn Dodgers before folding in 1943).

Even after leaving the NFL, Matsu continued to play amateur football. In 1930 he was named to a Virginia all-star team that played an all-star pro squad. While the professionals won the game 20–7, Matsu made the only score for the Virginians with a touchdown pass to Meb Davis, his former William & Mary teammate, and then kicked the extra point. Matsu married in 1927. His son, Arthur A. Matsu, was born two years later, and a daughter followed soon after. With a family to support, Matsu turned to coaching. In 1930 he was hired as the football coach at Asheville High School, in Asheville, NC. The next year he moved to Benedictine College in Richmond, Virginia.

In 1931 Matsu's old William & Mary coach, J. Wilder Tasker, was named head coach at Rutgers University. He invited Matsu to become one of his assistant coaches. It was a plum position, especially at the height of the Great Depression. Not only did Rutgers have prestige as a birthplace of

intercollegiate football, but it enjoyed a certain reputation for racial tolerance based on the brilliant football career of Paul Robeson, who had played
for the college a decade earlier.

After five years as backfield coach, in 1936 Matsu was selected to coach
the freshman football team. He would occupy the post off and on for two
decades. His coaching received mixed reviews. Quarterback Frank Burns, a
future Rutgers head coach himself, later termed Matsu, "[a] master of offen-
sive football, a true innovator." Another Rutgers athlete, Leonard Weissburg,
remembered Matsu as a very austere and strict man who rarely ever smiled
but was a very good coach. Arthur Victor Mann agreed that Matsu was a
great natural athlete, in spite of his short stature, and a great coach, but he
added that Matsu's great weakness was his insistence on calling all the plays
and not letting his players make decisions on their own. Toshimasa Hosoda,
a Nisei quarterback who played for Rutgers in the 1950s, recalled that Matsu
did not show him any particular favor based on their common ancestry but
grumbled at him as much as at the other players and did not welcome discussion on topics outside of football.

Matsu took several additional assignments during his Rutgers years. During
World War II he taught physical education and operated the physical fitness
program for the school's Army Specialized Training Corps. He also served
as the assistant sports publicity director. Matsu kept in fine shape himself. In
1948 he won the Rutgers alumni golf tournament, beating several younger
athletes. In 1955 he left Rutgers and some years later moved to Arizona, where
he sold real estate and served as a scout for Arizona State University. He spent
his last years near Phoenix, Arizona, where he died in 1987.

NISEI IN PRO BASKETBALL: WAT MISAKA AND DR. YANAGI

When center Wang Zhizhi joined the Dallas Mavericks of the National
Basketball Association (NBA) in early 2001 and Yao Ming achieved stardom
with the Houston Rockets, many commentators mistakenly referred to the
two Chinese players as the first Asians in the history of professional basketball. When Jeremy Lin joined the New York Knicks, commentators made
much of the new phenomenon of Asian Americans in pro basketball. In fact,
in the first years of the sport, the Knicks hired two Japanese Americans, and
both made their mark at different positions.

The first was Wat Misaka. Born in December 1923, Wataru Misaka grew up in Ogden, Utah, the son of a barber. He attended Weber College, a two-year-school, and then the University of Utah, around the time of Pearl Harbor, and joined the varsity basketball squad, the Utes. In March 1944, Mikasa and his teammates visited Madison Square Garden to play in the National Invitation Tournament (NIT). Kentucky defeated the Utes in the first round. However, the defeat was assuaged when another team was forced to bow out of the NCAA Men's Basketball Tournament following a group car accident, and the Utes were invited to compete for the NCAA championship. They traveled to Kansas City, where they swept their games to win the Western Regional title, then returned to New York for the national final against a heavily favored Dartmouth team. With help from Misaka, Utah won a stunning 42–40 overtime victory.

After a stint in the US Army, Misaka returned to Utah in the postwar years. In 1946–1947, he again led the Utes to the NIT. This time, Utah won their opening game, defeating Duquesne 45–44. Misaka clinched the victory with a foul shot in the game's closing moments. In the NIT final, Utah once again played Kentucky and prevailed 49–45, winning revenge for 1944. Misaka, playing small forward, starred on defense, limiting Kentucky's star scorer Ralph Beard to a single point during the first half. With the NIT championship, the Utes became the first team to post a winner in both major college tournaments. (A few years later, City College of New York would achieve the unprecedented feat of winning both tournaments in a single year.)

In 1947 the New York Knickerbockers of the Basketball Association of America (BAA) drafted Misaka (two years later, the BAA would merge with a rival league to form the NBA). Misaka's hiring, which came just months after Jackie Robinson broke Major League Baseball's color line, drew media attention. Misaka was both the first Asian and the first nonwhite player in the new league. (Incredible as it may seem today, when the majority of NBA players are African Americans, no blacks played in the NBA until four players, including the Knicks' own Nat "Sweetwater" Clifton, started in 1950.)

Misaka opened the season with the team on November 13, 1947. However, he played just three games, scoring only seven points, before he was released on waivers on November 25. No explanation was given for his sudden release, ordered by new coach Joe Lapchick. Racial issues may have played a role, although Misaka later insisted that he was treated like the other players and did not feel particular prejudice. Clearly, at 5-foot-7, he was at a disadvantage against taller players in the pros, although he had faced players of equal stature in college.

After leaving the Knicks, Misaka returned west. During a stop in Chicago, Abe Saperstein, owner of the celebrated all-black team, the Harlem Globetrotters, offered him a spot on the team; Saperstein had seen him play at an exhibition in Hawai'i some years earlier. Misaka turned down the offer and returned to the university to complete an engineering degree. He still lives in Utah, where he remains a pillar of the Nisei community. In December 2013, he celebrated his ninetieth birthday.

The other Nisei recruited by the Knicks, a man known as Yana, had a far longer career in New York than Misaka. However, he did not join the team as a player but as a physician. Dr. Kazuo Yanagisawa was born in Berkeley, California, on April 29, 1914, the son of a gardener. He graduated from the University of California, Berkeley in 1935. In his undergraduate years he showed scientific talent; in 1936 he published his first scholarly article. Perhaps because of limited educational opportunities in medicine for West Coast Nisei, he enrolled at the University of Maryland School of Medicine, graduating in 1940. He then moved to Boston, where he took up a residence in orthopedic surgery at Massachusetts General Hospital. Because of this, he escaped being confined with his family in the War Relocation Authority (WRA) camps during World War II, though he still experienced prejudice as a Japanese American. In 1942 Yanagisawa took a position in the department of orthopedic surgery at St. Clare's Hospital in New York City. The same year he married. His new wife, Eugenie, was an obstetrician and gynecologist. In the next years, the couple had five children. In addition to his work at St. Clare's, where he rose to head of the Orthopedics Department, he opened a private practice, served on the city's retirement board, and worked as a police surgeon.

In 1942, in search of employment (and money to support his growing family), Yanagisawa took a job as house doctor at Madison Square Garden. He became renowned for giving free medical treatment to arena employees and sometimes their families. In 1949 he was named the Knicks' team physician as well. "Dr. Yana" became a familiar figure at the Garden—the only person given the right to smoke in the team locker rooms. A gruff but kindly physician, he not only treated the athletes' bruises but acted as a confidant and supporter. By the 1960s, he was a leading figure in sports medicine. He successfully removed a bone spur from the leg of Willis Reed, operated on Phil Jackson's back, and saved the career of Dick Barnett with an operation on his Achilles tendon. Yana also worked as team physician for the New York Rangers hockey team. He performed successful spinal fusions on no less than five players—notably star Rod Gilbert, who later eulogized the doctor as his second father—and repaired goalie Jacques Plante's knee. A burly, bespectacled man with a shape (said one Garden employee) like a sumo wrestler, Yanagisawa would show off his powerful chest muscles by inviting players to punch him in the stomach as hard as they wished. However, his size concealed diabetes and heart ailments. On February 22, 1970, he died suddenly of a heart attack. So close had he become to the Knicks that when they won the NBA title that year, his family was voted a full share of the prize money.

EARLY JAPANESE AMERICANS IN ORGANIZED BASEBALL

Many chroniclers have documented the place of baseball in the lives of Japanese Americans. The Nisei Baseball Research Project's notable book and film documentary, *Diamonds in the Rough: Baseball and Japanese-American Internment* illuminate how baseball helped inmates in the War Relocation Authority (WRA) camps deal with their situation. North of the border, the National Film Board of Canada's documentary *Sleeping Tigers: The Asahi Baseball Story* has revived interest in Vancouver's formidable prewar Nisei team. A special focus of Japanese American pride and commemoration is the career of Wally Yonamine, the versatile athlete who played in the National Football League—and then in minor league baseball for the Salt Lake Bees—before starring in Japanese baseball during the 1950s. The community fascination with baseball is reflected in the numerous Nikkei who played professionally in recent decades, including major leaguers Ryan Kurosaki, Don Wakamatsu, Lenn Sakata, and Mike Nakamura.

It is interesting to look back at some historical figures. One is José Nakamura, a 5-foot-8 left-hander who was one of the first Nikkei in the pros. Nakamura was born in Cuba, the son of a Cuban mother and a Japanese father who had immigrated at the turn of the century and worked in a sugar mill. After pitching for the Havana Cubans, Nakamura was discovered by Joe Cambria, a scout for the Washington Senators, and debuted in 1949. (That same year, incidentally, the California League's Modesto Reds launched their notable "Japanese battery" of pitcher Jiro "Gabby" Nakamura—no relation to José—and catcher Hank Matsubu.) After stops in Abilene, Laredo, and Tampa, José Nakamura landed with Shelby, North Carolina, in the Class D Tar Heel League, at the bottom of the pro pyramid. Nakamura spent three seasons there, compiling a 49–22 record. In 1953 he tallied a 2.40 ERA—the best in the league—and attracted attention by striking out 238 batters in 248 innings while walking only fifty-five. To obtain further seasoning (and also to earn money to help put his sister through medical school), he pitched in the Mexican League in the offseason.

Nakamura's record earned him a promotion to the Charlotte Hornets of the Class A South Atlantic League (often called the Sally League), whose color line had only recently been broken by the young Hank Aaron. Although Nakamura won his first game in April 1954, his coaches feared that his small stature would not allow him to pitch complete games, and they sent him to the bullpen. Without sufficient work to keep sharp, Nakamura struggled. After the 1955 season, he quit Charlotte and moved to Colombia, where he pitched for the Merida Indios. In 1957 he signed with the Mexican League's Yucatan Lions. He won ten games and helped pitch the Lions to the pennant. He retired in 1958. In his later years, he managed a sugar-processing factory. A museum in Colon, Cuba, includes exhibits about his baseball career.

A second figure is pitcher Toru "Bill" Nishita, a 6-foot 175-pound right-hander. Born in Hawai'i in 1930, he played for St. Louis High, then moved to the mainland to attend college. After compiling a 16–1 record for Santa Rosa Junior College in 1950, he enrolled at UC Berkeley and joined the Cal team. In 1951, shortly after graduation, he followed Wally Yonamine to the Tokyo Yomiuri Giants. (Yonamine later recalled feeling motivated to improve his own game by both Nishita's example and his higher salary.) Nishita pitched three seasons for the Giants, punctuated by a two-year hitch in the US Army. In 1954 he attracted the interest of scouts when he pitched in Honolulu against a group of barnstorming major leaguers directed by Yankee pitcher Eddie Lopat. Nishita held the major leaguers to three hits, though he lost 2–1 in extra innings.

In 1956, after being released from his contract with Tokyo, a scout for the Brooklyn Dodgers urged Nishita to try US baseball. Encouraged, he paid his own way to the Dodgers' spring training camp in Vero Beach, Florida, for a tryout. He impressed club officials so much that they signed him to a contract. Brooklyn sent him to their chief farm club, the Montreal Royals, making him the first Nisei to play in Triple-A—just one step beneath the majors—raising hopes that he might soon become the first Asian American big leaguer. (The choice of Montreal, known for racial tolerance, may not have been altogether accidental—Jackie Robinson had signed to play for the Royals when he broke pro baseball's color line a decade earlier.)

Once in Montreal, Nishita immediately caused widespread excitement in the local Japanese community. He started fast, chalking up three victories against a single defeat. Japanese Canadians in different cities organized trips to see him play. However, by late summer his record stood at 6–7, and he was traded away. Nishita spent the rest of 1956 and 1957 in the Dodger organization, then returned to Japan in 1958, where he went 16–19 for the Toei Flyers. After several more years pitching for different Japanese teams, and a stint with the Hawaii Islanders of the Pacific Coast League, he finished his career in Japan in 1963. In later years he lived in Hawai'i, where he died in May 2003.

Perhaps the greatest Nikkei baseball figure is Yosh Kawano, the legendary Chicago clubhouse attendant. As with many legends, it is hard to know where the truth lies. What is certain is that Kawano was born in Seattle in 1921, grew up in Los Angeles, and while still in high school was hired as clubhouse boy for the Hollywood Stars of the Pacific Coast League. In 1935 he worked as a batboy and attendant for the Chicago White Sox when they held spring training in Pasadena, California, and became a team favorite. Kawano gained national attention when he traveled to New York to see them after they left for the season. Three years later, Kawano again served as Sox batboy in spring training. Denied permission to come east with the team, he traveled to Chicago anyway and was hired. During these years, he also worked for the Chicago Cubs during their California trips. (Kawano's job with the Stars was taken by his brother, Nobu, who was the longtime equipment manager for the Los Angeles Dodgers.)

In the period after Pearl Harbor, Kawano was confined in the WRA camp at Poston. When he sought to join the Army, and was refused because of his small stature, he secured the assistance of White Sox manager Jimmie Dykes, who arranged for him to be enlisted. After spending nineteen months in New Guinea and the Philippines, where he was decorated for bravery, he moved to Chicago and took a job as clubhouse man with the crosstown Cubs. In 1953 he was promoted to equipment manager. In the decades that followed, Kawano became an institution. More than an employee, he was a friend and confidant to many players, to whom he freely lent money and gave advice. Ryne Sandburg even invited him to be present when the star second baseman was inducted into the Baseball Hall of Fame. According to one report, when the Wrigley family sold the team to the Tribune Company in 1981, one clause in the contract provided that Kawano could not be fired. In 1985, the fiftieth anniversary of Yosh Kawano's service, the Cubs officially named the clubhouse at Wrigley Field after him, and in 1997 they celebrated Yosh Kawano Day. In 2008, despite being hospitalized with cellulitis, he served his sixty-eighth season before retiring.

The JACL and the Integration of the American Bowling Congress

Professional sports have been one of the most visible areas of society for the promotion of civil rights. The most famous example of this is Jackie Robinson, who broke professional baseball's unwritten law of racial segregation when he took the field for the National League's Brooklyn Dodgers in 1947. Not only did Robinson's on-the-field heroics provide substantial proof that African American players could compete on an equal basis with whites, but his courage in enduring a tidal wave of racial attacks and hostility earned him widespread respect. In the process, he helped push the larger society into opening up.

Other sports leagues soon imitated Robinson's example. In July 1947, Larry Doby became the first African American player in baseball's American League. Professional football and basketball also gradually lifted their color bar. Marion Motley and Bill Willis of the Cleveland Browns—part of the All-America Football Conference in 1946, then the National Football League after the 1949 season—became two of the first African Americans in pro football. As previously noted, Wat Mikasa, a Nisei guard, became the first nonwhite player in professional basketball with the New York Knicks in 1947, while the first black players made their appearance three years later. Even professional golf, long the most exclusive of sports, was forced to abandon its lily-white status. Following a determined campaign by black golfers, led by the celebrated boxing champion Joe Louis, the Professional Golfers Association gradually relaxed its rules, though it did not formally void the whites-only clause of its constitution until 1954.

Perhaps surprisingly, the most entrenched opponent of racial integration among sports associations, and the target of a widespread legal and political campaign, was the American Bowling Congress (ABC). Founded in 1895, the ABC first enacted a "white men only" bylaw in 1916. Additionally, the ABC would not permit official matches to take place at any bowling alley that sponsored other tournaments for mixed groups. During World War II, bowling exploded in popularity nationwide (thanks in part to promotion by the US Army), and the injustice of the segregation appeared more glaring. Thus, in the aftermath of the war, labor and civil rights groups launched a campaign to overturn the official exclusion of minorities. In April 1947, a coalition of groups, led by the NAACP and the United Auto Workers-Congress of Industrial Organizations (UAW-CIO), came together in Chicago to create the National Committee for Fair Play in Bowling (NCFPB). Hubert Humphrey, the future US vice president and senator who was then the mayor of Minneapolis, agreed to serve as NCFPB chairman, while pro golfer Betty Hicks was named vice chair.

Among the groups who sent representatives to the Chicago conference was the Japanese American Citizens League (JACL), and its national president, Hito Okada, was named to the NCFPB steering committee. The JACL's involvement reflected the grave importance of the campaign to Japanese Americans. Long before World War II, bowling had been wildly popular among Nisei both in Hawai'i and on the mainland, who created their own leagues and held tournaments. In the aftermath of wartime removal and resettlement, Nisei bowling enthusiasts spread across the country and formed teams; a JACL survey in late 1947 found over 200 Japanese American bowling teams within the continental United States and an equal number in Hawai'i. The ABC exclusion rule hit these bowlers hard, both because of its undemocratic nature and because it restricted the number of bowling lanes open to them. (Although Asian Americans in Hawai'i were permitted to bowl in ABC-sponsored meets there, they could not participate on the mainland.) JACL leaders responded to the ban with a dual strategy. First, they created their own association. In September 1946, the national JACL sponsored a local bowling league of twelve teams in its home base of Salt Lake City and invited teams to compete in a tournament in March 1947. The event was such a success that the JACL established a national bowling tournament, open to both men and women. Over the following years, the tournament blossomed into a multicity meet, in which Korean American and Chinese American bowlers also joined. Indeed, the leagues were so successful that in 1950 Gish Endo of East Oakland was appointed as the first national JACL bowling commissioner to run the sport.

Meanwhile, the JACL began working to overturn the ABC exclusion rule. In March 1946, after multiracial groups of protesters formed picket lines outside an ABC tournament in Buffalo, New York, JACL secretary Mike Masaoka announced that the JACL would support the protests and organize one of its own. In December 1947, the JACL joined an unsuccessful NCFPB campaign to persuade Michigan governor Kim Sigler to deny the ABC use of the state fairgrounds for its annual meeting until it lifted its exclusion policy. Okada, Masaoka, and Sam Ishikawa then attended the NCFPB conference in New York in February 1948, where delegates planned to have allies introduce an amendment at the ABC meeting in April. However, when the ABC met in Detroit, Michigan, the 500 delegates voted the measure down. Worse yet, when "The Hawaii Ambassadors," a Hawai'i-based ABC team made up of bowlers of Chinese and Japanese ancestry, traveled to the national tournament as dues-paying members, they were barred from competing— the team instead made a tour of the nation to promote racial harmony in bowling. Following the ABC vote, UAW activists briefly formed a rival league, the All-America Tournament. In May 1949, the NCFPB organized a protest against the exclusion policy outside the ABC national tournament in Atlantic City, New Jersey. Richard Akagi of the New York JACL walked the NCFPB picket line and posed for photographs alongside representatives of the NAACP and the Brotherhood of Sleeping Car Porters. However, the delegates at that meeting once again voted down an amendment to end the ABC exclusion policy.

In fall 1949, CIO national counsel (and future US Supreme Court justice) Arthur Goldberg announced that the union had petitioned state authorities in Illinois, where the ABC was chartered, to take action against the organization due to its discriminatory practices. Illinois attorney general John S. Boyle filed suit to revoke the ABC charter because it "incited racial discrimination." As a result of the pressure, the ABC was forced to move its 1950 tournament from Indianapolis, Indiana, to Columbus, Ohio. In January 1950,

New York State attorney general Nathaniel Goldstein likewise brought legal proceedings to ban the ABC from the state. The NAACP and its allies meanwhile filed suit in Wisconsin and Ohio. (For reasons that are not clear, the JACL did not become a party in these lawsuits, though JACL vice president Tom Hayashi announced that the organization offered its full cooperation.) ABC secretary Elmer F. Baumgarten, the most determined opponent of integration, dismissed the legal actions and claimed that the foundations of the "American way of life" would be threatened if the organization lost the right to select its members. While the cases proceeded slowly through the courts, they did raise public awareness of the exclusion policy.

Japanese American bowlers in Seattle soon became the focus of widespread attention. In October 1949, the ABC ordered the Boeing Bowling Association in Seattle, made up of teams of aircraft workers, to expel the Nisei Clippers (an all-Nisei squad) from the league on racial grounds. Boeing refused and publicly defied the ABC by voting to formally admit the Nisei members. (Boeing reached a temporary—and rather ludicrous—compromise with the ABC, under which the Nisei team remained in the league, but only the scores and averages of the seven other teams were reported to the ABC). The Seattle City Bowling Association backed Boeing by enacting a resolution calling on the ABC to strike the word *white* from its eligibility requirements. The JACL organ *Pacific Citizen*, which had devoted extensive coverage to the bowling ban, editorially praised the action and denounced the "Un-American Bowling Congress" for its exclusion policy. Several leagues in Spokane and Portland withdrew from the ABC over its exclusion of Asian American members. The JACL launched a further protest in March 1950, when Kenneth Koji, a veteran of the 442nd Regimental Combat Team who had settled in Sparta, Wisconsin, was removed from the Wisconsin State Bowling Tournament on racial grounds. In response to the ouster, state attorney general Thomas E. Fairchild brought suit against the ABC.

The final turning point came on April 21, 1950, when Illinois judge John B. Sbarbaro found the ABC guilty of having "abused its franchise." and ordered it to drop its "white men only" bylaw and pay a $2,500 fine, or else its charter would be revoked. According to one source, Sbarbaro was prepared to revoke the ABC charter immediately, but ABC counsel Floyd Thompson pleaded with him not to, assuring the judge that the organization would be meeting two weeks later and would act on its own. The ABC's Baumgarten

countered by proposing that the ABC build its own lanes and become a completely private organization with freedom over membership. It was clear,
however, that the handwriting was on the wall.

Thus, on May 12, 1950, Jack Bunsey, president of the Boeing league, who
stated that he was acting on behalf of all the ethnic Japanese and Chinese
bowlers on the West Coast, introduced a resolution at the ABC annual
meeting to overturn the national exclusion policy (at the behest of southern delegates, the resolution provided that all members affiliate with local
associations, a compromise that permitted chapters in the South to continue practicing racial discrimination). After ABC general counsel Michael
Dunn reminded delegates that the organization's "very life" was at stake,
as a result of the lawsuits and negative publicity, the motion was quickly
passed by a voice vote. JACL president Hito Okada immediately issued a
statement hailing the move and added that he was proud of the JACL's role
in bringing about democratic practices in bowling. JACL national secretary Masao Satow recommended that all JACL leagues join their local ABC
associations—ignoring the important fact that the organization still barred
women. The ABC 1951 national tournament in St. Paul, Minnesota, was the
first to include Nisei bowlers.

The full history of the National Committee for Fair Play in Bowling remains
to be written. It was a rare example of a successful coalition between labor
unions and civil rights organizations during the early postwar period. Perhaps
because its target was an explicit nationwide racial ban, and because the racial
bar did not encompass sensitive areas such as jobs, education, or housing, its
leaders (notably the dynamic, young Hubert Humphrey) brought together
diverse public and private forces to support their campaign. The JACL role
in the NCFPB was relatively minor compared to the CIO or the NAACP (or
several Jewish groups, which provided extra funding and lobbying support).
Still, the JACL was the only nonblack minority organization to join the coalition, though in 1950 an Indonesian team competed in New York under its
auspices. Indeed, given the continuing exclusion of African American bowlers in the South even after the National ABC integrated, it is conceivable that
Nisei formed the largest nonwhite group to be admitted to the ABC after
the national ban was overturned. In any case, bowling remained for many
decades the Nisei sport of choice.

8

Arts

JUN FUJITA: POET AND PHOTOGRAPHER

One particular preoccupation of Nikkei in prewar Chicago was photography. Professional photographer Shoji Osato (father of dancer and actress Sono Osato) produced notable pictures of Chicago cityscapes. Harry K. Shigeta, who moved to Chicago from Los Angeles early in the Depression era, established a successful commercial photography business. There were also the Kuwahara, Yamamoto, and Ise photo studios. Isamu Tashiro, a local Nisei dentist, prepared lectures with colored slides during the 1930s to introduce Americans to Japanese culture. Most striking of all was Jun Fujita. Fujita's name is by no means a household word today, but he was perhaps the most famous Japanese American in Chicago in the first half of the twentieth century. In addition to his brilliance as a photographer, Fujita developed a masterful command of the English language, its rhythms and its subtle nuances. As a result, he became one of the relatively rare authors and poets who, like Joseph Conrad, Samuel Beckett, and Yone Noguchi, produced notable literature in a second language.

DOI: 10.5876/9781607324294.c008

Jun Fujita was born in Hiroshima, Japan, on December 13, 1888. According to one story, he first started photographing at the age of eighteen, when his uncle, the editor of a Japanese publication, sent him to Canada to photograph the Canadian fishing and lumber industries. Fujita remained in Canada for a short period, then came to the United States in 1909. Once in Chicago, Fujita enrolled at the Armour Institute of Technology (today's Illinois Institute of Technology) and studied electrical engineering. In order to support himself, he got a job as a cameraman with the *Chicago Evening Post*, photographing the events of the day. Almost immediately he created a sensation. On July 24, 1915, an excursion ship, the *SS Eastland*, capsized. Fujita's photos, especially one image of a horror-stricken fireman carrying a little girl's lifeless body out of the ship, were reprinted in newspapers nationwide.

Fujita remained with the *Evening Post* until the newspaper folded in 1932. His photos were also carried by the Newspaper Enterprise Association news service. He became notable for his photos of soldiers during World War I (for which he won a prize from the Liberty Bonds campaign) and those of the race riot on Chicago's South Side in summer 1919. In one haunting series, Fujita recorded a mob of young white men pursuing a black man and stoning him to death. He also took photos of gangland Chicago during the 1920s— notably the bloody aftermath of the notorious St. Valentine's Day Massacre of February 1929, where Al Capone's troops wiped out Bugs Moran's gang at a garage on North Clark Street. Fujita had a knack for taking photographs amid dangerous or forbidden surroundings. Perhaps because of his Japanese racial identity, he could remain inconspicuous and escape attack. In 1925 he defied a courtroom ban on photographs of the sensational trial of William D. Shepard, accused of having killed a millionaire orphan, and obtained a snapshot of the proceedings. Fujita also became known for his portraits of famous people who came through Chicago, such as Frank Lloyd Wright, Al Capone, and Albert Einstein. During these years, he met a fellow journalist, Florence Carr, whom he later married.

After the *Evening Post* went under, Fujita opened a commercial photography studio, Photo Craft, and worked for clients such as Sears, Roebuck & Company and Stark Bro's Nurseries and Orchards Co. During 1935 and 1936, Secretary of the Interior Harold Ickes, whom he had known in Chicago, hired him to photograph various public works projects being built as part of the New Deal.

Even as Fujita developed an eloquent visual vocabulary, he distinguished himself by his command of written language. His poetic sensibility even appeared in newspaper pieces he wrote. For instance, in one 1918 article, he made a comic playlet out of the trial of an accused bigamist. In another, he rhapsodized about a set of Oak Park triplets (in cadences that anticipate the later Howard Dietz/Arthur Schwartz song "Triplets" from *The Band Wagon*):

> *The three girls*
> *Look alike.*
> *Talk alike.*
> *Walk alike.*
> *Dress alike.*
> *Play alike.*
> *Sing alike.*
> *Work alike.*
> *Laugh alike.*
> *From which you may judge that they ARE alike.*

Soon he began regularly contributing tanka (Japanese poetry) to *Poetry* (the magazine of the Modern Poetry Association) and placed another piece in *Literary Digest*. In 1922 he complained that poet Amy Lowell's haikus lacked an "essential Japanese quality." In response, he assembled a slim volume of his poems (most already published) and gave them to the master printer Will Ransom to publish. In 1923 Covici-McGee published 365 copies of the collection *Tanka: Poems in Exile*. His poems have also appeared in *Quiet Fire: A Historical Anthology of Asian American Poetry, 1892–1970* and *The New Anthology of American Poetry*.

Fujita pursued various leisure time interests. He painted Japanese watercolors and enjoyed music. He designed and built a log cabin on Rainy Lake in Voyageurs National Park in Minnesota. The cabin, situated on a rocky island and surrounded by pine trees, suggests a Japanese landscape. Fujita drew on his love for photographing outdoors by building a cottage in the Indiana Dunes, where he took color photos of wildflowers after the first color sheet film was introduced in 1938. A set of his color photos of the countryside, which he first used to illustrate an article in *Home & Highway*, was later placed in the photograph collection of the Art Institute of Chicago. He was an outboard motorboat enthusiast and won several prizes in regattas. In

1933 he was favored to win the runabout competition at the Chicago Century of Progress Exposition but lost in the final heat. (He nevertheless covered all the events for *MotorBoating* magazine.)

Fujita, who was called "Togo" in Chicago in honor of the famous Japanese admiral, achieved great renown during his lifetime. He was friends with local literati, such as playwrights Ben Hecht and Charles MacArthur and poet Carl Sandburg. In a sign of the esteem in which he was held, Fujita was granted American citizenship by a special act of Congress, introduced by Illinois senator James Hamilton "Ham" Lewis. In 1942, even as the federal government instituted the mass removal of West Coast Japanese Americans, Fujita volunteered for wartime service. Harold Ickes recommended Fujita to the Office of War Information and testified to his absolute patriotism.

Fujita remained in semiretirement in later years and suffered from poor health. Nevertheless, he assisted in mounting an exhibition of his wildflower photos at Laurence Technological University in Michigan in 1958. A similar show followed in Oshkosh, Wisconsin, in 1962. In 1964, a year after Fujita's death, his widow donated his collected photos to the Chicago Historical Society.

ROBERT KUWAHARA: CARTOONIST AND ANIMATOR

From the early days of Japanese settlement in the United States, cartoon art, manga, and anime of various kinds have held a special fascination for the Nikkei. Cartoons and animation have attracted outstanding producers as well as consumers—including Henry Yoshitaka Kiyama's pioneering *The Four Immigrants Manga: A Japanese Experience in San Francisco, 1904–1924*, published in 1931; the comic strips in wartime camp newspapers, such as Jack Matsuoka's Poston cartoons; and Jimmy Murakami's animated films, beginning in the 1960s. One brilliant and versatile figure is Bob Kuwahara, who brought to life Walt Disney's early cartoon creations, started his own comic strip—the first by a Japanese American to be featured in the mainstream press—and later produced animated features.

Robert S. Kuwahara was born in Tokyo on August 12, 1901. He was the youngest son in a family of five boys and a girl. After he had attended school for two years in Japan, his parents brought him to the United States in 1910. Kuwuhara's father tutored him in English for several months, then enrolled him in first grade at a local public school. Kuwahara later recalled that at first he was teased—as an older boy and a foreigner—but that the hostility subsided once he mastered English. By the time he entered Polytechnic High School in Los Angeles, he had lost his accent completely. Kuwahara joined Poly's tennis team and was selected as a cartoonist for the school newspaper, the *Optimist*. (He was also fond of golf and won renown as a virtuoso on the musical saw.) After his high school graduation in 1921, he enrolled at the Otis Art Institute in Los Angeles, where he studied painting and drawing, with a concentration in portraiture. His talent was publicly recognized in 1924, when he entered a student competition to paint murals of babies for a nearby children's hospital and received a prize for his work.

After several years at Otis, Kuwahara moved to New York to study at the Grand Central School of Art and struggled to find work as a commercial artist. (The 1930 census lists him as living in the Bronx with a fellow Issei, Thomas Hayakawa.) However, in the face of the Great Depression, he was forced to abandon the effort and return to Los Angeles. Kuwahara's career received a boost in 1930, when William Edwin Rudge commissioned him to contribute to a series of limited edition portraits of famous American authors. Kuwahara executed studies of Lafcadio Hearn and Ralph Waldo Emerson— the Emerson drawing was much reproduced. Similarly, he was commissioned by the *Los Angeles Times* to do a portrait of author Agnes Repplier.

In 1932 Walt Disney hired Kuwahara as a writer and animator. Over the following years, he was named head of the Story Division and was active in designing a set of short animated films—notably *Thru the Mirror* (1936) and the Academy Award–winning *Who Killed Cock Robin?* (1935). Kuwahara was also part of the team that worked on Disney's first full-length cartoon, *Snow White and the Seven Dwarfs* (1937). In the meantime, he married a local Japanese American woman, Julia Suski, and had two children, Denis and Michel (known as Miki). In 1937 Kuwahara was hired to head a division of the cartoon department of Metro-Goldwyn-Mayer Studios.

The coming of the war transformed Kuwahara's life and work. Removed from his home by the government, he and his family were confined at the Santa Anita Assembly Center before being shipped to the Heart Mountain camp. Kuwahara's Japanese birth made it difficult to secure work on his release. He later recounted that he moved to Chicago, where he had a con-nection with a motion picture studio doing war-related work, but as an enemy alien he was unable to get a security clearance and his employment application was denied. Meanwhile, he tried working at advertising agencies and in commercial art but found that his background as an animator was a great handicap in entering other artistic fields. In desperation, he worked up a comic strip titled *Miki*, which was sold to a New York–based syndicate. His job secured, Kuwahara settled in the New York suburb of Larchmont. He found New York refreshingly clear of the prejudice he felt as a Japanese American in California.

In January 1945, *Miki* premiered in eleven newspapers. Within a few years, the strip was syndicated in twenty-three newspapers nationwide, including the *Chicago Daily News* and the *Brooklyn Eagle*, and scattered newspapers abroad. It featured a set of running characters, most notably Miki—a young boy with a powerful imagination who is the hero of the strip—and Uncle Harry, whom Kuwahara termed "the visual translation of Miki's imagination." Uncle Harry simultaneously watches over Miki, provides magic help, and causes trouble. Kuwahara claimed that Mickey Mouse was a model for the strip, but its combination of an imaginative boy and the companion he dreams up can be seen as a distant ancestor of Bill Watterson's strip *Calvin and Hobbes*.

Kuwahara's intention in writing and illustrating the strip was to represent, as he put it "an average American lad of heroic qualities and likable traits." Still, his vision of "average," or at least his sense of his market, was largely white. Although much of the strip's material was inspired by Kuwahara's sons—especially the younger son after whom his hero was named—the strip's central characters were white and no Japanese American characters were featured. Moreover, he downplayed his own ethnicity by drawing the strip under the name Robert Kay. All that said, Kuwahara used his own name when discussing his work in interviews and during public testimony before a congressional committee in 1947 in support of the Judd bill amending the Immigration and Naturalization Act.

In 1950 declining circulation forced Kuwahara to give up the *Miki* strip. He returned to animation work at Paul Terry's Terrytoons studio, where he worked on various features. In 1959 the studio selected him to write and direct the *Hashimoto-san* cartoons. This series featured Hashimoto, a Japanese mouse and judo expert, and his family. Hashimoto recounted his adventures to an American reporter by the name of G.I. Joe. Although a white actor provided Hashimoto's voice and the character had some stereotypical features, later commentators have praised the series as the first positive representation of Asians in American cartoons. Over the following four years, Kuwahara wrote and directed fourteen Hashimoto-san shorts. These were shown theatrically at first and later were incorporated into the CBS television program *The Hector Heathcote Show*. He also worked on the TV cartoon series *The Deputy Dawg Show* and the short-lived *The Astronut Show*. Kuwahara died in 1964.

The "Double Life" of Conrad Yama

Some time ago I had the happy surprise of uncovering the "double life" of a remarkable Nisei. It was not that he had a secret identity, like one of those spies who appear to lead tranquil suburban lives. He simply moved from one field (political activism and journalism) to another (theater and movies) and, in the process, changed his name. Still, the upshot was that K. Conrad Hamanaka and Conrad Yama, two Japanese Americans whose very different work I had known and admired, were in fact one and the same man.

Kiyoshi Hamanaka was born in Fresno, California, in 1919. After attending Fresno High School, he enrolled at Fresno State College, where he majored in speech and psychology and became interested in acting. Inspired by reading Tolstoy, he absorbed himself in socialist and pacifist ideas (he took the English name Conrad because it sounded like "comrade"). In July 1941, Hamanaka was called under Selective Service. He asked to be excused as a conscientious objector, stating that he did not believe in using "arms to kill human beings to solve world problems." His request was refused, and he was sent to Jefferson Barracks, Missouri, and confined in the stockade.

As a rare Nisei conscientious objector, Hamanaka's stand was not well received by Japanese Americans desperate to prove the group's loyalty. Issei leaders pleaded with him to withdraw his opposition to military service, and he was informed that his mother was suffering from his actions. To resolve the situation, he agreed to a compromise and accepted induction in a noncombatant role as a medic. After serving seven months, he was released on February 12, 1942, and he immediately returned to Fresno State. However, a week later, Executive Order 9066 was issued. Hamanaka was forced to repack his bags and move with his family to the Fresno Assembly Center.

FIGURE 8.1. Conrad Yama.

At Fresno, Hamanaka threw himself into activity. He taught drama classes, acted as a scoutmaster, and organized discussion forums for adults. He also ran membership drives for the American Civil Liberties Union (ALCU). When an inmate newspaper, the *Fresno Grapevine*, was created, Hamanaka was named editor. He quickly stood up for free speech. When a talk by an outside speaker was banned and editorials were censored, he ran the newspaper with black boxes where the excised stories would have been and sent the texts of the banned stories and speech to outside supporters, notably ACLU attorney Ernest Besig and Socialist leader Norman Thomas (Assistant Secretary of War John McCloy denied that a *Fresno Grapevine* existed, whereupon Thomas sent him the evidence). Perhaps in retaliation, government officials separated Hamanaka from his family and sent him to the Jerome camp. (According to a family legend, the reason for his separation was that he quarreled with his family, who objected to his dating an *eta*, or *burakumin*, woman [the lowest Japanese social class] at Fresno.) At Jerome, Hamanaka was named editor of the camp newspaper, the *Denson Tribune*.

When registration was imposed on inmates in early 1943, Hamanaka faced a dilemma. He supported democracy and wished to leave camp, but he felt that his status as a conscientious objector and his refusal to do military service meant that his allegiance was, by definition, qualified. Thus, his honest responses to Questions 27 and 28 could only be "no-no." Although Hamanaka avoided being sent to Tule Lake, he languished in Jerome for a year, during which he had multiple leave clearance hearings (one examiner offended him by asking repeatedly why he was not a Christian). He met a woman in camp, with whom he fathered a child. Meanwhile, with editorial help from Norman Thomas, he drafted an article on Japanese Americans and the "loyalty" question. In it, Hamanaka criticized the questionnaires as meaningless and punitive, noting that the provisions asking Nisei to "foreswear allegiance" to Japan presupposed that they had a previous allegiance. Thomas tried, without success, to place the article with various magazines. (A version of the text ran in the *Pacific Citizen* in 1945.)

In December 1943, after Hamanaka received an official discharge from the Army, he decided to bring suit against the government over his confinement, at which point he was promised a leave permit. He applied to the University of Chicago to pursue a degree in psychology and was accepted. However, the promised permit was held up by administrative means, despite repeated efforts by Ernest Besig to push the War Relocation Authority (WRA). In May 1944, Hamanaka suddenly received notification of his leave clearance. It is conceivable that officials intended to trap him, since as soon as he and his newlywed wife arrived in Chicago he was arrested for draft evasion—government lawyers insisted that his conscientious objector status and discharge had been wiped out by the reinstitution of conscription on Nisei. He was freed only after heroic efforts by Besig and intervention by WRA director Dillon Myer.

In the years that followed, Hamanaka married and moved to New York City, where he attended The New School, contributed to its literary magazine, *12th Street*, and immersed himself in Manhattan intellectual and bohemian circles. According to his family, Hamanaka was close to the circle of Beat writer Jack Kerouac and may have provided a model for Kerouac's Japanese characters. During these years, he and his wife had two daughters, Lionelle and Sheila. (Sheila Hamanaka has become a notable author/illustrator of children's books on Japanese Americans and other subjects.)

At length Hamanaka decided to become a professional actor and took the name Conrad Yama. In 1958 Yama received his first break when he was cast in the original production of Rodgers and Hammerstein's musical *Flower Drum Song*. He received glowing reviews for his performance as Dr. Li, the immigrant Chinese father of the heroine, played by Miyoshi Umeki. He remained with the play throughout its Broadway run and continued in touring productions thereafter. His next years were less successful, although Yama made guest appearances on TV's *Naked City* and *The Patty Duke Show*. In 1964 he opened on Broadway as a Coney Island concessionaire in the short-lived musical *I Had a Ball*, starring Buddy Hackett. (An early experiment in racially integrated theater, the play featured a multiethnic cast directed by an African American, Lloyd Richards.)

In 1968 Yama scored a notable coup. Based on his resemblance to Mao Zedong, he was cast as Mao in Edward Albee's avant-garde play *Box-Mao-Box*, which premiered in Buffalo and opened on Broadway in October. As a result, he won the small but showy role of Mao in the film *The Chairman*. Although the film, a rather silly thriller with Gregory Peck as an American scientist spying in China, was not a success, Yama was hailed for his performance—advertising agencies even hired him to portray Mao. He played a similar role in *The Virgin President* as a Chinese prime minister. (His daughter Lionelle portrayed the character's daughter.) Yama's work soon led to his being cast in other movies, including *Midway*, *The King of Marvin Gardens*, and *The Taking of Pelham One Two Three*. He even had a bit part as a fruit seller in *The Godfather*!

He likewise continued his theater work. In 1974 Yama starred opposite Pat Suzuki in Frank Chin's *Year of the Dragon* at the American Place Theatre, playing Pa, a domineering Chinese patriarch who speaks English with luscious malapropisms and refuses to understand Caucasians. He repeated the role in a TV production in 1975, with George Takei as his son. Yama returned to Broadway in Steven Sondheim's *Pacific Overtures* in 1976 and provided comic relief as a Burmese ambassador in David Hare's off-Broadway drama *Plenty* in 1982. After living in retirement in New York for many years, Conrad Yama died in 2010.

REIKO SATO: ACTRESS AND DANCER

Asian American performing artists of the postwar era (has it changed so much since?) had difficulty finding sufficient work, let alone parts that allowed them to transcend stereotypes. One exceptional actress and dancer, Reiko Sato, won recognition for her talents, but her career soon stalled. Today, long after her early death, her luminous talent still shines through her few, mostly brief, screen appearances. An intriguing aspect of Sato's career was her intimate relationship with Marlon Brando, a closely guarded secret during her lifetime.

Reiko was born in Los Angeles. She later claimed in interviews that her father was a Zen Buddhist priest. Whether this was real or invented, it is certainly true that Tonazo Sato came to the United States from Japan in 1906, at the age of twenty-four, after completing three years of university training. He settled in Southern California, where he made his living as a farm operator. By 1930 Tonazo was living as a boarder in Los Angeles. That year, he met and soon married Chieko Koyogaku, a young Japanese woman twenty-two years his junior who had just arrived in America (just how she was able to enter, during the time of the Japanese exclusion, is not clear). Chieko, like many Issei wives, was well educated by the standards of American women: she had attended two years of college—most likely a teacher's college—in Japan. Reiko, their first child, arrived on December 19, 1931. Her brother Koji followed two years later. (An older half-brother, Toshio, born in Wyoming in 1922, also lived with the family.) Sato later recalled that she took up dancing at the age of four. However, she was barely ten when the United States declared war on Japan. The Sato family was moved to Turlock and then confined at the Gila River camp.

After the war's end, the Sato family returned to Los Angeles, where Chieko managed an apartment building. Reiko later said that her two brothers served in the armed forces—one in the Army, the other in the Air Force. Reiko finished high school and enrolled in college, intending to study mathematics and languages. Despite her tiny size—she stood less than five feet tall and weighed barely ninety pounds—she radiated presence, and her mother encouraged her to perform. Reiko soon received a break when she was chosen for the role of Suki in a (forgettable) Dorothy McGuire movie, *Mother Didn't Tell Me* (1950). That same year, she also appeared in an Ann Sheridan thriller, *Woman on the Run*.

FIGURE 8.2. Reiko Sato.

She soon concentrated on dance and was accepted into the Jack Cole Dancers. Cole was a founder of modern jazz dance; he taught Gwen Verdon and influenced Bob Fosse. In 1953 Cole became the choreographer for the Broadway musical *Kismet*, an adaptation of an old *Arabian Nights* play that featured songs adapted from the music of Alexander Borodin (most famously "Stranger in Paradise"). Cole selected Reiko as one of the three "Ababu princesses," a trio of prospective brides for the Caliph, who performed a bravura staccato dance to the song "Not Since Ninevah." *Kismet* was a hit, and

Sato remained on Broadway with the show for almost two years. In 1955 she repeated her role in the MGM film version in which she was featured opposite Vic Damone. Sato found *Kismet* an enjoyable and familiar vehicle. (She would play in several revivals, including a West Coast tour in 1962 and a production at New York's Lincoln Center in 1965.) In 1956 she was given a chance to show off her acting talent when she accepted a lead role in the national tour of the Pulitzer Prize–winning play *The Teahouse of the August Moon*, in which she starred opposite Larry Parks.

Sometime during the early 1950s, Sato met Marlon Brando, who was notable for his attraction to Asian women. In June 1954, columnist Dorothy Kilgallen publicized the relationship with an item in her column, stating that Brando was romancing Reiko Sato. It was true that the two saw a lot of each other, although Brando was not, to say the least, a monogamous lover. Nevertheless, at some point, he asked Sato to marry him, a proposal she appreciated but declined. He also allegedly pushed to have her cast alongside him in the film version of *The Teahouse of the August Moon*. However, she considered the part demeaning and refused. It is not clear how long their romance lasted. Presumably it had cooled by the time Brando married Anna Kashfi in fall 1957. Nevertheless, the two remained close friends and companions for the rest of Sato's life.

Meanwhile, in early 1959, Sato had another chance to appear on Broadway when she was picked for the cast of the musical *Destry*, starring Andy Griffith as an unlikely gunslinger. Sato performed as Ming Li, one of a multiethnic chorus of prostitutes from Paradise Alley. She remained in *Destry* until the following year.

In 1960 Sato moved to Hollywood and was cast in *Hell to Eternity*, the film biography of war hero Guy Gabaldon, a Mexican American raised by a Japanese American family. The film has some historical importance as the first Hollywood picture to portray the wartime removal and confinement of Japanese Americans, though the product was, at best, uneven. Whether because of Sato's experience playing a prostitute in *Destry*, or just her appeal to prurient male interests, her role as a Nisei bar hostess from Hawai'i consisted primarily of a wild striptease dance (apparently somewhat edited amid fears of censorship). Once again, Vic Damone appeared with her.

The following year, she was granted a role at the other end of the spectrum. In the film version of *Flower Drum Song*, she was cast in the featured role of Helen Chao, the seamstress with a major unrequited crush on James Shigeta's Wan Ta, who sings the ballad "Love, Look Away." A young Marilyn Horne dubbed Sato's singing voice. However, she executed a powerful dance routine, some of which involved flying through the air on wires.

In her next role, Sato benefited professionally from her connection with Brando, who arranged for her to be cast in his film *The Ugly American* (1963), in a role originally planned for Brando's new wife, Tarita. Sato played the wife of an Asian revolutionary leader (played by Eiji Okada of *Hiroshima Mon Amour* fame). Her part, though small, was well received. After the film's release, Sato told an interviewer that she intended to stick to dramatic roles because musical and dance parts were so difficult to find. It was not to be, however. In 1966 Jack Cole invited her to join the cast of *Chu Chem*, a "Chinese-Jewish" musical. However, it closed out of town. Afterward, she gradually withdrew from the stage. In later years, she divided her time between Los Angeles and Brando's private South Sea island of Tetiaroa, which she helped manage. Reiko Sato died of a brain aneurism on May 28, 1981. Half of her ashes were sent for placement in a Buddhist temple; the other half were "spirited away" for burial in Tetiaroa.

The Unknown Life and Art of Miné Okubo

Miné Okubo gained a certain renown within Japanese American circles during the war years—first as the artistic editor of the magazine *Trek* in the War Relocation Authority camp at Topaz, then, most enduringly, as the creator of the 1946 book *Citizen 13660*, the first and perhaps finest camp memoir to see print. Okubo's years before and after camp form an untold story, or rather several stories. Interestingly enough, when Okubo died in 2001, her friends and family scheduled separate memorial services in Riverside, California; the San Francisco Bay Area; and New York City, as each had been home to her and represented a distinct period of her life and character. This article roughly follows that spatial and temporal division.

Miné Okubo was born in Riverside on June 27, 1912, one of seven children of Tamestugu and Miyo (Kato) Okubo. While she later described her father as a landscaper/gardener and occasional farmer, he seems to have taken on other jobs to feed the family; the 1910 census lists him as a tailor running a clothes shop and the 1920 census lists him as a dishwasher at a confectionary.

FIGURE 8.3. Miné Okubo's cover image for *Trek*, 1943.

According to family lore, Miyo Okubo was an honors graduate of the Tokyo Art Institute who was sent to the United States by the Japanese government to work as a calligrapher in the Japanese Arts and Crafts show during the

1904 St. Louis World's Fair. (While many Japanese, including a group of Ainu, were indeed "imported" for the Japanese pavilion, Miyo may not have been among them, since by the time the fair opened on April 30, she would already have been several months pregnant, and showing herself in public would have been shocking.) Miné later recalled that her mother used to paint at home and always encouraged her seven children to pursue artistic careers—nevertheless, Miné added, her mother often lost patience with her early artistic efforts because Miné could never copy anything precisely. After Miyo died in 1940, Miné would pay tribute to her with the painting *Miyo and Cat*, which portrayed her with Bible in hand.

In addition to Miyo, the family included numerous artists. One of Miyo's brothers, who also left Japan at the turn of the century, became a skilled impressionist-style painter and died young in France; Miné later treasured a set of photos of her uncle's lost canvases. Another artistic presence was Miné's brother Benji (Bunji) Okubo, a pioneering Nisei painter and director of the Art Students League of Los Angeles. (Legend also has it that Benji became the first Nisei movie actor when he took on the uncredited role of Trouble, the biracial son of Mary Pickford's Madame Butterfly, in the 1915 silent film adaptation of the story.) Miné was evidently not close to Benji, who was eight years her senior, and her artistic style differed from his, so she tended to minimize his impact on her. Still, he clearly served as a role model of artistic creativity and independence. Conversely, her sister Yoshiko Okubo (Tanaka), some five years older, was perhaps a stronger influence. Yoshi attended Riverside Junior College (today's Riverside Community College, or RCC), where she majored in art. In 1929 two of her paintings were featured in the Kane Art Exhibition in Riverside. After graduation, Yoshi opened a gallery in Riverside's downtown Mission District but closed it soon after she married. However, when Miné started having local exhibitions, her sister helped organize receptions for her.

The Okubos were among the few Japanese families in Riverside, and Miné made a diverse group of friends growing up. Her talent for friendship would remain a central part of her character. Another characteristic that she developed early on was a love of cats. Cats would remain a central subject in her art and in her life—she would later make her living for a time as a cat sitter. Moreover, whenever she signed autographs, she would include little drawings of cats next to her signature.

During her youth, Miné later recalled, she was interested in science, but she ultimately decided that science "was a man's world" and that she should choose something else. She settled on art, she added, as the highest form of human attainment, one that she wanted to master at as high a level as possible. After attending Poly High School, she followed her sister and enrolled at Riverside Junior College in 1930, though sources differ as to whether she graduated in 1932 or 1933. The RCC yearbook, for which she provided designs, was her first published work. Curiously, Miné did not contribute writings or artwork in those years to the local Japanese vernacular newspapers, *Kashu Mainichi* and *Rafu Shimpo*, the way other artistic-minded Nisei did. (After World War II, however, she agreed to create the artwork for *Kashu Mainichi*'s annual holiday issue, a tradition that would last for at least twenty-five years.)

Miné left Riverside for San Francisco soon after graduation and never returned to live there. Apart from her first solo show, which opened in the swank Mission Inn in November 1937, she did not show her work in Riverside for many years. However, in 1974 she was invited back to RCC as Alumna of the Year, in conjunction with an Okubo exhibition at the school's art gallery. In interviews she spoke with warmth and nostalgia about her time in the city. She was sufficiently impressed by the reception given her that in her will she left RCC her papers and the bulk of her private art collection. In February 2006, a street on the campus was officially renamed Mine Okubo Avenue in her honor.

Sometime around 1933, Miné was awarded a fellowship by the University of California, Berkeley, and she enrolled there in pursuit of both bachelor and master of fine arts degrees. In the late 1930s, after graduation, she took a job with the Federal Art Project, a branch of the New Deal–era Works Progress Administration—Miné was one of the relatively few Nisei to obtain public employment in California, where anti-Asian discrimination was overt. In addition to producing paintings directly for the project, she assisted John Haley, her former UC Berkeley professor, and Beckford Young in painting a set of murals for a building on Government Island (today's Coast Guard Island).

In 1938 Okubo won a Bertha Henicke Taussig Memorial Traveling Fellowship, which allowed her to spend eighteen months studying art in Europe. Miné visited museums in numerous cities. She loved to tell stories of roaming alone through Europe in winter wearing a large parka to protect against the unfamiliar chill—when asked her identity, she would cheerfully answer, "I'm an Eskimo!"

In September 1939, war broke out in Europe. Okubo caught one of the last boats home to the United States. Back in the Bay Area, she became active with the San Francisco Art Association (SFAA) and joined its annual painting and watercolor exhibitions at the San Francisco Museum of Art (today known as SFMOMA). She won an anonymous donor prize in the 1940 SFAA annual. The following year, her painting *Miyo and Cat* won the Anne Bremer Prize and was purchased by the Oakland Museum of California. (Her other 1941 entry, *Chapel Hill*, a study of African Americans at prayer, also aroused critical attention.)

In fall 1940 and 1941, Miné put on solo shows of gouaches in the SFAA gallery in the San Francisco Museum of Art. She also exhibited there with the San Francisco Society of Women Artists. Four Okubo paintings were included in the Society's fall 1940 annual, leading critic Emilia Hodel of the *San Francisco News* to declare Okubo "the star of the show." The next year, Okubo's gouache *Fishing Boats* won honorable mention in the Society's exhibition of watercolors. Okubo also displayed her work in the East Bay. In 1940 she won first prize in the University of California Art Exhibition and then displayed her watercolor works in the lobby of the now-demolished Telenews Theater in Oakland. She also contributed artwork to a show in the California section of the Palace of Fine Arts at the 1940 Golden Gate International Exposition on Treasure Island. That summer, Okubo was selected to assist the famous Mexican painter Diego Rivera in painting murals at the fair—she also enjoyed hanging out with his wife, artist Frida Kahlo, who accompanied him. Today the murals can be found at the City College of San Francisco.

In spring 1942, Okubo was working on murals for the Servicemen's Hospitality House in Oakland when Executive Order 9066 was issued. Friends advised her not to leave the West Coast so that she could complete the job; she received special permission to travel after dark in violation of curfew so that she could finish her work. The Okubo family was divided soon after by the official removal. Okubo's father was arrested and interned in Missoula, Montana. (Miné later explained that her father had likely been arrested due to the fact that he had joined the Japanese Union Church. However, he had no political connections or interests and joined primarily for some company after his wife's death.) Meanwhile, her siblings were incarcerated in different camps: Benji Okubo was confined at Heart Mountain, where he opened an art school. The others went to Poston.

Miné and one brother were confined at the Tanforan Assembly Center, then moved to Topaz. At Topaz, Okubo taught art classes and helped found a literary review, *Trek*, for which she drew cover designs and illustrations. She produced over one thousand drawings of life in camp, some of which she transformed into formal drawings and paintings. She continued her close association with the SFAA and the San Francisco Museum of Art. In early 1943, her drawing of camp sentries won a prize at an SFAA show, and a reproduction appeared in the *San Francisco Chronicle*. The publicity attracted the editors of *Fortune* magazine, who hired Okubo to work on a special issue on Japan in conjunction with two other Japanese American artists, Yasuo Kuniyoshi and Taro Yashima. With the employment guarantee, Miné left Topaz and moved to New York, where she lived for the rest of her life. Okubo's illustrations in *Fortune* caused a sensation, especially the selection of her camp sketches that accompanied an article on Japanese Americans. With *Fortune*'s blessing, the San Francisco Museum of Art mounted a special exhibition of the original *Fortune* artwork by Okubo and her colleagues in August 1944.

While Okubo never again lived in the Bay Area, for several years she continued to exhibit in established venues there. In 1945 and 1946, her watercolors won honorable mentions in SFAA shows at the San Francisco Museum of Art. In 1948 her painting *Strike* won honorable mention at the SFAA's 65th Annual Painting and Sculpture Exhibition, and the following year her painting *Cat and Cradle* won the Anna Elizabeth Klumpke prize at the 66th exhibition. Her success as a mainstream California artist climaxed in 1949, when her painting *Clown and Horse* received the prestigious James D. Phelan Award; Miné doubtless appreciated the irony of winning prize money endowed by the estate of California's race-baiting anti-Japanese senator. In 1950 she was an instructor of art for the University of California, Berkeley summer session and spent several months in San Francisco. While Okubo scaled down her West Coast activities after 1950, she still considered herself a California artist, and her chief collectors—Roy Leeper, Gaylord Hall, and Mas Yonemura—were all Bay Area residents. It was therefore fitting that *Miné Okubo: An American Experience*, the first major retrospective of her art, premiered at the Oakland Museum of California in 1972. Furthermore, in 1983 she was one of twelve women featured in the state Department of Education's educational guide "California Women."

As noted, Okubo left Topaz in 1944 and settled in New York, with help from *Fortune*. The magazine's editors found her a rent-controlled studio apartment in Greenwich Village. She would live and work there until the last months of her life. (Her studio's location shaped her art: out of deference to her fellow tenants, Okubo generally painted with acrylics—oils, she feared, would smell too strong.) She stubbornly outlasted several landlords who tried to get her out so that they could develop the building and who punished her by turning off her heat or removing her rear balcony. She joked that after one particularly recalcitrant landlord dropped dead of a heart attack, the later ones left her alone!

Once in New York, Okubo met M. Margaret Anderson, editor of *Common Ground*, a liberal pro-immigrant quarterly. With Anderson's encouragement, Okubo assembled a show of her camp sketches and other art, which opened at *Common Ground*'s offices in March 1945. It moved briefly to the New School for Social Research and subsequently toured the West Coast, including Gumps department store in San Francisco and Pasadena's Fountain House bookstore. When the show played the Seattle Art Museum, *Time* magazine ran an article on Okubo.

Meanwhile, Okubo arranged her sketches into a book-length narrative and drafted the accompanying text. Columbia University Press published the work, *Citizen 13660*, in September 1946. *Citizen 13660* recounts Okubo's removal experience and her life at Tanforan and Topaz. Its words and images depict the multitudinous features of camp life—the dust storms, the lack of privacy, the (barely) converted horse stalls where inmates were housed, the schools, the loyalty exams, even the gangs of radical inmates who beat up suspected informers.

While later commentators, including Okubo herself, emphasized the protest angle and subversive nature of *Citizen 13660*, many reviewers did not perceive the work in such terms when it first appeared. Rather, mainstream critics unanimously lauded the text as an objective record of the camp experience and underlined Okubo's humor and warmth. In a typical commentary, proletarian novelist Jack Conroy wrote in the African American newspaper *Chicago Defender*, "The story is told with authentic simplicity rather than recrimination or bitterness." While the Japanese press was also generally positive, certain Nisei publications, such as *Nisei Weekender* and the *JACD Bulletin*, criticized Okubo for soft-pedaling the horrors of the camp experience. In response, Alice Togo, herself a former inmate, snapped in *Pacific Affairs* that even if the text did not directly address the ethics of removal and the damage to the inmates, the images did: "[Okubo] draws no conclusions for her reader, but any thoughtful person examining her drawings of the disorganized classrooms, the crowded living quarters which offer no privacy, and the institutionalized mess halls can form his own judgment." (The *Hokubei Shimpo*, which noted that Okubo had powerfully shown the difficulties of life in camp, also enthused over her humorous depiction of Issei, with faces resembling those in Ukiyo-e prints.)

Even before *Citizen 13660* came out, Okubo threw herself into making art. She participated in several group shows: one of her first—an exhibition of New York Japanese American artists that opened in summer 1947—was, by pleasant coincidence shown at the city's Riverside Art Museum. She then had a solo show at the Mortimer Levitt Gallery in 1951. However, Okubo could not support herself by selling her canvases. As before the war, she took on commissions for mural projects. Most notably, in 1948 she was invited by American Export Lines to provide a set of eight 8-foot-high 17-foot-wide murals for the salons of a quartet of new ships, the *4 Aces*. (The canvases were so large that the only way Okubo could fit them into her studio/apartment was to place them diagonally, bisecting the living room.) Miné's murals, stylized route maps of the Mediterranean with small city symbols, attracted praise by *New York Times* art critic Aline Loucheim.

Still, Okubo faced a dilemma: How could she support herself yet find time and resources to paint? At first, she struggled to make a reputation as a commercial artist and illustrator. Her drawings were accepted for publication by magazines such as *Saturday Review of Literature, Life, Survey Graphic*—even *The Spirit*, house organ of the Standard Oil company. Under the aegis of M. Margaret Anderson, her work appeared regularly in *Common Ground*. In 1945 she illustrated one of the first published articles by Chinese American writer Jade Snow Wong. Two years later, her drawings accompanied an article by Bradford Smith. Okubo's drawings were also featured in the *New York Herald Tribune* and the *New York Times*. *Times* book review editors reprinted selections from Okubo's camp sketches in reviews of three different books (as well as her own), during the late 1940s. The editors then commissioned

Okubo to do marginal drawings for three articles on non-Asian American topics during the years 1950–1952.

Nonetheless, newspaper and magazine work proved too erratic and sporadic in nature to be a stable source of support, and Okubo may also have wished for a chance to extend her talents. She thus phased out magazine work and discovered another field of art through which she could not only earn money but use her creativity: book illustration. Although art historians have rarely studied Asian American commercial book art, it represented one of the first mainstream venues for Nikkei artists to display their talent, at least under their own names. In the first part of the twentieth century, artists such as Gazo Foudji, Sanchi Ogawa, and Genjiro Yeto (aka Genjiro Kataoka) gained attention with their designs for works by authors such as Lafcadio Hearn, Onoto Watanna (Winifred Eaton), and Yone Noguchi. Conversely, few postwar Japanese Americans, apart from Isami Kashiwagi and Henry Sugimoto, won contracts for book illustrations (Gyo Fujikawa and Taro Yashima illustrated other people's books but were best known for their own).

It is not altogether clear how Miné began illustrating books, but it was likely due to the involvement of Toru Matsumoto. Matsumoto was a Japanese Christian who migrated to the United States in 1935 and enrolled at Union Theological Seminary, then stayed on in New York during the war. After being ordained as a Reformed Church minister in 1944, Matsumoto concentrated his efforts on pastoral care and support for Japanese American resettlers. In 1948 Matsumoto wrote an autobiographical novel about his boyhood in Japan called *The Seven Stars*. Friendship Press, the publishing arm of the National Council of Churches (then called the Federal Council of Churches), agreed to publish the work, then commissioned Miné to create images for it. Despite her Japanese background, Okubo had never been to Japan and did not know Japanese art well. Rather then imitate orientalist stereotypes, she responded with a set of tiny square "decorations" which used classic Japanese motifs— pine trees, village rooftops, rice pickers—stylized within rapidly sketched, almost impressionist drawings. Friendship Press's art editors were evidently pleased because they selected Okubo to illustrate a half-dozen more books about Japan and international relations over the following years. (She meanwhile did a frontispiece for Robert W. O'Brien's 1950 book *The College Nisei*, a history of the National Japanese American Student Relocation Council, portraying a typical Nisei framed against a college campus.)

In 1960 Okubo, perhaps seeking more varied work, left Friendship Press. She agreed to illustrate a psychology book, Walter Toman's *Family Constellation: Its Effect on Personality and Social Behavior*, for the German publisher Springer. Her humorous, childlike drawings of family members complemented Toman's text. She was thus assigned to do further illustrations for Springer. Notably, in 1965 she provided illustrations for the anatomy textbook *Clinical Coordination of Anatomy and Physiology*. Okubo stated later that she carefully studied and memorized anatomical details for the drawings. Shortly after, she decided to give up illustrating and concentrate entirely on painting. In 1968 she mounted an exhibition of her art, the first in nearly twenty years.

By this time, Miné's camp experience and artwork had faded from view, although she appeared in "The Nisei: The Pride and the Shame," an episode of the 1965 CBS TV documentary series *The Twentieth Century*. During the 1970s, Okubo joined the nascent redress movement, even as her work was rediscovered. A new edition of *Citizen 13660* appeared in 1983 and won an American Book Award. Okubo was asked to contribute to shows of art by camp inmates, and her work was officially recognized. Miné was perhaps proudest of an award she received from New York comptroller Alan Hevesi, for her contributions to her adopted city. She continued to paint and to mask her warm heart with a brusque exterior. She died in 2001.

GYO FUJIKAWA: ARTIST AND AUTHOR

During much of the twentieth century, Japanese American artists, like other Asian Americans, had a difficult time pursing their careers. They shared the troubles of other artists in publicizing and selling their work in a market-driven economy, where art was either treated as a commodity or ignored altogether. They also experienced additional difficulties as nonwhites. With a few notable exceptions, Japanese Americans remained outside the kind of social networks where they could meet patrons and secure commissions—especially for portraits—that aided so many painters and sculptors. Art magazines did not feature their work and mainstream galleries were out of their reach. They did not even have any source of direct philanthropic support equivalent to the Harmon Foundation, which subsidized black artists and fostered the growth of African American painting.

The public art programs of the New Deal during the 1930s were of only limited assistance to Nikkei artists. Federal authorities quickly restricted hiring to US citizens, thereby discriminating against the mass of Issei creative artists barred from citizenship on racial grounds. West Coast Nisei, likewise, remained largely excluded from federal support by biased administrators and struggled to promote their work. Japanese Americans were forced to rely on whatever scarce financial support they could obtain from their own communities. Artists mounted their own shows or combined their artistic endeavors with related work, if they could. Seattle painters Kamekichi Tokita and Kenjiro Nomura opened a sign-painting business to support themselves. In the face of these formidable obstacles to success, it was not surprising that many budding artists gave up and entered other careers. Yet Gyo Fujikawa, a multitalented Nisei, managed to achieve renown in a few different areas of visual art despite facing professional barriers as a Nisei and additional ones as a woman.

Gyo Fujikawa was born in Berkeley on November 4, 1908, to Mr. and Mrs. Hikozo Fujikawa. The family later moved to Southern California. Gyo excelled in art from a young age. She won a drawing contest in high school and displayed such talent that a teacher recommended her for a scholarship at the prestigious Chouinard Art Institute. Fujikawa enrolled, despite the opposition of her parents, who feared that an artist's life would be too uncertain and urged her to attend an academic college. Following her graduation in 1932, she spent a year in Japan studying Japanese brush painting. She later claimed that her studies in Japan helped school her in patience and concentration. Following her return to the United States, she taught at Chouinard. Meanwhile, she took up work at Walt Disney Studios, which maintained a whole stable of Asian American animators (the most notable being famed painter Tyrus Wong). Fujikawa prepared various brochures and advertisements promoting the movie *Fantasia*.

After several years at Disney, Fujikawa was lured to New York as art director for William Douglas McAdams, a pharmaceutical company. Because she was living in New York at the time World War II started, she was able to continue her commercial work during the war and was not confined in government camps, though her family was confined at Rohwer. After the war, Fujikawa began work as a freelancer, doing commercial drawings and designing Christmas cards. She designed one notable campaign for

Beech-Nut baby food. Fujikawa put together drawings of Mother Goose characters that could be strung together to make a minibook. In 1964 she was commissioned to design a cover for the *Saturday Evening Post*. Her design, a picture of a parakeet in a cage pressed up against a window to see a bird in the snow outside, received widespread publicity when her original painting was stolen from a car in Washington, DC, after the reproduction for the cover had been completed.

Meanwhile, Fujikawa became active in book design. In 1952 she produced a set of drawings of Disney characters for *McCall's* magazine. The drawings attracted the attention of children's book publishers Grosset & Dunlap, which hired her to illustrate a new edition of Robert Louis Stevenson's *A Child's Garden of Verses*, first published in 1953. Its success led the publisher to commission additional book illustrations. Fujikawa's edition of Clement Clarke Moore's *The Night Before Christmas* (1961) and her edition of *Mother Goose* (1968) became particular favorites.

Not content with providing pictures for other authors's work, in 1963 Fujikawa persuaded the publisher, Grosset & Dunlap, to publish two original children's books she had written and illustrated, *Babies* and *Baby Animals*. The two books quickly became children's bestsellers. Absorbed by the process of creation, Fujikawa gradually withdrew from commercial art and concentrated on writing and illustrating children's books. In the two decades that followed, she produced some forty different works, of which the best known was *Gyo Fujikawa's A to Z Picture Book* (1974). Other well-regarded titles included *Oh, What a Busy Day!* (1976), *Gyo Fujikawa's Come Follow Me . . . to the Secret World of Elves and Fairies and Gnomes and Trolls* (1979), *Welcome is a Wonderful Word* (1980), *Jenny Learns a Lesson* (1980), *That's Not Fair!* (1983), *Shags Finds a Kitten* (1983), and *Are You My Friend Today?* (1988).

Fujikawa's books attracted a large audience and were translated into French, Spanish, and Dutch. She became one of the first children's authors to command author's royalties instead of a flat fee. Her picture books were also notable as being among the first to include children of various racial groups. She later noted that she preferred seeing things from a child's view and almost never put grownups in her works. Her obituary in the *New York Times* later quoted her on the subject: "Although I have never had children of my own, and cannot say I had a particularly marvelous childhood, perhaps I can stay I am still like a child myself. Part of me, I guess, never grew up."

Another notable aspect of Fujikawa's oeuvre was her work designing US postage stamps. In 1960 she designed a four-cent stamp commemorating the one hundredth anniversary of a US-Japan trade agreement. The image, colored in pink and blue, featured a view of Washington, DC, with the Washington Monument seen through the cherry trees. The stamp design gained extra publicity when it was featured at an official welcome ceremony for Crown Prince Akihito—the future emperor of Japan—who praised its "felicitous" design. In 1964 she was commissioned to produce a second stamp in support of Lady Bird Johnson's campaign to beautify the country (which included the removal of road signs and opening gardens). Fujikawa's stamp, inaugurated in 1966, resembled the first. It also included cherry trees and a Washington landmark—this time, the Jefferson Memorial. In 1982 Fujikawa produced her third stamp, commemorating the fiftieth anniversary of the International Peace Garden, which spans the border of Manitoba and North Dakota. The stamp featured a Canadian maple leaf (a rare rendering in official US art of a symbol of another nation) and a red rose. Three more stamps with designs by Fujikawa would see the light in the 1990s. In 1993 her design for a twenty-nine-cent stamp featured the image of a red rose. She followed it with a thirty-two-cent pink rose design two years later. In 1997, at the age of eighty-nine, her last design, for a thirty-two cent stamp, contained a yellow rose. On November 26, 1998, three weeks past her ninetieth birthday, Gyo Fujikawa died in New York.

Shinkichi Tajiri: Sculptor

Amid the innumerable topics that make up the tapestry of Japanese American history, one little-noticed theme is that of Nisei in Europe. While the exploits of the 442nd Regimental Combat Team in Italy and France during World War II have been thoroughly studied and commemorated, the large presence of Nisei students, soldiers, and expatriates in the surrounding years has passed largely unnoticed. Fortunately, a series of Nisei memoirs over the years has afforded us insight into the lives and careers of some of the individuals who have resided in Europe. Sono Osato's *Distant Dances* (1980) covers the years she spent as a schoolgirl in Paris and then as a ballerina touring with the Ballet Russes in the 1930s. The journalist Gene Oishi's *In Search of Hiroshi* (1988) tells the story of his military service in postwar Europe and his stint as

FIGURE 8.4. Shinkichi Tajiri in Chicago, 1948.

a jazz musician in a band in Verdun (he would go on to spend four years as a newspaper correspondent in Europe). Paul Okimoto's recent *Oh! Poston, Why Don't You Cry For Me? And Other Stops Along the Way* (2011) recounts his medical studies in France.

Particularly prominent and striking is the contribution of Nisei in the arts, beginning in the years before the war. In 1929 singer Agnes Yoshiko Miyakawa moved from Sacramento to Paris, where she earned international renown singing *Madame Butterfly* at L'Opéra Comique. In 1936 soprano Toshiko Hasegawa started an opera career in Italy that led to her becoming a lead singer at Teatro alla Scala in Milan. In the late 1930s, Newton Tani moved from San Francisco to Paris to study piano. The well-known artists Henry Sugimoto and Isamu Noguchi studied art in Europe in the late 1920s. They mixed with such eminent Japanese-born creative artists as painter Leonard Foujita (Tsuguharu Fujita) and dancer Michio Ito. Miné Okubo, thanks to a fellowship, toured Europe in 1937 and 1938 and studied the great masters.

In the years after the end of the war, new connections were made. Lillian Oka Tcherkassky danced with Les Ballets de Monte Carlo. Steve Shigeo Wada used the GI Bill to travel to France and study painting with Fernand Léger. Hiroshi Tamura was awarded a fellowship in Paris by the Art Institute of Chicago. Hawai'i-born Dorothy Furuya studied for three years at L'Académie Julien in Paris. Poet Kikuko Miyakawa (Packness), who won a fellowship to study silver work in Copenhagen, married a Danish official and settled down there.

Probably the most eminent, and surely the most versatile, of the Nisei artists who went to Europe was Shinkichi Tajiri, a California-born Japanese American who became a nationally known figure in his adopted nation of the Netherlands. He was born Shinkichi George Tajiri on December 7, 1923 (he would turn eighteen on the day of the Pearl Harbor attack), one of the six surviving children of Ryukichi Tajiri, a descendant of a samurai family, and his wife, Fuyo. He spent his childhood in a multiracial area of South Central Los Angeles, where he later noted that all of his friends were African Americans.

When George (as he was then known) was thirteen, his father found a new job as representative of the San Diego Fruit & Vegetable Growers Association, and the family moved to San Diego, where the young Tajiri attended high school. He suffered successive shocks, first when his father died suddenly, and then when he was struck by a prolonged illness that kept him bedridden for months. By this time, he had already grown interested in art. In summer 1941, he attended a Work Projects Administration–financed sculpture class in San Diego's Balboa Park. The instructor, Ruth Ball, brought him to sculptor Donal Hord, a modernist famous for his Aztec-inspired stoneworks and buildings. Hord took him on as a pupil and instructed him in sculpture and drawing.

By this time, George's older siblings were out of the house and beginning to make a name for themselves. His eldest brother, Larry Tajiri, would become the era's most prominent Nisei journalist, as editor of the *Pacific Citizen* during and after World War II and then as a columnist and drama critic for the *Denver Post*. (After Larry's sudden death in 1965, his younger brother agreed to serve on the board for the Larry Tajiri Memorial Award for Outstanding Accomplishment in the Performing Arts, established in his honor, and to design the statuettes for the award, dubbed the "Larry.") George's brother Vincent Tajiri, who was a sports reporter and short story writer for the *Nichi Bei*, would go on after the war to become the founding photo and art director of *Playboy* magazine.

The young George and his family were caught in the roundup of West Coast Japanese under Executive Order 9066 and were removed to Santa Anita and Poston. (During the war, their home in San Diego was literally pulled up and carted away with all the furnishings inside, and after being sold at auction, it disappeared forever.) At Santa Anita, Tajiri took art classes with Hideo Date. While at Poston, he met Isamu Noguchi (a warm friend of his brother Larry), with whom he helped lead Poston's art department. He passed the time in camp by making crayon drawings using art materials donated by Donal Hord. In May 1943, he had his first exhibition at Poston High School of his paintings and charcoal drawings.

After the US Army established an all-Nisei volunteer combat unit (the future 442nd Regimental Combat Team) in early 1943, Tajiri decided that, being the family's oldest son in camp, he should volunteer as a patriotic gesture. He may also have thought that at 110 pounds, with a heart flutter, poor eyesight, and a history of pneumonia, he would not likely be accepted. In any event, he enlisted. After eleven months of intensive training (during which time he also served as a staff illustrator of the unit's yearbook), he shipped out with his unit to Italy, where he took part in the battle of Anzio. On July 9, 1944, he was wounded in one leg. After six months recovering in an Army hospital, he was transferred to noncombatant duty as a postal worker and hotel concierge. Along with his friend Milton Hartfield, he was then assigned to Special Services, where he drew portraits of displaced persons.

In 1946 Tajiri was discharged and went to join his family, who had resettled in Chicago. With help from the GI Bill, he enrolled at the Art Institute of Chicago. He helped form the Gaka Art Guild—a cooperative of Nisei and white artists—and eventually served as its president and supervised the Guild's exhibit at the Southside Community Art Center, which included his stone sculpture *Father and Son*. However, embittered by wartime confinement and distressed by the anti-Japanese prejudice he encountered in postwar

Chicago, Tajiri decided to leave the United States. He resolved to return to Europe, where he could perfect his art. He remained in "self-imposed exile," as he later termed it, for the rest of his life. In the process, he decided to drop the name George—from then on he would be known only as Shinkichi, or simply by the name Tajiri.

In fall 1948, Tajiri sailed to France in order to study with the noted sculptor Ossip Zadkine. He also took painting classes from Fernand Léger and studied at the Académie de la Grande Chaumière. His work centered on abstract forms constructed of iron and plaster. He soon undertook what he called his Junk series, sculptures of recycled split bronze from rubble heaps around abandoned factories that he welded together with wire or brass (he scoured the banks of the Seine for discarded metal). He also began his Brick series, small-scale bronze sculptures formed from a mold of carved firebricks. After meeting artist Karel Appel in Paris, Tajiri grew close to the members of COBRA, an avant-garde art and social protest group that was later celebrated. He participated in their 1949 show at the Stedelijk Museum Amsterdam, then a second one in 1952.

After his GI Bill stipend ran out in 1951, Tajiri supported himself for a time by teaching art and designing patterns for a wallpaper factory in Wuppertal, Germany. He returned to Paris in 1953. He sold some of his sculptures and gave seminars on the use of the acetylene torch in sculpture but was forced to take odd jobs to support himself (he received some support from his first wife, a nurse at the American Hospital of Paris in Neuilly, who had cared for him after he contracted hepatitis). Soon after, he met Ferdina "Ferdi" Jensen, a young Dutch sculptor and jewelry designer who would become his second wife and chief muse. He also discovered filmmaking. In 1955 he and filmmaker Baird Bryant won a Golden Lion award at the Cannes Film Festival for their short film *The Vipers*. The work, set to a soundtrack by Stan Kenton's band, explored in surreal imagery the "high" experienced by a marijuana smoker. Following this success, Tajiri produced his second film, a documentary on Ferdi's jewelry designs.

Even as his films enjoyed success, his artistic career picked up. He had one-man shows in Paris, Brussels, Amsterdam, and The Hague and participated in various group shows in Europe and Chicago and at the Carnegie International in Pittsburgh. He exhibited at three of the famous Documenta shows in Kassel, Germany. Around this time, the Museum of Modern Art in New York acquired one of his pieces for its collection. In 1959 he won the William and Norma Copley prize for achievement in sculpture, and a John Hay Whitney Fellowship the following year. One of his large sculptures won the Mainichi Shimbun prize at the Tokyo Biennale and was installed in the garden of the city's Meiji Yasuda Life Insurance Company. Another of his pieces was placed in the garden of the Stedelijk Museum Amsterdam. The city of Arnhem (Ferdi's birthplace) commissioned him to create a giant sculpture for its town square to commemorate the rebuilding of the city, and other commissions followed. So much of Tajiri's work, in fact, was placed in outdoor spaces that he abandoned iron sculpture for bronze, which would stand up better to the elements.

Beginning in the 1960s, Tajiri's sculpture concentrated on two themes. One was the warrior. Partly because of his own wartime experience, Tajiri held strong antiwar sentiments and deplored the waste and danger of the arms race. In 1964 he made a series of eight large machines inspired by streamlined Formula One cars (automobiles and, especially, motorcycles, were an undying love of his), jets, and rockets. At the same time, he was drawn to Japanese folklore and the figure of the samurai. In later years, he would begin work on a monumental series based on the 47 Ronin, the masterless samurai of Japanese legend. Meanwhile, in 1967 he started work on his Knots series, a set of curving sculptures that he thought had a universal and multiple human significance (he spoke with amusement about the many questions he received regarding the presence of sexual imagery in his work).

In addition to sculpture, Tajiri pursued many other arts. He illustrated books for authors ranging from Henry Miller and Christopher Logue to Margaret Randall. He also practiced photography, creating a set of notable stereoscopic images of the entire Berlin Wall and reviving the long-defunct art of daguerreotypes (early photographic images on a metal plate). In 1970, while in Copenhagen, he produced the documentary *Bodil Joensen: A Summer Day*, about the Danish actress and porn star of that name. Tajiri was also a pioneer in working artistically with videotape and creating experimental videos. He published several art books as well as his memoirs (which appeared in an illustrated bilingual English-Dutch edition).

In 1956 Shinkichi and Ferdi moved to the Netherlands. They first settled in Amsterdam, where their two children, Giotta Fuyo and Ryu Vinci, were born (like the early American painter Charles Willson Peale, Shinkichi named his daughters for famous artists). However, in 1962 the couple discovered the small town of Baarlo, and near it, Kasteel Scheres, a castle with a tower and a set of wings surrounding a courtyard. They purchased the site and relocated their studios and assistants there.

Tajiri was proud of his acceptance by the Dutch, who commissioned several works and asked him to represent the Netherlands at the 1962 Venice Biennale. In the next years, he had numerous exhibitions of his work in Amsterdam, Arnhem, and other cities. He was invited to do a show at the Tokyo Gallery and in 1963 made his first trip to Japan, a six-week voyage to Tokyo. A year later, he visited the United States, thanks to a residency in Minnesota as a visiting professor at the Art Institute of Minneapolis, and he also toured Mexico. Using the Art Institute's foundry, he created twenty-five bronze sculptures, which he displayed at the school and that served as the centerpiece of his first show in New York, at the André Emmerich Gallery. He also created a monumental public sculpture for the neighboring city of St. Paul.

In February 1969, Ferdi died in an accident, leaving the family devastated. Shinkichi threw himself into work and began commuting to Berlin, where he was employed as a teacher at the Hochschule für bildende Künste. He remained a professor there until 1989. Despite his punishing schedule, he also struggled to become close to his daughters. He later explained that his wife's death had made him realize that, despite his love for his daughters, he had been so consumed by his artistic creations that he had neglected his family. He invited a new woman, Suzanne van der Capellen, to live with him and care for the children. The two were married in 1976 and would remain together until Tajiri's death.

Tajiri attracted some American collectors. His *Granny Knot*, purchased by Nelson Rockefeller, eventually became part of the Rockefeller Foundation's collection. In 1981 his sculpture *Friendship Knot*, representing the "unity between two cultures," was installed in the Weller Court in Los Angeles's Little Tokyo. He nonetheless remained little known in the United States, compared to his celebrity status in Holland. In 1992 Tajiri was named an officer in the Order of Orange-Nassau, a high honor for Dutch people akin to knighthood for the British. He continued working well into his eighties. He pursued his Ronin series and put together a tribute to Ferdi and her art. During this period, he had the proud pleasure of exhibiting in shows that included art by his daughter, Giotta, and her children. A highlight of his career came in 2007, when *De Wachters* (the Sentinels), a set of four of his sculptures, was installed on a bridge near his home; the ceremony featured an unveiling by the queen of the Netherlands. Shinkichi Tajiri died in Baarlo on March 15, 2009.

9

The Queer Heritage of Japanese Americans

Not long ago, when actor/activist George Takei publicly affirmed that he is gay, it was a major step forward for Japanese Americans. It might seem odd that in this day and age, the coming out of even such a celebrated representative of the community could cause much of a stir. After all, gays and lesbians have become increasingly accepted in Japan, even as LGBT Asian Americans generally have become visible in diverse fields. Redondo Beach mayor Mike Gin, a Republican, and former Oakland City Council member Danny Wan, a Democrat, have each achieved a measure of renown in the political arena. Lawyer Urvashi Vaid opened doors for other Asian Americans as chair of the National Gay and Lesbian Task Force. In media and the popular arts, actors Alec Mapa and B. D. Wong, journalist Helen Zia, filmmakers Gregg Araki and Arthur Dong, and ambisexual comedian Margaret Cho are examples of well-known Asians who have spoken publicly about their queer sexual orientation. [Author's note: since this was published, actor Sab Shimono

DOI: 10.5876/9781607324294.c009

and model Jenny Shimizu have also come out publicly.] Pauline Park has pioneered the movement for transsexual rights.

Yet Japanese Americans have generally been less open about homosexuality, in part because the community has not always been welcoming. Even in San Francisco, the gay capital of North America, many Nikkei probably still think that gay and lesbian Japanese Americans do not exist or are not really part of the community, that antigay discrimination is not their concern.

Nevertheless, a few noteworthy Japanese (North) Americans have joined struggles on behalf of both groups. The late Tak Yamamoto, who was confined in Poston as a boy, was named first president of Asian/Pacific Lesbians and Gays, even as he worked for redress and led pilgrimages for the Manzanar Committee. Stan Yogi, a longtime activist with the National Coalition for Redress/Reparations, has been active in gay/lesbian community work. In Hawai'i, Al and Jane Nakatani helped organize the 1998 campaign against a proposed anti-marriage amendment to the state constitution, saying that it was an assault on American freedom. (In 1996 the Honolulu chapter of the Japanese American Citizens League [JACL] introduced an official resolution at the national conference supporting same-sex marriage as a matter of equality. With its adoption, the JACL became only the second nationally based civil rights organization—the ACLU was first—to go on record as supporting equal marriage rights.)

North of the border, a lone Japanese Canadian defied the odds and won the fight. In 2002 Joy Masuhara, a Sansei physician from Vancouver, brought suit in a British Columbia court to gain the right to marry her partner, Jane Eaton Hamilton. In her brief to the court, she explicitly connected the silencing and shaming she felt as a lesbian with her experience growing up in a Japanese Canadian family that had been incarcerated during World War II. In May 2003, the court found for Masuhara and Hamilton. The decision led to North America's first same-sex marriage laws.

Perhaps the most outstanding example of LGBT activism among Japanese Americans is that of Kiyoshi Kuromiya. Steven Kiyoshi Kuromiya was born in Heart Mountain on May 10, 1943. His uncle was Nisei draft resister Yosh Kuromiya. He grew up in Monrovia, California. In 1961 Kiyoshi (then known as Steve) enrolled at the University of Pennsylvania, where he studied architecture with the famed designer/philosopher W. Buckminster Fuller (he would later collaborate with Fuller on the 1981 book *Critical Path* and the 1983

FIGURE 9.1. Joy Masuhara, *left*, and Jane Eaton Hamilton.

work *Cosmography: A Posthumous Scenario for the Future of Humanity*). In his Penn years, Kiyoshi was celebrated as a gourmet and helped support himself through school by compiling a Philadelphia restaurant guide. At the same time, he was energized by the nonviolent civil rights movement. He joined the campus NAACP chapter and participated in a sit-in at a bus terminal in Aberdeen, Maryland. The following year, he attended the famous March on Washington. In early 1965, Kiyoshi went south as an activist for voting rights for black Americans. On March 16, following the violent repression of demonstrators in Selma, Alabama, he joined a nonviolent march on the Alabama State Capitol in Montgomery. The marchers were chased and set upon by local sheriffs. Kiyoshi was clubbed so badly that he was hospitalized with scalp lacerations.

Although Kiyoshi had known of his homosexuality for some time, his work on behalf of black Americans (and, later, his protest against the Vietnam War) made him aware of the need to protest injustice against gays and lesbians. He is said to have been one of some forty gays and lesbians who formed a picket line in front of Independence Hall on July 4, 1965, an event widely considered the first-ever gay rights demonstration. In the following years, he continued to seek more "rational" laws on sexuality.

In June 1969, police raided the New York bar the Stonewall Inn. Instead of dispersing quietly and shamefully, as usual, the bar's patrons reacted to police repression with anger and self-defense efforts. The three-day Stonewall Riot opened the door to a nationwide Gay Pride movement, in which thousands of young people (and some not so young) came out of the closet. Within weeks, a new political group, the Gay Liberation Front (GLF), had been organized, modeling itself after the black power and other minority pride movements. Kiyoshi threw himself into the movement, and helped found the GLF's Philadelphia branch. The same year, he attended a convention of the Black Panther Party as an openly gay delegate and helped persuade Panther chief Huey Newton to make a statement on behalf of gays and lesbians. Throughout the 1970s, he worked on behalf of LGBT causes. He remained interested in justice for Japanese Americans as well.

In the early 1980s, Kiyoshi discovered that he was HIV-positive. He soon became absorbed with treatment issues and improving the quality of life for people with AIDS. He helped found a Philadelphia chapter of the AIDS activist group ACT UP in 1987. Two years later, he created the Critical Path Project. Critical Path served as both newsletter and website for information on AIDS treatment options and as a space for people with AIDS to express themselves. Kiyoshi himself read widely on AIDS research and became an encyclopedic authority on medical care. He simultaneously remained active on behalf of free speech and peace issues. In 1996 Kiyoshi volunteered as the plaintiff in an ACLU lawsuit challenging the Communications Decency Act, a federal Internet censorship law. In 1998 the case went to the US Supreme Court, which struck down the law as an infringement on freedom of speech. The next year, he brought another lawsuit, *Kuromiya v. US*, in which he tried, without success, to obtain marijuana for medical purposes for people suffering from serious diseases. Kiyoshi died on May 10, 2000. The Kiyoshi Kuromiya Memorial Community, a community gathering space, was founded in his honor.

Sexuality from Issei to Nisei (2008)

My first queer Japanese American heritage column focused on a small number of visible, self-affirming gay and lesbian figures, notably George Takei, Tak Yamamoto, Joy Masuhara, and Kiyoshi Kuromiya. (One might now add writer/poet Dwight Okita of Chicago, whose 2011 book, *The Prospect of My*

FIGURE 9.2. Hideyo Noguchi's statue in Ueno Park, Tokyo.

Arrival, was among the top three finalists for the Amazon Breakthrough Novel Award.)

The reason for this selection was that most often, when gays and lesbians have received a measure of tolerance it has been on the largely unspoken condition that their difference remain hidden, so as not to make others uncomfortable. As Yale law professor Kenji Yoshino, himself an openly gay Nikkei man, most provocatively put it in his book *Covering: The Hidden Assault on Our Civil Rights* (2006), it is not so much being queer or Asian American that remains stigmatized as it is acting out, such as by publicly proclaiming one's identity or protesting discrimination. Thus, Japanese Americans who use their Japanese first names or same-sex partners who hold hands in public (let alone marry) arouse particular hostility. My first column was intended as a reminder that sexual minorities— particularly outspoken ones—did and still do compose a vital element of the Nikkei community.

That said, much of the queer side of the Japanese American past is secret, guarded, and uncertain: desire between persons of the same sex must be inferred, guessed at, or interpreted from the sources. The very definitions of love and sexuality must be qualified when we look at ethnic Japanese society—notably the immigrant generation—for the good reason that Issei couples were often united for family reasons rather than romance. Conversely, a large percentage of Issei laborers, both in Hawai'i and on the mainland, were "old bachelors" who immigrated alone and then would not or could not find wives locally or in Japan. Instead, their living spaces, and their most intimate relationships, were shared with other men—a pattern that Nayan Shah has called "queer domesticity," in speaking of Chinese immigrants. (In this line, chronicler Richard Akagi told the compelling story of Mr. K—, an Issei who ran a boardinghouse for other bachelors. Mr. K loved to play female roles in full drag whenever the community performed a *shibai* (Japanese play) and sometimes acted as a woman offstage.)

We do not and cannot know to what degree these men, who shared rooms and often a bed together, had actual sexual relations with each other; yet the romantic friendships that evolved must frequently have had an edge. Witness this wonderfully sexually charged scene between the scientist Hideyo Noguchi and his roommate Miyabara, recounted on page 157 of Gustav Eckstein's 1931 biography of Noguchi:

> To Miyabara [Noguchi] lets out also his vexations, talks often of one colleague who comes with silk gloves and a cane, pronounces the silk in a particular way, as if the whole colleague might be made of that commodity. Which is certainly no reason for being vexed at the man, and perhaps no one is vexed. The man wears perfume . . . Presently [Noguchi] is himself wearing silk gloves and carrying a black cane.
> "Look at my body. It is little. But every organ in it is powerful." He is naked when he says that and about to get into the tub. He struts back and forth. Miyabara loves him. Miyabara may gall him and he may gall Miyabara but they gall each other as two people who love each other."

There is even clearer evidence of poet Yone Noguchi's bisexuality. As scholars Amy Sueyoshi and Edward Marx have noted, Noguchi's correspondence reveals that he had intimate attachments with both travel writer Charles Warren Stoddard and with a fellow Japanese immigrant, Kosen Takahashi, even as he pursued affairs with woman (including Léonie Gilmour, with whom he fathered sculptor Isamu Noguchi).

Whatever the impact of these individual histories, which were known to some Nisei, little if any real awareness of same-sex desire filtered down to the next generations. Even today it is almost impossible to acquire information from Nisei on the lives of gays and lesbians in the community during the first half of the twentieth century. As one older Nisei later described the climate, "The closet was deep and dark."

There were, it is true, scattered hints of various queer behaviors in Japanese America, subsumed under other labels. In 1931 twenty-six Nikkei in Los Angeles were among those fined for vagrancy and indecent exposure after police raided a screening of "obscene pictures." Four years later, a biracial Nisei woman was arrested for vagrancy after she hitchhiked from San Diego to San Francisco with a female companion. In 1948, after the bodies of a ten-year-old Nisei boy and his friend were recovered from the Chicago River, police investigating a sex slaying broadcast the name of a local Japanese American man who they had targeted for questioning because he was "friendly with the boys." A Japanese American newspaper proceeded to print his name.

The Nisei press also gave a few glimpses of queer life outside. In 1931 the *Nichi Bei Shimbun* carried a photo of pioneer sexologist and gay propagandist Magnus Hirschfeld. Ten years later, the *Rafu Shimpo* carried a photo of a "female lothario" who had passed as a man and seduced other women. Journalist Joe Oyama, who had ridden the rails as a hobo and mixed in artistic circles, regaled Nisei readers with various tales of drag queens shopping for jewelry in Little Tokyo and of a French man who was betrayed by his wife with a woman in male dress.

Whatever these glimmers, most Nikkei, like most other Americans, long remained hostile to any notion of homosexuality. A select few found community outside. John Nagatoshi Nojima, a former inmate at Manzanar camp, joined the pioneering homophile organization Mattachine Society after it was created in 1950 and later was active in the allied group ONE Incorporated.

For thirty years, Nojima was the lover of gay activist W. Dorr Legg. Still, most remained isolated. Progressive minister Rev. Lloyd K. Wake of Glide Memorial Church, who in 1971 began celebrating commitment ceremonies for gay and lesbian couples, wrote an open letter deploring the treatment of queer Japanese Americans by their own community:

> I have counseled with a number of Japanese homosexuals. It is heartbreaking and agonizing to hear the problems that have come down on them because of the cruel and inhuman attitude of family and friends. The Japanese community, like any other community, is slow to accept the fact of homosexuality in its midst. It is just as slow to affirm it as a valid orientation and life style. Consequently, many of us counsel with people who have been dehumanized by an insensitive and "uptight" community. This certainly includes the church community.

Conditions have changed a good deal since Wake's letter. Today, queer Japanese Americans need not feel the shame and isolation their forebears did. Nikkei civil rights organizations have defended the rights of gays and lesbians. Nevertheless, Japanese American communities still have a ways to go to build a climate of acceptance and inclusion toward their children who are "different."

THE RISE OF HOMOPHOBIA IN JAPANESE AMERICAN COMMUNITIES (2009)

Since I started writing The Great Unknown in 2007, I have marked LGBT Pride Week each year with a column on the queer heritage of Japanese Americans. The struggle for equality by gays and lesbians is of special importance to Japanese communities, not just because Japanese Americans have themselves been targets of bigotry and injustice, but because the increasingly visible presence of gays and lesbians within Nikkei circles ensures that antigay discrimination touches the community directly and powerfully.

My first column focused on the contributions of proud, self-affirming Nikkei activists such as Joy Masuhara, George Takei, Tak Yamamoto, Stan Yogi, and especially Kiyoshi Kuromiya, who participated in redress and other struggles on behalf of Japanese Americans and defended gay and lesbian rights. The goal of the column was to remind readers that gays and lesbians have always comprised an essential element of Japanese communities. I was highly honored and gratified when Harry Honda, the legendary Nisei journalist and longtime editor of the *Pacific Citizen*, later praised and endorsed this piece in his own *Pacific Citizen* column.

My second column focused on the hidden history of queer sexuality among Japanese Americans. My main argument, which took off in part from the groundbreaking scholarship of Amy Sueyoshi and Nayan Shah, was that conventional categories of homosexual and heterosexual are not terribly helpful for understanding the lives of Japanese Americans, particularly the Issei. Through an article by Ken Kaji, I have since learned of the life of one immigrant, Jiro Onuma. Onuma came to the United States in 1923, never married, collected erotic male photo magazines, and developed close relationships in camp with younger Japanese American men.

Interestingly, no arrests of Japanese bachelors for sodomy have as yet come to light, in contrast to several cases in which Chinese were prosecuted. For example, in 1895 Ah Fook, a cook in Los Angeles, was arrested for a "crime against nature" with a Scandinavian sailor. In 1901 Quong Ho and Charles Wong were imprisoned in North Adams, Massachusetts, for rape and "unnatural crime," while in 1904 Charlie Lum, a laundryman in Worcester, Massachusetts, was formally charged with sodomy following the complaint of a local white boy who was revealed to be suffering from "an infectious disease."

My question today is how the varied (and sometimes freewheeling) sexuality of the Issei gave way to silence and suspicion of alternative sexuality among many Nisei and Sansei. While causality is always complex, we can say in historical terms that Issei tended toward Japanese views. In traditional Japanese culture, unlike in the West, male homosexuality was not a sin but something essentially private, separate from marriage. There was even some history of glorification of same-sex love among samurai, as demonstrated by Ihara Saikaku's renowned 1687 collection *The Great Mirror of Male Love*. In imperial Japanese society, where the sexes often remained separated, same-sex social relations flourished. Issei artist Chuzo Tamotsu, an antimilitarist, later recalled that when he did his military service, circa 1900, a superior officer propositioned him for sex while they were in the bath. When Tamotsu resisted, his superior reported him for disobedience. Fortunately, Tamotsu persuaded the high commander that the emperor did not expect him to do such things as part of his oath of allegiance.

Once settled in America, Japanese immigrants and their children seem to have absorbed dominant views of homosexuality as contemptible and unmentionable. Under the influence of Protestant missionaries, Issei were pressured—and pressured each other—to conform to heterosexual norms. (The preaching was apparently less successful at curbing endemic gambling and prostitution within Japanese communities.) As John Howard reveals in his provocative book *Concentration Camps on the Home Front: Japanese Americans in the House of Jim Crow* (2008), internal community policing was augmented during World War II by official policies of enforced heterosexual interaction between Nisei soldiers and women from camp via USO dances. Nisei men, frequently relegated to gardening or domestic labor and sensitive over dominant stereotypes of Asians as unmasculine, may also have wished to distance themselves from homosexuality as effeminate. The result was that gays and lesbians were largely invisible and unwelcome in Japanese communities. I have heard various Nisei women recount the story of an unnamed boy—or maybe several different ones—a gentle and scholarly Nisei whom everyone knew to be "different," who no doubt faced constant harassment and suffered so badly that he committed suicide at a young age.[1]

Worse, even as the larger society began changing in the 1970s and 1980s, homophobia and denial remained rampant, even among Nikkei progressives. S. I. Hayakawa, a conservative who nonetheless championed black equality, called himself "deeply, deeply, deeply offended by homosexuality." In 1977 he endorsed the failed Briggs Initiative, a ballot measure in California that would have barred gays and lesbians from teaching in public schools. Two years later, Hayakawa publicly asserted a link between marijuana and homosexuality, which led him to oppose decriminalization. James Omura, who denounced Executive Order 9066 as totalitarian and bravely supported the Heart Mountain draft resisters, was not equally supportive of rights for homosexuals. Because a fellow Japanese American worker once made a pass at him during his early years when he worked in fish canneries in Alaska, he claimed, he developed a strong prejudice and opposed equality for gays and lesbians (Omura added that homosexuals were generally disdained and ostracized by Issei as well).

Perhaps the most striking example of a homophobic civil rights activist was William Marutani, the long-serving Japanese American Citizens League (JACL) attorney and judge, who was confined as a teenager at Tule Lake.

During the 1960s, Marutani spent summers in Louisiana as a volunteer law-yer defending African Americans, and in 1967 he represented the JACL in the Supreme Court's famous case *Loving v. Virginia*, which struck down all laws against interracial marriage. Marutani's was the first-ever argument by a Nisei lawyer in any civil rights case before the high court. In 1980 he was selected as a member of the US Commission on Wartime Relocation and Internment of Civilians, whose report led to the granting of redress. In 1982 Marutani remarked in his *Pacific Citizen* column that he felt an instinctive aversion and moral abhorrence for what Issei pejoratively called *hentaisei* (which he trans-lated as "abnormal" or "sexual perversion") and the Nisei called "queers"; he did not know any homosexual Japanese Americans himself and did not wish to. While Marutani conceded that those practicing homosexuality (he refused to use the term *gay*) should not be arbitrarily persecuted, he felt that the "practice should not be encouraged or advanced." Thus, he opposed civil rights for gays and lesbians, such as the right to teach in public schools. When challenged by a reader, Marutani countered that his view reflected the views of the vast majority of Nisei, if not of all Nikkei.

It is unclear, and doubtless unknowable, how right Marutani was in 1982. Nonetheless, since then, many Nikkei have clearly changed their minds, as a new generation—gay and straight—has come of age free of the culture of silence and shame. We must give credit to various mentors who pointed the way. There is Dana Takagi, author of pioneering essays on politics and sexuality. There is Kenneth K. Kumashiro, editor of *Restoried Selves* (2004), the collection of autobiographies by LGBT Asian American activists. There is Seattle's Yoshiko Matsui, who came out in 1992 at seventeen (moving in with her partner's family because she found living at home impossible) and organized groups for local lesbians. But perhaps we should stop here and save more for next year's column.

THE RISE OF HOMOPHOBIA: PART 2 (2010)

Writing a LGBT Pride Week column on the queer heritage of Japanese Americans, a tradition I began with *Nichi Bei Times*, is one that I am happy to carry over to *Nichi Bei Weekly*. Such discussion seems particularly rele-vant at the present time, when conservative and Christian movements have appealed to Asian Americans to support legal discrimination against gays and

lesbians in the guise of family values. (Hak-Shing William Tam, an evangelical Christian, has expressed such virulent antigay bigotry during testimony in
court challenges to Proposition 8 that he has thereby been transformed into a
poster boy of sorts for the LGBT movement.) People of all backgrounds have
a strong interest in learning about the vital, if often hidden, history of the
queer members of the Japanese American family. Today's column serves to
update and expand on these columns with new information that I have found
since their appearance.

In the first year's column, I told stories of some of the few visible gay and
lesbian Japanese Americans and traced their struggles to win equal rights
for different groups. One figure I mentioned was Stan Yogi. Yogi—adding
historian to his repertoire of skills and service—has coauthored (with Elaine
Elinson) *Wherever There's A Fight: How Runaway Slaves, Suffragists, Immigrants,
Strikers, and Poets Shaped Civil Liberties in California* (2009), the first multigroup,
comprehensive study of civil rights in California. This excellent volume has
just won a Gold Medal at the California Book Awards.

The second year's column discussed the state of research on same-sex
relations within early Japanese communities. It brought together original research by several scholars who have done duty as historical sleuths.
Since that time, I have been pleased to discover the amazing work of lesbian artist/archivist Tina Takemoto. Last year, as part of a show at San
Francisco's GLBT Historical Society, *Lineage: Matchmaking in the Archive*, she
did a project on Jiro Onuma, an Issei bachelor who lived in San Francisco
before being sent to camp at Topaz. Drawing on Onuma's surviving papers,
Takemoto dramatized his isolation and hardships in camp by creating the
"Gentleman's Gaman: A Gay Bachelor's Japanese American Internment
Camp Survival Kit."

In the third year's column, I discussed the turn of the Issei away from
Japanese culture, with its long homoerotic tradition, and the growth of
endemic community homophobia in the early twentieth century. I was very
proud that the piece drew the most favorable comments from readers of any
of my columns to date. Still, not everyone agreed with my suggestion that
the rise of antigay hostility was a product of the influence of Christianity—
especially white Protestant missionaries—on the Nikkei. Instead, readers
suggested that lack of tolerance for homosexuality reflected larger community taboos about sex—one Nisei woman said that until she married she had

no idea where babies came from—plus the desire of Japanese Americans to prove their good citizenship by conforming to the moral codes of the dominant society. This meant distancing themselves from anything stigmatized and shaming transgressors, though without any violent hatred.

There is, to be sure, a good deal of truth in this. As mentioned, gay Nikkei legal scholar Kenji Yoshino has argued in powerful terms in his book *Covering: The Hidden Assault on Our Civil Rights* (2006) that a major part of prejudice against racial or sexual minorities results not from their existence itself but their visibility. (This is demonstrated in extreme form by the US military's "don't ask, don't tell" policy: the Army admits that sexual orientation has no impact on the ability of gays and lesbians to serve since they are not barred altogether, but they are allowed only on the strict condition that they not reveal themselves and make others aware of them.) Certainly, many mid-century Nisei and Sansei viewed homosexuality as unspeakable, denied that there were any gays or lesbians in the community, and greeted all mention of the topic with embarrassed silence. Male homosexuality, because of its association with effeminacy, represented a special threat to Nikkei men anxious over their manhood. As journalist Edward Iwata noted some thirty years ago, tongue only partly in cheek, the main element in the "inexcusable ignorance" of Japanese Americans about sexual minorities was fear: "There is only one thing that most Asian Americans fear more than speaking in public or finding bad skiing conditions, and that is homosexuality. It is the last taboo, it is tainted ground. If one is religious, homosexuality is a filthy sin. If one is a Nisei, it is *verboten* to discuss. If one is a Sansei, it is a netherworld full of lisping, limpwristed men."

Furthermore, the discomfort often became internalized. One small window on such attitudes can be found in Joanne Oppenheim's recent book, *Stanley Hayami, Nisei Son: His Diary, Letters, and Story from an American Concentration Camp to Battlefield, 1942–1945* (2008). This charming volume reprints the diary entries and letters of Stanley Hayami, a teenaged Nisei who was confined at the Heart Mountain camp and later served in the 442nd Regimental Combat Team, where he met his untimely death. (Hayami's papers, donated by his family to the Japanese American National Museum, also form the basis for Ann Kaneko and Sharon Yamato's documentary, *A Flicker in Eternity.*) In his writings, Hayami makes no mention of his attraction to any females or males, and his profile drawing of a muscular male nude represents the sole conceivable marker of any erotic interest. Yet, in his diary entry for June 27, 1943, he speaks of his moodiness and frequent wish to be alone amid nature and then quickly adds, "I don't tell this to anyone because they'll figure that I'm a queer (Maybe I am)." This awkward confession not only provides our only clue as to Hayami's sexual identity but suggests how thoroughly all deviance from community social norms was tarred with the brush of homosexuality.

Wherever the force of overall community strictures, it is clear that the most overt opposition to gay and lesbian equality within Japanese communities, as among other ethnic groups, has long come from those speaking in the name of Christianity. A vivid illustration is the actions of Allen Kato. In 1994 the Japanese American Citizens League (JACL) National Board, by a 10–3 vote (plus three abstentions), approved resolutions in favor of full equality for gays and lesbians and called the freedom to marry a constitutional right that should not be denied to any American regardless of sexual orientation. The JACL thereby became the first national civil rights organization, apart from the American Civil Liberties Union, to formally support equal rights to marriage for gays and lesbians. Kato, JACL legal counsel, publicly resigned his position over the issue. While he objected on procedural grounds to the board's action, he admitted that the center of his opposition was religious: "As a Christian, I believe the issue of same-sex marriage is a moral issue and not a civil rights issue. I believe homosexual marriage is morally wrong." While Kato pronounced himself in favor of laws to protect gays and lesbians from discrimination (what he called "prohibitory laws"), he did not explain how he proposed to afford same-sex couples equal benefits with married couples. Instead, he insisted that recognition of civil marriage for gays and lesbians would violate his religious freedom.

Kato's views remain widely shared within Japanese communities. In September 2008, when Proposition 8 was on the ballot in California, a national Asian American survey found that a majority of ethnic Japanese voters in California intended to support the measure. Still, the widespread opposition to Proposition 8 by those under forty-five years old across all racial groups strongly suggests that as the younger generation of Japanese Americans—both gay and straight—assumes community leadership, they will produce a more open and less fearful community.

Postscript (2012)

This column, on how Western-style homophobia grew up in West Coast Japanese communities, sparked some debate. As noted, in the course of my discussion I quoted the entry from the camp diary of Stanley Hayami, in which he spoke of his moodiness and his frequent wish to be alone amid nature. He confided to his diary, "I don't tell this to anyone because they'll figure that I'm a queer (Maybe I am)." I used this "confession" as evidence for the proposition that social nonconformity among Japanese Americans became tied up with gender nonconformity—that is, any people who were somehow different, and who stuck out from the general crowd, were stigmatized as "queers." I added in passing that there was no hard evidence in the diary of Hayami's sexual orientation and that the only conceivable hint in any direction was some drawings he did of muscular men.

Some readers proceeded to jump on my comments and complain that I was presenting Hayami as gay. One noted that, despite Stanley's comments, the diary shows him to be a normal teenager who was not antisocial and who liked parties. Various friends also contended that I might have made too much of Stanley's use of the word *queer* in reference to himself, since it was a common word among Nisei (like other Americans of the time) that meant "strange" or other things with no connection to homosexuality—as indeed, Stanley uses the word at other places in the diary where there is clearly no sexual dimension.

My reply to all these comments was this:

As you will note, my main point is not to speculate on Stanley Hayami's sexuality, much less to make a definitive interpretation. Stanley says that he is reluctant just to tell people that he wants to be alone, because that might mark him as a queer. I picked up on that as a sign of just how stigmatized all difference in character was, and how it became tied up in people's minds with sexual difference.

That said, there remains a question about how to treat Stanley's private comment to his diary. The point about the generalized use of the adjective "queer" is well taken. However, in this one particular case Stanley uses it, not in adjectival form as elsewhere [à la "queer ideas"], but as a noun: "a queer." This too was a well-recognized usage: Bill Marutani, to give just one example, has stated that that Nisei of his generation routinely referred to homosexuals as "queers." [Marutani was just two years older than Stanley Hayami.] Of course, there were more symbolic uses of the label as a generalized undesirable: for instance, in Milton Muramaya's novel *All I Asking for Is My Body*, which takes place in Hawai'i in the late 1930s, a plantation Nisei character praises his white school teacher, whereupon another [young Nisei] scoffs that there are no "good" haoles—if a white guy is nice, he is either "a communist or a queer."

We can agree that the Hayami diaries (at least the published part) do not give any much evidence one way or the other about ANY sexual interest. Whether Stanley attended parties or not, and whether he was social or antisocial, there simply is no statement of erotic interest in girls, [unlike] lots and lots of guys in camp who DID express heterosexual inclinations. Stanley's silence on the subject could indeed be regular teenager behavior. It could also be something else. Conversely, when I say that the only conceivable sign of any sexual desire at all is his nude male drawing, this is just precisely what I mean—it is the ONLY thing that could by any stretch of the imagination even be so interpreted. It is at least equally conceivable that there was no such [sexual] interest associated.

In sum, I do not mark Stanley as attracted to men, but in the absence of clear evidence I do not assume that he was straight either, and I do not consider it over-reading or stigmatizing to leave the question open, though my main point is elsewhere.

I do not know whether I satisfied my critics, but I did not receive any further comments. More recently I came upon an intriguing corollary to the matter, something that serves as an odd sort of confirmation of my analysis of Stanley Hayami's comments in his diary. As noted, in 1982 William Marutani mentioned in his column in the *Pacific Citizen* that in the years when he was growing up, he and other Nisei called gay people "queers," while the Issei referred to them as "hentaisei," a phrase which Marutani translated as "abnormal" or "sexual perversion." (Since then, I have found no other corroboration that Issei regularly employed this term—perhaps some Nisei readers could enlighten me as to whether their parents actually used it.) Intrigued, as I always am by Issei Japanese lingo, I mentioned Marutani's statement to a group of friends from Tokyo. To my surprise, they responded that, in Japanese, hentaisei means "nonconformist" or "deviant," with a connotation of "antisocial" in the sense of being opposed to dominant social norms. As such language would imply, it was not so much that, in Japanese eyes, same-sex activities were shameful or unnatural, as Marutani would have it, but that they disrupted the traditional, fixed social structure. Indeed, this sense of hentaisei reminded me of nothing so much as the classic Japanese proverb about the nail that sticks up being hammered down. If this is the intellectual framework that Nikkei communities took from Japan, it is no wonder that Stanley Hayami internalized the association of queer behavior with queer sexuality.

HAWAI'I 1986: THE SHIFT TO EQUAL RIGHTS (2011)

This piece represents a fifth entry in the series of annual columns I have produced on the queer heritage of Japanese Americans. It represents an anniversary column in a rather broader sense as well, in that it marks twenty-five years since the years 1986–1987. That period was a time of notably strenuous conflict over the issue of equality for gay and lesbian Americans, including those of Japanese ancestry, and the founding moment of what would soon be called queer activism. In retrospect, we can identify two principal catalysts for the attention to gay and lesbian concerns and the revival of militancy in the mid-1980s.

The first was the AIDS crisis. By 1986 an estimated 1 million Americans were HIV-positive, and the rate of new infections was increasing. Although the AIDS-related death of actor Rock Hudson in late 1985 had brought the first mainstream visibility to the epidemic, it remained a source of shame and stigma to most Americans, gay and straight. When federal and state governments failed to make treatment and research a funding priority, in March 1987 ACT UP—the AIDS Coalition to Unleash Power—was formed in response. ACT UP militants campaigned for new legislation, more money to care for the stricken, and greater access to experimental AIDS medications. Their tactics, which included creating posters and videos and staging "die-ins" and other demonstrations, would serve as a model for a generation of activists.

The other cause was the US Supreme Court's ruling in *Bowers v. Hardwick*, announced at the end of June 1986. Michael Hardwick, a Georgia man whose home was entered by police, was discovered having sex with another male. After being arrested on sodomy charges, he challenged the law. While a lower court threw out the conviction, by a narrow 5–4 majority, the Supreme Court ruled that state anti-sodomy laws were constitutional as enforced against same-sex couples and that there was no "constitutional right" to engage in homosexual sodomy. (The Court would overrule itself seventeen years later in the case of *Lawrence v. Texas*, in which it overturned all remaining sodomy laws—the majority opinion termed the *Bowers* ruling an "insult" to gay and lesbian Americans.)

Japanese American Citizens League leaders, like their counterparts in other mainstream Asian American organizations, did not concern themselves with antigay discrimination in any visible way during the 1980s. Not only was their attention fixed on urgent matters, such as redress for wartime confinement and prosecuting the murderers of Vincent Chin, but much of their membership likely shared, to some degree, the general discomfort over homosexuality. Meanwhile, it must be admitted, mainstream gay and lesbian organizations made little effort to engage with Asian American groups or issues.

Still, individual Japanese Americans, especially in progressive Hawai'i, did begin to make their voices heard during this time on the side of equal treatment for all. In the wake of the *Bowers* decision, Roy Takumi, a future state legislator then working for the American Friends Service Committee, in a letter to the editor of the *Honolulu Star-Bulletin*, contended that because heterosexual sodomy was not similarly outlawed, "The ruling implies that the Court believes that identical conduct by heterosexuals is not subject to state action: thus it is not the action but who does it that makes it illegal. It marks the first time since the Dred Scott decision that the Court has carved out a category of people for special treatment, reversing decades of movement to apply rights equally." Tokumi concluded, "The rights of every minority must be vigilantly protected because the rights of one are the rights of all."

Meanwhile, in response to the decision, in July 1986, a multiracial set of activists formed the Hawaii Democrats for Lesbian and Gay Rights. The group endorsed a slate of eleven candidates for the fall elections. Its biggest coup came in September, when powerful US senator Daniel K. Inouye agreed to address a group meeting organized at Hula's Bar and Lei Stand, a well-known gay nightspot in Waikiki. Inouye had been, for some time, a quiet supporter of equality for gays and lesbians and in 1980 signed up as an early cosponsor of a bill to extend to sexual minorities the protections of the

Civil Rights Act of 1964 against employment and housing discrimination (the ancestor of today's still-not-enacted Employment Non-Discrimination Act).

Inouye told his audience at Hula's that, while he recognized the difficulties involved in coming out of the closet, gays and lesbians needed to speak out: "If you want to hide, that's up to you. But if you want to stand up and be counted, I think there is greater hope for you." Inouye concluded that gays and lesbians had "many friends" in Congress and that they would eventually triumph, as other groups had, over "unreasoning prejudice." He received a standing ovation. While various polls indicated that he was comfortably ahead in his race for reelection against his Republican opponent, Frank Hutchinson, his presence at the meeting caused a public stir. Hutchinson charged that by speaking at a gay bar, Inouye was "endorsing homosexuality." The senator's defenders responded blandly that he was simply meeting constituents.

Inouye's careful message of support was seconded soon after by an unlikely source. In early 1987, the Catholic bishop of Honolulu, Joseph Anthony Ferrario, took a public position in favor of a proposed bill to protect the state's gays and lesbians from housing and employment discrimination. While he stated that he followed church teaching against homosexuality, Ferrario added that he distinguished between opposition to sinful acts and the equal right to dignity of all individuals. When a conservative group called Concerned Roman Catholics of America, claiming to speak for the majority of the faithful, decried the bishop's position, D. H. Matsuda publicly praised Ferrario, asserting tartly in a letter to the editor that if the bishop's critics indeed spoke for Catholics, "it is better to be a human being than . . . a Catholic."

In the fall 1986 election, Democrats regained the majority in the Senate that they had lost six years earlier. A group of senators, including Daniel Inouye, supported an increase in funding for AIDS research and treatment. In reaction, conservative senator Jesse Helms proposed the first of his notorious "Helms amendments," forbidding any federal funding for AIDS treatment or any other activities that would "promote or encourage, directly or indirectly, homosexual activities." Although the provision represented exactly the type of "unreasoning prejudice" Inouye had told gays and lesbians that their friends would defeat, the senator recognized that the wall of prejudice was still formidable. In order to secure passage of the legislation,

Inouye voted in favor of the amendment—as did all senators of both parties, apart from Democrat Daniel Patrick Moynihan of New York and liberal Republican Lowell Weicker of Connecticut. (Partly because of Weicker's stand, conservative groups formed a coalition during the 1988 election to support his challenger, Democrat Joseph Lieberman, who won the seat and thereby launched his Senate career.)

In sum, the support from Japanese Americans that gays and lesbians received in their struggle for equality during the late 1980s was modest, low-key, and largely the product of individuals. Yet even such modest beginnings paved the way for more organized efforts during the 1990s, as queer Japanese Americans gained increased visibility within ethnic communities and the larger society in Hawai'i.

Postscript (2012)

When I wrote this column about the rise of LGBT politics in Hawai'i, I did not know about the inspiring story of Blake Oshiro. Oshiro, a Honolulu Democrat, was first elected to the state's House of Representatives in 2000 and subsequently rose to the position of majority leader. In Spring 2010, as the House was considering a bill to legalize civil unions for same-sex couples, Oshiro publicly announced that he was a gay man, hoping to signal the importance of the legislation to him. While little noticed in the rest of the country, his action made him the nation's first openly gay legislative chief. (The bill passed but was vetoed by Governor Linda Lingle; a subsequent bill was signed into law in 2011 by her successor, Neil Abercrombie, and it remained in effect until same-sex marriage was legalized in the state in 2013.)

Oshiro's coming out incited Christian conservatives to back a primary election challenge to the majority leader by another Nikkei, Honolulu city councilman Gary Okino. That spring, Okino testified before the Hawaii Senate Judiciary and Government Operations Committee against the civil unions bill. Calling homosexuality a "perversion," Okino had warned of "the medical dangers of a homosexual lifestyle." After Oshiro prevailed in the primary, Okino endorsed Republican candidates against him in the general election. In the face of pressure over his bigoted views and party disloyalty, Okino later resigned from the Democratic Party. Oshiro won reelection in November 2010, then left his seat a year later to become Governor Abercrombie's deputy chief of staff.

THE JACL's HISTORIC VOTE FOR EQUAL MARRIAGE RIGHTS (2012)

As most Americans are aware, on May 9, 2012, President Barack Obama made the landmark announcement that he supported the right of same-sex couples to marry. Obama explained that, as a Christian, he had faced a long struggle over what position to take, but that in the end, the Golden Rule won out. His announcement was greeted with jubilation by LGBT Americans and straight supporters of equality but bitterly denounced by religious conservatives and right-wing spokespeople as an attack on both Christianity and marriage.

Whatever the political calculation present in the president's change of position, and the limitations of that support in terms of changing existing law, his statement marks the first time that a sitting president has placed the moral authority of his office behind the principle of full equality for gay and lesbian couples. Obama's action in taking sides before election time was also a courageous move, given the opposition to marriage rights for same-sex couples among voters in various swing states.

The game-changing nature of President Obama's statement, as well as the sharply opposing reactions it sparked, were mirrored nearly twenty years ago, on a smaller scale, in regard to the adoption of a resolution in favor of marriage equality by the Japanese American Citizens League (JACL). The JACL's action, in mid-1994, made it the first nationally based minority civil rights organization to grant official support to marriage for same-sex couples (the national NAACP, in vivid contrast, only did so in mid-2012, after Obama's announcement). Remarkably, the measure was adopted a full five years before Vermont became the first state to enact civil unions and a decade before Massachusetts became the first state to legalize same-sex marriage. The JACL's action was the subject of bitter division within the Japanese community and led to an unusually public airing of disagreements and, ultimately, a referendum to repeal the vote of the organization's ruling board.

The origins of the marriage resolution apparently lie with various JACL chapters—most notably in Hawai'i. In 1993 the question of marriage rights first gained nationwide attention when Hawai'i's state Supreme Court ruled in *Baehr v. Lewin*—a suit that included two Filipino Americans and their same-sex partners who sought to marry—that refusing marriage licenses to gay couples constituted unconstitutional sex discrimination (Hawai'i voters ultimately voided the decision by adopting a constitutional amendment limiting marriage to heterosexual couples). The Hawai'i JACL, which had sent a letter of support for the couples, decided to bring the matter to the organization's national leadership. Bill Kaneko, national vice president from the Honolulu chapter, initially presented the resolution to the National Board, with support from Ruth Mizobe, governor of the Pacific Southwest District Council. Meanwhile, progressive JACL chapters in the San Francisco Bay Area and Los Angeles—urban areas with more visible gay populations—moved to lobby for its adoption. Many of these backers had previously worked for Japanese American redress. Some were themselves gay or lesbian, like Tak Yamamoto, a founding member of Asian/Pacific Lesbians & Gays, or former JACL staffer Lia Shigemura. Others, like longtime activists Trisha Murakawa, Ruth Mizobe, and Chizu Iiyama, supported the proposal on general principles of equal rights.

The fact that such a measure could even be considered was surprising. In contrast to its longtime championing of racial equality and affirmative action, the JACL had never been visibly supportive of the rights of gays and lesbians. On the contrary, in 1982 longtime JACL national counsel William Marutani stated in the *Pacific Citizen* that he opposed civil rights for "queers," like the right to teach in public schools, in order to ensure that homosexuality "not be encouraged or advanced." He added that his view surely reflected the feelings of the vast majority of Nisei, if not all Nikkei.

In 1988 the JACL adopted a new constitution. It included "sexual orientation" for the first time on its list of categories in regard to which it opposed discrimination and sought equal justice. This addition was not debated at the time of ratification and was probably little noticed at the time—it may have been simply boilerplate antidiscrimination language. It was not until 1993 that the JACL National Board first formally voted to endorse the rights of gays and lesbians to legal protection from discrimination in housing and employment as well as the right to serve in the military. The board's action followed the passage in Colorado of Amendment 2, an initiative to strip gays and lesbians of all legal protections against discrimination, and in the wake of the debate over opening military service to LGBT Americans that led Congress to establish the "don't ask, don't tell" policy. To take up such a "cutting edge" rights question (in the words of national youth council director Kim Nakahara) as same-sex marriage just a few months later represented something of a revolution for the JACL.

In February 1994, Bill Kaneko presented a resolution to the JACL National Board supporting "the concept of marriage as a constitutional right that should not be denied because of a person's sexual orientation." Legal prohibitions on same-sex marriage, it stated, violated constitutional guarantees of equal protection and human rights. The board voted to table the resolution temporarily, in order to consult member chapters. At its next meeting in May 1994, following the consultation, the JACL's National Board approved the Kaneko resolution by a vote of 10–3 (with two abstentions).

The board's action catalyzed a storm of protest. JACL legal counsel Allen Kato resigned, publicly stating that, as a Christian, he considered homosexual marriages to be "morally wrong" and the board's action was an affront to his religious freedom. Esteemed journalist Bill Hosokawa accused the board of moving the JACL past the purposes of its founding, which was to focus solely on issues of direct and paramount importance to Japanese Americans (the existence of LGBT Japanese Americans, and the impact on their own rights, went ignored in Hosokawa's discussion).

Meanwhile, numerous individuals sent letters to the *Pacific Citizen* deploring the vote as an endorsement of homosexuality. A writer from Renton, Washington, complained that the JACL now favored granting same-sex couples the same benefits granted to "normal married couples to protect them and their children." A Redondo Beach, California, reader proclaimed, "If the JACL constitution says that we should support a person's civil rights regardless of sexual orientation, change it! Otherwise we must support people engaged in paedophilia [*sic*], incest, and bestiality." A reader from Dublin, California, called on the JACL to stand for the "traditional family." While Buddhists remained silent on the religious question, several authors, following Allen Kato, couched their opposition to the measure in explicitly Christian terms. One correspondent from Stockton, California, thundered against "same-sex" as the sin of sodomy, an affront by the perpetrator "against the maker and against his own flesh." Another from Santa Ana, California, stated that "civil rights" could never take precedence over "moral rights" in a nation founded on Christian principles.

Various local chapters protested the board's action as unauthorized. The JACL's Mount Olympus chapter, based in heavily Mormon Salt Lake City, brought a resolution to have the JACL National Council—composed of representatives from all chapters—vote on repeal of the board's resolution.

Hoping to defuse the debate, Mike Hamachi, of the Diablo Valley chapter (following a proposal by Peggy Sasashima Liggett), introduced a competing resolution to support domestic partner legislation rather than marriage and explicitly respect the right of JACL members to disagree about whether domestic partnerships could be considered a matter of civil rights.

For veteran JACLers, it must have seemed like déjà vu—the tone of the debate was eerily reminiscent of a similar controversy over civil rights that the organization had faced a generation previously. In early 1963, the JACL National Board accepted Rev. Dr. Martin Luther King, Jr.'s invitation to send representatives to that summer's March on Washington. Several local chapters had then protested that the JACL should not identify itself too closely with the black freedom movement, since it was not their struggle and the JACL's presence would alienate useful white allies. Local chapters also charged that the national JACL was exceeding its authority. The *Pacific Citizen* published a number of letters from Nisei, most advising against marching. In the end, President K. Patrick Okura called an emergency National Board meeting to set policy; he set the meeting in his hometown of Omaha, Nebraska, far from local West Coast pressures. The delegates there approved the right of JACL members to attend the historic march, though only a few dozen actually did so. [With apologies for the self-promotion, I direct readers wishing a fuller account of this conflict to the final chapter of my book *After Camp: Portraits in Midcentury Japanese American Life and Politics* (2012).]

In summer 1994, there was a showdown over marriage at the JACL's national convention in Salt Lake City. In hopes of blunting the Christian-based opposition, Bill Kaneko presented articles written by religious leaders, such as Rev. Joan Ishibashi of the United Church of Christ in Honolulu and Rev. Mark Nakagawa of Sacramento, California, who endorsed the same-sex resolution. He also introduced letters of support from the Asian Law Caucus, the Asian Bar Association, and the National Asian Pacific American Legal Consortium. Perhaps surprisingly, given both his reputation as a moderate consensus-seeker and his vulnerability as an elected official to negative publicity, then congressman Norman Mineta proved to be one of the most forceful advocates of the National Board's resolution. Mineta asked the delegates rhetorically, "Where would we be today if the NAACP, or the National Council of La Raza, or the Anti-Defamation League of B'nai Brith, or the National Gay & Lesbian Task Force had taken the position that redress was a Japanese American issue—and had nothing to do with African Americans, Hispanic Americans, Jews or gay and lesbian Americans?" In more practical terms, he reminded JACLers that Representative Barney Frank, the first sitting congressman to come out voluntarily, had been a leading actor in moving redress through Congress and that Japanese Americans had a debt to repay to their champion.

Following the end of debate, the JACL National Council voted 50–38 to uphold the National Board's resolution. Four chapters split their vote and eleven more abstained. (By a large majority, the National Council then passed the Hamachi resolution on domestic partnerships, though it had been rendered effectively moot.) Carole Hayashino, the JACL's associate director, later stated that while she had not expected the National Board resolution to actually be overturned, the closeness of the vote showed how difficult it was for the various chapters to accept it: "It was an emotional discussion." Two years later, JACL executive director Herb Yamanishi added that the decision, which remained controversial, had cost the group part of its membership.

Now, a generation later, when the president and—according to public opinion polls—a majority of Americans (including a large majority of those under thirty) support extending marriage rights to same-sex couples, the JACL's action appears forward-looking and responsible. In another generation, young Nikkei may look back with puzzlement that there was ever any controversy in the community over marriage rights for the LGBT community.[2]

NOTES

1. I have since found this precise story documented in Larry Tajiri's January 5, 1935, "Vagaries" column in *Nichi Bei*.

2. In June 2015, the US Supreme Court declared all state laws barring marriage by same-sex couples unconstitutional.

10

A New Look at the Unknown Great

While the story of ethnic Japanese in Louisiana, whether in the metropolis of New Orleans or the bayous, is rather unknown, even to locals, Nikkei have had a surprisingly large impact on the state's history.

Possibly the first Japanese settler in Louisiana, and certainly the most notable, was Jokichi Takamine. Takamine was only in his late twenties when he traveled to New Orleans for the Cotton Centennial Exposition of 1884 as co-commissioner of the Japanese delegation, but he was already well known as a scientist. He appreciated New Orleans so much—and in particular a local white woman named Caroline Hitch who he met there—that after the exposition he and Hitch got hitched, and the couple remained in town part time through 1888. While living in New Orleans, Takamine met the writer Lafcadio Hearn, who had previously settled there. According to legend, Takamine so intrigued Hearn with his stories of Japanese life that he inspired Hearn to move to Japan, where he subsequently achieved renown for his stories of languid Japanese. Takamine himself, after returning briefly to Japan,

DOI: 10.5876/9781607324294.c010

FIGURE 10.1. Imahara family at Afton Villa in Louisiana.

settled permanently in New York. In 1901 Takamine developed the process for isolating and synthesizing the hormone adrenaline, thereby achieving worldwide fame and a considerable fortune.

Takamine helped cement a special relationship between Louisiana and Japan. In 1896 he escorted a group of six Japanese businessmen to New Orleans, where they placed the first large orders for cotton. Within two

FIGURE 10.2. Japanese Americans in Louisiana in 1941.

decades, the cotton trade expanded so much that New Orleans reportedly did more business with Japan than with all of Central America. In 1922 Japan opened a consulate in the Crescent City. In 1928 businessman Neal Leach founded the Japan Society of New Orleans; by 1937 it had 175 members.

Meanwhile, white agriculturalists, led by a planter with the delightful name of Seaman A. Knapp, turned to Japan to revive southwest Louisiana's once proud rice industry, which had fallen on hard times. With aid from the US Department of Agriculture, Knapp visited Japan as an official agent and explored various rice plants. On Knapp's recommendation, the department invested $18,000 in Kyushu (some sources say Kishu) rice—its grains could stand up to the rolling mills used to process rice without breaking, thus making mass mechanization possible. Knapp then recruited Japanese experts to plant this rice (locally dubbed "Jap rice") and teach farmers their ancestral techniques for rice cultivation. As a result of the new techniques, plus better irrigation, rice fields in the Gulf Coast region boomed. Within five years, farmers increased their rice acreage threefold and the value of their lands tenfold.

Although the 1900 census listed only seventeen Japanese in all of Louisiana, the establishment of such commercial and agricultural ties led some locals to encourage settlement by groups of Japanese farmers—and some immigrants to consider it. Yet racial prejudice and fears of economic competition destroyed plans for mass settlement of ethnic Japanese. In March 1905, Jiro Harada, a Japanese commissioner from San Francisco and a University of California, Berkeley graduate, announced that he had made arrangements for the development of a large Japanese rice-growing colony in southwest Louisiana to be composed mainly of already-established Issei who had grown weary of prejudice on the Pacific coast. When town officials in Crowley announced that two hundred Japanese farmers would be settling there, a statewide outcry of influential whites protested any such "colonization," on the grounds that it would make the state's already intractable race problem even worse. A decade later, after the California Alien Land Law of 1913 barred Issei from land ownership, West Coast Issei, encouraged by real estate and railroad interests, once more began to consider establishing themselves in Louisiana. Again local whites protested, both openly on racial grounds and more indirectly against what they termed an oriental "invasion." In 1921 Louisiana enacted its own alien land law. Ironically, in the face of hostility from Louisiana whites, many settlers ended up establishing themselves in Texas. Promoters envious of Louisiana's profitable rice fields attracted Japanese investors to Texas to build up the industry, and eventually a prosperous colony of Japanese-owned plantations sprang up around the Texas Gulf Coast (most famously the legendary Saibara clan, who settled in Webster), while merchants opened shop in downtown Houston.

Still, some Japanese did migrate to Louisiana, and by the 1930s, the local community had expanded to between forty and fifty permanent residents, a population composed of farmers, importers, and fishermen. In 1904 Tomehitsu Hinata, a US Navy veteran of the Spanish-American War, arrived in New Orleans, and with his wife, Katsue, he opened a Japanese art and curio store on Royal Street in the French Quarter. Their daughters Yuki, Toshi, and Kyo—the first Louisiana-born Nisei—attended college in the 1930s. Toshi and Kyo were hired as teachers in the New Orleans public schools. By way of comparison, before World War II, there was not a single teacher of Japanese ancestry in any Los Angeles–area public school. Namyo Bessho, another US Navy Spanish-American War veteran, who was one of the rare Issei to become naturalized before 1922, settled in the district of Algiers with his wife, Koh, and their children.

By 1940, according to Tokumi Hamako, a Nisei employee at the New Orleans consulate who wrote a set of columns for the West Coast vernacular press on life in the Deep South, the local population included ten consular officials plus "Two Nisei doctors from Hawaii . . . a chick-sexer; a young Nisei girl from the good ol' city of Los Angeles; a ship chandler who has a French wife, two children and a bad case of asthma; a shrimp dealer who is a Stanford graduate, and his family; and a fisherman with a red face." With assistance from the consulate and the Japan Society, in 1931 the city's first Japanese school opened in the Hotel Monteleone. Hisashi Nomasa, a Loyola University student, was the first permanent language instructor; he was one of several Nikkei to study in the region. In 1937 Roger Yawata of Oakland enrolled at Loyola, becoming the only Nisei collegian in New Orleans, and took over teaching at the language school. Minoru Kimura, a Nisei from Hawai'i, graduated from Tulane University School of Medicine in 1936. In 1941 Clifford Uyeda enrolled in medical school at Tulane, and during World War II, he worked as an intern at the city's Charity Hospital.

A handful of Issei and Nisei settled outside New Orleans. In 1927 Sam Nagata opened a trucking business, hauling produce between New Orleans and New Iberia, Louisiana. His brother, Josie, and his wife, Edith, relocated to the region in the mid-1930s and opened a fruit market/grocery store in Eunice, Louisiana, in Cajun country, near Lafayette. Their son, Joe Nagata, set records as a high school football player; he enrolled at Louisiana State University (LSU) on a football scholarship and played as a first-string back in the 1944 Orange Bowl. In 1928 Manabu and Saki Kohara, who had run a photo studio in Omaha, Nebraska, moved to the central Louisiana town of Alexandria with their five children. After an abortive effort at truck farming, they opened a photo studio, which survived the Depression and prospered during the war when a pair of nearby Army camps housed GIs (including Nisei soldiers). All of their children attended LSU. Their eldest daughter, Kay Kohara, became one of the early Nisei women physicians, working as a resident physician at Charity Hospital in New Orleans before marrying and moving to Baltimore.

Despite the barriers to their settlement, throughout the prewar era, Japanese Americans in Louisiana were not treated as "colored," unlike blacks. Indeed, by all accounts, Louisiana was one of the few places in prewar America where Japanese were always granted courteous service in hotels and restaurants and routinely addressed as "sir" or "ma'am." Clifford Uyeda, who arrived in New Orleans in mid-1941, later recounted taking his first streetcar ride and being reproved when he unknowingly took an empty seat in the colored section of the segregated car; the conductor soon settled the matter by taking the "colored" sign out from the slot in front of Uyeda's seat and sliding it in back of him, thus moving him into the "white" section. Uyeda added that when he studied at Tulane, he was treated as just another student.

The Second World War hit Louisiana's Japanese population hard. On December 8, 1941, the Japanese consulate closed its doors, and its Japanese alien employees were interned. Japanese shrimp boats were grounded and the Hinata art store in New Orleans closed its doors. The Hinata daughters, anticipating dismissal from their public school teaching posts, voluntarily offered their resignations to the city school board, but their resignations were refused and they were granted certificates of commendation.

World War II brought Nikkei from all over the Americas into Louisiana. First, a group of Issei men—largely from Hawai'i—who had been arrested and interned after Pearl Harbor were shipped to Louisiana and up to 1,200 were held during 1942–1943 at Camp Livingston, near Alexandria. Meanwhile, New Orleans served as the post of debarkation for over 2,000 ethnic Japanese from Peru and other Latin American countries who were kidnapped from their home countries during 1942 as part of a deal with the US State Department and shipped for internment in the United States. Then, in mid-1943, Japanese American soldiers from the 100th Infantry Battalion were detailed for training at Camp Livingston. Masses of Nisei trainees visited nearby Alexandria, where the Kohara family put them up, establishing a virtual USO in their house.

In early 1944, the War Relocation Authority (WRA) opened an area office in New Orleans. Few of the inmates paroled from camp had resettled in the Deep South, where land was cheap and well irrigated and where there was room for development. Government officials saw an opportunity for successful resettlement. They found a strong local booster in Roku (Dairoku) Sugahara, a Nisei businessman who had migrated with his wife to New Orleans. WRA officials proceeded to lead groups of Issei and Nisei farmers on tours of Louisiana and to propose resettlement. In the last days of 1944, the Southern Area WRA office put together a several-page English-language "letter" designed to attract Japanese American farmers to Louisiana (it was produced together with a second pamphlet, addressed to both Issei and Nisei, regarding resettlement in Texas). The Louisiana letter provided information on climate and ways of acquiring land. It included a letter to "Japanese evacuee brethren," produced under the signature of Masami Hata, an Issei resettler identified as working as a gardener in Baton Rouge. Sugahara extolled New Orleans as a "melting pot of many races" where "understanding and tolerance reigned." Left ostentatiously off the list of "races" enjoying such tolerance and understanding were the African Americans, who formed about 30 percent of the city, and Native Americans.

Despite the WRA's efforts, only a few farmers actually migrated to Louisiana. In early 1945, notably, Kozo Hattori took over a chicken farm just outside the city in St. Bernard Parish; he hired three other inmates as workers and made daily deliveries of produce to New Orleans. WRA officials were frustrated by the lack of a more significant response and opined that the reluctance of inmates to resettle in Louisiana was a product of exaggerated fears of prejudice. Ironically, those fears would soon appear less than exaggerated, for despite the WRA's almost total failure to encourage Japanese American resettlement in the area, rumors quickly spread that the government was engaging in a plot to use government loans to "colonize" Japanese people in the area. In February 1945, a police jury in Jefferson Parish, near New Orleans, enacted a resolution formally opposing any such settlement and called on farmers and real estate agents to not lease or sell land to Japanese of whatever citizenship. Leander Perez, a New Orleans lawyer (and outspoken segregationist) who was district attorney and political boss of St. Bernard and Plaquemines Parishes, quickly jumped on the bandwagon. Under his leadership, in May 1945, the two parishes adopted ordinances barring anyone of the "Japanese race" from owning land within their borders. In the face of such hostility, the WRA was forced to curtail its project.

Yet almost no sooner had the anti–Japanese American movement raised its head than the tensions dissipated. Despite the (largely symbolic) anti-Japanese ordinances, an estimated 190 Japanese Americans resettled in Louisiana during 1945–1946 and worked in the shrimp industry, in greenhouses, or as chick sexers. Yamato Kikuchi, who came from Topaz with his three sons, worked in a supermarket. Some Nisei took jobs in flower markets. Although many resettlers ultimately left, some remained and made a name for themselves. James Imahara, a Nisei farmer, opened up a landscaping and greenhouse business near Baton Rouge and ultimately became a million-aire. New Orleans housed resettlers with a variety of occupations. Kyokuzo Tomoda, an Issei from Stockton, California, moved to town with two daughters and started the K.T. Manufacturing Co., which sold roach powder and bug repellent. Another Stockton Issei, Testsuo Ijuin, opened a sandwich and coffee shop on Tulane Avenue near the Charity Hospital but died suddenly only a month later, after which his wife, Kiyo, and three daughters took over the shop and ran it for several years.

The Crescent City slowly resumed its status as a magnet for accomplished Nisei, and an estimated fourteen families were in residence by 1950. Roku Sugahara, after a stint in the Army, returned to New Orleans part time, where he operated a real estate appraisal business and served as a local correspondent for the *Pacific Citizen* until his untimely death in 1952. The Yenari family settled in the suburb of Gretna. The emperor of Japan would decorate Hajime Yenari, a jeweler and watchmaker, for his service to US-Japanese relations. His wife, physician Katsu Oikawa Yenari, undertook a residency in pediatric medicine at Tulane, then opened a private practice in Gretna. Hajime's brother, Ted Yenari, a Nisei optometrist, also set up shop. George Asaichi Hieshima, an ex-GI, received his medical degree from Tulane University, while Kazuo Watanabe, a former MIS officer, graduated from Tulane University Law School.

Sometime around 1950, the Japanese consulate in New Orleans reopened its doors, further boosting the size of the regional ethnic population—the 1960 census listed 519 ethnic Japanese statewide—and their prestige. By the mid-1960s, Japan had become the city's chief foreign trading partner. In 1972, for example, New Orleans had a higher value of exports to Japan (including a booming business in soybeans) than to all of Europe. During the decade ending in 1976, an average of 200 Japanese ships a year called in New Orleans. Japanese tourists became a common sight on the Crescent City's streets and Bourbon Street remained a spiritual home (and pilgrimage center) for Japanese and Nisei jazzman.

A few Nikkei residents gained widespread attention. After serving in the celebrated 442nd Regimental Combat Team, football star Joe Nagata returned to Eunice and spent thirty years coaching local high school football teams. In 2003 he was elected to the Louisiana Sports Hall of Fame. Linebacker Scott Fujita of the New Orleans Saints earned even greater fame in recent years, both for his playing and his community activism. Dr. Akira Arimura was named a professor of medicine at Tulane in 1965 and served there for thirty years, leading a circle of Japanese endocrinologists working in the Nobel Prize–winning medical research team of Dr. Andrew Schally. Charles H. Shindo, a California native, has served as a professor of history at Louisiana State University for over a decade.

Still, not every aspect of the Japanese presence in Louisiana was as positive. In 1992 sixteen-year-old Japanese exchange student Yoshihiro Hattori was shot dead in Baton Rouge by a meat market manager, Rodney Peairs, after Hattori and a white friend knocked mistakenly on his door in search of a Halloween party. The national Japanese American Citizens League inquired in vain why Peairs had shot only the Japanese boy and not his white companion. At his trial, Peairs was acquitted of manslaughter, though the student's family subsequently won a large award for civil damages from him.

Some of the old connections between Louisiana and Japan have dimmed. Trade declined sharply after Japan's economic boom went bust in the early 1990s. Conditions have been especially difficult in recent years. In 2008 the New Orleans Japanese consulate closed its doors, citing lack of business, and relocated to Nashville, Tennessee. The move, coming at a time when the city was struggling to rebuild after the devastation wrought by Hurricane Katrina, was a blow to locals and attracted fierce criticism and unsuccessful petitions. Still, one can find remnants of the former closeness between Japan and Louisiana and the financial and cultural exchange between them. One of the most unique is the Café du Monde, a New Orleans institution that has survived for 150 years. Thanks to an exclusive concession agreement, there are some thirty branches of the iconic café in Japan—the only branches in the world outside Louisiana—serving its menu of chicory coffee and beignets.

JAPANESE AMERICANS IN PREWAR CHICAGO: AN OVERVIEW

Scholars have been taking increased interest lately in Nikkei life in Chicago during the mid-1940s. There is, to be sure, a good deal still to discover. (It would be a great service for some bilingual scholar to translate Ryoichi Fujii's grand historical study *Shikago Nikkeijinshi* into English.) Their curiosity is natural. Chicago was the chief center of resettlement for Japanese Americans leaving the wartime camps. By the first years after the war, the city and its suburbs had become home to some 22,000 Nikkei, while as many as 30,000 may have passed through the city at some time. Issei and Nisei in Chicago developed a vibrant group life and formed multiple community-based newspapers and social agencies, most famously the *Chicago Shimpo* and the Chicago Resettlers Committee (still going strong as the Japanese American Service Committee).

By contrast, scant attention has been devoted to Japanese Americans in Chicago in earlier decades, perhaps because of the small size of the Nikkei community during the prewar period; according to the 1940 census, the city was home to barely 400 people of Japanese ancestry. Yet, even that tiny prewar population bears exploration, as it included extraordinary intellectuals, professionals, and creative artists.

The procession of significant Nikkei residents begins in the nineteenth century, when poet Yone Noguchi and missionary/educator Tel Sono migrated to the city from California before eventually moving to New York. Sono attended the city's deaconesses training school in 1889 and worked for the Woman's Christian Temperance Union. Noguchi, who arrived circa 1899, wrote lyrically about daily life on Chicago's streets for the *Evening Post*. (Several other Japanese writers who passed briefly through Chicago—notably Kanzo Uchimura, Kafu Nagai, and Jenichiro Oyabe—left vivid descriptions of their experiences in the city.)

Another fascinating early figure was Japanese Socialist Kiichi Kaneko, who moved to Chicago circa 1906 after marrying Josephine Conger. The couple founded and coedited a magazine, *The Socialist Woman* (later *The Progressive Woman*), which pushed socialism and women's suffrage. Kaneko returned to Japan in 1909 and died young of tuberculosis, while Conger kept the periodical going. Meanwhile, the pioneering Nisei writer Kathleen Tamagawa grew up in Chicago at the turn of the century (the daughter of Sanzo Tamagawa, a silk salesman). She later related her childhood experiences there—such as attending John Dewey's school—in her 1932 memoir *Holy Prayers in a Horse's Ear: A Japanese American Memoir.*

Universities—notably the University of Chicago—were magnets drawing talented Japanese during the prewar era. Early in the century, Chicago's Political Science Department hired Toyokichi Iyenaga, an expert on Japanese diplomacy. Iyenaga gained a nationwide readership for his writings on US-Japan relations and politics. He also was a frequent commentator on the status of Japanese Americans, most prominently in his 1921 book *Japan and*

FIGURE 10.3. Radio star Betty Ito.

the California Problem (which he coauthored with Kenoske Sato). Conversely, in 1933 the Political Science Department at Northwestern University hired Ikuo Oyama, a former leader of Japan's progressive Labour-Farmer Party, who had been forced to flee Japan due to his opposition to militarism. He remained there until after World War II, working in the university library. He later returned to Japan, where the Soviet Union awarded him the Lenin Peace Prize in 1951 for his opposition to nuclear weapons and "Strengthening Peace Between Nations."

Meanwhile, Chicago attracted numerous graduate students from Japan. The most celebrated was political scientist Sterling Tatsuji Takeuchi, author of the influential 1935 book *War and Diplomacy in the Japanese Empire*; others were sociologist Tadao Kawamura and religious scholar Takeichi Takahashi. Chicago's Sociology Department also educated a pair of brilliant Nisei—Jitsuichi Masuoka and S. Frank Miyamoto—while Kansuke Kawachi of Hawai'i received his master's degree there.

The city's institutions also drew natural scientists. In 1902 Kenji Toda, a student at the Tokyo Academy, was invited to join the University of Chicago's Department of Zoology. He remained there for more than fifty years. Toda attained international renown for his scientific drawings of animals and human endocrine glands for science classes and textbooks. He was equally famous as an expert on Asian art and the author of books on Chinese scrolls and Japanese painting.

Similarly, Tokumatsu Ito arrived in the United States in 1903 and opened a Japanese goods store. He ultimately spent a long career dividing his time between work in the Anthropology Department at the Field Museum of Natural History, where he also served as a curator of Chinese screens, and the Department of Oriental Art at the Art Institute of Chicago. (One may suppose that Toda and Ito must have met with their junior colleague Frank Nakamura, a professor in the Botany Department at the University of Illinois, during some of his frequent trips to Chicago.)

Ito's daughter, Elizabeth (Betty) Ito, gained various laurels of her own. She enrolled at the University of Chicago as a German literature major and was selected Phi Beta Kappa. After graduation, she became well known as a radio actress. She first appeared in 1936 as Martha Yamoto, a doctor's daughter, on the WGN hospital drama *Healing Hands* and on the NBC serial *Jack Armstrong, The All-American Boy*. In August 1937, NBC signed Ito to a contract, and she became featured player in the serial *Young Hickory*, playing a white woman, Alice Carter. However, she was hired soon after to play the part of Lotus, the notorious "oriental siren," in the radio version of the famous comic strip *Don Winslow of the Navy*. Betty Ito served during World War II in the Office of Strategic Services and met her future husband, sociologist and professor Barrington Moore. The two fell in love and married in 1944—his elite white American family was shocked by the interracial union. Elizabeth Ito Moore lived with her husband for almost fifty years, serving as his editor and collaborator, until her death in 1992.

Another group of celebrated Nisei performers were the Taka Sisters (née Takaoka), a vaudeville trio of exotic Japanese dancers (supposedly from Tokyo) who billed themselves as "the only Japanese triplets on the stage" and combined dance steps with violin, piano, and koto playing. They headlined at Harry's New York Cabaret during 1935–1936, until a jealous white lover murdered the eldest sister, Mary, in mid-1936 (a crime that broke up the act).

Ballet dancer Sono Osato was a more classical performer; her family called Chicago home. Sono's father, Shuji Osato, was a professional photographer who also worked for the Japanese tourist office and the national railways. Sono made Chicago her base between European tours with the Ballets Russes and Ballet Theater but later moved to Broadway as a musical theater star.

JAPANESE AMERICANS AND THE DEATH PENALTY

Since the beginning of Japanese settlement in the United States, commentators have often remarked upon the supremely law-abiding nature of the Nikkei. Sociologists and criminologists have offered various theories as to why Japanese Americans have such an outstanding record in this regard. They have pointed variously to the impact of close-knit family structures, feelings of collective responsibility, and fear of intervention by outsiders on preserving collective morality and reducing illegal activities. Such good citizenship became a point of pride for Issei and Nisei before World War II. In the same way, wartime defenders of Japanese Americans underlined the community's low crime rate—first as an argument against mass incarceration under Executive Order 9066, later to promote their desirability as neighbors after their return from the War Relocation Authority camps. (A similar public statement was made by a progressive Santa Maria minister with the wonderfully apropos name of Aaron A. Heist.)

In actual fact, the prewar Japanese population had its share of petty lawbreakers (even ignoring the mass evasion of alien land laws and other discriminatory legislation that Nikkei perpetrated). In particular, gambling was widespread among Issei men on the West Coast, and bootlegging was popular with the same demographic during the era of Prohibition. Still, a certain truth could be found in the reports of pro-Japanese boosters. According to official statistics, arrest rates were extremely low within the Japanese community, especially in comparison to those of other minority groups, with violent crime exceedingly rare. Nevertheless, in the half-century before World War II, the grisly crimes of three notable Japanese American felons attracted public notice, and their capital cases made a large public impact.

The first case involved Jugiro Shibuya, an Issei sailor living in a boardinghouse in Brooklyn. In 1889 Shibuya was convicted of murder and sentenced to death by electrocution—New York's was the first such law in the country—for stabbing a fellow Japanese sailor to death during a brawl following a card game. The electric chair, like the guillotine one hundred years earlier, immediately became a gruesome—and controversial—symbol of death, and the law was controversial, especially after William Kemmler became, in August 1890, the first criminal to be executed by electrocution. Roger M. Sherman, a distinguished lawyer and opponent of capital punishment who had served as Kemmler's counsel, applied for a writ of habeas corpus on Shibuya's behalf, attracting nationwide attention to the case. A federal district court refused to issue a writ of habeas corpus. Sherman then appealed the decision to the US Supreme Court, which heard the appeal on November 12, 1890. Sherman argued that the electric chair was "cruel and unusual punishment" under the Eighth Amendment, since "burning by wire" did not kill the prisoner instantaneously but tortured him to death by jolts to his body. Two weeks later, the high court upheld the lower court decision without issuing an opinion.

Shibuya was scheduled for execution in January 1891. Sherman then commenced another habeas corpus petition, in which he alleged, among other points, that following his initial conviction, Shibuya had been assigned a lawyer who was not admitted to the bar. Meanwhile, lawyers for a fellow prisoner who had also been scheduled for execution—an African American named George Wood—protested his conviction on the grounds that blacks were regularly excluded from jury service in New York and there had been none on the jury that convicted him. Sherman took a leaf from their book and argued that Shibuya's sentence was unconstitutional because no Japanese were permitted on *his* jury. In May 1891, the US Supreme Court ruled in the two cases that nothing in New York's law barred members of minority groups from jury service, so any protests over the informal practice of exclusion should have been brought up at trial. Since they had not, the high court could not intervene to uphold constitutional rights. (It took seventy-five years, in the case of *Swain v. Alabama* (1965), for the high court to overturn a death penalty conviction because of the deliberate exclusion of minorities from juries.) On July 7, 1891, Jugiro, Wood, and two other prisoners were fried in the electric chair, the next victims after Kemmler.

A second capital case, involving Japanese immigrant Enichi Kato, was more poignant than grisly. In February 1937, Kato, a thirty-five-year-old Issei truck farmer and his family disappeared from their home in Auburn, Washington. All their belongings were still inside the house, and after no trace of the family had been seen for two weeks, Japanese community members grew concerned and launched a search. Soon, the bodies of Mrs. Kato and the four children were found together in a low patch of ground near a neighbor's house. Suspicion immediately fell on Enichi. A neighbor boy recalled that he drove Kato to the train station, and the ticket clerks confirmed that a man answering his description had bought a ticket to Sacramento, California. Police began a search for Kato in the Portland and Sacramento areas. Meanwhile, Mr. Z. Itayama, the owner of a flower shop in Richmond, California, decided that the new employee whom he had hired on February 19 was acting very strangely. Itayama confronted him, and the employee admitted that he was Enichi Kato and that he had slain his family.

Itayama immediately took Kato to the police station, where he confessed. Kato told police that he had killed his wife, Tora, and their four children. His wife had been ill for several years, he stated, and he had been unable to find work and earn sufficient money to care for the family. Unable to obtain relief, Mrs. Kato had finally expressed the desire to die. After a family conference, Kato agreed to kill his wife. Feeling hopeless without her, and pitiful because he could not feed his hungry children, he resolved to end their suffering as well. Thus, on February 12, he shot his wife and the older two children—nine-year-old Tom and seven-year-old Betty—then strangled ten-year-old Sam and five-year-old Mary with scarves knotted around their necks. He buried their bodies in a shallow grave under a mattress. He had intended, he explained, to kill himself as well, but he insisted that the sect that he was a member of (identified in newspaper articles as the Konkokyo Shinto Church) required all graves to be marked with a tombstone. He therefore resolved to earn the money needed for the tombstones before killing himself as well.

Kato was arraigned rapidly and brought to Auburn to stand trial. He refused counsel, explaining through an interpreter that he needed to keep what little money he had to buy gravestones for his family. Superior Court judge Hugh Todd then appointed a pair of lawyers to represent him. Kato's case went to trial in May. He pleaded guilty and was sentenced to death by a jury. Either Kato reconsidered his wish to die or still hoped to earn money for his family's tombstones before dispatching himself, as he authorized further moves to save his life. His lawyers successfully appealed the conviction on the grounds of juror misconduct, and he went through a second trial. During the second trial, Kato's lawyers argued that he went insane due to excessive consumption of polished rice. In the end, he was found guilty and sentenced to life imprisonment, after which his story remains lost to history.

The capital case that inspired the most widespread publicity in the mainstream press was the Jamieson murder in Hawai'i, in which a Nisei was the accused. On September 18, 1928, Gill Jamieson, the ten-year-old son of prominent local banker Frederick Jamieson, was called out of school and told that his mother had been injured in an automobile accident. A young Japanese American in a white coat, who resembled a hospital orderly, had picked him up at the school entrance and took him away. In fact, the young man was nineteen-year-old Nisei, Myles Yutaka Fukunaga. Fukunaga worked eighty hours per week in the pantry at a local hotel, but he made little money and desperately needed more in order to assist his destitute parents. A lonely, antisocial boy wounded by prejudice against Japanese Americans, he was inspired by reports of child murderers—notably the case of Nathan Leopold and Richard Loeb four years earlier in Chicago—to show his courage and intelligence by performing "the perfect crime." He thus plotted the kidnapping and ransom of Gill Jamieson, the son of the man whose bank had humiliated Fukunaga's parents by attempting to evict them from their home.

After kidnapping young Jamieson, Fukunaga took the boy to a hideout and killed him by beating him over the head with a steel chisel. He then sent a ransom note to Jamieson's parents, demanding $10,000 for the boy's safe return, and signed it "the Three Kings." That evening, Fukunaga telephoned Frederick Jamieson with instructions on how to meet him. His face hidden by a handkerchief and armed with a hammer, Fukunaga took $4,000 from the banker, promising to return with the boy, but then vanished.

The kidnapping shocked Honolulu's *haole* (white) society. Police immediately set up roadblocks to search cars and Boy Scouts and local volunteers organized into posses to conduct house-to-house searches. The "oriental" phrasing of the ransom note and the racial identity of both the chauffeur and the note's sender led the police to quickly suspect that the kidnappers were local Japanese. Harry Kaisan, a discharged former chauffeur of the Jamieson family, was called in for questioning by police and drugged in order to get him to confess to the crime.

Fukunaga eventually decided to end the suspense and halt the useless searching for the abducted boy. On the morning of September 20, he sent a note, along with a piece of the ransom money to authenticate it, to the offices of the *Honolulu Star-Bulletin* newspaper. The note read "Mas. Gill Jamieson, poor innocent lad, has departed for the unknown, a forlorn 'Walking Shadow' in the Great Beyond, where we all go to when the time comes." The letter promised to reveal the identity of the Three Kings in five days. Later that day, the boy's body was found in a glade near the Ala Wai canal.

Meanwhile, suspicion heightened against the local Japanese community, and a dozen local Japanese were detained and questioned. As terror gripped the larger population, Issei parents frightened of race riots warned their children to come home straight after school and not play outside. Japanese community organizations telegraphed condolences to the Jamieson family, offered rewards for the killer's capture, and volunteered to help search for the criminals. (Ironically, Fukunaga himself, remorseful and confused over his deed, offered to help police search for the Three Kings but was refused on the grounds that he was too young and small to help.)

On September 22, Fukunaga visited his old hometown of Waialua. The agent at the railroad station where he purchased his return ticket to Honolulu recognized the bill Fukunaga used as part of the ransom money and warned police of his identity. Police searched the Fukunaga family home and found evidence linking Myles to the crime. With the aid of his younger sister, police tracked him down the following evening. He admitted that he alone had killed the Jamieson boy and made a full confession at the station. As he arrived at the station, a siren sounded from Honolulu's Aloha Tower to signal the apprehension of the Three Kings.

With vigilante mobs howling for lynching or immediate execution of "the Kiawe Killer," Fukunaga's case went to trial just ten days later. Fukunaga did not deny his crime, but the judge refused to permit him to plead guilty. Despite the serious evidence that the defendant was mentally disturbed and an open letter from Professor Lockwood Myrick of the University of Hawaii that Fukunaga was insane, the court-appointed defense counsel called no witnesses to testify regarding his sanity. The defendant's boyishness and polite demeanor nonetheless impressed the counsel and members of the jury, some of whom shed tears as the foreman announced the guilty verdict. Three days later, the judge sentenced Fukunaga to death by hanging.

The Japanese community had been heavily stigmatized by the crime and the summary nature of official justice. In a protest against discrimination, community leaders, guided by *Hawaii Hochi* editor Fred Makino, launched a series of appeals, saying that the conviction was unjust because Fukunaga was insane. The Supreme Court of the Territory of Hawaii denied the petition, and the US Supreme Court refused to hear an appeal. On November 19, 1929, Fukunaga was hanged in Honolulu. The sensational crime and the racial bias shown in the trial would heavily foreshadow the 1932 Massie-Kahahawai case, in which five young men of various nonwhite ancestries (including one Nisei, Horace Ida) were falsely accused of raping a white woman.

The involvement of Issei and Nisei defendants in sensational murder cases has not been much studied. Obviously, it is an aspect of the community's history that most people would prefer to conceal rather than commemorate. Still, it is worth noting the community's role in both the Kato and Fukunaga cases (there was no community to speak of at the time of the Shibuya case) against legal injustice. In both cases, Japanese Americans were quick to assist authorities in apprehending the assailants. At the same time, the Japanese press expressed sympathy for the disturbed killers, without approving their actions, and reported their cases to ensure that justice was done. Their actions reveal a fine combination of community spirit and humanity.

THE OTHER SIDE OF THE HOOD RIVER STORY

Today's column is a tribute to the late broadcaster Paul Harvey's long-running radio series, *The Rest of the Story*. In that series, Harvey would tell a seemingly familiar or commonplace tale and then finish with an unusual twist that took listeners by surprise. Let's tell a tale about Japanese Americans and racial prejudice and see if you can find THE REST OF THE STORY.

Hood River, Oregon, which sits on the Columbia River, at the famous Columbia Gorge, has some of the most beautiful scenery in the United States. Today it is a popular resort and windsurfing mecca. In the past, though, the town and the surrounding county were famous for the apples, strawberries, and cherries grown there.

Historians such as Linda Tamura and Lauren Kessler tell us that Japanese immigrants began to settle the area around the turn of the twentieth century, working in lumber, sawmills, and orchards. Although handicapped by Oregon's alien land law, the immigrants gradually amassed plots of land. Their skill and hard labor brought them prosperity. By the 1930s, Japanese farmers produced one-fourth of the local apple crop and dominated the market in strawberries and asparagus.

The town of Hood River was a beacon for Japanese farmers in the region. They could attend events at the community hall or congregate and shop at the grocery store run by an enterprising Issei, Masuo Yasui. Yasui started the grocery store with his brother shortly after arriving in the United States in 1905 and used the profits to acquire considerable property. Yasui raised a large family in town. His children—notably his son Minoru, a lawyer—would achieve renown among Japanese Americans.

The success of the Issei farmers and merchants brought them acceptance, if sometimes grudging, from local whites. However, as in other communities, the climate in Hood River dramatically changed with the coming of war. Masuo Yasui, arrested after Pearl Harbor, remained interned for six years. With the advent of Executive Order 9066, Issei and Nisei alike were forced to abandon their homes and leave for confinement. Local whites, always resentful of the economic competition of the Nikkei, cheered their departure. A delegation from Hood River appeared before the Tolan Committee in spring 1942 to lobby for mass removal. A year later, a poll by the *Hood River Sun* revealed that 84 percent of those surveyed did not wish Japanese Americans to return.

Hostility among local whites, and their determination to keep Issei and Nisei out, became palpable once former inmates began to return to town. In November 1944, representatives of the local branch of the American Legion, made up largely of World War I veterans, ordered the names of sixteen Nisei servicemen erased from the honor roll in front of city hall. One of the names was that of Frank Hachiya, a Military Intelligence Service staffer who had been killed while on duty in the Philippines.

The incident was reported in *Life* magazine and soon attracted international outrage. (One interesting protest took place in Evansville, Indiana, where Dr. Charles E. Rochelle, a World War I veteran and the first African American to be awarded a doctor of education degree from the University of California, Berkeley, mobilized the local branch of the Colored American Legion to rally on behalf of the Nisei veterans.) Stung by the bad publicity and under pressure from the national American Legion, as well as from locals who supported racial tolerance, the Hood River post finally reversed its policy in April 1945. By that time, however, the small town had become a national watchword for bigotry. The Hood River incident shocked the conscience of a nation, laying bare the naked racism behind the exclusion of Japanese Americans. It is said that the events in the town inspired the 1955 movie *Bad Day At Black Rock*. When Spencer Tracy's character arrives in a small town to hand the posthumous medal earned by a Nisei soldier to his father, he finds that the man has mysteriously (been) disappeared.

Yet the locals, whether white or Issei, might have been excused for failing to anticipate the widespread revulsion caused by these bigoted actions. For this was not the first time a minority group had been harassed and excluded in Hood River.

In spring 1932, in the depths of the Great Depression, white and Issei farmers recruited hundreds of young men from the Philippines to work in Hood River County. Filipino Americans were new to the region—the 1930 census listed only nine in the entire county—but there were apple trees to be pruned and "grass" (asparagus) to tend, and the "Pinoys" were willing to work for low wages. During their off hours, the young men visited the Yasui grocery store, buying rice or canned fish—they referred to the proprietors as "poppa" and "momma."

These were very difficult times for Filipinos in the United States. Unemployment was high, and even though the immigrants (technically US nationals) were relegated to the kind of stoop labor and other tasks most white laborers refused to perform, their low wages, mixed with their foreign appearance and culture, aroused white hostility.

Race rioting against Filipinos had already erupted sporadically along the West Coast. As with African Americans in the South, fears of interracial sexuality and the attraction of Filipinos to (and for) white women fueled and justified the repression. In 1930, for example, a mob of four hundred white vigilantes invaded a Pinoy dance hall in Watsonville, California, killing one man and injuring several more.

In Hood River, too, local townspeople grew anxious. The Pinoys were all men—young and strong and vibrant. And then something happened—different versions describe just what it was. According to one account, a Filipino driving home offered to give a lift to a fifteen-year-old white girl, and that simple neighborly act led to an innocent friendship, in which the two occasionally went to the movies together. Another story had it that a Filipino invited a young woman out, but either the effrontery of the invitation or a sense that he was leering at her led the insulted girl to complain. (One newspaper account from the time alleged that three Pinoys had been arrested for molesting a twelve-year-old girl, but this seems unlikely, as there were no reports of trials or convictions.)

Whatever happened, vigilantes in the white community, including World War I veterans—members of the same American Legion post that would later strike the names of Nisei from the town honor roll—spread charges that a Filipino had attacked a girl. On March 18, a crowd estimated at eighty people visited every ranch in the area and invaded the bunkhouses where Pinoy workers were living. The workers were roused and ordered at gunpoint to leave. The entire Filipino population hurriedly packed their bags and fled for their lives. To this day, no Filipino American community has reappeared in the Hood River Valley.

The Issei and Nisei of Hood River seem to have regretted the loss of their fellow Asian workers and customers. They may have been outraged by the violation of civil and human rights, the collective punishment for individual (and likely imagined) crimes. Or they may have been confused as to how so many people could have suddenly just disappeared and wondered what really happened. They seem to have spoken about it among themselves, in hushed tones. But they did not speak up and protest in public or even send the news to the Japanese vernacular press elsewhere. Apart from bare or distorted accounts in the mainstream press, the only accounts of the incident were reported by Filipino American journalists. So, when a decade later, the Japanese Americans were forced at gunpoint from their homes and the American Legion plotted to keep them from returning, perhaps they remembered THE REST OF THE STORY.

S. I. HAYAKAWA: JAZZ SPECIALIST AND CIVIL RIGHTS SUPPORTER

Samuel Ichiyé Hayakawa (1906–1992), a complex and colorful figure, was arguably the most controversial Nisei of the twentieth century. Although Hayakawa was well known as a semanticist and professor at San Francisco State University (SFSU), his lasting fame (or notoriety) stemmed not from his scholarly achievements but his conservative politics and opposition to student protesters. In 1968–1969, a "Third World" coalition of students at SFSU launched a strike, demanding ethnic studies programs and protesting the Vietnam War. When the college's president resigned, Hayakawa took over the post. He became notable for his outspoken opposition to the strikers; on one occasion, he even ripped out the wires from their sound truck at a demonstration. Upon retiring from San Francisco State in 1973, he became a newspaper columnist, then parlayed his newfound popularity into a successful campaign for the US Senate on the Republican ticket in 1976.

With this victory, Hayakawa became the first—and so far, the only—senator of East Asian ancestry from a mainland state, and at seventy, among the oldest freshman senators ever elected. During his single term, he aroused the ire of Japanese Americans when he publicly opposed official apologies and redress for wartime incarceration in a speech before the Japanese American Citizens League (JACL) and expressed his conviction that the Nisei were better off for the experience (Hayakawa's remarks stung his audience even more because he had never been confined in a War Relocation Authority [WRA] camp). Instead, he called on the Nisei to do their part to help improve relations with Tokyo and curb Japan bashing. After leaving the Senate, Hayakawa became a consultant on East Asian relations. He sparked further liberal outrage by cofounding US English, a lobbying group dedicated to making English the official language of the United States. Yet, if the story of S. I. Hayakawa's public career is familiar, his earlier biography is little known and his ideas resist easy classification.

First, he was not born in America, but in Vancouver, British Columbia. Hayakawa's father had immigrated from Japan to San Francisco at the dawn

FIGURE 10.4. S. I. Hayakawa.

of the twentieth century, returned to Japan, then settled with his wife in Canada. He worked as a labor contractor and journalist for a local Japanese newspaper before opening a struggling import/export business. Samuel Ichiyé was the eldest of four children. The family migrated across Canada during his youth, and he grew up in Cranbrook, Calgary, and Winnipeg, Manitoba. In Winnipeg, the Hayakawas were the only Japanese family in a Scottish and Jewish immigrant neighborhood (Hayakawa later was renowned for sporting a tam o'shanter, which he donned in tribute to his Scots associations). In 1926–1927, around the time that Hayakawa received his BA from the University of Manitoba, the family split up. His parents and two younger sisters moved to Japan, where his father became a wealthy businessman. Hayakawa moved with a brother to Montreal, where he earned a master's degree at McGill University, supporting himself in part by working as a taxi driver.

In 1929 Hayakawa left Canada and enrolled at the University of Wisconsin; he was so studious that friends nicknamed him "Don," which stuck with him thereafter. Hayakawa also wrote verse, and several of his poems and articles appeared in *Poetry* magazine over the next years. He cut a dashing figure at Wisconsin. One roommate, Robert Frase, later recalled how Hayakawa, who loved motorcycles, bought his bike upon graduation. Hayakawa then gave him a lift to commencement, with the two of them scooting through campus in cap and gown. Meanwhile, Hayakawa met and subsequently married a white woman, Margedant Peters. In 1935, following completion of a thesis on the poet/essayist Oliver Wendell Holmes, he received his doctorate (the thesis led to his first book, a coedited anthology of selections from Holmes's writings, in 1938). After graduation, Hayakawa traveled to Montreal, where his brother had established himself as a businessman. He intended to remain to Canada but could not find work. He returned to Wisconsin, took a job lecturing on English literature in the university's extension division, and contributed to the *Middle English Dictionary*.

Around this time, Hayakawa was invited (one might say summoned) by his parents to visit them. He recounted his visit to his ancestral homeland in "A Japanese American in Japan," a pair of articles published in *Asia* magazine in March-April 1937, which provide evidence of Hayakawa's literary gifts. (These articles represented not only Hayakawa's first published prose but were among the first appearances by a Nisei in a mainstream magazine.) He started by explaining that, before his visit, he knew little of Japanese culture—for example, while he knew most of the words and music to Gilbert and Sullivan's *The Mikado*, he was pretty vague on the 47 Ronin! He also had troubles communicating with his Japanese family. While his father spoke fluent English, he could converse with his mother only in a mixture of Japanese baby talk and literary English. His youngest sister, who had returned to Japan at the age of five, had felt such pressure to not be "different" in Japan that she had deliberately forgotten all English.

In the articles, Hayakawa described several scenic parts of Japan—notably Lake Biwa, where he went out on a picnic boat and ate fresh-sliced fish and fresh tempura. He was enthralled by the public Shinto shrines and Buddhist temples (which he compared with his pallid Protestant upbringing) and moved by the women who wept as they prayed. Hayakawa's comparison of American democracy and Japanese feudalism was alternately humorous and poignant. For example, he described how he had been welcomed on his arrival and given generous presents by a deputation of his father's employees.

Conversely, his father put on formal visiting clothes and stayed up half the night with the family of a deceased employee to pay his respects. In the end, Hayakawa was fascinated by Japanese civilization, which he was anxious to study, and "the achievements of Japanese ethical and esthetic discipline." However, he felt uneasy in Japan. He was a teacher, he said, and the teacher in Japan was only secondarily a seeker after truth and primarily an instrument for inculcating national greatness. He was too American, too much the skeptic and empiricist, to survive in the close-knit and hierarchical confines of Japan. Even before the Japanese invasion of China, Hayakawa clearly sensed the approach of militarism.

In 1939 Hayakawa was named professor of English at the Armour Institute of Technology (now the Illinois Institute of Technology) and moved to Chicago. He became attracted to Alfred Korzybski's doctrines of what he called general semantics. Korzybski argued for systems of thinking and language that reflected the fluid nature of reality. Hayakawa was fascinated by the idea, as he put it, of "an examination of language as a preliminary to an examination of the problems stated in language." He sought to popularize Korzybski's epistemological theories by means of a textbook, and in 1939 he published the first version of *Language in Action* with a small Chicago press. The book attracted such attention for its lucid and entertaining style that it was taken up by a major New York publisher. In December 1941, just before Pearl Harbor, the book became a Book-of-the-Month Club selection, assuring it large sales. It would go through numerous editions and make its author known nationwide.

The young Hayakawa repeatedly expressed a determination not to be limited or pigeonholed by his Japanese background. Part of his interest in general semantics was its emphasis on environmental factors over heredity and the resistance of reality to fixed Aristotelian categories of truth. Meanwhile, in the shadow of fascism, he grew increasingly conscious of the dangers of propaganda and racial hatred and how people substituted facile stereotyping for thought. He concluded that ethnic particularism and ghettoization invited social division, while assimilation and participation in democratic society promoted positive communication and equality. This would remain throughout his life his most consistent principle (aside from perhaps contrarianism).

As a result, Hayakawa opposed ethnic-based organizations on principle. He was willing to participate in struggles for civil rights in the name of furthering democracy. Most notably, in 1936 he visited Ottawa as part of a delegation from the Japanese Canadian Citizens League and lobbied unsuccessfully for voting rights for Nisei in British Columbia. Nevertheless, he favored multigroup action on a nonracial basis for economic democracy, particularly organizations of consumer cooperatives and cooperative housing—his wife, Margadent, edited the *Chicago Co-operative News*. He remained self-consciously cosmopolitan. In particular, because of his passionate love of jazz—on which he later claimed a somewhat spurious expertise—he became a familiar figure in Chicago's African American communities (and as a jazz pianist at café society parties). While it is too easy to read Hayakawa's interest in assimilation and distance from Japanese communities as simply a product of his rootless and itinerant youth, family and psychological factors, as well as intellectual ones, undoubtedly contributed.

Hayakawa's principles were tested during Word War II by the removal of West Coast Japanese Americans. While Executive Order 9066 represented exactly the kind of racist and undemocratic action that he deplored, he was wary of anything resembling special pleading for his own group. His response was twofold. First, he quietly assisted resettlement efforts so that Nisei could leave camp and enter the larger society. In 1942 his old Wisconsin roommate, Robert Frase, contacted him. Frase had been recruited to join the WRA by director Dillon Myer. In part through knowing Hayakawa, Frase was convinced that Japanese Americans were loyal; he and his supervisor, Tom Holland, opposed confinement and lobbied Myer to authorize immediate resettlement. When Frase visited Chicago to establish a resettlement office there, Hayakawa hosted him at his house and advised him on securing jobs and housing for resettlers.

Meanwhile, in 1943 Hayakawa joined the African American newspaper the *Chicago Defender* as a weekly columnist; he continued his column until January 1947. While he surely appreciated that its editors hired him partly as an expression of solidarity with Nisei, he refused to speak solely as a Japanese American. Rather, he maintained a stance of objectivity. When he sporadically—and reluctantly—addressed issues of confinement or anti-Japanese discrimination, he did so within a larger context of promoting American democracy. Ironically, as C. K. Doreski has noted, poet Langston Hughes was more critical of government treatment of Japanese Americans in his *Defender* column than was Hayakawa. Conversely, Hayakawa was forthright in his criticism of racism against blacks in both his *Defender* column and his lectures on race relations.

Hayakawa's interactions with Japanese communities remained uneasy through the postwar years. During this period, due in part to the efforts of Robert Frase, Chicago became the focal point of Japanese American resettlement. Most of its ethnic Japanese newcomers—a population that reached some 20,000 by 1946—were forced by discrimination and the housing shortage, as well as their impoverished state, to squeeze into slums and racially changing neighborhoods and take menial, low-paying jobs. Hayakawa was genuinely sympathetic to Nisei victimized by official prejudice (disdaining euphemisms, he spoke of Japanese Americans having been "herded into concentration camps"). However, his powerful faith in assimilation and resistance to ethnic particularism led to clashes. Sociologist Setsuko Matsunaga Nishi later recalled that when she asked Hayakawa to serve on the advisory board of the Chicago Resettlers Committee, which was trying to open housing and find jobs for Japanese Americans, Hayakawa resisted and scornfully responded, "Why do you want to pull me back? Can't I just be a model of what a person of Japanese ancestry can achieve by assimilating?" He reluctantly agreed to serve and made a large financial contribution. (He may have been impressed by Nishi's own involvement in African American communities, or perhaps by the fact that the board already boasted such prominent Chicagoans as department store magnate Marshall Field and Inland Steel president Edward L. Ryerson.) Meanwhile, because of Hayakawa's agreement with its platform of assimilation and multiracial civil rights, he likewise bent principle regarding opposition to ethnic organizations and joined the JACL.

Before long, however, Hayakawa reversed his position. In summer 1952, he publicly announced that he would no longer contribute to the Chicago JACL's Anti-Discrimination Committee because of the organization's support for the McCarran-Walter Act. The act, a product of Cold War xenophobia and exaggerated concerns over security, gave the government new powers to strip naturalized US citizens of their citizenship and exclude or deport aliens suspected of subversive tendencies. However, the act overturned the exclusion of Japanese immigrants (albeit in token numbers, within existing discriminatory national origins quotas) and granted naturalization rights to Issei. Because these were two primary goals of the JACL, the organization's leaders reluctantly gave the larger bill their support; and after President Harry

Truman vetoed the bill, the JACL helped lobby Congress to override the veto. In letters to the *Pacific Citizen* and *Chicago Shimpo*, Hayakawa accused the JACL of opportunism. By supporting a "heartless," repressive, and illiberal bill in order to secure naturalization rights for Issei, Nisei were putting their own interest ahead of that of the many aliens and immigrants who would be damaged by the law. Hayakawa was not alone in his opposition: journalist Togo Tanaka had already condemned the JACL's actions. Still, it represented an impressive statement of principle, especially since Hayakawa himself stood to gain from the legislation. While Hayakawa was a Canadian citizen, he was barred from US naturalization because of his Japanese ancestry. It was only after the passage of the McCarran-Walter Act that he was able to become an American citizen himself.

After the dispute over McCarran-Walter, Hayakawa again distanced himself from Nisei communities. By this time, he had become a well-known educator and semanticist. In 1950 the University of Chicago hired him as a lecturer and five years later, he was appointed professor of English at San Francisco State. He likewise served as editor of the professional linguistics journal *ETC.* Hayakawa remained opposed to separate ethnic-based organizations, and he stirred up further controversy when he declined an invitation to speak to a West Coast Nisei student federation and counseled students to avoid forming separate organizations, which he referred to as a "crutch."

Still, on two occasions in the coming years he joined forces with Japanese community members for libertarian goals, though both times the interventions carried his own individual mark. First, in August 1963, at the time of the March on Washington, Hayakawa delivered a widely publicized lecture on the "Negro problem," in which he expressed his sympathy for African Americans and asserted that the way the nation handled the civil rights question would determine its place in the world. Hayakawa called for a number of special public-private measures to assure equality, including initiatives by labor unions and businesses to recruit minorities, the end of segregation in public accommodations, and incentive bonuses to attract talented teachers to schools for the underprivileged. His advocacy of special government recruitment efforts for minorities prefigured the creation of affirmative action programs and magnet schools.

At a time when the JACL was paralyzed over Rev. Martin Luther King, Jr.'s invitation to attend the March on Washington, this was a controversial position among Nisei. Hayakawa implicitly rejected the argument, pressed by conservatives, that blacks should improve their situation by their own efforts and that Nisei would jeopardize their good relations with white allies by supporting equality for African Americans. Although Hayakawa had not delivered the lecture to a Japanese American audience, he granted the progressive newspaper *New York Nichibei* permission to serialize extracts from it over the following weeks, with the goal of winning further Nisei support for civil rights.

The other occasion when Hayakawa assisted Japanese communities was in his strong support for Iva Toguri d'Aquino, who had been arrested after World War II and charged with broadcasting for Japan as "Tokyo Rose." In the mid-1970s, as Japanese Americans undertook the movement for redress (which Hayakawa opposed, as noted above), investigators discovered that Aquino's conviction was tainted by perjured testimony and postwar hysteria. A campaign grew to win her official pardon from President Gerald Ford. Hayakawa was recruited to lend his support (presumably by his friend Clifford Uyeda, a leader of the pardon movement). He responded with a pair of newspaper columns examining Aquino's case. He noted that the reason Aquino had been indicted for treason, unlike the others who broadcast on Japanese radio during World War II, was that she had refused to renounce her American citizenship, even under duress. He insisted that such courage merited reward, not blame. In addition to publishing the columns, he telephoned the White House to lobby Ford administration officials. The pressure, especially from a newly elected Republican senator, may well have helped. Ford issued Aquino a pardon on January 19, 1977, one day before leaving office.

S. I. Hayakawa, no doubt because of his idiosyncratic style and his shift to right-wing politics, has been largely excluded from history, especially that of Japanese Americans. Little attention has been paid to him. (The distinguished novelist Gerald W. Haslam, a onetime student of Hayakawa's, produced a biography, *In Thought and Action: The Enigmatic Life of S. I. Hayakawa*, in 2011.) This seems unfair. He was a distinguished scholar with authentic, if protean, ideas, and he climbed to the heights of public office with his election to the Senate (although once in office, he was caricatured as "sleeping Sam" after an incident where he dozed on the Senate floor). He stands as a monument to self-creation and social mobility.

ANNE REEPLOEG FISHER AND MORTON GRODZINS:
THE CENSORSHIP OF CONFINEMENT

The story of Executive Order 9066 and the mass removal and confinement of Japanese Americans during World War II is a difficult one for many people to wrestle with, even today. The inability of Americans to deal fully with the wartime treatment of Japanese Americans can be demonstrated by looking at two different incidents of censorship during the early postwar years, involving books on the subject by Anne Reeploeg Fisher and Morton Grodzins.

Anne Reeploeg Fisher (1900–1994) was a Socialist and a member of the Interracial Church of the People in Seattle. When Gordon Hirabayashi went to trial in mid-1942 for breaking curfew regulations and refusing to register for "evacuation," Fisher attended his trial and took stenographic notes of the proceedings. She also wrote to members of Congress during 1942 and 1943 in order to secure better treatment for camp inmates. Still, her interest in the question remained minor until April 1945, when she went to San Francisco to report on the inaugural United Nations conference for the Socialist newspaper *The Call*. According to Fisher's account, while in California, she attended a meeting of a vanguard of Japanese Americans recently returned from camp. She was surprised to learn of the mounting antagonism against the returnees and all the difficulties they were having securing housing. She also visited the Manzanar camp, where she found the inmates apprehensive about leaving the relative security of the camp and returning to the larger society.

After Fisher returned to Seattle, she began writing an article on the Japanese American question, in order to educate the public about the returnees. However, once she started, she found more and more to say. After six months of typing twelve hours a day, six days per week, she had an enormous book manuscript, titled *Exile of a Race: A History of the Forcible Removal and Imprisonment by the Army of the 115,000 Citizens and Alien Japanese Who Were Living on the West Coast in the Spring of 1942*. Once the manuscript had been cut in half to save on printing costs, Fisher began seeking a publisher. In early 1946, she submitted it for a Scribner prize in history, a $10,000 award that also brought guaranteed publication by the prestigious Scribner publishing company. The judges expressed approval of Fisher's research and writing. However, she received information that a prizewinning historian had objected to the book on political grounds: "I did not like reading it—it is a humiliating book." Because he felt that facing such recent injustices hurt one's pride in one's country, he opposed awarding a prize to the book.

The negative assessment not only helped cost Fisher the Scribner prize, she later claimed, but it was fatal to her chances of publication. Although she received inquiries from Doubleday, nothing solidified, and she waited another twenty years—until 1965—before she undertook publication of *Exile of a Race*. By that time, no works on the camps had been produced for over a decade, and the nation had settled into a comfortable silence over what had occurred. Using the Peninsula Printing Company, a small British Columbia firm, she self-published 2,000 copies to be sold to libraries and schools in Canada. In order to extend copyright, she then produced 1,000 more via Seattle's F&T Publishers for sale in the United States. The book was sufficiently popular to ensure a new printing in 1970, and, in 1987, a new edition with a supplement. While the appearance of *Exile of a Race* heralded a slew of major studies of Executive Order 9066 in the late 1960s and early 1970s, it never achieved the prominence and influence it would have had it been chosen for publication by a major mainstream press in the first years after the war.

A second example of censorship is the affair of Morton Grodzins. Grodzins (1917–1964) was a graduate student at the University of California when he was hired as a researcher by the Japanese Evacuation Research Survey (JERS), a giant social science study of mass confinement headed by University of California sociologist Dorothy Swaine Thomas. Grodzins combed through multiple sources and compiled vital information for the project. In 1943, for example, he made a research trip to Washington, DC, and interviewed Justice Department officials. The following year, he submitted his thesis, "Political Aspects of the Japanese Evacuation," which was accepted in 1945. In 1946 he was listed as a coauthor on Thomas and Richard Nishimoto's study of "disloyals" at Tule Lake, *The Spoilage: Japanese-American Evacuation and Resettlement During World War II*, published by the University of California Press in 1946. The preface to that volume noted that as part of their series, the editors next intended to publish a monograph on "political and administrative aspects of evacuation and resettlement" (presumably, some version of Grodzins's work). Meanwhile, Grodzins was hired as a professor in the Political Science Department at the University of Chicago.

Following disagreements with Thomas, Grodzins decided to seek publication elsewhere, and in 1948 William T. Couch, the director of the University of Chicago Press, agreed to publish his work. In the book *Views From Within*, anthropologist Peter Suzuki details at length the attempts of Thomas, University of California chancellor Robert Sproul, and others to influence the University of Chicago Press to not publish the book. Although the pretext for denying publication was that Grodzins's manuscript was composed of confidential material belonging exclusively to the JERS project, Suzuki argues, with some justice, that University of California officials, in fact, objected to its portrait of elite California farmer and commercial groups and racist West Coast political leaders as chiefly responsible for mass removal.

When Thomas was unable to provide any evidence of a written agreement by Grodzins to not seek outside publication, Couch decided to publish the book as a contribution to public knowledge. University of California officials protested so strongly that University of Chicago chancellor Robert Hutchins moved to suppress the manuscript. Meanwhile, University of Chicago president Ernest C. Colwell ordered Couch to desist from publication, insisting that "interuniversity comity" was more important than freedom of the press.

Ordinarily, such maneuvers, however improper, would have killed the project, but the University of Chicago officials had not reckoned with their man: for Couch, it was history repeating itself. William Terry Couch (1901–1988), the son of a Virginia-based Episcopal minister, had become an editor at the University of North Carolina Press while still an undergraduate and had become its director in 1932. As a liberal white southerner, he was concerned about race relations and encouraging interracial dialogue. Thus, in 1936 he approached the distinguished African American educator Rayford W. Logan about producing an anthology of "Negro" opinion on the race question. Over the following years, Logan commissioned essays from a galaxy of distinguished black figures. The result, a manuscript called *What the Negro Wants*, was submitted in 1943–1944. While the contributors espoused different strategies for ending racial discrimination, they all agreed on one fundamental issue: racial segregation was harmful and should be abolished—a bellwether moment of consensus.

Although he had commissioned the book, Couch was shocked by the results. He firmly believed that the contributors were courting danger by attacking segregation instead of trying to develop all-black institutions. He asked Logan to alter the manuscript, but Logan refused. Out of personal principle (plus the threat of a lawsuit) Couch gave in and agreed to publish the manuscript as it stood, though he added an editor's introduction expressing his firm disagreement with the contributors. *What the Negro Wants* appeared in 1944. It swiftly became a classic of African American thought, and it remains in print and is much cited today. Nevertheless, even in North Carolina, considered the most liberal state in the South, any book challenging Jim Crow in 1944 was regarded as scandalous. Despite Couch's expressed dissent with its ideas, he was forced to resign from the press for allowing its publication, a move which prompted Chicago to hire him shortly after.

In the end, thanks to Couch's insistence on informing the public on issues of importance, in 1949 the University of Chicago Press published Grodzins's book under the title *Americans Betrayed*. As the first full-scale scholarly treatment of the decisions and events behind Executive Order 9066, it underlined the primary role of California "pressure groups" in bringing about mass removal. It was well reviewed and remains much studied by historians. However, Couch suffered once more for his defiant reliance on principle. In 1950 Hutchins summarily dismissed him, despite protests by sixteen distinguished University of Chicago faculty members and the resignation of the press's humanities editor, Fred Wieck. A year later, in a stunning shift, Morton Grodzins himself was selected as a University of Chicago Press editor, taking over from Couch. The circumstances surrounding the offer of the position to Grodzins, and his acceptance, were not publicly reported. In a further irony, Dorothy Swaine Thomas and the University of California Press would respond to Grodzins's book by commissioning and publishing a separate manuscript that grew out of the JERS study. *Prejudice, War, and the Constitution: Causes and Consequences of the Evacuation of the Japanese Americans in World War II*, coauthored by Jacobus tenBroek, Edward N. Barnhart, and Floyd W. Matson, though less focused on West Coast pressure groups and their role in agitating for removal, was more critical than Grodzins of the actions of the executive and the judiciary branches of government.

The examples of Anne Reeploeg Fisher and Morton Grodzins point up the various feelings of shame and defensiveness that elite Americans continued to feel in the postwar years regarding the wartime treatment of Japanese Americans, in reference to the West Coast interest groups that had clamored for their removal and the government which had arbitrarily denied their rights. Thus, even well researched and highly regarded studies by non-Japanese were subjected to censorship. It would not be until the 1970s, when Japanese Americans themselves rose to tell their stories and lobby for reparations, that the widespread urge by the nation's citizens to forget the wartime events would be overcome.

Gordon Hirabayashi's Surprising Postwar Career

In the annals of the wartime removal of Japanese Americans, one outstanding figure to celebrate is Gordon Hirabayashi, a man of principle whose legal challenge to official injustice went all the way to the US Supreme Court. Jeanne Sakata's 2007 play, *Dawn's Light*, has brought Hirabyashi's wartime exploits to countless audiences. However, many aspects of Hirabyashi's career remain understudied.

Let us recount what is generally known of Gordon Hirabayashi's life. Born in 1918 and raised in Auburn, Washington, Hirabayashi later said of his youth, "I grew up on a farm: I can recall year after year of our family just barely making ends meet. In fact, many were the years that our summer's crops merely paid off the winter's grocery bills, so that the following winter loomed before us without much financial cushion on our part."

In 1937 Hirabayashi enrolled at the University of Washington. Impressed by the Quakers, whose philosophy resembled that of the Japanese Christian sect in which he had been raised, the Nisei student joined in their pacifist activities on campus. In the wake of Executive Order 9066 and the imposition of a special curfew on Japanese Americans, he protested the violation of his rights as a US citizen by turning himself into the FBI and building a legal case against official policy. He was placed in a holding cell on the eleventh floor of the city-county building in Seattle, where he would remain for the next nine months. Following a trial, Hirabayashi was convicted of violating curfew regulations and declining to register for "evacuation." Hirabayashi appealed, and in early 1943 the Supreme Court took up his case. He was granted bail and released on the proviso that he move outside the West Coast excluded area. Thus, accompanied by a pair of marshals, he relocated to Spokane. During this time, he worked as a restaurant waiter, a night watchman, an emergency room orderly, and a clerk in a university bookstore.

In May 1943, the Supreme Court heard the case of *Kiyoshi Hirabayashi v. United States* (since Hirabayashi's given name is Gordon—a fact later veri-fied on his birth certificate by his family—naming the case with his Japanese middle name represents a subtle but telling indication of official racism). Meanwhile, as in the more famous Supreme Court case of *Korematsu v. United States* a year later, the Army engaged in egregious manipulation and with-holding of evidence to strengthen its case.

The Court unanimously upheld his conviction. The justices, ruling in the middle of the war, showed extreme deference to military claims of a danger to national security—a claim that Eric Muller has since convincingly demon-strated to be based on knowingly false statements by military officials about the possibility of a Japanese invasion of the West Coast. Since the govern-ment produced no proof of any disloyal activity by Hirabayashi (or any other West Coast Japanese American), the decision, in essence, legitimized racial stereotyping and popular prejudice as grounds for official action.

The legal limbo of the Nisei, confined without charge for the crime of looking Japanese, was reflected in Hirabayashi's punishment. As he had asked to be incarcerated at a road construction camp and the government refused to pay for his transportation to a camp outside the excluded zone, he was forced to hitchhike to the Catalina Federal Honor Camp, near Tucson, Arizona, where he was confined. (In his honor, in 1999 the site was renamed the Gordon Hirabayashi Recreation Area.) Even government officials recog-nized the exceptionally upright nature of their convict, as he made his trip completely unguarded. Because of his late arrival in Arizona, prison officials there could not find the paperwork in his case and discussed letting him go. Hirabayashi claimed that this would look suspicious. Finally, after dismissing their putative prisoner and persuading him to take in dinner and a movie and then return, they found his paperwork and incarcerated him for his term.

Almost no sooner had he been released from prison than he was inspired to join the movement of Nisei draft resisters, who protested the government's forcing them into military service while they and their families were denied their citizenship rights. Rather than registering as a conscientious objector, as he had done in 1940, Hirabayashi refused to register at all. Arrested once more and convicted of draft evasion, he was sentenced to a year in the penitentiary at McNeil Island, near Seattle. (He would later be included in the blanket pardon President Harry Truman offered to the draft resisters at Christmas 1947.)

In 1944 Hirabayashi caused a fresh public stir when he married a white woman, Esther Schmoe, the daughter of renowned peace activist and humanitarian Floyd Schmoe. The young couple was targeted by hostile press coverage. Esther bravely went through with her wedding in the face of racist hate mail about her marrying a convict and member of an "enemy" race. She and a set of baby twin daughters would be waiting for Hirabayashi when he emerged from prison.

So much for the known Gordon Hirabayashi. However, there is a good deal more to Hirabyashi's life and contributions than just the war years—and it is fascinating to discover his unknown postwar life. In September 1945, following his release from prison, Hirabayashi returned to Seattle. He found housing with his wife and new daughters in a low-income housing project, where a son, Jay, was born in 1947. Gordon enrolled at the University of Washington to complete his studies. He swiftly finished the credits for his BA, then enrolled in graduate work in sociology and was hired as an instructor. In spring 1948, as part of his MA thesis, he put together a sociometric survey of Nisei students about their attitudes toward other groups. He found a large percentage of Nisei preferred to socialize in-group, though they also expressed hostility to various other Nisei.

Completion of the survey had two important results. First, with support from sociology professor Robert O'Brien (who had worked as director of the National Japanese American Student Relocation Council during the war and was known to be sympathetic to Nisei), in 1949 Hirabayashi and a fellow student, Keith Griffiths, won a $2,000 fellowship from the Seattle chapter of the Anti-Defamation League of B'nai B'rith to conduct a large-scale survey of public attitudes toward racial and religious minorities on behalf of the Seattle Council of Social Agencies. Over the months that followed, Hirabayashi directed interviews of several hundred people from a variety of backgrounds. He found that a large percentage of local whites were still actively hostile to Japanese Americans and other minorities. While Japanese Americans, in turn, expressed less negative attitudes toward minorities, a large number expressed hostile sentiments: 27 percent would not invite an African American into their home for a social evening, and 75 percent would oppose permitting their children to date one.

Meanwhile, Hirabayashi's work on the survey put him into contact with the late journalist Budd Fukei, editor of the fledgling Seattle Nisei newspaper the *Northwest Times*. Fukei invited Hirabayashi to discuss his survey in the newspaper's New Year's 1949 issue. When the article was received favorably, Hirabayashi was engaged as a regular feature writer, producing columns in rotation with Fukei's own. Although they were contemporaries, Fukei and Hirabayashi made an odd pair. Fukei was a seasoned newspaperman who had gained experience working for the Japanese press before the war, while Hirabayashi, despite his academic credentials, was a journalistic neophyte. Furthermore, Fukei was a staunch supporter of the Nisei soldiers of the 442nd Regimental Combat Team and later became the editor of the Nisei Veterans Committee newsletter. Thus, he was an unlikely champion of the pacifist and draft resister Hirabayashi.

Hirabayashi inaugurated his weekly column, Just Among People, in February 1949. He would continue producing the columns, with some pauses, through the middle of 1951. The columns reveal both his sensitivity and talent as a writer. In one column, for example, he spoke with admiration of a set of married women students in his class who bravely pursued their education, though doing so meant continually juggling child care schedules and family finances. "And I thought I had a tough row to hoe," he concluded. In another, he expressed relief that a bill in the Washington State Legislature to grant release time in public schools for religious instruction had been defeated. He insisted that even a supposedly voluntary program of religious education would lead to pressure for conformity and stigmatization of minorities. He illustrated the point with homey examples:

> Children are all too anxious to pick on differences. Remember the red-haired kid in the class? What about the skinny tall one or the big fat blonde? What about the Japanese kid who brought "onigiri" for lunch instead of sandwiches like the rest of the kids? He was made fun of so heartlessly that he ran home crying. Kids exercise little discretion: somebody else's differences are their jokes and fun.

In his columns, he regularly drew insights from his own experience, including his wartime confinement and interracial marriage, though he softened such discussions by means of humor (often self-deprecating):

> When I look at my economic standing, I see "red"; my occupation is merely part-time instructor because I'm so busy. I'm only a part-time parent. I seem

to be only half-baked in no matter what category I consider myself. About the only thing I have done fairly thoroughly appears to be "in-mating" at seven different institutions of "correction" (University of Washington excluded).

One of his best pieces told of a class trip he led to McNeil Island, where he had been imprisoned during the war. Hirabayashi noted sardonically, "The last time I visited the island penitentiary, I was given a free trip, awarded a room and board scholarship, and didn't take the return trip for a year. This was my second trip, and I made sure that I returned the same day."

Hirabayashi did not shy away from controversial issues in his columns. In one of his first contributions, he argued on behalf of a national health insurance bill (sixty years before Barack Obama's administration). He also opposed restrictive covenants—because they restricted the rights of minorities and whites. However, while he was progressive-minded, he was equally ready to question liberal pieties. For example, he insisted that discrimination, in the sense of choosing one's associates and expressing preferences, was perfectly normal and indeed essential, provided such choices were not on irrational grounds such as race or religion. Similarly, when he attended a program of speeches on democracy, he remarked with asperity that it was too easy to talk about democracy rather than actually doing something about it: "What use are good intentions if we lack the techniques to implement them?"

Fukei, his editor, did not seem to have interfered with his contributor's outspoken commentary. However, in summer 1950, following the outbreak of the Korean War, Hirabayashi expressed opposition to military conflict and called for negotiation and accommodation with the Soviet Union to prevent war. Fukei agreed to publish the piece but added a disclaimer that Hirabayashi's views did not necessarily reflect those of the newspaper. His position did not seem to excite any opposition or hostile mail in the *Northwest Times*. Presumably, Nisei readers were well aware of his position on war.

In 1951 Gordon Hirabayashi defended his doctoral thesis in sociology. His subject was the adaptation and status of the Doukhobors in British Columbia's Slocan Valley. It was an interesting choice of subject. Members of this sect of pacifist Christians from Russia, who believed in holding land communally and refused to serve in the military, had been persecuted by the Tsarist regime. They had migrated to western Canada at the turn of the twentieth century in search of freedom but would face continuing government persecution there as well because of their refusal to assimilate (they attracted further opposition by their practice of staging mass nude protest marches against policies they opposed). Although Hirabayashi seems not to have had a deep knowledge of Doukhobor culture, the parallels between their treatment and the experience of Japanese Americans likely impressed him (the more so as many Doukobors had formed friendly connections with Japanese Canadians removed from the West Coast and confined in the Slocan Valley during World War II). Ironically, in 1953, barely a year after he completed his study, British Columbia's government would seize 150 children from a radical Doukhobor faction—the Sons of Freedom—and forcibly intern them in residential schools.

Following the completion of his doctorate, Hirabayashi began his career as a professor. (One odd legacy of the wartime Japanese American cases is that Hirabayashi was able to become a professor and Minoru Yasui would retain his license to practice law without hindrance. Conversely, their fellow defendant, Fred Korematsu, was barred from obtaining a license as a real estate broker in the postwar years because the conviction on his record rendered him ineligible for the required "good character" citation. This is not because academics and lawyers have lower ethnical standards than real estate agents but due to the odd fact that Hirabayashi's and Yasui's offenses were technically misdemeanors, while Korematsu's was a felony.) In 1952 Hirabayashi headed to Lebanon with his family to take up a position as an assistant professor of sociology at the American University in Beirut. He later explained that he wanted some international experience and that this was the first job offered to him. He remained in Lebanon for three years, then moved to the American University in Cairo, Egypt, in 1955–1956. (When war threatened the region and Hirabayashi was invited to evacuate, he retorted that as a Japanese American he had always refused to evacuate his home.) During his time in the Middle East, he published his first scholarly articles—on communication networks and political awareness in Egypt, social change in Jordan, and Lebanese village networks.

In 1959 Hirabayashi returned to North America and accepted a position as professor of sociology at the University of Alberta in Canada. He later explained that his return was largely for family reasons, as he thought his children could get a better secondary education in North America. Hirabayashi remained at the University of Alberta until his retirement in 1983 and served as the department chair from 1962 to 1970. During his years in Alberta,

Hirabayashi worked as a specialist in race relations, especially on the subject of the Métis (mixed-race native peoples). He also helped establish the new field of Asian Canadian studies. His most important contribution in this area was the 1980 anthology he coedited with K. Victor Ujimoto, *Visible Minorities and Multiculturalism: Asians in Canada*.

Although Hirabayashi had long been an obscure figure, he became an icon to the activists of the Japanese American redress movement of the 1970s and 1980s. His name and his wartime challenge to Executive Order 9066 gained renewed national attention in the early 1980s, when he authorized a petition to overturn his original conviction for curfew violation on the grounds of official misconduct and overreaching by means of the seldom-used writ of coram nobis. His legal team—headed by Rod Kawakami, Camden Hall, and Kathryn Bannai, who drew on research by Peter Irons and Aiko Herzig-Yoshinaga—presented evidence of fraud and manipulation of essential evidence in the original Supreme Court case, which led Federal District judge Donald S. Voorhees to schedule a full evidentiary hearing.

The case was heard in June 1985 in the federal courthouse in Seattle, the site of Hirabyashi's original trial forty-three years earlier. Following an inconclusive ruling by Judge Voorhees, both sides appealed. In September 1987, the Ninth Circuit Court of Appeals, in a unanimous opinion by Judge Mary M. Schroeder, declared that Hirabayashi and his counsel had presented convincing evidence that the government had doctored the record in his case and ruled that his convictions on all counts were vacated. His victory, along with that of the other coram nobis petitioners, may well have been decisive in persuading Congress to enact the Civil Rights Voting Restoration Act the following year, granting redress to all the West Coast Japanese Americans who had been affected by Executive Order 9066.

However, if this was Hirabayashi's most celebrated contribution to redress, it was by no means his only one, nor was his involvement confined to the essentially symbolic role he took in bringing the coram nobis case. Rather, even before his case was retried, Hirabayashi had expressed interest in the developing redress movement. In a speech before a Japanese American Citizens League (JACL) council in 1972 (one in which he urged Japanese Americans to attack problems of inequities facing all social groups), he noted that a legal subcommittee was discussing reopening his case. While he admitted that such an action was unlikely to succeed, he noted, "I fully endorse this effort and hope the opportunity can be had to correct the records as a con-tinuing precedent and national embarrassment." In February 1976, the JACL Pacific District Council honored him at a dinner in Los Angeles. He used the opportunity to urge Nisei to work for reparations as compensation for their loss of freedom during the war. While any successful movement would require a massive public education effort, he said, it was worth it to make America "[a] little better symbol we can identify with." At a Seattle JACL dinner shortly afterward, he added that the success of reparations would not only raise public awareness of wartime injustice and avoid such a thing happening again, but it would permit Nisei to stop aping whites: "We need to be ourselves and take stock of our unique aspect of American citizen-ship." Conversely, during an interview in New York, he deplored the apa-thetic response to redress proposals of most Nisei, which made him fear that they would go along if the government decided to order mass confinement again. In 1978 he suggested that Japanese Americans needed to be willing to "rock the boat" and suggested they approach redress with the same dauntless heroism that the Nisei soldiers of the 442nd had displayed.

In the period that followed, Hirabayashi remained an active supporter of political campaigns for redress. When disagreements arose over the form of such restitution, and a set of advocates—most notably Mike Masaoka of the JACL—proposed renouncing individual payments in exchange for a large trust fund for community assistance and human rights projects, Hirabayashi pub-licly deplored such ideas as irresponsible: "If injustice is to be admitted, then justice should follow with some kind of direct compensation to the victims."

In addition to his support of redress for Japanese Americans, Hirabayashi took action on behalf of Japanese Canadians. In 1977, two years after he became a Canadian citizen, he agreed to direct events in Alberta for the cen-tennial of Japanese Canadian settlement. Although he stated that year that "[p]olitical participation by Japanese Canadians is still a generation away," he threw himself into the developing redress movement in Canada. It was an act of great generosity; unlike in the United States, Hirabayashi did not stand to benefit personally from any redress award.

While a complete history of Gordon Hirabayashi's involvement in Canada's long redress struggle—a movement that sparked strong divisions among var-ious activists and organizations in the Japanese community—still remains to be written, it is clear that he served on numerous committees and attended countless meetings as president and spokesperson of the Edmonton Japanese Community Association and as a member of the National Association of Japanese Canadians (NAJC). As in the United States, he repeatedly urged payment of individual reparations. As he put it in 1985, a time when many Japanese Canadians urged settling with the government for a lump sum payment to the community, redress meant "establishing a meaningful, significant figure which would be granted across-the-board to all victims." Hirabayashi's prestige may have helped persuade Japanese Canadian leaders to hold out for such payments, which were granted in the final redress package in 1988. In recognition of Hirabayashi's contributions, in 2003 he was awarded the biennial award of the NAJC, which recognizes an outstanding member of the community.

Hirabayashi, who suffered from Alzheimer's disease in his last years, died in 2012.

Afterword

I hope that you have enjoyed your tour through The Great Unknown. I can honestly say that writing these pieces has been a good deal of fun, rather more so than in the case of my scholarly works—though there is some over-lap between the two. It has the extra thrill of bringing me close to an imag-ined community of readers, from whom I enjoy hearing.

Probably the question that readers most often ask me—sometimes with flattering wonder in their voices—is how and where I collect the wide-ranging bits of information that go into the articles. Since my mission is centered on exploring unknown aspects of Japanese American history— whether it means celebrating less-known people or bringing to light hid-den sides of famous figures—I generally cannot rely on existing reference works. Instead, I make use of other methods to trace these persons missing persons from history.

In most cases, unless I am adapting something I have already written somewhere else, the search for information starts with the material I come upon in the course of my ongoing research. In the past fifteen years or

DOI: 10.5876/9781607324294.c011

so, I have visited countless archives around North America. Sometimes I arrive with a particular project or files in mind; at other times I just look through finding aids to see what is available. I read through files of government agencies, collections of personal papers, and numerous newspaper and magazine backfiles; as I mentioned earlier, there is a very rich trove of information to be found. I thank my lucky stars that so much of the ethnic Japanese press, especially for the prewar years, survived the wartime removal and the upheavals afterward.

Once I start going through material, my discoveries begin. My usual practice is that whenever I see something that strikes me as unusual or potentially interesting, I will copy the text, if possible, or at least make a note of it. Later on, when I am done for the day or week, I sort through my pile of clippings and papers and arrange everything by subject, as I think most useful. I then slip items into existing folders (computer or manila) or create new ones. Of course, most of the things I turn up are filed away indefinitely, and the most important parts go into my more scholarly works. Still, I always seem to discover unusual bits that I think are especially fun or intriguing but that do not fit as well there. My column thus gives me a place to let people "lick the spoon" of my research and enjoy using it in a different way.

In any case, once I have enough in my Hisaye Yamamoto folder, say, or my prewar Chicago folder, I consider writing an article on the subject. I then look for more information elsewhere. I rummage through the books I have in my home library to look for material or check other folders for material that may be housed separately. I speak to friends with expertise on a particular subject to find out whether they know anything. One good part of writing about Japanese Americans is that I get to know people—both professional scholars and amateur and family historians—who are happy to share sources and insights. I also check my notes of past interviews with Nisei that I have done (or, in a few cases, that colleagues have given me). While I have not done full-scale recorded oral histories in the manner of Densho, I have been lucky enough to find various witnesses of the past who were ready to tell me their stories—some of whom even became friends in the bargain. A good deal of the material that I included in my article on John M. Maki, for example, came from our correspondence and an interview I did with him some years ago. Sometimes it is the siblings or children of subjects who are my sources. Fred Oyama, who joined his Issei father, Kajiro, as litigants in the postwar Supreme Court case *Oyama v. California* and won a historic victory over alien land legislation, kindly filled me in on some family history.

What I have described thus far might be said to derive from some fairly classic tools of the historian: archival research, microfilm reading, and interviews. The one new element is that many archives these days allow researchers to bring digital cameras and photograph documents or use scanners, both of which are faster and easier processes than taking notes or making photocopies. However, once all that is done, I also make use of online databases via the Internet—a fairly new development and, to my mind, a quite magical one. (I do a certain amount of online research using general search engines, but I generally find it to be of limited use.) Until recently, historians who wanted to consult published material—notably newspapers or magazines—had to go to a library that happened to have hard copies and then read through masses of pages (with help from a few published indexes such as the *New York Times Index* or the *Readers' Guide to Periodical Literature*). Now, however, the field of history has been transformed. Historians can sit at home at their computers and do much of their research by searching through online databases. For example, ProQuest has scanned all past issues of the *New York Times* and other top newspapers, while other services offer databases of local newspapers. One can also find different organs of the ethnic press. Densho's archive contains files of WRA camp newspapers, while the JACL has now undertaken the digitization of the *Pacific Citizen*.

What is more, once I sign into these various newspaper databases, I can often simply plug in the name of the person whose career I am researching and get results. Thanks to keyword searching, which allows readers to zero in on references to a specific person or thing, information that in the old days a historian could find—if at all—only though months of intensive research, can now be accessed virtually instantaneously. Several years ago, I read through a vast store of microfilm of old issues of African American newspapers and spent weeks looking for material on Japanese Americans. It was with a mix of joy and chagrin that I reviewed recently some of my old research, by repeating the process online. Within a few hours, I located the vast majority of what I had previously found (though not all, I proudly noted), plus some other items I had missed the first time. Similarly, in many cases, journals and books, in whole or in parts, can now be consulted onscreen. I also use genealogical databases, as they provide information such as birth and marriage records and scanned census sheets. (With the same kind of anticipation with which some folks await the NBA playoff season, I long counted down the days to April 2012, when the 1940 census records started becoming publicly available.) I also consult various oral history databases, looking for mentions of the person or event I am researching.

After all the historical research is done, sometimes I also have to take up a little of the reporter's trade as well and locate potential sources who will answer questions and fill in gaps in my information. It is always nice when a knowledgeable friend can introduce me to a good source, especially surviving friends and relatives of my subjects. More often, I must seek out people myself and try to locate them through professional directories or university alumni offices. If the family name is an unusual one, I can look in telephone directories for contact information. (The bane of my existence is women who marry and change their last name in the process, which makes tracking them down much more difficult.)

Once I have contact information for potential sources, I much prefer to write letters or e-mail them if I can, rather than call, but sometimes I have no choice. Being a rather shy fellow (yes, really!), I find it takes a lot of effort for me to bring myself to call total strangers and ask questions over the phone—especially about difficult times in the lives of their family members. Sometimes it can be agonizing to explain who I am and what I want, but I am glad to report that, in most cases, people are gratified by my interest or are at least gracious about it. In a few cases, we have had extended conversations.

So now you know all my secrets—I hope you will be inspired to read my newer columns in *Nichi Bei Weekly* and keep on enjoying them!

Selected Bibliography

Austin, Allan W. *From Concentration Camp to Campus: Japanese American Students and World War II*. Urbana: University of Illinois Press, 2004.

Azuma, Eiichiro. *Between Two Empires: Race, History, and Transnationalism in Japanese America*. New York: Oxford University Press, 2005.

Bird, Kai. *The Chairman: John J. McCloy and the Making of the American Establishment*. New York: Simon & Schuster, 1992.

Black, Allida M. *Casting Her Own Shadow: Eleanor Roosevelt and the Shaping of Postwar Liberalism*. New York: Columbia University Press, 1996.

Bosworth, Allen R. *America's Concentration Camps*. New York: Norton, 1967.

Carter, John Franklin. *Power and Persuasion*. New York: Duell, Sloan and Pearce, 1960.

Chuman, Frank F. *The Bamboo People: The Law and Japanese-Americans*. Del Ray, CA: Publisher's Inc., 1976.

Collins, Donald E. *Native American Aliens: Disloyalty and the Renunciation of Citizenship by Japanese Americans during World War II*. Westport, CT: Greenwood, 1985.

Daniels, Roger, ed. *American Concentration Camps*. 9 vols. New York: Garland, 1989.

Daniels, Roger. *Asian Americans: Chinese and Japanese in the United States since 1850*. Seattle: University of Washington Press, 1988.

DOI: 10.5876/9781607324294.c012

Daniels, Roger. *Concentration Camps USA: Japanese Americans and World War II*. New York: Holt Rinehart, 1971.

Daniels, Roger. *Prisoners Without Trial: Japanese Americans in World War II*. New York: Hill and Wang, 1993.

Daniels, Roger, Sandra C. Taylor, and Harry Kitano, eds. *Japanese Americans: From Relocation to Redress*. Revised edition. Seattle: University of Washington Press, 1991.

Doreski, C. K. "'Kin in Some Way': The *Chicago Defender* Reads the Japanese Internment, 1942–1945." In *The Black Press: Literary and Historical Essays*, edited by Todd Vogel, 161–87. New Brunswick, NJ: Rutgers University Press, 2001.

Duus, Masayo. *The Life of Isamu Noguchi: Journey without Borders*. Princeton, NJ: Princeton University Press, 2004.

Duus, Masayo Umezawa. *Unlikely Liberators: The Men of the 100th and the 442nd*. Honolulu: University of Hawai'i Press, 1987.

Eckstein, Gustav. *Noguchi*. New York: Harper & Bros., 1931.

Endow, Kay Karl. *Transpacific Wings*. Los Angeles: Wetzel, 1935.

Farago, Ladislas. *The Broken Seal: The Story of "Operation Magic" and the Pearl Harbor Disaster*. New York: Random House, 1967.

Farmer, James. *Lay Bare the Heart: An Autobiography of the Civil Rights Movement*. New York: Plume, 1985.

Fisher, Anne Reeploeg. *Exile of a Race: A History of the Forcible Removal and Imprisonment by the Army of the 115,000 Citizens and Alien Japanese Who Were Living on the West Coast in the Spring of 1942*. Kent, WA: F&T Publishers, 1965.

Franklin, Jay [John Franklin Carter]. *The Catoctin Conversation*. New York: Scribner's, 1947.

Fujikawa, Gyo. *Babies*. New York: Grosset & Dunlap, 1963.

Garrison, Dennis M., ed. *Jun Fujita, Tanka Pioneer*. Baltimore: Modern English Tanka Press, 2007.

Genensman, Deborah, and Mindy Roseman. *Beyond Words: Images from America's Concentration Camps*. Ithaca, NY: Cornell University Press, 1987.

Girdner, Audrie, and Anne Loftis. *The Great Betrayal*. New York: Macmillan, 1969.

Grodzins, Morton. *Americans Betrayed*, Chicago: University of Chicago Press, 1949.

Hansen, Arthur A., ed. *Japanese American WWII Evacuation History Project*. 5 vols. Westport, CT: Greenwood, 1992.

Hatiyama, Leslie T. *Righting a Wrong: Japanese Americans and the Passage of the Civil Liberties Act of 1988*. Stanford, CA: Stanford University Press, 1993.

Hayakawa, Samuel I. "A Japanese American Goes to Japan." *Asia* (March 1937): 269–73.

Hayakawa, Samuel I. "My Japanese Father and I." *Asia* (April 1937): 331–33.

Hayakawa, S. I. *Language in Action*. New York: Harcourt Brace, 1941.

Hirasuna, Delphine. *The Art of Gaman: Arts & Crafts from the Japanese American Internment Camps 1942–1946*. Berkeley, CA: Ten Speed, 2005.

Hohri, William Minoru. *Repairing America*. Pullman: Washington State University Press, 1988.

Hosokawa, Bill. *JACL in Quest of Justice*. New York: William Morrow, 1982.

Hosokawa, Bill. *Nisei: The Quiet Americans*. New York: William Morrow, 1969.

Howard, John. *Concentration Camps on the Home Front: Japanese Americans in the House of Jim Crow*. Chicago: University of Chicago Press, 2008.

Ichioka, Yuji. *The Issei: The World of the First Generation Japanese Immigrants, 1885–1924*. New York: Free Press, 1988.

Ichioka, Yuji. "The Meaning of Loyalty: The Case of Kazumaro Buddy Uno." *Amerasia Journal* 23, no. 3 (Winter 1997).

Irons, Peter. *Justice at War*. New York: Oxford University Press, 1983.

Ishigaki, Ayako. *Restless Wave: My Life in Two Worlds*. New York: Feminist Press at the City University of New York, 2004 [1940].

Ito, Kazuo. *Issei: A History of Japanese Immigrants in North America*. Translated by Shinichiro Nakamura and Jean S. Gerard. Seattle: Japanese Community Service, 1973.

Japanese-American Relocation Reviewed: Interviews. 2 vols. Berkeley: University of California / Bancroft Library, Regional Oral History Office, 1974.

Kashima, Tetsuden. *Judgment Without Trial: Japanese American Imprisonment during World War II*. Seattle: University of Washington Press, 2003.

Kearney, Reginald. *African American Views of the Japanese: Solidarity or Sedition?* Albany: State University of New York Press, 1998.

Akemi Kikumura-Yano, Akemi, ed. *Encyclopedia of Japanese Descendants in the Americas*. Walnut Creek, CA: Rowman & Littlefield, 2002.

Kitagawa, Daisuke. *Issei and Nisei: The Internment Years*. New York: Seabury, 1967.

Kurashige, Lon Y. *Japanese American Celebration and Conflict: A History of Ethnic Identity and Festival, 1934–1990*. Berkeley: University of California Press, 2002.

Kurashige, Scott. *The Shifting Grounds of Race: Blacks and Japanese Americans in the Making of Multiethnic Los Angeles*. Princeton, NJ: Princeton University Press, 2008.

La Violette, Forrest L. *Americans of Japanese Ancestry: A Study of Assimilation in the American Community*. Toronto: Canadian Institute of International Affairs, 1945.

Mackey, Mike, ed. *Guilt by Association: Essays in Japanese Settlement, Internment, and Relocation in the Rocky Mountain West*. Powell, WY: Western History Publications, 2001.

Maeda, Daryl J. *Chains of Babylon: The Rise of Asian America*. Minneapolis: University of Minnesota Press, 2009.

Maki, John M. *Japanese Militarism: Its Cause and Cure*. New York: Knopf, 1945.

Maki, John M. *Voyage Through the Twentieth Century*. Amherst, MA: privately issued, 2004.

Maki, Mitchell T., Harry H.L. Kitano, and S. Megan Berthold. *Achieving the Impossible Dream: How Japanese Americans Obtained Redress*. Urbana: University of Illinois Press, 1999.

Masaoka, Mike, with Bill Hosokawa. *They Call Me Moses Masaoka*. New York: Morrow, 1987.

Matyas, Irene. *Die Internierung Japanisch-Stämmiger Amerikaner Während des Zweite Weltkrieges*. Vienna: Böhlou Verlag, 1990.

McWilliams, Carey. *Prejudice: Japanese-Americans: Symbol of Racial Intolerance*. Boston: Little, Brown, 1944.

Melendy, Brett. *The Oriental Americans*: Boston: Twayne, 1972.

Miyakawa, Masuji. *Powers of the American People, Congress, President, and Courts (According to the Evolution of Constitutional Construction)*. New York: Baker & Taylor, 1908.

Muller, Eric L. *American Inquisition: The Hunt for Japanese American Disloyalty During World War II*. Chapel Hill: University of North Carolina Press, 2007.

Muller, Eric. *Free to Die for Their Country: The Story of the Japanese American Draft Resisters in World War II*. Chicago: University of Chicago Press, 2001.

Myer, Dillon. *Uprooted Americans*. Tucson: University of Arizona Press, 1971.

Nakagawa, Karl S. *The Rendezvous of Mysteries*. Philadelphia: Dorrance, 1928.

Niiya, Brian, ed. *Japanese-American History: An A to Z from 1868 to the Present*. New York: Facts on File, 1983.

Oda, James. *Heroic Struggles of Japanese Americans: Partisan Fighters from America's Concentration Camps*. Hollywood: printed by author, 1981.

Okihiro, Gary Y. *Cane Fires: The Anti-Japanese Movement in Hawaii, 1865–1945*. Philadelphia: Temple University Press, 1991.

Okimoto, Daniel I. *American in Disguise*. New York: Weatherhill, 1971.

Okubo, Miné. *Citizen 13660*. Seattle: University of Washington Press, 1983 [1946].

Oyabe, Jenichiro. *A Japanese Robinson Crusoé*. Honolulu: University of Hawai'i Press, 2009.

Ozaki, Milton K. *The Cuckoo Clock*. Chicago: Ziff-Davis, 1946.

Anonymous [Kenneth Ringle]. "The Japanese in America: The Problem and the Solution." *Harper's* 185 (October 1942): 489–97.

Robinson, Greg. *After Camp: Portraits in Midcentury Japanese American Life and Politics*. Berkeley: University of California Press, 2012.

Robinson, Greg. *By Order of the President: FDR and the Internment of Japanese Americans*. Cambridge, MA: Harvard University Press, 2001.

Robinson, Greg. "Internationalism and Justice: Paul Robeson, Asia, and Asian Americans." In *AfroAsian Encounters: Culture, History, Politics*, edited by Shannon Steen and Heike Raphael-Hernandez, 358–81. New York: New York University Press, 2006.

Robinson, Greg, and Sanae Kawaguchi Moorehead. "On the Brink of Evacuation: The Diary of an Issei Woman, by Fuki Endow Kawaguchi." *Prospects: An Annual of American Cultural Studies* 28 (2003): 155–83.

Robinson, Greg. *A Tragedy of Democracy: Japanese Confinement in North America*. New York: Columbia University Press, 2009.

Robinson, Greg, and Elena Tajima Creef, eds. *Miné Okubo: Following Her Own Road.* Seattle: University of Washington Press, 2008.

Robinson, Greg. "Norman Thomas and the Struggle Against Japanese Internment." *Prospects: An Annual of American Cultural Studies* 29 (2004): 419–34.

Robinson, Greg. *Pacific Citizens: Larry and Guyo Tajiri and Japanese American Journalism in the World War II Era.* Urbana: University of Illinois Press, 2012.

Sasaki, Yasuo. *Ascension: Poems of Vintage, 1967.* Privately printed, 1967.

Sasaki, Yasuo. *Village Scene, Village Herd: Poems of Vintage 1968 and Sequel.* Cincinnati, OH: Balconet, 1986.

Seigal, Shizue. *In Good Conscience Supporting Japanese Americans During the Internment.* San Francisco: AACP, 2006.

Shaffer, Robert. "Cracks in the Consensus: Defending the Rights of Japanese Americans During World War II." *Radical History Review* 72 (June 1998): 84–120.

Shimano, Eddie. "Blueprint for a Slum." *Common Ground* (Fall 1943): 77–79.

Schrager, Adam. *The Principled Politician: The Story of Ralph Carr.* Golden, CO: Fulcrum, 2008.

Sono, Tel. *The Japanese Reformer: An Autobiography.* New York: Hunt & Eaton, 1892.

Sueyoshi, Amy. *Queer Compulsions: Race, Nation, and Sexuality in the Affairs of Yone Noguchi.* Honolulu: University of Hawai'i Press, 2012.

Tajiri, Shinkichi. *Autobiographical Notations: Autobiography, Words and Images, Paintings, Sculptures, Printed Matter, Photography, Paperworks, Computergraphics.* Eindhoven, NL: Kempen, 1993.

Takahashi, Jere. *Nisei/Sansei: Shifting Japanese American Identities and Politics.* Philadelphia: Temple University Press, 1998.

Takaki, Ronald. *Strangers from a Different Shore: A History of Asian Americans.* New York: Penguin, 1989.

Tamagawa, Kathleen. *Holy Prayers in a Horse's Ear.* New Brunswick, NJ: Rutgers University Press, 2008.

Tamura, Eileen H. *Americanization, Acculturation, and Ethnic Identity: The Nisei Generation in Hawaii.* Urbana: University of Illinois Press, 1994.

Tateishi, John. *And Justice For All: An Oral History of the Japanese American Detention Camps.* New York: Random House, 1984.

Thomas, Norman. *Democracy and the Japanese Americans.* New York: Postwar World Council, 1942.

United States Commission on Wartime Relocation and Internment of Civilians. *Personal Justice Denied.* Washington, DC: Government Printing Office, 1982. Reprint, Seattle: University of Washington Press, 1997.

US Congress House Select Committee Investigating National Defense Migration. *National Defense Migration. Report of the Select Committee Investigating National Defense Migration, House of Representatives . . . Preliminary Report and Recommendations on Problems of Evacuation of Citizens and Aliens from Military Areas. March 19, 1942.* Washington, DC: Government Printing Office, 1942.

US Congress House Special Committee on Un-American Activities. *Report and Minority Views of the Special Committee on Un-American Activities on Japanese War Relocation Centers.* Report No. 717. Washington, DC: Government Printing Office, 1943.

US Department of the Interior War Agency Liquidation Unit. *People in Motion: The Postwar Adjustment of the Evacuated Japanese Americans.* Washington, DC: Government Printing Office, 1947.

US Department of the Interior War Relocation Authority. *WRA: A Story of Human Conservation.* New York: AMS Press, 1978 [1946].

Weglyn, Michi Nishiura. *Years of Infamy.* Seattle: University of Washington Press, 1996 [1976].

White, G. Edward. *Earl Warren: A Public Life.* New York: Oxford University Press, 1982.

Yamamoto, Hisaye. *Seventeen Syllables and Other Stories.* New Brunswick, NJ: Rutgers University Press, 2001.

Yoneda, Karl G. *Ganbatte: Sixty Year Struggle of a Kibei Worker.* Los Angeles: UCLA Asian American Studies Center Press, 1983.

Yoo, David K. *Growing Up Nisei: Race, Generation, and Culture among Japanese Americans of California, 1929–49.* Urbana: University of Illinois Press, 2000.

Yoshino, Kenji. *Covering: The Hidden Assault on Our Civil Rights.* New York: Random House, 2007.

SELECTED ARCHIVES

John Franklin Carter Papers, American Heritage Center, University of Wyoming

Alan M. Cranston Papers, Bancroft Library, University of California, Berkeley

Bill Hosokawa Papers, Denver Public Library

Carey McWilliams Papers, Hoover Institution, UCLA, Claremont Colleges

Isamu Noguchi Papers, Isamu Noguchi Foundation, New York City

Miné Okubo Papers, Riverside Community College

Norman Thomas Papers, New York Public Library

Minoru Yasui Papers, University of Colorado Denver, Auraria Library

PERIODICALS

The Japanese American Press

The Bandwagon

Chicago Shimpo

Continental Times

Crossroads
Doho
Gyo-Sho
Hawaii Hochi
Heart Mountain Sentinel
Hokubei Mainichi
Hokubei Shimpo/New York Nichibei
Honolulu Record
JACD Newsletter
JACL Reporter
Japanese American Courier
Japanese American Mirror
Japanese American Review
Kashu Mainichi
Manzanar Free Press
New Canadian
New World Sun (Shin Sekai)
Nichi Bei Shimbun (California Japanese-American News)
Nichi Bei Times
Nisei Weekender
Northwest Times
Pacific Citizen
Rafu Shimpo
Reimei
Sangyo Nippo
Scene
Trek
Tule Lake Dispatch

Index

abortion rights, 166–73

activist(s) and activism, 17–20, 23, 24, 34, 35, 38, 46, 54, 68, 85, 110, 112, 113, 129, 153–91, 241, 242, 248, 257, 258, 262, 275, 302, 306, 307; black, 175; civil rights, 130, 133, 190, 241–48, 250; Fellowship of Reconciliation (FOR), 90; interracial, 173–76; JACL, 125; LGBT/Queer, 241–48, 251; Nikkei, 248; progressive, 89; religious, 39; union, 204

actresses, 207, 217–20, 237, 278

African Americans, xii, xix, 16, 23, 51, 57, 86, 87, 90, 94, 96, 112, 133, 143, 159, 160, 164, 174–78, 180, 183–86, 194, 197, 202, 206, 224, 229, 234, 251, 265, 273, 280, 286, 287, 294, 295, 298, 299, 302; attorney(s), xii, xviii, 15, 96, 125, 164; community(ies), 292, 293; leader(s), 174–79; newspaper(s), xviii, 46, 86, 88, 226, 292, 311

Alien Land Act, xii, 146, 157, 270

allies, 22, 204, 205, 264, 295

American Civil Liberties Union (ACLU), 15, 96, 97, 127, 146, 161, 163, 174, 214. 242, 244

animator(s), 210–13, 230

Anti-Japanese/Anti-Japanese American Racism, 44, 63, 76, 123, 137; discrimination, 292; movements, 273; ordinances, 273; prejudice, 15, 98, 123, 122, 153, 235; press, 77, 142

art, 6, 23, 31, 44, 53, 148, 169, 181, 185, 220–32, 234–39, 270, 272, 278; Art Institute [Los Angeles], 222; Art Institute of Chicago, 209, 234, 235, 278; Art Institute of Minneapolis, 238; Chouinard Art Institute, 230; criticism, 8; Federal Art Project, 223; Gaka Art Guild, 235; Poston, 235; Riverside Art Museum, 227; San Francisco Art Association (SFAA), 224, 225; San Francisco Museum of Art, 224, 225; Seattle Art Museum, 226; Southside Community Center, 235; University of California, 224

assembly center(s), 130, 161, 162; Fresno, 213–15; Puyallup (Camp Harmony), 63, 64, 75; Santa Anita, 15, 55, 134, 146, 182, 189, 211, 235; Tanforan, 225, 226

Attorney General, 161

baseball, 59, 193, 202; American League, 202; California League, 200; Japanese Americans in, 199–202; Japanese leagues, 199; Lefty O'Doul, 59; Major League Baseball, 197; National League, xviii, 193–96; Nikkei baseball figure, 201; Nippon Stars Baseball Team, 56; Nisei Baseball Research Project, 199

basketball, 52, 71; Basketball Association of America (BAA), 197; NBA, 196; Nisei in, 71, 196–202

bowling, 202–6; American Bowling Congress, 202–6; Boeing Bowling Association [Seattle], 205; National Committee for Fair Play in Bowling (NCFPB), 203, 204, 206; Seattle City Bowling Association, 205

California, xi, 10, 12, 15, 22, 31, 33, 52–57, 77, 86, 93, 94, 96, 98, 109, 124, 126, 136, 138, 143–47, 150, 155, 157, 159–61, 164, 173–75, 177, 181, 183, 198, 201, 212, 213, 217, 220, 223–26, 230, 234, 242, 250, 252, 254, 263, 264, 274–76, 281, 287, 296–99, 311; California Institute of Technology, 157; Californian(s), 124, 129, 138; California Race Relations Commission, 125, 144, 164; California State Assembly, 177, 179; California Supreme Court, 159; Lieutenant Governor, 177; Oakland Museum of California, 224, 225; University of California Berkeley, 23, 78, 174, 198, 223, 224, 225, 270, 286, 297; University of California Los Angeles (UCLA), 173; University of Southern California, 181; Women's Bar Association, 15

camps (relocation centers), 60, 67, 94, 110, 113, 174, 198, 199, 201, 220, 275, 279, 288; Amache (Granada), 15, 141, 146; Gila River, 131, 217; Heart Mountain, 45, 67, 68, 211, 242, 250, 253; Jerome, 55, 215; Manzanar, 85, 96, 110, 111, 128, 146, 147, 177, 178, 242, 247, 296; Minidoka, 64, 75, 96; Poston (Colorado River), 23, 24, 88, 89, 201, 210, 225, 233, 235, 242; Rohwer, 230; Topaz (Central Utah), 94, 220, 225, 226, 252, 273; Tule Lake, 88, 94, 215, 250, 297

cartoonist(s), 210–13

censorship, 65, 72, 76, 125, 219, 244, 296–300

Chicago, xviii, 15, 16, 24, 26, 28–35, 38–43, 46, 94, 97, 106, 127, 135, 183–86, 188, 190, 198, 201–3, 207–12, 215, 226, 233–36, 244, 247, 275–79, 282, 291–94, 297–99, 310; Japanese American Service Committee, 183, 276

civil rights, xii, 22, 33, 38, 39, 81, 90, 125, 128, 133, 135, 141, 153–91, 202, 206, 241, 242, 245, 251–54, 262–64, 288, 291, 293–95; activists, 130, 133, 190, 250; Civil Rights Act (1964), 259; Civil Rights Movement, 38, 39, 63, 86, 186, 243; Japanese Americans and, 22, 111, 139, 153, 156, 159, 248; organizations, xviii, 203, 206, 242, 248, 254, 261; sit-ins, 38; US Commission on Civil Rights, 186

Congress of Racial Equality (CORE), xviii, 38, 39, 90

culture, 5, 60, 133, 155, 238, 251, 286; American, xv, 67; Doukhobor, 305; Indian, 23; Japanese, 63, 64, 67, 207, 249, 252; Jewish, 133; Native American, 31

dancer(s), 19, 22, 207, 217–20, 234, 279

death penalty, xviii, 279–84

Executive Order 9066, 21–24, 31, 33–35, 44, 85, 88, 95, 96, 110, 111, 113, 120, 125, 127–30, 134, 138, 139, 141, 145, 147, 159–61, 163, 165, 170, 179, 182, 213, 224, 235, 250, 279, 285, 292, 296, 297, 299, 300, 306

feminism/feminists, 5, 17–20, 22

football, 193–99, 202

gay/lesbian (LGBTQ), xii, 241–66; activists, 242, 248; anti-gay bigotry and discrimination, 242, 252, 258, 262; Asian/Pacific American: 241, 242, 247, 251, 262, 263; community, 242, 265; equal rights, 242, 243, 254, 257, 261, 262; Gay Liberation Front (GLF), 244; Hawai'i Democrats for Lesbian and Gay Rights, 258; homophobia, 248–57; Japanese Americans and, 242, 245, 248, 252, 253; organization(s), 241, 258, 264; pride movement, 244, 248, 251, 252, 260

Hapa (Mixed-Race Japanese Americans), 21–47

Hood River, Oregon, 284–87

immigration/immigrant(s), 3, 4, 9, 12, 49, 55, 115, 136, 137, 156, 210, 226, 246, 249, 252, 285, 286; Anglo-Irish, 24; Asian, 161; Chinese, 246; German, 44; Japanese, 4, 9, 28, 65, 153, 156, 157, 247, 250, 281, 285, 293, 294; Jewish, 289

Issei, 11, 12, 19, 22, 121, 128, 130, 131, 136, 139, 141, 143–47, 149, 150, 181, 211, 213, 217, 227, 230, 249–52, 256, 270, 271, 273, 274, 276, 279, 281, 283–87, 293, 294, 310; Anti-Issei Discrimination, 175; artists, 18, 249; attorneys, 153–57; business-men, xvi, 33, 44; men, 5, 272, 280; sexuality, 245–48; West Coast, 11, 12, 99, 270, 280; women, 3–17, 19, 20

Japanese American Bar Association, 15
Japanese American Citizens League (JACL), 32–34, 55, 69, 75, 78, 80–82, 84, 85, 90, 109, 110–12, 125, 128, 132, 135, 146, 147, 159–61, 163–65, 174, 175, 177, 181, 190, 194, 202–6, 242, 250, 251, 254, 258, 261–65, 275, 288, 293, 294, 306, 307, 311
Japanese American Committee for Democracy (JACD), 24, 112, 128, 227
Japanese American Historical Society, xii
Japanese American History Archives, 173
Japanese American National Museum (JANM), 91, 140, 186, 253
Japanese American Personality and Acculturation Study, 183
Japanese Americans (Nikkei), xi, xii, xv, xvi, xviii, xix, 5, 10–15, 20–24, 28, 30, 33, 38, 39, 44–46, 52, 53, 55, 57, 59, 61, 63, 67, 71, 82, 83, 88, 89, 94, 99, 103, 108–10, 115, 116, 120, 122, 123, 131, 135, 137–39, 141, 143, 153, 155, 201, 203, 205, 207, 210–12, 219, 220, 225, 227–29, 234, 242, 244, 246–50, 252–53, 260, 264, 265, 267, 272, 273, 274–76, 279, 280, 282, 285, 290, 293, 295, 296, 305; citizenship rights, xix, 66, 181, 246, 257, 276; community, xii, 15, 60, 61, 148, 173, 176, 185, 248–51; history, xvii, 95, 147, 187, 232, 309; literary magazines, 54; Pro Japanese, 19, 52, 67, 69, 71, 75, 76, 111, 124, 280; sexuality, 244–48, 255–57
Japanese Canadians, XIX, 201, 305, 307, 308
jazz, xviii, 143, 171, 218, 233, 274, 288–95

lawyer(s), xviii, 13–17, 31, 33, 35, 93, 94, 97, 127, 133, 153, 159–61, 164, 165, 173, 215, 241, 251, 273, 280, 282, 285, 305
legal cases, 15, 75, 94; Ex Parte Endo, 93; Hirabayashi v. United States, 95, 164, 165, 195, 300–302; Korematsu v. United States, 95, 145, 146, 164, 165; Oyama v. California, xii, 146, 147, 157–60, 311; Regan v. King, 146;

160–66; Takahashi v. California Fish and Game Commission, 33, 147, 175; Wakayama v. California, 96, 110, 146
Library of Congress, 6–8, 123
literature, xii, 7, 9, 11, 13, 49–92, 166, 170, 278, 311; Asian, 7; Asian American, 13; Chinese, 166; English, 290; Japanese, 7; Japanese American, 185
Louisiana, 251, 267–75

military service, 38, 41, 110, 213, 232, 249, 262, 301

National Japanese American Student Relocation Council, 101, 130, 182, 228, 302
Newspapers and Periodicals, Japanese American, 13, 54, 56, 62, 68, 69, 71, 80, 87, 135, 136, 167, 247, 302; camp newspapers, 165, 311; Chicago Shimpo, 34, 276, 294; Doho, 22; Fresno Grapevine, 214; Gyo-Sho, 54, 62; Hawaii Hochi, 284; Heart Mountain Sentinel, 45, 75; Hokubei Shimpo, 20, 227; Honolulu Record, 112; Japanese American Courier, 61, 66, 71, 75; Kashu Manichi, 78, 87, 167, 181, 223; Manzanar Free Press, 85, 111; New York Nichibei, 295; New World Sun, 54, 59, 77, 78; Nichi Bei, xi, xii, xiii, xvi, xvii, 57, 59, 78, 133, 134, 169, 188, 235, 265; Nichi Bei Shimbun, xi, xvi, 5, 56, 78, 247; Nichi Bei Times, xi, xvi, xvii, 82, 147, 251; Nichi Bei Weekly, xi, xiii, xvii, xx, 251, 312; Nikkei Heritage, xx; Nikkei Voice, xx; Nisei Weekender, 55, 227; Northwest Times, 136, 303, 304; Poston Chronicle, 88, 165; Rafu Shimpo, 5, 17, 19, 86, 90, 125, 129, 151, 169, 170, 223, 247; Reimei, 54, 167, 167; Sangyo Nippo, 5, 84; Trek, 220, 221, 222
New York, 16, 20, 22, 23, 26, 41, 44, 51–53, 60, 65, 90, 97, 128, 138, 156, 171, 174, 175, 185–89, 195–99, 201, 202, 204–6, 211, 212, 215, 216, 220, 227, 230, 237, 244, 260, 279, 280, 291, 295; New York Times, 6, 7, 108, 148, 227, 231, 311
Nisei, xviii, 5, 6, 9–11, 21–24, 28, 32–36, 39, 42–45, 53, 55–57, 59–66, 80, 81, 84–90, 93–117, 121, 125, 128–30, 134–36, 138, 139, 141, 145, 146, 149, 150, 159, 160–66, 167–70, 173, 174, 177–79, 182, 185, 187, 188, 190, 193, 196, 198, 199, 201–3, 205–7, 213, 215, 219, 222, 223, 227–30, 242, 250, 251, 253, 255, 256, 262, 264, 270–74, 276, 278, 279, 282, 284, 287, 288, 290, 292–95, 301, 302, 304,

307, 310; activist(s), 43, 175; artist(s), 22, 55, 233–35; attorney, 31, 32; author, 24–28, 167; civil rights, 22, 111, 295; GIs/soldiers/veterans, 125, 132, 134, 135, 143, 235, 250, 271, 286, 303, 307; journalist(s), 22, 67–77, 89, 185, 234, 249; lawyers, 31, 33; LGBT/queer, 251, 253; literary, 62, 86, 167; Nisei Writers and Artists Mobilization for Democracy, 22, 55, 134; novels, 56, 87; pro basketball, 196–99; sexuality, 245–48; students, 45, 99, 101–3, 108, 130, 187, 232, 294, 300, 302; wartime confinement, 93–117; woman/women, 13, 30, 45, 81, 94, 146, 250, 252, 271; writers, 22, 43, 54–56, 89, 134, 169, 170, 173, 181, 276

photographers, Japanese American, 108, 207–10, 279
photography, 4, 39, 71, 106, 130, 188, 207–10, 222, 235, 237, 247, 249, 271, 311
poetry, 5, 11, 34, 167, 170, 173, 209, 290
poets, Japanese American, 7, 13, 16, 21, 53, 112, 137, 166, 181, 207, 209, 210, 234, 244, 247, 252, 276, 290, 292

Redress Movement, Japanese American, xii, 83, 94, 138, 177, 179, 262, 306

sculptor(s) and sculpture, 21, 55, 134, 229, 232, 234–39, 247
sport(s), xii, 89, 171, 193–206, 235, 274, 289

War Relocation Authority (WRA), 23, 24, 45, 89, 94, 97, 131, 132, 141, 146, 185, 215, 272, 273, 292
West Coast, Japanese Americans on, xviii, 6, 13, 22, 44, 45, 52, 69, 77, 80, 85, 89, 93, 94, 96, 97, 101, 113, 114, 125, 129, 130, 138, 142, 150, 159, 160, 173, 177, 219, 224–26, 264, 271, 287, 296, 298–300; defense commander, 121; Issei, 11, 99, 270, 280; Japanese, 235, 301; Japanese Americans, xix, 10–12, 63, 85, 110, 122, 123, 128, 130, 139, 146, 150, 170, 210, 292, 299, 301, 306; Japanese Canadians, 305; Japanese community, xvii, 149, 157, 255; Nisei, 64, 76, 99, 110, 125, 198, 230, 294
World War II and Japanese Americans, xvi, xvii, xix, 8, 10, 11, 17, 21, 41, 56, 60, 65, 67, 68, 71, 76, 83, 94, 96, 99, 103, 104, 108, 109, 113, 114, 117, 118, 123, 125, 135, 136, 137, 138, 139, 142, 143, 170, 175, 177–79, 188, 196, 203, 210, 219, 230, 232, 234,

237, 270, 271, 278, 279, 280, 295, 296, 299, 300, 305–307; activism, 21; anti-Japanese prejudice, 15; army and civilians, 123; Governors of Western States, 139–43; Japanese Canadians, 242, 305; mass removal/confinement: 5, 67, 77, 93, 109, 110, 113, 119–51, 164, 177, 185, 186, 190, 199, 235, 252, 258, 275, 288, 300, 303, 310; Supreme Court and internment cases, 15, 75, 94; US Commission on Wartime Relocation and Internment of Civilians, 178, 186, 251. See also assembly centers, camps

PEOPLE

Abe, Sanji, 113–17
Abiko, Kyutaro, xvi, 5
Abiko, Yonako, 5
Ariyoshi, Koji, 109–13

Carter, John Franklin, 148–51
Chino family, 28–39; Frank (Haruka), 28; Franklin Kyoshi, 30, 31; James Elbert (Yone), 30; Mercelia, 28; Robert Asahi, xviii, 29, 34, 38, 39
Collier, John, 23, 24, 89, 132
Cranston, Alan M., xviii, 23, 130, 136–38

Dymally, Mervyn, xii, 176–80

Endo, Gish, 204
Endo, Mitsuye, 93–95, 159
Endow, Kay Karl (Karl Shigeru Nakagawa), 56–60

Farmer, James, 38, 39, 174
Fisher, Anne Reeploeg, 296–300
Fisher, Galen, 97
Foujita, Leonard (Tsuguharu Fujita), 234
Fujikawa, Gyo, 228–32
Fujita, Jun, 227–30
Fujita, Scott, 213, 294
Fujita Rony, Tom, 130

Glenn, Evelyn Nakano, 3
Grodzins, Morton, 296–300

Hayakawa, Samuel Ichiyé, 138, 250, 288–95
Hayakwa, Sessue, 39
Hayakawa, Thomas, 211

Hirabayashi, Gordon Kiyoshi, 94, 95, 98, 136, 146, 164, 165, 296, 300–308
Hohri, Samuel Shiro, 44, 83–86, 87, 89, 125
Hohri, Daisuke, 83
Hosokawa, Bill (Kumei William), xviii, 61, 63, 67–77, 80, 263

Ishigaki, Ayako, 5, 17–20, 22
Ishigaki, Eitaro, 18, 22

Kanai, Lincoln Seiichi, 95–98, 110
Kawaguchi Family, 13; Fuki Endow, 9–13, 20; Sakujiro, 12, 13; Sanae, 20
Korematsu, Fred, 95, 98, 145
Kuromiya, Kiyoshi, 241–44, 248
Kuwahara, Robert, xii, 12, 207, 210–13, 227, 230–33

Macbeth, Hugh Ellwood, xii, xviii, 96, 125, 143–47, 159, 164
Maki, John M., 60–66
Malkin, Michelle, xvi, 67, 119–23
Matsu (Matsuzawa), Arthur, xii, xviii, 193–96
McCloy, John L., 114, 121, 122, 123–25, 214
Misaka, Wat (Wataru), 196–99
Miyakawa, Agnes Yoshiko, 233
Miyakawa, Kikuko, 234
Miyakawa, Masuji, 153–57
Miyakawa, T. Scott (Tetsuo), 68
Muller, Eric L., xvi, xx, 67, 301

Nakano, Naomi, 98–109
Nakano, Yosuke (Nick), 103
Nishis/Nishi Family, 184, 185; Ken, 183; Setsuko Matsunaga, xviii, 180–91, 293
Noguchi, Ayako, 87
Noguchi, Hideyo, 22, 245, 246
Noguchi, Isamu, 21–24, 55, 78, 134, 138, 234, 235, 247
Noguchi, Yone, 21, 207, 228, 247, 276

Ohi Family, 28–39; Kamatsu Elizabeth, 15, 30, 31, 32; Sidney Tokichi, 28, 30
Okubo Benji (Bunji), 222, 225
Okubo, Miné, xviii, 137, 183, 187, 220–29, 234
Omori, Chizu, xii, 89
Oyabe, Jenichiro, 49–53, 276
Oyabe, Massayoshi (Joe), 53
Oyama, Fred / Fred Yoshihiro, 157–60, 310

Oyama, Ikuo, 277
Oyama, Joe, 87, 173, 181, 247
Oyama, Kajiro, 146, 157, 160
Oyama Mittwer, Mary (Molly), 54, 87, 169, 170, 173
Ozaki, Milton K, xviii, xx, 39–43

Robeson, Paul, 23, 133–36, 196
Roosevelt, Eleanor, xviii, 9, 32, 85, 129–32, 138, 151
Roosevelt, Franklin Delano, xviii, 22, 23, 35, 91, 122, 129, 134, 145, 146, 148–51, 156, 182

Sakanishi, Shio (Shiho), 6–9
Sasaki, Sasabune (Shuichi), 166
Sasaki, Yasuo, 87, 166–73
Saito, Mito, 56
Saito, Reiko, 217–20
Sato, Kenoske, 277
Sato, Robert Yoichi, 101
Shimano, Eddie, 22, 53–56, 62, 87, 187
Sono, Tel (Teru), 13–17, 276
Sono, Tesai, 15
Stafford, Yoné U., 43–47, 88, 89
Sugihara, Ina, 85, 173–76

Taguma, Kenji, xi–xiv, xvi, xvii, xx
Tajiris / Tajiri Family, 80, 82; Marion / Guyo, 77–83; Ryukichi, 134; Shinkichi George, 232–39; Tajiri Larry, xvii, 22, 55, 59, 68, 77, 78, 82, 89, 112, 135, 138, 167, 234, 235, 265; Vincent / Vince, 39, 235
Tamagawa (Eldridge), Kathleen, 24–28, 276
Thomas, Norman M., 85, 125–29, 141, 145, 151, 174, 214, 215
Truman, Harry S., 132, 151, 294, 301

Uno, Edison, 68, 177
Uno, Kazumaro (Buddy), 67–77

Yama, Conrad (Kiyoshi Conrad Hamanaka), 213–16
Yamamoto, Frank Yikata (Yuke), 87
Yamamoto, Hisaye, 5, 43, 45, 46, 83, 86–92, 173, 310
Yamamoto, James Tsutomu, 89
Yamamoto, Mitsu, 102, 108
Yamamoto, Sannosuke, 102
Yamamoto, Tak, 242, 244, 248, 262
Yanagi (Yanagisawa), Kazuo, 196–99